Hosts with Ghosts
Historic Haunted Hotels in the Southeast
Second edition

Kathleen Walls

Hosts With Ghosts © 2024 K Walls

ALL RIGHTS RESERVED

No part of this book may be produced in any form, by photocopying or by any electronic or mechanical means, including information storage or retrieval systems, without permission in writing from both the copyright owner and the publisher of this book, except for the minimum words needed for review.

ISBN: 978-0-9861109-8-6
Library of Congress Control Number 2007907544

Edited by Barbara Sachs Sloan
Interior Design by Kathleen Walls
Cover Design by Kathleen Walls
Front Cover Art by Kathleen Walls

Published by Global Authors Publications

"Filling the gap in publishing"

Dedication:

To my faithful animal companions who stayed home while I traveled to get the information for this book and to Martin Walls, my faithful human companion, who stayed home and fed the animals.

Acknowledgement:

I owe a big thank you to all the CVB, DMO, and media companies who hosted me. Without them, it would have been impossible to travel around and gather this information.

Table of Contents

Chapter 1 Alabama 1
Selma 1
Tallassee and Montgomery Area 8

Chapter 2 Florida
Cedar Key 28
Carrabelle 33
Apalachicola 39
Amelia Island 44
Tampa - St Petersburg Area 51
Jacksonville and its Beaches 68
St. Augustine 76

Chapter 3 Georgia 106
St. Marys 106
Jekyll Island 114
Americus, Plains, and Andersonville 119
Macon 128
Warm Springs and Pine Mountain 143
Adairsville and Northeast corner of Georgia 149

Chapter 4 Kentucky 171
Harrodsburg 171
Perryville 176
Taylor County 177
Green River Lake 177
Greensburg 178

Chapter 5 Louisiana 181
New Orleans 181

Chapter 6 Mississippi 212
Natchez 212
Vicksburg 237

Chapter 7 North Carolina 259
Fayetteville 259

Chapel Hill, Durham, and Raleigh   270

Chapter 8 South Carolina 300
Charleston   300

Chapter 9 Tennessee 326
Chattanooga   326
Nashville 339

Chapter 10 Texas   364
San Antonio   364
Austin   391
Port Aransas   406
McAllen   412

Chapter 11 Virginia 426
Virginia Beach   426

Introduction

The South has long been famous for its Southern Hospitality. Hotels throughout Dixie vie with one another to offer their guests more service and more amenities. They strive to make each visitor feel like a cherished family member instead of a paying customer.

When you visit a hotel, you expect more than a temporary roof over your head while you travel. You want to immerse yourself in the flood of history that has engulfed the spot you visit. Perhaps you seek a Colonial ambience in Virginia or a touch of Civil War drama in Georgia or Alabama. Or you may want to relive the brash frontier past of Texas, Kentucky or Tennessee. Maybe you wish to experience the Creole flavor of Louisiana or Mississippi's rural heritage. In Florida, much of its history has been influenced by its tropical and subtropical climate. Some of the states included in this book, like North and South Carolina, have a culture so diverse, you can expect to find a totally different experience awaiting you depending on which part of the state you visit.

You want to experience this flavor when you travel. This book is set up for you as a traveler. I have offered the most interesting sights whether they are historic places, fun attractions or off the wall less known sights that might be missed in some guidebooks. In some cases, I have arranged them in chronological order to give you a better historical picture of the area. Sometimes, I placed them for convenience of driving to them. I included both haunted and non-haunted, as I know you want to see all each area has to offer.

Many of the most interesting hotels in the southeast are housed in historically significant buildings. All old buildings retain a trace of the historical elements that shaped their destiny. Ah, if only their walls could talk! Of course, I can't tell you all about all the best hotels in Dixie. There are far too many. But I can let you in on the secrets hidden behind the doors of some of the ones with that little something extra, their very own historical spirits. Some are large, corporate-owned resorts. Some are so tiny they are now considered bed and breakfasts or inns even though they were once hotels. Some are not what you would consider a traditional hotel even. They all do have one thing in common. These are the Hosts With Ghosts!

Chapter 1 Alabama

Selma

St. James Hotel

Indian lore says Selma is built where Chief Tuskaloosa met with explorer DeSoto. Whether that is true or just myth, no one knows for sure, but one thing is sure: Selma is filled with history -- and ghosts. So much has happened in Selma since 1820 when it was officially incorporated. It was planned and named by William Rufus King who later became Vice President of the United States under President Pierce. He is interred in its Live Oak Cemetery, one of the few cemeteries in the South on the National Register of Historic Sites. The cemetery is the resting place of many other famous people, including Elodie Todd Dawson, staunch Confederate supporter and sister-in-law of Abraham Lincoln; Harriet Hooker Wilkins, a Selma suffragist who became the first woman elected to the Alabama Legislature; and Frances Hobbs, a real-life Scarlet, who sewed her jeweler husband's most valuable stones into her petticoats, saving them from Union Army looters.

Strange that the history of Selma is most often associated with two historic epochs titled with the word "Civil": The Civil War and The Civil Rights Movement. Neither was at all "civil." Much bloodshed and tragedy marked both events; thus most of the ghosts in Selma relate to one of these eras.

During the Civil War, Selma was one of the South's main military manufacturing centers until April 2, 1865, when Union General J. H. Wilson's troops captured Selma. It produced much needed supplies, munitions and Confederate warships such as the ironclad Tennessee. It touches a personal note with me as my great-great grandfather, Captain John Roy, fled New Orleans when it fell to Admiral Farragut in April of 1862 to go to Selma. There he worked with local cannon makers and possibly helped design a Confederate submarine.

For important visitors to Selma in the mid-19th century, the hotel of choice was The Brantley. This elegant hotel was built in 1837 high on a bluff facing the Alabama River. Today it is known as the Saint James Hotel.

During the Battle for Selma, the hotel became the Union headquarters and afterward was used as home for the occupying officers. Perhaps this is why the hotel was spared the fiery end so many other building along Water Street suffered due to the explosions and burning of so many arsenals and munitions factories.

When the hotel's owner, Dr. Gee, went to serve in the Confederate Army, he turned the hotel over to Benjamin Sterling Tower, his slave who was later to be the first African-American ever elected to Congress. At the time of his management, Tower added to the hotel and increased his own wealth so that by the end of the war, he was believed to be wealthier than his former master.

Prominent businessmen and plantation owners enjoyed the luxury the Saint James offered. Other not-so-savory visitors also took refuge at the Saint James as well. Two of those infamous guests were Jesse and Frank James.

Sixteen-year-old Jesse along with his older brother Frank joined Quantrill's Raiders, a volunteer unit of guerilla fighters that harassed Federal troops and sympathizers behind Union lines. After the war, Jesse and Frank continued their violent ways. By 1869, the brothers were notorious criminals with a huge reward on their heads. For some Confederate sympathizers, the brothers had a kind of Southern Robin Hood image of desperate men struggling to restore the old order. This image was due in part to John Newman Edwards, a Kansas City Times editor with dreams of restoring the Confederacy.

The brothers visited the hotel in March of 1863. They came to visit a cousin, John Green Norris, who had lived near them in Missouri. Norris had moved to Selma and become a respected citizen there. At the time of the James brothers' visit, he was a city councilman. When the James brothers arrived in Selma, using the aliases of "Williams," Norris courageously offered to let them stay at his home. Realizing the danger this would create for their cousin if they were found there, the brothers declined. They chose instead to stay at the Saint James. They felt safe enough to have a photograph taken during their stay. While at the hotel, they shot pool with the hotel manager, James Dedman, who later described the brothers as well-mannered and perfect gentlemen.

However, the Pinkertons were hot on the trail, and the brothers fled Selma just ahead of their pursuers. Rumor has it the outlaws escaped by diving into the Alabama River and swimming to safety.

By 1892 the hotel had become an Alabama version of Skid Row. It wasn't until the 1990s, when it had sunk to the level of a tire-recapping factory, that it was rescued and restored to its former glory and renamed the Saint James.

As might be expected, Jesse James' shade is frequently spotted in the hotel. A male apparition dressed in 1880 cowboy garb, boots and spurs has been seen exiting guest rooms 214, 314 and 315. Jesse has also been observed in the bar sitting at his favorite corner table just to the left of the bar. He is not alone in the hotel.

An attractive, black-haired female spirit has been seen. She is believed to be his girlfriend, Lucinda. She most often appears to be floating and sometimes seems to stare at guests. Observers have noticed the scent of lavender when she is around. Her picture hangs downstairs.

An interesting phenomenon is a phantom dog believed to be Jesse's pet that has been heard running around and barking in an upstairs room although the hotel is not pet friendly now..

Many other incidents have occurred here that cannot be explained by "normal" means. In the courtyard area, voices and barking have been heard when no one was there. No living being anyway. The Alabama Foundation For Paranormal Research has investigated the hotel, and the Foundation's psychics have seen spirits dressed in 1800s clothing both in the courtyard and other places in the hotel.

In the Brantley Ballroom, Brad Kendrick, former sales and marketing director with the hotel, and several hotel employees heard a male voice. When a psychic used an EVP recording device there and asked, "Is anyone here?" they got back a reply on the tape: "Well, that's a stupid question."

Kendrich also had another odd experience. A guest sent him a picture he had taken outside the manager's office of a figure in white hovering in the air in the hallway. It was in a position that could not have been a reflection.

Psychics also recorded voices in room 304. One departed soul stated he was angry because he died before he could finish what he wanted to do.

The entities there do seem to be aware of the living inhabitants that share the space. Once an angry bartender yelled "Stop it!" when glasses behind the bar were clanging for no apparent reason. They stopped moving immediately.

This is one of the most haunted hotels in Alabama, so enjoy your stay but remember to hang on to your wallet if a strange-looking cowboy approaches. Jesse James was known to rob train passengers, demanding their wallets.

Grace Hall

The Saint James is not the only spot in Selma inhabited by spirits.

Grace Hall was once the home of Miz Eliza. In the late 1800s she presided over her gracious home and her four children and looked after boarders as well. She is still doing that today. When the home was maintained as a bed and breakfast, guests, especially women and children, would see her frequently. She is not a lonely ghost as an old gentleman is also seen. He is believed to be the spirit of an attorney, Mr. Satterfield, who was a long-time boarder who fell in love with one of Miz Eliza's daughters. Because of their great age difference, they never married. It's a private home now.

Old Cahawba Archaeological Park

The Old Cahawba Archaeological Park was Alabama's capital between 1820 and 1826. Due to its propensity to flood, the capital was moved to Tuscaloosa. The city was nearly abandoned but then rebuilt when the railroad put in a line, which passed nearby. It became a major distribution point for cotton to be shipped on the Alabama River. During the War Between the States, it was the site of a Union prison. During reconstruction, it became an enclave of former slaves who divided the city into small plots of land to farm and freedmen who used it as a relatively safe place to discuss political strategy. Today, it is preserved by the state and offers an interesting glimpse into the past. You can wander the ruins and speak with an archeologist about the significance of the site.

You can also see one of the area's most intriguing ghost lights. It is referred to as Pegues' Ghost but actually is a light or brightly glowing orb. The phenomena first occurred in 1862 on the grounds of Colonel Pegues' home, then the social center of the area. Interestingly enough, the colonel, who was the leader of the Cahaba Rifles, Fifth Alabama Regiment, had returned to recruit more soldiers for his regiment. He was killed in June of the same year, so perhaps it warned of his eminent death. Or perhaps it foretold the death of the town a few years later. Whatever its cause, the story is fascinating.

A young couple was wandering around the lushly wooded grounds, perhaps trying to forget the turmoil devastating the land, when they spotted a large glowing ball of light. The gentleman tried to capture it, but it eluded him and eventually disappeared before their startled eyes.

On two Saturdays in October, they hold Haunted History Tours.

Sturdivant Hall

Even though so much of Selma was lost to the fires that accompanied the city's fall to Union forces, much has also been saved. A good place to view the best of Selma's antebellum homes and buildings is in the Old Town Historic District. It is Alabama's largest historic district. Beautiful Sturdivant Hall is one of the district's showpieces.

The house was designed by a cousin of General Robert E. Lee, Thomas Helm Lee, for Colonel Edward T. Watts. It was built in 1852-1853. The Watts only lived in it for 11 years, and in 1864 Mr. John McGee Parkham purchased the home. Parkham and his family seemed to prosper while he lived in the home. He became president of the bank where he worked. However, Mr. Parkham was dealing in cotton futures and using bank money. When the futures fell, the Federal Authorities who were still occupying Selma during reconstruction, arrested him and sent him to the former Confederate prison at Cahawba.

Parkham was a popular man in Selma. Friends believed he was unjustly imprisoned as most other bankers were doing the same thing. So they bribed one of the guards to leave his cell door open. Parkham rushed out to a waiting boat, but one of the guards shot and killed him. His wife sold the house and left Selma in disgrace.

Parkham was buried in the old Live Oak Cemetery, but apparently he preferred his comfortable home. Many people have heard or seen his spirit, mostly upstairs. He's not lonely there either; his little girls are often glimpsed peeping out a window. Docents in the museum will tell you about doors that open and close mysteriously. They usually bid him a polite

"Good evening, Mr. Parkham" when this happens. Upstairs, beds that are carefully made up the evening before appear rumpled and slept in in the morning.

A few years ago during a "battle ball" for the re-enactment of the Battle of Selma, one of the guards went upstairs to investigate a sighting of children playing in the off-limits upstairs rooms. In spite of the fact that three different people had reported seeing children up there, he found no one there when he went to investigate.

An African-American worker, whose grandfather had worked in the home after the Parkhams left, reported an unusual occurrence. The old gentleman was plowing, and the mule reached a spot in the yard that it would never pass. The man told his grandson he believed Mr. Parkham was buried in that spot. Today, it's a museum open Tues.-Sat. 10:00 am - 4:00 pm

Brown Chapel

One of Selma's landmarks that spans both the Civil War and the Civil Rights Movement is Brown Chapel. Built in 1866 by Freedmen, it was the first African Methodist Episcopal Church in Alabama. In 1965 national attention focused on the striking Byzantine-style church. Six hundred African-American protesters gathered there on March 7 with plans to stage a peaceful march to the state capital. When the marchers reached the Edmund Pettus Bridge, just six blocks away, local deputies and state troopers began beating the marchers with clubs. The clubs and tear gas dispersed the marchers, but a new movement swept the South.

Civil Rights for all were now demanded! It had been promised in the earlier Civil Rights Act of 1964, but without the all-important right to vote, that legislation was worthless. Now as images of the Selma March and its consequences flashed into homes across the nation, history was unfolding. ABC called it "Bloody Sunday," and like all battles, it had consequences.

From a tiny church in Montgomery, a new general stepped in to command his bloodied but unbeaten army. Then-little-known Rev. Martin Luther King, Jr., marshaled his troops for another peaceful assault on the old powers that be. On March 9th, he led a symbolic march to the bridge. There the authorities again stopped the marchers. King avoided bloodshed and instead had his people kneel and pray. This march was never intended to be anything but a symbol focusing even more attention on Alabama. Then on March 21st, after winning a federal injunction allowing the march, he set out again from Brown Chapel with around 3,000 followers. When he arrived in Montgomery, he was at the head of a triumphant 25,000 marchers, both Black and white. Within five months of that fateful day, President Lyndon Johnson signed the Voting Rights Act of 1965. Perhaps the ghosts of murdered Civil Rights workers still stand in awe in front of Brown Chapel. You can sSchedule a personal or group tour of Brown Chapel African Methodist Episcopal Church but being a religious organization, they probably won't mention any residents spirits.

Other places

Selma offers a do-it-yourself ghost tour that you will want to take. Other haunted spots in this historic town include a Rhineland-inspired castle, the Trotter Home.

Selma also has the honor of being the home of one of America's premier ghost storytellers, Kathryn Tucker Windham who passed away in 2011, and her resident ghost, Jeffrey. Her museum is located nearby at the Thomasville Campus of Alabama Community College. Selma has so much more to see and do, so before you take your own trip to Montgomery, you may want to visit the Old Depot Museum, Vaughan-Smitherman Museum, Voting Rights Museum, Slavery and Civil War Museum, and by all means visit Historic Water Street and The Historic Village.

Tallassee and Montgomery Area

Montgomery

Montgomery is a dichotomy. The county of Montgomery was established in 1816 and named after Major Lemuel P. Montgomery, the first soldier to die at the Battle of Horseshoe Bend in 1814. At almost the same time, two separate cities were established. Alabama Town and New Philadelphia both struggled to be named the county seat. In a way both won. In late 1819 they merged and incorporated as the city of Montgomery. This time in honor of a different hero, Major Richard Montgomery, who fought in the Revolutionary War. It was made the state capital in 1846 but was still a quaint village rather than a booming metropolis.

The town's duality continued, and what turned Montgomery into a national player instead of a quiet backwater was the event that led to the state's most stunning disaster. On January 11, 1861, Alabama was the fourth state to secede. It invited delegates from the other seven seceded states to come to Montgomery and draft a constitution. In February, Jefferson Davis took the oath of office as first President of the Confederacy at the Montgomery State Capitol Building. No wonder it's nicknamed "Cradle of the Confederacy."

Ironically, Montgomery is also considered the birthplace of the Civil Rights Movement. But this diversity has made it a more interesting place to visit. From Civil War to Civil Rights, Montgomery is one fascinating city.

And as icing on the cake, it was the home for many years of the all-time King of Country Music, Hank Williams.

Naturally, Montgomery also has its college, and you know all colleges have a ghost story or two.

The Greystone Hotel

The Greystone Hotel in Montgomery was built in 1928 and bragged it had "150 Rooms, Bath and Showers, Running Ice Water Each Room." The 10-story classic brick hotel on Commerce Street was the last collaboration between architect Frank Lockwood and builder Algenon Blair. In later years the building became run down and was rented as residence to transients. Later it was a bank and office complex. When the Riverfront area became popular, the Hampton Inn chain bought it and renovated it to its former splendor.

One remnant of its historic past remains. Legend says once a woman died in the Greystone. She was either a female hotel worker or a newly married bride and died the fourth floor of the hotel. Apparently, she loved the hotel, and her spirit reportedly is glimpsed in the hallways of the fourth floor. Haunted Hearse Tours of Montgomery includes the hotel in its tours.

Riverfront Park and Union Station Visitors Center

It's only fair to start where it all began, at the river with the railroad. Those two factors made Montgomery what it is today. The station was built by the Louisville and Nashville Railroad in 1898. The brick and limestone three-story building and its sheds were perched on a high bluff along the Alabama River. Today, it is the centerpiece of the Riverfront Park and home of the Visitors Center. There are also an interpretative museum, a gift shop and all the answers you need to enjoy Montgomery.

Old Alabama Town

Would you like to take a trip back in time to late 19th and early 20th century Alabama? You don't need a time machine. Just take a trip to Old Alabama Town in Montgomery. It's more than a museum. It's traveling back in time among through 50 authentically restored structures with "residents and workers" doing the everyday tasks of that time along six blocks of downtown Montgomery.

When I visited, there were two of the docent's children in period costume dashing about much as their counterparts did a hundred years age. It made it so much more authentic than just an adult guide ever could.

I was able to visualize myself back in the 1800s as I walked through this village. But the centerpiece for anyone interested in the paranormal is the Lucas Tavern. Lucas Tavern was originally located about 15 miles east of Montgomery on a stage line. Walter and Eliza Lucas raised their children there and welcomed weary travelers. The most illustrious traveler to partake of the tavern's welcome was the Marques de Lafayette, who stayed there in 1825.

Apparently, Eliza is still doing what she enjoyed in life. Many visitors have seen her, and she has made her presence felt at staff meetings. She is most frequently glimpsed in the tavern doorway as a small woman dressed in Victorian clothing. She has also been known to act as a docent and pose for photographs for visitors in other buildings as well. One gentleman who was taking pictures in the old schoolhouse after hours was pleased to find what he assumed was a guide posing with a McGuffy Reader there. The woman was about 5'3" and smiled but did not speak to him. He snapped several pictures and was astounded when the "guide" vanished into thin air. When the pictures were developed, there was a bright light in the area where the "guide" had stood.

Eliza was always a gracious Southern hostess and believed in settling disagreements in an amicable manner. She once reacted in a staff meeting when she felt one member was acting too hostile. A puff of smoke blasted from the fireplace covering the offending member with soot and ashes.

On another occasion, two members of the staff were discussing the historical district critically. The door to the room where they were seated flew off its hinges and fell to the floor. Yes, Eliza may be a small friendly phantom, but she believes good manners should be observed at all times.

Of course, there is so much more to see there. Possibly other spirits still hang around. The "Town" is divided into three sections; a Living Section, a Working Section, and Along the Street.

Three blocks of the town is a working block that shows how potteries, blacksmiths, even musicians plied their trade There is the Oliver Cotton Gin dating back to 1900. On most days, re-enactors are there showing off their town.

A blacksmith was the backbone of every community then. They were even more important than modern mechanics, as they not only kept the wagons rolling but also made things needed for everyday life, like axes, tools, household utensils, and nails. Daniel Webster Boatwright originally opened this shop in Fleahop in Elmore County in 1893 and it remained in operation by his family until the 1940s.

There's a gristmill, old pharmacy, print shop, and many more buildings. Travel back to when these were an everyday part of peoples' lives.

Visit the living block where people of the time go about their everyday lives. Visit classrooms where students leaned the latest reading, writing, and arithmetic. This was not too different from today in appearance but decades away in technologically. Here are desks with inkwells and slates, not computers and tablets.

The corner grocery store was part of everyday life before the coming of chains. This one dates to 1892 when it began life as Daniel O'Leary's Grocery and Saloon son morphing into just a grocery store.

Churches were more than a place of worship then. They were a meeting and socializing place. They built this one around 1885. It was the First Colored Presbyterian Church of Montgomery.

Every town needed a doctor. Dr. Thomas David Duncan built this doctor's office in 1938 in his parents' backyard and operated out of it all his life. Doctors served as dentist and sometimes veterinarians then. They got paid in eggs, poultry or however their patients could pay them. Those unenlightened days, if you were sick you got treated whether you had money or insurance. Doctors weren't part of huge corporations charging over $400 a visit. Ever wish you could go back to a more peaceful time?

Along the Street Section is where old building are recycled and are in use today. Many of the homes became bed and breakfasts but some are put to other uses. You can visit Shaffer Garden filled with native plantings that show what a 19th century central Alabama garden might have looked like.

One building is almost a circling back to the original premise of Old Alabama Town. Rescued Relics is located in the 1920s Wilbanks Warehouse that once serviced those newfangled horseless carriages. Today, it's a not-for-profit salvage business that raises money to restore and maintain the historic structures at Old Alabama Town. It sells historic architectural elements and materials from pre-1960s building that are being razed and sells them to people wishing to incorporate antique elements into their projects around Montgomery and the central Alabama region. As the old song goes, let the circle be unbroken.

State Capitol

When the state capital was once again moved from Tuscaloosa to Montgomery, a Capitol building was designed and built by a Philadelphia, Pennsylvania, architect. That capitol burnt in 1849 but was then rebuilt following the original plans in 1851. Today, it stands proudly on Goat Hill. It also served as Capital of The Confederacy for a few months. Two of its most striking architectural features are the domed rotunda and the floating staircases. It was placed on the Register of Historic Places in 1982.

When Gov. Winston was sworn in on the steps in 1853 he used a special Bible purchased for that purpose. It has since been used to swear in every governor of Alabama to this day. When the Bible is not being used at an inauguration, it resides at Alabama Department of Archives and History's third-floor Nineteenth-Century Gallery. It is known as the "Jefferson Davis Bible" because it was used for the swearing in of the only president of the Confederacy as well. In fact, there is a note on the front flyleaf by Judge John Phelan, the 1861 Alabama Supreme Court Justice, verifying Davis' use of the book.

Davis' massive stature rises up just before you enter the massive white granite building. Within, the Wallaces, George and Lurleen, take over. Their portraits are prominently displayed. But the ghosts in the capitol itself seem to be from the Civil War era, not the Civil Rights one. A custodian had reported seeing the spirit of a woman in Confederate clothing in the second floor halls. The governor's reception area restrooms seem to have a haunt of their own also. The faucets turn off and on by themselves.

Now when you move into the Governor's Mansion, that is an interesting story. The pictures of some Confederates seem to have a mysterious presence. So much so that former Governor Fop James' wife, Bobby, removed several including a portrait of Confederacy President Jefferson Davis. Davis' image was replaced with a reproduction of the Ten Commandments. It is questionable in this time of political correctness, whether it was the ghost of Davis or the ghost of an era many would like to forget ever happened. Paranormal investigators claim there is a widow of a Civil War solidier who seeks her husband's spirit there.

There are too many reminders of the earlier divisions between races. A bronze star marks the spot Jefferson Davis stood as he took his oath of office. Images of Governor George Wallace at his first inauguration speech in 1963 delivering a message that would remain in the minds of all even after his turnabout regarding to racial equality: "Segregation now! Segregation tomorrow! Segregation forever!"

First White House of the Confederacy

Even if Davis had been ousted from the Governor's mansion by Bobby James, he still is reputed to roam in his own domain, The First White House of the Confederacy, just across the street. When I visited I was transported back in time.

I was with a group of travel writers, and we were given a deluxe tour. Everything looked as it had in the days when the Davises enjoyed this graceful stucco Italianate home as a residence.

We were served tea in china cups just as Varina Davis might have served her guests in those elegant days at the start of the worst war in our country's history.

Along with memorabilia from the Davis occupation, there are many relics of other War Between the States soldiers, both the generals and the privates. One of the most moving is a letter from a dying soldier to his family about where his body should be laid to rest.

Dexter Ave. King Memorial Baptist Church & Parsonage

In the ultimate duality, just across the street from the capitol is Dexter Avenue King Memorial Baptist Church, the small house of worship that launched an American hero, Martin Luther King, Jr. The Selma debacle would give King his chance at national fame, but it was his unique philosophy that made him truly great. Where others returned violence for violence, King espoused peaceful methods. In the end, his way had gained respect of both races and made him a national icon.

The one thing most visitors comment on about the church is, "It is so small!" How appropriate that such a great page in history was started in such humble beginnings.

The original church was located father down the block in a old slave trader's pen in 1877. At first it was called the Second Colored Baptist Church. At the time, the street was called Market St. In January 1879 the congregation had prospered enough to buy a small lot on the corner of Market and Decatur streets, where the current church is still located. They built a small wood frame that they used for both church and school. The red brick building we see today was constructed between 1883 and 1889. After its place in the Civil Rights Movement was fixed in history, the church was designated a national historic landmark on June 3, 1974. The name changed again to Dexter Avenue Baptist Church, when Market Street became Dexter Avenue honoring Andrew Dexter, "New Philadelphia's" founder. In 1978 the name once more was changed to Dexter Avenue King Memorial Baptist Church, to honor its 20th century pastor, Dr. Martin Luther King, Jr.

To round out the vision of Dr. King's mission in Montgomery, visit the parsonage, located several blocks away. It was home to the pastors of the Dexter Avenue Church from 1920 to 1992.

Civil Rights Monument

The Civil Rights Monument designed by Maya Lin in 1989 is inspiring. It is a circular table with the timeline of all-important events in the Civil Rights Movement beginning with the Supreme Court ruling to integrate schools in 1954 and continuing to Dr. Martin Luther King, Jr's assassination in 1968. It immortalizes the 40 men, women and children who lost their lives in the fight for racial equality. The backdrop is a black granite wall engraved with a portion of Dr. King's most famous speech. "We will not be satisfied until justice rolls down like waters and righteousness like a mighty stream." This is the passage that inspired the fountain.

The memorial appropriately sits in front of the Southern Poverty Law Center, an organization that seeks to abolish hate crimes.

Rosa Parks Memorial and Library

A simple act of civil disobedience by a simple woman sparked a movement that changed the country. In 1955, a tired African-American seamstress refused to give up her seat to a white man. Rosa Parks was arrested for this small act and started a conflagration that began with the Alabama Bus Boycott and culminated in a ruling by the Supreme Court of the United States that bus segregation was illegal anywhere in the country.

The museum dedicated to Rosa Parks, who has been called the Mother of Civil Rights, is located on the very block where she boarded the bus that fateful day. It is on the campus of Troy State University. It houses the University Library.

The museum leads you through the plight of African-Americans during segregation beginning with a bus that provides a literal window into the past. Six different sections lead you through the history and the story of Rosa Parks as a person. As an educational tool for children and adults alike, this is not to be missed.

Huntingdon College

Montgomery is a college town. And as you know almost all colleges have ghost stories. Huntingdon College has its share. The college didn't start life in Montgomery or as Huntingdon College. It began as Tuskegee

Female College, when its charter was signed by Alabama Governor John Winston on February 2, 1854.

It soon became apparent that the school would thrive better in a larger city. So it was renamed Women's College of Alabama and relocated to Montgomery in 1910. It soon became co-educational and was renamed Huntingdon College in 1935. Its gothic style buildings lend themselves to ghost stories. One of its earliest spirits originated in a tragedy when the college was still located in Tuskegee.

A young lady named Martha from New York was requested by her father's will to attend his mother's alma mater, Woman's College of Alabama. She was unhappy at the campus and did not make friends with other students easily. Being a Northerner in a very Southern city, she did not fit in. The other young women taunted her about everything and especially about her choice of clothing color. She always wore red and even decorated her dorm in red. No one wanted to be her roommate, and finally after one girl Martha believed to be slightly friendly toward her had asked to be moved to another room, Martha committed suicide.

Although the death occurred before the college's move to Montgomery, apparently Martha has relocated as well. She has been seen on campus by many students. She is said to frequent the fourth floor of Pratt Hall where many of the sorority chapter rooms are located.

The Red Lady is far from lonely as she haunts Huntingdon College. In fact she has a male counterpart called The Ghost on the Green. His girlfriend broke up with him, claiming he was too possessive and demanding. He tried to regain her affection, but she would not take him back. Desperate and unwilling to seek a new companion, he went out on the green one night and shot himself. Although he is not seen, he is felt. Many students have felt him tugging on their clothing, rumpling their hair or even breathing on them. That would be reason enough to make anyone nervous about walking the green at night, but there are other spirits on the green as well.

The most endearing specter on campus is Billy, a little boy who was visiting his older sister in the 1970s. Billy was playing ball near the pond and lost his ball. He wandered into the water and drowned trying to find the ball. Students have spotted a small boy in old-style clothing scampering around the pond area of the green.

The saddest ghost on the green is that of a young woman who was brutally murdered as she returned from the library to her dorm. He body was found in a wooded area, strangled. Her friends believed they knew who the killer was, but no one was ever convicted. It is said if you encounter her spirit at night, she will call out the name of her killer to you.

Male students resideimg in Searcy Hall have their own phantom girlfriend. Students have been amazed to see a beautiful young woman who is clad only in a towel. She smiles and then disappears into thin air or walks through a wall, leaving her admirers awestruck in more ways than one.

Naturally, the library has to have its own ghost. Frank the Library Ghost is rumored to rearrange entire rows of books. Library staff report the dumbwaiter moving between the floors when no one was operating it. He frequents the fourth floor, and visitors there are liable to go in pursuit of a noise just outside their view only to find nothing but a blast of cold air and the sound of distant giggling.

F. Scott and Zelda Fitzgerald Museum

The F. Scott and Zelda Fitzgerald Museum is a small museum dedicated to the memory of the Fitzgeralds. Zelda met Scott when he was stationed in Montgomery during the war. The Fitzgeralds rented this house for a short time: October 1931 to April 1932. Only the bottom floor is a museum, but for those interested in Fitzgerald's work, it's a must. Many paranormal groups have visited the home and claim there is a presence. Is it Zelda?

Montgomery Zoo

The Montgomery Zoo was originally founded in 1920. It covers 48 acres and is home to more than 700 different species of animals from five different continents including South America, Asia, Africa, Australia and North America.

Hank Williams Sites

The Hank Williams story didn't begin in Montgomery, but much of his musical career's highlights are there. Whether you are a Hank fan or not, visit the Hank Williams Museum in Montgomery. I visited it several years ago and had the good fortune to meet one of his original Drifting Cowboys, Lum York. Lum is gone now, too, but his memory lives on.

We became friends when I wrote about Lum for a British publication, and I learned much about Hank that was only known to his close friend.

"Growing up in rural Alabama, the depression days of the 1930s and early 1940s were rough," Lum York remembers. "I only had two pairs of overalls. My mother washed on Wednesdays, so I had to wear them all week long."

Not far away in Georgian Alabama, another child was born in 1923 whose life was destined to link with Lum's in the creation of the most-enduring legend country music has ever known. Hank had won a talent contest at the Montgomery Empire Theater singing an original song entitled "WPA Blues" in December of 1937. For that he received $15, his first income as a singer. There was no stopping his music career from that moment. He worked local clubs and did a show on WSFA, a Montgomery radio station.

In 1944 Lum and his big bass fiddle joined Hank's band, The Drifting Cowboys. Lum told me about the first time he played music with Hank, "We had got to be friends working together in the shipyard. One night I went where he was playing. I had bought a bass and was learning to play it. I was also a friend of the guy who was playing bass that night, and he asked me to sit in while he went to the bathroom. Hank and Audrey were dancing while I played the set. When the music ended, Hank asked me 'You want a job playing with the band?' I told him, 'Hank, I don't know how to play too good.' He said, 'You want to learn? I'll pay you $20 a week and room and board.'"

The two men worked together and collaborated on songs for many years.

Lum was also the unwitting inspiration for Hank's "I Saw the Light." Hank, Audrey and the band, six people altogether, were crammed into a 1942 Chevy. As you can imagine, it was hard for any of them to rest comfortably. Lum raised up to change positions. He looked out the window and as he lay back down, he stated, "We're getting close to Montgomery. I saw the light." He was referring to a beacon light near town that was always a landmark for the band as they returned home from shows.

Hank began mumbling that that was a good title for a song, and by the next day when the band gathered for their show on WSFA, he was picking out the tune to "I saw the Light." Many versions about the origin of this song have been advanced over the years, but Lum felt that this is the truest.

Hank played his last gig in Montgomery also. It was a benefit on Dec. 28, 1952, at the Elite Casino Lounge. Three days later, he would be dead in the back seat of his baby blue Cadillac enroute to a performance in Ohio. He had not yet reached his 30th birthday, but he had already become a legend in not only country music but pop where many of his songs were and still are played. In five years he had recorded 225 songs and written more than half of them. Twenty-eight had made Billboard's Top 10. No other artist has accomplished this record.

The Hank Williams Museum is located in an unpretentious building in downtown Montgomery. Inside, the singer's life and legend come to life. Personal memorabilia, clothing, the mike he used in his last performance, and the piece de la resistance, his 1952 Cadillac, are housed in the museum.

Cecil Jackson founded the museum in 1999 to honor a man who had inspired him for years. Their first meeting was when Hank bought him a Coke at 8 years old. Today his daughter, Beth Petty, manages the museum.

As so much of his professional life was played out in Montgomery, it is only fitting that he be recognized. Recently, a stretch Highway 65 leading to his boyhood home in Georginia, Alabama, was named "The Lost Highway" in his honor.

His life-sized statue graces Lister Hill Park in downtown Montgomery. Ironically, it's located just across from the City Auditorium where Hank's funeral service was held.

From the statue to the graveyard is just a short drive. Hank was laid to rest in Oakwood Cemetery Annex. The epitaph on his tomb was composed by his first wife, Audrey,

"Thank you for the love you gave me
There could be nobody stronger
Thank you for many beautiful songs
They will live long, and longer"

She could only suspect how prophetic the words were. His songs are still re-recorded today, over half a century after his death.

Although it says "RIP" on the grave, it is hard to believe that this hard-living legend who died so young could rest in peace. Perhaps he doesn't but prefers to still move among the living. Many of you know Alan Jackson's 1990 hit "Midnight in Montgomery," but did you know that it has a basis in fact?

Since his death, fans have swarmed to Hank's gravesite. So much so that Hank Williams, Jr., has posted a sign asking fans to respect his father's grave and not leave beer cans and trash strewn around. According to an AP story, two Alabama fans, Tanner Broughton of Birmingham and Jeremy Gossett of Pell City, were visiting his grave one Halloween night and actually saw his restless spirit, wearing his trademark cowboy hat leave his tomb and walk toward the nearby woods.

So when you visit Montgomery, be prepared for anything. As Alan Jackson sings, "It's midnight in Montgomery. Hank's always singing there." **Hank's died in 1953 in his Cadillac en-route to a concert. He and Audrey are buried in Oakwood Cemetery Annex. The gravesite is easy to find and clearly marked.**

US Ghost Adventures offers tours of many haunted Montgomery sites.

Indian Lore of Tallassee

Before the European settlers put their mark on this part of Alabama, it was home to the Creek Nation. The last Creek capital city of Tukabatchi was just a mile south of present day Tallassee. As the 1700s rolled into the 1800s, the Creeks thrived in this city believed to be the second largest in North America. The focal point of their village was a huge oak called the Great Council Tree. It was under its ancient branches that tribal business was conducted.

In 1811 one of the Creek's most fateful decisions occurred beneath the Council Tree. The great Shawnee chief, Tecumseh, visited the Creek chiefs. He pleaded with them to join his people in a strong stand against the "white man." The Creeks were undecided about such a risky proposition, and Tecumseh left in a huff. He threatened to return to his own people and stamp his foot so hard the Creeks would feel the reverberations.

The Creeks scoffed at such bravado, but several days later when there was a small earthquake, the Shawnee's words came to mind. They agreed to join the Shawnee in the battle, thus signing their own doom. When Andrew Jackson and his Cherokee allies defeated the Creek and Shawnee alliance at nearby Horseshoe Bend, they were forced to sign the Treaty of Fort Jackson and cede 23 million acres, the majority of their homeland, to the United States. The power and prestige of the Creeks was lost forever.

Their Council Tree outlived the Creek city by more than a century. It was destroyed by a storm in 1929. That same year, the Alabama Anthropological Society placed a granite monument to mark the site. The monument was moved to Bicentennial Park in 1975.

Confederate Armory

Another "Lost Cause" is represented in the only remaining Confederate Armory left in existence. Colonel Gorgas, Confederate ordnance chief, ordered the armory moved from Richmond, Virginia, to Tallassee in the spring of 1864 when the Confederacy feared they could not protect the original location. It was relocated to an old 1844 cotton mill. It barely missed being destroyed by Union forces on two occasions. Major General Rousseau bypassed it in 1864, and a second raid by General Wilson was misled by a faulty map and also failed to locate and destroy the armory. It is still standing but not in good shape.

Rose Hill Cemetery

Find time to browse in the shops on historical Tallassee and visit Rose Hill Cemetery where the remains of William Parker, one of Andrew Jackson's servants during the war of 1812, is buried. When you need a little outdoor time, visit Lake Talisi for great fishing, boating or swimming.

Sign about the Selma to Montgormey March

Exhibit at F. Scott Fitzgerald Hiouse

Sculptures at Legacy Memorial

Dexter Parsonage

Hank Williams's grave

Rosa Parks stature at museum

Lum York at Hank Williams Museum

Dining room at Lucas Tavern

First White House of the Confederacy

State Capitol

Former Greyhound Bus station now Freedom Rides Museum

Former Greystone Hotel

Chapter 2 Florida
Cedar Key

Island Hotel

When I drive into Cedar Key, no matter how harried my day or how tense I am, I feel the magic by the time I cross the bridge entering the island town, and my relaxo-meter always kicks in. I watch several lazy brown pelicans perch on posts, all that is left of an abandoned stilt house that was blown away by one of the many hurricanes that are also drawn to this exposed community perched on the edge of Florida's northwestern coast. The birds and the posts are reflected in the shallow waters of the gulf. Closer in, toward the end of the dock, oyster bars peer through the ripple of the waves. This is Cedar Key. Welcome to Island Time!

Cedar Key can hold its own in any comparison with Key West, Marathon or any of the better known keys. This is the heart of Florida's "Nature Coast," and it has everything except the crowds.

This tiny artist refuge and fishing town is still what Florida used to be before the population boom. Artists are drawn to the fishing and crabbing village like bees to honey because of the fantastic scenery, balmy climate and breathtaking sunsets. The April Sidewalk Arts Festival draws visitors from all over. The Seafood Festival in October also draws crowds. When I stroll along the waterfront, I am tempted by a multitude of choices. Along with the many galleries, featuring a variety of creative endeavors, there are unique shops and food-and-drink establishments. You can have a quiet drink in the company of sea birds on a deck overlooking the gulf. If you are in the mood for a more romantic setting, enjoy supper in a glass-enclosed dining room perched high atop a dock as the golden orb of the sun paints the western sky with pink and lavender streaks. At night, the live music is mellow as you dance with a star-drenched sky for a backdrop.

Whether you spend a day or a week on Cedar Key, the easygoing rhythms of the island will remain in your memory. It has no skyscrapers, no theme parks and no huge enterprises. It just has a timeless natural beauty and friendly atmosphere that will bring you back time and time again. This quaint village is one of the few places left where you can glimpse the Florida of another time. Spend a few days feeding the pelicans at the dock or watching dolphins gambol off its shore, and you will never want to leave.

The place to stay if you are in the mood to search for local spooks is the Island Hotel. Cedar Key was hit hard by Hurricane Helene bu towner, Andy Blair, said, only the basement was flooded and he can resume operation as soon as power was restored.

At the Island Hotel, Cedar Key's most famous vintage inn, there are several unseen (most of the time) guests from days gone by who refuse to leave. The building is drenched in history and lore. Dining in its restaurant will transport you back to the Victorian era. The huge underwater mural behind the bar dates back to the 1930s. The hotel is listed on the National Registry of Historic Places. If there were a National Registry of Haunted Places, it would surely be on that, too. Since its construction in 1859, it has played host to many colorful characters: the kind of people who enjoyed life too much to leave it without a fight.

Originally used as a general store and post office, it collected its first ghost shortly before the end of the Civil War when the manager hired a nine-year-old black boy to help around the store. One day he saw the child put something in his pocket; believing the boy to be stealing, the manager chased him. When the manager could not find him and the boy never returned to his job, not too much thought was given the matter. About a year later workers relining the basement cistern made a grisly discovery; the skeleton of a child was found in the cistern. Perhaps as he ran to hide from the angry manager, the child fell into the cistern and drowned. To this day, the spirit of that scared child still hides in the dark basement.

During the Civil War, the hotel was quarters for both sides, at different times, of course. It is one of the Southern soldiers who stands guard just inside a door leading to a second-floor balcony. This is the most frequently sighted haunt in the hotel but definitely not the most interesting one.

Over the years the hotel has functioned as many things. It was a brothel and speakeasy during the prohibition years. A holdover from that period seems to be the wandering soul of a prostitute. She never does any harm, just sits on the side of a guest's bed and offers a gentle kiss.

Some of the hotel's reputed 13 ghosts departed life due to foul play. One of these is the spirit of a former owner, Simon Feinberg. Word reached Mr. Feinberg that his manager, W. L. Markham, was operating an illegal whiskey still in the hotel. They met over dinner. Markham professed his innocence. Feinberg fell asleep that night and never awoke. He died of "food poisoning." It was commonly believed Markham was the poisoner. The question of Markham's innocence remained in limbo until 1999. The then owners found remains of circular copper piping that would have been used in a still hidden in the hotel. Feinberg is believed to roam the hotel, perhaps in search of Markham, but he is quite harmless toward guests.

In 1946 Bessie and Loyal Gibbs bought the then-unlivable hotel and began to revitalize it. Bessie was a flamboyant hostess and drew a clientele of some of the time's most interesting guests. The Neptune Bar downstairs, so named for the mural of King Neptune, was a favorite of actor Jack Palance. Pearl Buck, Vaughan Monroe, Tennessee Ernie Ford, Francis Langford, Myrna Loy, Richard Boone and John MacDonald were some of the other notables who frequented the hotel during the Gibbs' ownership. Bessie continued to operate the hotel after Loyal's death. After her death in 1975, her spirit appears in what was her quarters when she ran the hotel, room 29.

Today, the Island Hotel is owned and operated by Andy Bair and his wife Stanley. One of the most recent encounters with resident spirits occurred shortly after they bought it. They had been in residence since January of 2004 and naturally had heard stories of strange happenings. Stanley explained to me, "We didn't pay too much attention to them until my daughter had an unnerving experience."

It was in June 2004 when Stanley and Glen had gone to Atlanta for Andy's daughter's graduation. Stanley's 37-year-old daughter, Elizabeth, was minding the hotel for them. Stanley recalls, "Elizabeth is very level-headed, not given to flights of fancy. She was sleeping in her room in the annex when her cat woke her by pacing over her. She pulled the cat closer to her and then looked up to see what had upset the cat. She saw a man staring down at her."

She pulled the cat close to her for mutual comfort and closed her eyes and somehow managed to fall back asleep. Naturally when she awoke next morning, she told one of the housekeepers. The woman led Elizabeth to a picture in the upstairs hall of the main building. Elizabeth recognized him at once as her nocturnal visitor. It was Mr. Markum, the former manager who may have dispatched his inquisitive employer so many years ago.

The Blairs, their daughter and presumably the cat as well are now firm believers in the hotel's spirit population.

Cedar Key Museums

Two museums transport you back through time to the early days of the island. The Cedar Key Historic Society, located on SR 24 and 2nd Street, depicts the town's development through photographs, artifacts and tools. It can also provide you with a self-guided tour of the city.

The Cedar Key State Museum is just north of the downtown area. It contains household articles, dioramas and one of the most extensive shell collections ever assembled. It also has a restored home typical of the early area settlers. The town has a checkered history. Its location made it a haven for blockade-runners during the Civil War. Because of its extensive cedar forests, it was a lumbering and pencil manufacturing center for many years. A devastating hurricane leveled much of the original town in 1896.

Even before the arrival of the settlers, fishing, crabbing, and oystering provided much of the town's economic base. Today, due to contamination of many of the oyster beds, clams are fast becoming an important commercial crop.

Other Keys

Cedar Key is located on a barrier island. Hwy. 24 connects it with the mainland by means of three bridges. There are dozens of other islets in the area, also, but they must be reached by boat. The most interesting of these is Seahorse Key. It has a lighthouse, built in 1851 and abandoned in 1915. Today, it houses the University of Florida Marine Research and Environment Education Center. It was used as a military outpost and hospital and during the Civil War as a prison. It is also the highest point on the Gulf Coast, rising 52 feet above sea level. It is one of the thirteen islands designated as Cedar Keys National Wildlife Refuge. The refuge is home to a large variety of water birds and a thriving reptile population. Due to the scarcity of fresh water, there aren't many mammals on these islands. With the exception of Seahorse Key, which is closed to the public from March through June, the beaches of all the islands are open for boaters. The only island interior that is open is Atsena Ortie Key. These beaches are great places for swimming, bird watching, photography and shell collecting.

Lower Suwannee National Wildlife Refuge

Just north of town, on Hwy 347, you can hike or drive the diverse habitats of the Lower Suwannee National Wildlife Refuge. More than 52,000 acres, bisected by the famed Suwannee River, compose one of the largest undeveloped river delta systems in the country. Its varied ecosystems support abundant plant and animal life. Alligator, osprey, eagle, white-tailed deer and a multitude of other wildlife roam the preserve.

Shell Mound

Shell Mound, a county park located at the south end of the refuge, is the site of an ancient Timacuan Indian mound. Shell Mound Trail crosses the midden at its 28-foot peak. From here you have a spectacular view of the estuary and the Gulf. For an almost guaranteed sighting of hosts of wading birds, ramble down the Dennis Creek Loop Trail. It is quite possible you may spot something else as well. Something far more eerie. In the late 1800s, a young woman named Annie Simpson used to walk the area with her wolfhound. Pirates also frequented the secluded spot to bury treasure. On one of her evening walks, Annie and her dog discovered them at work hiding their ill-gotten loot. Neither Annie nor her dog was ever seen alive again.

Treasure hunters claims to have found the remains of old chests and the skeleton of a large dog, but Annie's remains have never been found. People wandering the mounds have reported seeing a beautiful girl with long dark hair accompanied by a wolfhound. Could Annie be tied to this, the last earthly spot she visited?

The park also boasts an inexpensive campground with electric and water hookups for short-term visitors. For more deluxe or longer term RV parks, there are several in the area. Cedar Key RV Park is located in town. It is a short walk from downtown and is on the Gulf.

For the best free entertainment in town, you can sit in the beach park or on the end of the pier and watch the pelicans swoop back and forth on the roof of an abandoned boathouse perched on stilts a few hundred feet from shore. If you're lucky, you might see a pair of dolphins frolicking in the waves or a few West Indian Manatees lazily turning in the water.

The best thing about Cedar Key is that they have managed to stave off the full-scale development that has altered most of Florida's gulf coast. You still drift along on island time on Cedar Key.

Carrabelle

Old Carrabelle Hotel

The Old Carrabelle Hotel iowners, Kathy and Skip Frink, have worked hard to preserve the 1880-era hotel's original Key West style but added modern comforts. As the hotel is the premiere place to stay in downtown Carrabelle; many hundreds of complimentary guest comments have been left behind, almost all with the promise that they'll be back. Some would be mighty difficult to honor, though, as visitors have come from as far away as Switzerland; Togo, West Africa; and Italy.

While neither Skip nor Kathy has actually seen anything supernatural, they have had guests say they felt a presence. Their normally laid-back dog, Sassy, appears aware of something the human inhabitants can't see. She refuses to go into a particular upstairs bedroom near the back of the house.

The Regatta Room is renovated and decorated in a nautical style, but Kathy pointed out the door, which has a slight discoloration. She explained, "We put several coats of Kilz stain on it and then the paint, but it still has a reddish color bleeding through which will not be covered. Kilz covers everything but not this door. It was not painted that red color when we bought the house. It was dark blue. It also seems to have been kicked in at some time."

She said there may have been a murder committed in the house once, but she was not sure of the victim. Two people definitely died in the house: a former owner, Captain Leon Langston, and his wife. The captain probably died in what is now the dining room. He was very ill during his last years and had closed off all but the front two rooms. His wife, who had died years before, may have died in that upstairs room. She suffered from agoraphobia and seldom left the house.

Skip told me of their latest experience. "We had a guest in Regatta one week who had a bad night's sleep. She was awakened by two events: first, the sound of gunshots, then later a baby crying. I explained it to her simply: The baby was crying because its mother got shot. But then I'm not very imaginative."

Skip and Kathy brought in the Panhandle Paranormal Investigators in 2003 to check out the entire building. The PPI group said by far the most "activity" they documented occurred in the Regatta Room.

Whatever the reason, the unearthly activity seems to have increased lately. Skip has a theory about that. He commented, "For our first four-plus years here, we worked hard on the inn and real estate, and we were doing fine. Then the national and local economies went into a slowdown. Since then, we have noticed strange things like the case above."

He sees the connection thusly: "We know that Captain Langston, who owned the hotel for about 30 years, was a major charter captain and died on the south side of the hotel, the same side as Regatta. This may be a stretch, but he was a prime mover in the development of sport fishing in Carrabelle.Could it be that he is trying to show his displeasure with the things that the City is doing?"

He continued, "The Carrabelle Boat Club had its Open House in 2006. This will be the greatest concentration of boats in one place (285) ever in Carrabelle. That day was two days after the 'gunshots' incident cited above. The city did not cooperate with the opening of the Boat Club. Maybe Leon is trying to object in his own way? Also, the young family that is developing the Club stayed in Regatta on their first trip to Carrabelle!"

Downtown Carrabelle

The development of tourism and related businesses will change the personality of the town. Many who come as tourists will be charmed by the Key West -- like the atmosphere of the town -- and will return as residents. At present, Carrabelle's waterfront combines the authenticity of a working waterfront with the fun of recreational fishing and boating. The Boat Club is one more draw for visitors who want to enjoy Carrabelle's untarnished beaches and water fun.

The town has been the site of two movies. "Ulee's Gold" starred Peter Fonda. The "gold" in the movie refers to a special type of Tupelo Honey found only in this area. "Coast Lines," starring Josh Brolin and Sara Wynter, was partially filmed there in 2005. The actors and crew stayed at the Georgian Motel, which had developed a real Parrot Head image. When you visit the Georgian, you are guaranteed to hear lots of Buffet music and find an inviting pool to splash around in.

Riverwalk

The town is quite proud of its Marine Street Riverwalk. You can spend a relaxing half hour wandering past shrimp boats, sailboats, sportfishers and the ruins of once-bustling commercial fishing buildings and docks. To be completed in 2008, Carrabelle's new Wharf will feature boat ramps, parking, wet slips and a dockmaster's office right on the Riverwalk. Numerous licensed sea captain-guides will be happy to take you fishing or cruising. The charter boat captains, will also be happy to take you to Dog Island.

Carrabelle Lighthouse

Carrabelle's tiny lighthouse stands guard over a stretch of Florida's most pristine coast. Crooked River Lighthouse is an unimposing 103-foot metal-frame structure but striking in its simplicity. It is almost a twin to the Sanibel Lighthouse. Built in 1892, the light is supported by steel beams rather than the more common round masonry tower. Neighboring pine trees have grown up almost to the light room on top. Interestingly enough, although there is no electricity connected, many people driving by have observed the light turned on and casting its welcoming beam out to sea. Rumors say it also has a resident ghost, a former keeper, who is responsible for the inexplicable light.. It is flanked by the keeper's house and the assistant keeper's house. The keeper's house, is a museum of seafaring history.

Tate's Hell

For nature lovers, wilderness areas abound in the area. More adventurous souls may want to go hiking or canoeing in Tate's Hell. Beware! The pristine nature preserve between Carrabelle and the Apalachicola National Forest is 144,508 acres of untamed woodland and swamp inhabited by wildlife including bears, deer, wild turkey, snakes, unlimited bird life, and lots of insects. You might be fortunate enough to spot a bald eagle or red cockaded woodpecker.

Be cautious there or you could end up like Cebe Tate, the man for whom the place is named. The legend recounts that the farmer journeyed into the great swamp in the late 1800s. He was searching for a panther that was killing his cattle. He followed his dogs into the heart of the wetlands. Gradually, the panther killed all the dogs. Tate lost his shotgun and was bitten by a water moccasin. He wandered for days delirious and feverish. When he finally emerged near Carrabelle, his only explanation of his whereabouts was "My name's Tate, and I've just been through Hell."

The Landing Site

Another tale that could curdle the blood of even the least sensitive reader centers around a circle of barren land on the west side of Timber Island. Timber Island was created by the dredging of the river to permit larger boats entrance to the gulf. The east side of the island is normal. Several businesses are there.

It's the west side of the island that is a different story. As you cross the Carrabelle Bridge, you will spot a circle of sand where nothing grows. According to Amanda Marcum, a lifelong resident, the place is known locally as "The Landing Site." Local legends claim people have disappeared there, possibly abducted by aliens. Indeed, strange lights have been seen there only to disappear before investigators can cross the bridge. There is even a story of a pair of teenaged lovers who parked there to indulge in a favorite teenage pastime. The deserted car was found later with a dead battery and a pair of panties on the back seat. No sign of the amorous couple was ever discovered.

Perhaps an incident that occurred in that area over two centuries ago is still reverberating. History records the case of a Frenchman and his lover who were shipwrecked east of St. George Island. To survive the trek toward St. Marks, they beat their slave to death with tree limbs somewhere on the west bank of the Carrabelle River, possibly near that same barren spot. Kindling a fire, they roasted the corpse's head and ate it. They smoked the remainder of his flesh and still had some left when they arrived in St. Marks. Could "The Landing Site" refer to a different type of travelers besides space aliens?

The World's Smallest Police Station

Carrabelle has a lot going for it besides its overabundance of ghosts. Pristine beaches, a temperate location and a low crime rate should tempt many of the snowbirds that flock to Florida to escape the winter snow up north. One unique attraction is the World's Smallest Police Station, which has been featured on Real People, Ripley's Believe It Or Not and the Today Show, and was actually used as a police station. It came into being on March 10, 1963. The city had a police phone bolted to the side of a building at the corner of U.S. 98 and Tallahassee Street, but people kept using the phone to make unauthorized long-distance calls. Johnnie Mirabella, who was the phone company's only Carrabelle employee at the time, tried to help. He moved the phone, but that did not end the calls. He also noticed there was no shelter to keep the policemen dry when it rained. He came up with an ingenious solution: The phone company was replacing its phone booth in front of Burda's Pharmacy with a new one, so he took the old booth and put the police phone into it at its present location. People still were sneaking in and making illegal calls. So eventually the dial was removed, solving that problem. The original World's Smallest Police Station now resides in the entry of City Hall, and a replica is still on the street where visitors take photos daily. If you come with a camera, stand with your hands behind your back for best effect.

Camp Gordon Johnson Museum

Camp Gordon Johnson Museum relives the little-known events of the amphibious assault forces in World War II. During the war, all the beach and waterfront land around Carrabelle was converted to a camp for the purpose of training amphibious soldiers and their support groups for the Normandy invasion. Originally it was named Camp Carrabelle after the community but later renamed Camp Gordon Johnston. However, soldiers stationed there were more likely to refer to the camp as Hell-by-the-Sea (before air conditioning and bug spray). The camp trained over a quarter million men for amphibious assaults during World War II. It also served as an interment base for German and Italian prisoners.

Today, the museum honors the soldiers with exhibits that retell the exploits of the overseas activities and life in a wartime camp of that era.

Florida State University Marine Lab

A unique attraction is the Florida State University Marine Lab. It is located there because the purity of the environment creates a hospitable place for research. It is not always open to the public, but be sure to visit if there is an open house when you are in the area. Also they offer a Coastal and Marine Conservation Lecture Series on the second Tuesday of the month at 7 p.m. in the auditorium.

Dining in Carrabelle

After exploring or lazy water fun, wading or just tanning at Carrabelle Beach, when all that water brings on a raging appetite, you have plenty of choices. Dining ranges from places like Carrabelle Junction, which offers simple breakfasts and lunches, to Saint James Bay Golf Resort, which provides upscale dining. My favorite is Fathoms Steam Room and Raw Bar. You can dine inside, but my favorite spot is on the deck overlooking the river. At dinnertime, there is a band. There is a decided Key West feel here. All the seafood choices are great, but remember they rate Apalachicola Bay Oysters as one of the best in the world so that's my first choice. In Eastpoint, Red Pirate Family Grill and Oyster Bar is a rustic seafood choice with music and a mini golf course. If you want to experience Carrabelle nightlife, try Harry's. It crosses Florida with New Orleans vibes.

Dr. Julian G. Bruce St. George Island State Park

A large part of the island is Dr. Julian G. Bruce St. George Island State Park. It's a magnificent park with a dual personality. Its Gulf of Mexico side offers about nine miles of white sandy beach for pleasant swimming or just lying around. You will see sea gulls, maybe a few sea turtles, and possibly some dolphins will entertain you with their leaping. On the Bay side, it's marshy and wild. You may see many birds like osprey and egrets. You may see a bald eagle or red-cockaded woodpecker. Reptiles and small mammals like raccoons and opossums live in the swampy underbrush.

Besides the swimming and sunning, bird watching, stargazing because of dark skies, geocaching, shelling, hiking, biking, fishing, kayaking, and canoeing are popular here. There are two ramps for boat access to Apalachicola Bay for small boats only. For picnickers, there are six beach shelters with picnic tables and grills.

If you can't get enough of the island, you can camp in one of the 60 campsites with electricity and water hookups in the pine woods behind the dunes. A dump station is available in the park. There is primitive camping for the more adventurous.

Carrabelle may call itself "The Pearl of the Forgotten Coast," but one thing is sure; once you visit Carrabelle, you will never forget it.

Apalachicola

Gibson Inn

Apalachicola is just a short drive over the bridge from Carrabelle. In the 1860s, it was the third-largest port on the Gulf, exceeded only by New Orleans and Mobile. In fact, in 1836 it was known as "The City of Granite Fronts" because of its 43 three-storied brick cotton warehouses and brokerages with granite columns that lined Apalachicola's waterfront.

When the railroad replaced shipping as the best way to move cotton, the town began to exploit its rich lumber sources. When that resource became depleted, they turned to the sea. The Apalachicola River dumps into the bay and eventually the Gulf, creating the most favorable conditions for shellfish harvesting. Today, it is famous for its oysters, but there is more than seafood to be found at its most interesting hotel.

In 1907 the Franklin Hotel was built by James Fulten "Jeff" Buck, a native of South Carolina. When it came into the hands of the Gibson Sisters, it was renamed The Gibson Inn.

Ginger Butler, a former employee of the Gibson Inn, told me of many guests commenting about a presence in room 309. She recalled one instance: "One guest, when checking out, thanked her companion for covering her last night, 'it was getting chilly.' 'I didn't!' the companion replied."

She hastened to clarify, "They are all good stories. Like he is looking after the guest's comfort. People have frequently felt like someone brushed up against them on the stairs. Often people will be watching television and the channels will change for no reason. Most things happen in room 309. That's where Captain Willard died."

Chef Wilhelm Bogan, a former chef at the Gibson Inn, is also familiar with the ghost at the Gibson Inn. In his version, Willard was in love with one of the "Gibson Girls."

"The captain would go to San Francisco to pick up cargo and be gone for about six month at a time. Then he was lost in a storm at sea. The Gibson sisters were so distraught, they sold the hotel. When he returned as a ghost, he stayed on in room 309. He tried to maintain the earlier spirit of the hotel. One person on checking out said, 'I didn't know you had a service where you polished people's shoes.' The clerk replied 'No, we don't.'

The ghost would often take guests shoes and put them outside the door, as they did in his time, to be polished."

Chef Wilhelm even had a personal experience with Captain Willard. "We were sitting at the bar one evening and all of a sudden stuff began to be thrown down the stairs, paper towels, soap, stuff like that. Everyone ran up stairs to 309 to find the ghost had rampaged the whole room. The beds were turned over! He did a number! Nobody knows why that room."

Even ghost busters need to refuel sometimes. In Apalachicola you will have lots of choices, but seafood is the way to go. If you want an upscale experience, The Gibson recently opened Avenue Sea. The husband/wife team, Chefs David and Ryanne Carrier, come from a very upscale background, but David states, "Our food style is very friendly, as are our personalities, and although we come from restaurants that deal with things on a very hoity-toity level, that's not really what we're about. Our food is less cerebral than those restaurants we come from. We're not trying to recreate anything here."

Delores's Sweet Shop

A great way to get a feel for the old Apalachicola is to visit Delores's Sweet Shop. Delores Roux grew up in the area and has many interesting tales to tell of the way things were. If you ask nicely, she may even tell you about her own personal ghost. One wall of her restaurant is covered with photographs of old Apalachicola: the waterfront, the old courthouse and many others scenes of the old town.

Ormon House

There are several other homes in Apalachicola that lay claim to their own ghosts. One is the Ormon House. It was the home of Thomas Ormon and his family. He was a wealthy Cotton Commissioner and ordered his home precut and delivered to its present site on the bluff overlooking the river in 1838. During the War Between the States, it was used as an infirmary, and perhaps that is the root of the ghost story. For years, the two-story, vernacular Greek revival-style home stood deserted and decaying. Today, the house and grounds are one of Florida's newest state parks. Whether in jest or not, in the bill to purchase the property, Attorney General Bob Butterworth added an amendment requiring DEP Secretary David B. Struhs to spend a night alone in the house. I haven't learned if he did, but the sellers do acknowledge that there is a "presence" in the historic home.

Flatauer House

Another great old Apalachicola house with a spirited history almost didn't survive the wreckers. The Flatauer House now houses the Gulf State Bank. David Butler, the bank's president, told me, "My first idea when we acquired the property was to have someone move the house elsewhere; it had deteriorated so badly that it was considered an unattractive nuisance. It had been converted to apartments back in the '20s. I even took out a full page ad offering it free to anyone who would take it and restore it. No takers. Then the idea of restoring it took hold. We only had one early photograph to use, so we had to rely on structural analysis."

The house chronicles the story of one family. In 1908, Adolph Flatauer was on top of the world. He built a magnificent home for his family with elegant oriental carpets and elaborate woodwork. In 1919, disaster struck. His wife, Regina, died during the flu epidemic. Adolph, unable to live without her, took his own life just a few months later. Sitting in front of the beautifully tiled fireplace in their master bedroom, he shot himself. The distraught widower desired only to join his beloved, but fate was not so kind. He died of the wound but only after suffering for three days. The spot where the bullet exited his head and struck the fireplace still remains chipped. On the tile of the hearth, there is always a spot resembling a bloodstain that will not clean no matter how hard it is scrubbed.

Emily Crumb, a former bank employee, recalled when the bank finally finished the restoration in 1982 and held an open house to proudly display its accomplishment. "Many of the Flatauer family came. Various family members told stories about the house being haunted." One person told Emily of being in the house as a child. "She said she and a friend heard a noise during the night. The two girls crept out to investigate. In the main hall, they saw an image of a man on the stairs carrying a bowl dripping with what looked like blood. They ran to get an adult to investigate, and when they returned there was no man, no blood. The experience really spooked her out."

As Emily points out, most of what occurred in the house has been told to her just as hearsay, but there are some things that she and other bank employees have witnessed themselves. "Frequently when we come in the morning, our desks have been disturbed. Typewriters have been overturned. Papers have been scattered on the floor."

Ghost or not, the house is a magnificent structure. It has been brought back to its original floor plan, and the bank is proud to show it to visitors.

Gorrie Museum

Picture living in Florida without air conditioning, then say "thank you" to Dr. John Gorrie. Dr. Gorrie was a physician during the 1841 yellow fever epidemic. He was desperately seeking some way to cool his feverish patients and devised a precursor to the air conditioner. It is on display at the John Gorrie Museum in town. The museum also features exhibits on the early history of Apalachicola.

Chapman Home/Weichert Realtors

There are so many beautiful old homes in Apalachicola, it is only natural many of the former residents still remain to look after what was their prized possession in life. Dr. Alvin Wentworth Chapman's home is one such place. Dr Chapman was a botanist who moved to Apalachicola in 1847. He was originally from Massachusetts but remained in Apalachicola until his death in 1899. During the War Between the States, Dr. Chapman's wife, Mary, who was from North Carolina, disagreed so strongly with her husband's political views that she left him and moved to Marianna. After the war they reconciled.

His home is a classical design that originally had a central hallway both upstairs and downstairs with two rooms on either side of the hallway. In those days, the kitchen was usually separate from the house. In 1921 the house was extensively remodeled. Today it is the office of Weichert Realtors. Investigators from Big Bend Ghost Trackers found many orbs and cold spots.

It is convenient that the Chapman Home is next to the Chestnut Street Cemetery. That makes it convenient for Dr Chapman to spend eternity in his home, since he is buried there along with his wife.

Chestnut Street Cemetery

Chestnut Street Cemetery dates back to at least 1831. Most of the town's original settlers are interred there. There is also a large contingent of shipwreck victims, some Confederate soldiers and a lot of Yellow Fever victims.

Perhaps two of the saddest burials in the old cemetery are the Messina children, Louisa and Frank. They were playing on the dock while they parents served supper to the older men in 1878. The younger child, Louisa, slipped and fell into the water. Frank jumped in to try and save his sister, but they both drowned instead. Perhaps Frank and Louisa still frolic among the old tombstones.

Shopping

Several of the old Cotton exchange buildings are renovated as shops and art galleries. The sponge exchange building, built in 1836, is now renovated into a boutique that sells natural sponges. Antique and art galleries abound.

Dixie Theater

Lest you think Apalachicola lacking in cultural events, think again. The Dixie Theater is a reconstructed gem. The original Dixie Theater opened in April 1913 as a venue for live entertainment. It progressed into a movie theater until 1967 then deteriorated until it was just a crumbling pile of bricks by 1994. That's when it was discovered by a pair of well-known Broadway veterans, Rex and Cleo Partington. They wanted to restore it as it had been in its heyday, but there were no reliable pictures and the structure was too far gone to give enough clues. However, they did reconstruct the facade and were able to restore the original ticket booth as it had been in its glory days. In 1998, it opened its doors again and offers classics like *Driving Miss Daisy, Steel Magnolias* and *Always - Patsy Cline*.

They have reinstated a tradition that gives new meaning to "we'll leave the light on for you." When the theater is unoccupied, a small-watt light bulb casts its eerie luminescence across the Dixie's stage. This custom traces its roots back to the days of ancient theater when stage managers provided a small light for the benefit of performers who had passed to the after-life. It's referred to as a "ghost light."

That's the way Apalachicola is. They view visitors as friends they haven't met, so they always leave the light on for you. Besides the theater welcoming you, the town also offers you a chance to visits historical homes on the first Saturday in May at the Tour of Homes each year and a chance to sample the incomparable seafood at the Florida Seafood Festival on the first Saturday in November.

Amelia Island

Florida House

David Levy Yulee was one of the first of the railroad barons. He was born "David Levy" and later added Yulee to his name. He married well, the daughter of the governor of Kentucky, and developed a 5,000-acre plantation on Florida's Homosassa River that produced lumber, sugar, and other products as well as a sugar mill to process the sugar cane. By 1857 David Yulee's Florida Railroad -- his planned Railroad from Fernandina to Cedar Key -- was to be the first cross-state railroad, linking the two important ports, one on the Atlantic Coast and the other on the Gulf Coast. Fernandina at that time had the largest and deepest harbor south of Chesapeake Bay. Both were important ports to the lumber and naval stores industry.

Although he had been elected to the senate, he resigned when Florida left the Union. Yulee's Homosassa mansion was burned by Union soldiers. The Confederacy stripped the steel rails from his railroad tracks to build the railroad lines that were needed in the interior of the state to move Confederate armies. After the war, he was sent to prison for being a rebel, but President U.S. Grant pardoned him. He lived out the rest of his life in Washington, D.C., where he died in 1886 at age 75.

He had helped make Amelia Island "the place to visit" for wealthy northern travelers before Henry Flagler's new railroad lured them farther South. The oldest hotel in Florida is Yulee's Florida House. It is still operating but has been vastly remodeled since the days David Yulee built his small Vernacular "Cracker" style house in 1857 to accommodate travelers on his railroad.

One of the reasons Yulee opened the hotel was so the wealthy and prestigious visitors would have a suitable place to stay. It certainly achieved that goal. Since its opening, The Florida House has played host to notables like Ulysses S. Grant, Cuban poet and freedom fighter Jose Marti, Mary Pickford, Laurel and Hardy, and various Rockefellers and Carnegies.

The War Between the States disrupted the small port town as well as Yulee's life. Union forces took over Fort Clinch and used the hotel to house federal officers. After the War, Major Leddy, who had served as Provost Marshall at Ft. Clinch, and his wife acquired the Florida House. They constructed an addition in 1865 to provide personal living space and a dining room that served boarding-house style meals. Mrs. Leddy continued to run the hotel and dining room after her husband's death. The modest dining room of the Leddys' day has evolved into The Frisky Mermaid Bar and Grill, one of Amelia Island's dining experiences. It offers elegant dining with an international flair and a full-service bar. Diane Warwick, the inn's former owner, appreciates the unique history of Florida House.

When you stay at the inn, you are apt to experience another brush with the inn's history in the "person" of one of the two friendly resident ghosts. One is a tall young man whose girlfriend who died in childbirth here at the inn. He seems to prefer the oldest part of the building but has been seen all over the inn. One guest claimed she spoke with him for several hours one night. She described him as "nice" but "very depressed."

Diane said several people have seen him and he seems to be searching and confused but friendly. Diane also told me the inn had been a brothel at one time and the madam was killed in room 12. That room had a lot of activity at one time. The Madam doesn't seem to like women. She moves makeup and turns on and off the television. Or at least she did until Diane repainted her room in blue and white, a very peaceful decor, and she had been quiet since then. Diane feels that the Madam was probably tired of the same color scheme and wanted the room freshened up.

Aside from these two specters, there seems to be other presences. Diane said she has had psychics stay at the inn at different times. They all told her the dining room is a very active area. During Yulee's time, this was the place where politicians would meet to discuss the affairs of the city. The psychics sense that the spirits of these men are still meeting in their usual place late at night when the dining room is closed.

Diane recalled when they had the innkeeper's quarters above the dining room, she would often wake at night and hear chairs scraping as if they were being moved around. She said, "I just let them have their meetings. When I went down there next morning, all would be just as I left it."

She recounted that her dining room workers often experience "something." "They set a table and leave the room then when they return to continue the setup, the silverware has been moved around."

Many of them have reported seeing something in the darkened room and when they turn on the lights to look no one is there.

The strangest experience Diane had occurred one day when a housekeeper had left a broom in the hall. She said, "I brought it into the office and had it sitting propped against the wall. Just when I was getting ready to close the office, a friend and her grandchildren stopped by to see if I wanted to go to the ice cream parlor down the street. Just at that moment, the broom moved to a flat position on the floor and then rose back to its original position against the wall."

Everyone present saw this happen. There was no normal explanation for it. Perhaps the spirits of the Florida House Inn were trying to tell Diane something. The woman visiting Diane was a self-proclaimed sensitive, it possibly had something to do with her presence.

Today, you can enjoy the historic ambiance of Florida House along with modern conveniences. Since it is pet-friendly, you can even share your accommodations with your best friend of the four-legged persuasion.

Eppes House

Fernandina is filled with grand old homes. Looking at them I could understand why the original owners would want to hang around. One is the Eppes House on Ash and 10th streets. It was built around 1885 and was the home of T. J. and Celeste Eppes. Celeste was a raven-haired beauty who desired attention at all costs. Once just to make her husband jealous, she lied and told him a family friend, Maj. Ferdinand Suhrer, was making inappropriate advances to her. She succeeded beyond her expectations and was horrified to learn that her enraged husband had shot and killed the innocent Major. The guilt must have eaten away at Celeste for years. When she and her newborn child died during childbirth, they were buried in the St. Peter's Episcopal Church graveyard nearby. But she could not rest in peace. She still roams her former home trying to make amends. A 20th century owner of the Eppes House reported seeing a woman with flowing raven hair that now had a white streak in it. The apparition spoke to the woman and told her the white streak was caused by the guilt she felt for causing the death of an innocent man.

The home is not open to the public but is part of the island's history and has been beautifully restored.

Thompson Houses

There were three historic houses built for the Thompson family in Fernandina in the late 1800s. The first of the Thompson Houses was built around 1872. It was the home of the most prominent family member, William Naylor Thompson, who was a state senator.

The Lucy Cottage was built around 1877 for his sister, Miss Lucy O. Thompson. It still remains in the Thompson family.

The last of the Thompson houses was built in 1882 for the senator's brother, Pratt Thompson. It was the city's first brick residence. His wife, "Miss Nettie," loved the old home. In fact she is still there. Called "a tease, not a terror," she still rattles the beds and rearranges the items on the dressers in what she still considers "her home." All three homes are listed on the walking or driving tour.

The Bailey House

There is a ghost story attached to this magnificent Queen Ann Style Victorian. Katherine MacDonell was born in 1874 on Amelia Island. When she was 13 she saw a picture of a beautiful home in a magazine and was so enthralled by its graceful lines and ornate gingerbread, she cut it out and told all her family and friends it was her "dream home."

A few years later, the teenaged Kate met a charming older man, Effingham W. Bailey, who was a steamship agent from Charleston, South Carolina, stationed in Fernandina Beach. He was smitten, and they planned to marry as soon as she was 18. When his young fiancée showed him the picture of the house, he promised to build it for her.

He kept his word, and the home still stands today in all its magnificent glory. Miss Kate was a determined woman. And a story is told about her run-in with the authorities.

At one time the city decided to cut down a giant, ancient, live oak tree on Ash Street, near her home. Miss Kate informed the city manager that no one had better "dare put an axe to that tree." She sat on her porch with a shotgun to protect her tree while the workers paved the street. The oak is still there, and some say Mrs. Kate's ghost is still guarding that tree from her porch. Formerly a B and B, it is now a private home but is occasionally open for the history museum special events.

Witches

One of Fernandina's oldest phantoms may be the ghost of a young girl who was accused of practicing witchcraft. She was hanged in the 1600s, but her spirit still guards her grave. Legends say if you approach her grave, you will feel the ground shaking. Other times you are allowed to approach, but a part of her leaves with you, and you will dream of her for two nights; then if you return to the gravesite, you will actually see her. Want to check for yourself? The grave of the girl is located on the narrow path just across from Fernandina Beach High School.

There are legends in town about another witch, Felipa, who practiced her magic in the old part of town.

Old Depot

Be sure to stop at the Old Depot to get all the latest information on Fernandina. It is the home of the Chamber of Commerce. This is also the starting point for the History Tour.

Old Jail

The Old Jail is one of the best places to start your tour of Fernandina at the Amelia Island Museum of History. It is the only spoken-history museum in Florida. Naturally, it has its own ghost who was hanged there more than a century ago.

The pirate, Luis Aury, arrived in Fernandina in 1817 to take over the island. He claimed to be a Mexican officer and raised the flag of the Mexican Republic annexing Amelia Island to Mexico. When he was finally captured three months later, he was imprisoned in the jail and then hanged out back. His ghost is said to still haunt the jail house He is one of the best-documented ghosts on the island. More than 100 volunteer guides give details of the island's past at the museum and on walking tours of the historic district. The Historic Society also sponsors a Ghost Tour that will give you a glimpse of what the area's early days were like as well as acquaint you with many of the island's phantoms.

Palace Saloon

The Palace Saloon is Florida's oldest saloon still operating in its original location. It was reported to be the last bar in the entire country to close for prohibition. During the hiatus, it served ice cream instead of its famous Pirate's Punch. It also has its resident ghost, Charlie Beresford, a former bartender who died there in 1960. Many have glimpsed him in the mirrors behind the huge mahogany bar. In the late 1880s, it was the haunt of America's wealthiest, such as the Vanderbilts, Duponts and Carnegies. Although damaged by a fire a few years ago, it has been restored to its original condition, and you can still belly up to the bar and watch for Uncle Charlie.

Amelia Lighthouse

One landmark that has stood the test of time well on Amelia is the lighthouse. Peeping above the trees, Florida's northernmost lighthouse has a strange history. In 1820, it began its life as Georgia's southernmost light on the southern tip of Cumberland Island. Then, in 1837, it was dismantled and moved to its present location.

Today, it is still in good shape and just recently has been opened to the public, but tours are limited. You MUST call the City of Fernandina Beach Parks & Recreation at least 24 hours in advance. Tours are at 10:00 a.m. the first and third Wednesday of the month

As in many lighthouses, it has its tragic ghost story. It is said to be haunted by the spirit of a former keeper and his young bride. The young woman died tragically, and the grief-stricken keeper killed himself at the top of the lighthouse. Visitors have experienced putrid smells inside the lighthouse. One of the doors is always found unlocked even though caretakers are careful to lock it when they leave. A radio will mysteriously come on at night for no reason.

Another ghost who reportedly inhabits the old lighthouse is Amos Latham, the first keeper, who died 1842.

Even the sandy beach the lighthouse stands guard over has some eerie stories. During the days when Fernandina was a big port city, pirates frequented the town. Supposedly some left behind a cache of buried treasure. It is reputedly marked by a chain hanging from a big oak named the "Money Tree." Many people have supposedly found the tree with its chain, but when they return with their shovels, they find that the tree and chain have mysteriously vanished.

Fort Clinch

On the coast looking toward Georgia's Cumberland Island, Fort Clinch stands as a silent sentry, a witness to American history's greatest tragedy. It was started in 1847 by the federal government, and the construction continued during the Civil War. In 1961 it was taken over by the Confederates who later withdrew by order of General Lee in 1862.

Of course, it was promptly occupied by the Federal troops. During the skirmishing between the two sides, several Union soldiers were killed.

After the Civil War, it was reduced to an almost standby position, only to be briefly reactivated in 1898 for several months during the Spanish-American War. Today it is a state park. Its remarkable state of preservation lends itself well to the reenactments conducted there regularly.

Among the Union soldiers killed at the fort was one man who promised his wife in a letter that he would not die until they were together again. He is believed to be one of the soldiers who haunt the fort today. Re-enactors at the fort often see a ghost in the courtyard who seems to be looking for someone. Many of his comrades have also been spotted.

One soldier appears in a window and has been seen by many people. He is in Yankee uniform and appears to be glowing.

Many other people have spotted a woman dressed in white, possibly a nurse. There are also those who have heard the cries of a ghostly baby. There are stories that a female spirit is often spotted searching for her baby. Could this be the same crying baby ghost? During the depression, homeless people lived in the tunnels of the fort. It is said the ghost baby is one of the homeless who died in the cold damp conditions. Four headless ghosts have also been sighted marching along the rampart at Fort Clinch

Along with all the sightings, there have been many reports of mysterious footsteps and jangling keys in the night.

After almost a century, Amelia Island has been rediscovered by visitors from the North. The construction of Amelia Island Plantation once more brings the richest and most influential Northern visitors to Fernandina Beach. The locals, they know they have had the "good life" here all along, whether anyone else "discovers" it or not.

Tampa - St Petersburg Area

Don CeSar

The classic ghost story is found at the Don Cesar Hotel. This St. Petersburg landmark grew out of one man's ill-fated romance. Perhaps the dashing "Don Cesar" and his beautiful Maritana were doomed from the start. Then again, perhaps they have finally reunited in the afterlife and are now living their dream "life" for all eternity in their castle by the sea overlooking the azure waters of Tampa Bay. You decide for yourself.

He was an orphaned American raised by his Irish grandfather. He was sent to England for an education and there met a young opera singer named Lucinda. She was singing the female lead in Thomas Rowe's favorite opera, Maritana. The two fell madly in love and planned to elope and spend their lives in a pink castle by the sea.

It was not to be. Lucinda's parents intervened and, on the day they were to depart for the United States, kept Lucinda secreted away. The brokenhearted young Rowe had no choice. He had to return home as his guardian required, but he never forgot his first love. He wrote to her at first, but the letters came back unopened.

Throughout the ensuing years, Thomas became a wealthy man. Forced by ill health, he moved to Florida. It was there that he bought 80 acres of an island on the shores of Tampa destined to become St Petersburg Beach. He had since married another woman, but his heart still yearned for the dream he had shared with his Lucinda. Now, a man of 42, he had the location and the means to build what he had promised his first love as a young student.

He divided the acres of his island paradise into tracts and sold lots. The streets were named for characters and places in Maritana. But the crowning jewel in his kingdom by the sea was the 10-story Moorish Mediterranean pink hotel. It could only be called the "Don Cesar." In the sunroom on the first floor, Rowe placed the fountain he had once promised to Lucinda. A winged angel poured water from a vase into a pond below encircled by swans.

The setting was gorgeous, the location was perfect, but the timing was terrible. The Don opened on January 16, 1928, with a scene that would have fit an F. Scott Fitzgerald novel. However when the stock market crashed in October 1929, the reverberation was destined to shake even the 10-foot-thick walls of Rowe's dream hotel.

Through receivership, hurricanes and prohibition, Rowe managed to hang on to his management of the hotel. Finally, he received a note from his lost love. Lucinda wrote on her deathbed to her beloved, "Time is infinite. I wait for you by our fountain . . . to share our timeless love, our destiny is time." Rowe died in the hotel on May 5, 1940. On his deathbed, he attempted to will the hotel to the staff. However, his doctors stated he was too ill to make a rational decision. His estranged wife, Mary, inherited it instead and took over the management. The hotel declined.

During the war years, the army purchased it. It became a hospital, a convalescent center, a veteran's administration office, and finally a derelict almost ready for the demolition ball. During the time of government ownership, its angel fountain was removed and the floor tiled over. Why? Probably the same reason they painted it Government Issue Green.

Then in the '70s, it was rescued and on its way to being a world-class hotel again. It was at this time that Thomas Rowe and his ladylove, Lucinda, began to be sighted by guests and staff alike.

The hotel passed through several hands and a few restorations, but the two spirits still seem to be there. They have been joined by some from the era when the building was used as a hospital also.

People who worked with him reported smelling a foul odor like his cigarettes. Thomas had asthma and had to smoke certain cigarettes the doctors prescribed that contained a medicine that got to his lungs. They had a particularly nasty smell.

Susan Owen, Guest Experience Manager, recounted when the sightings began in earnest. "It was during the renovation. Workmen would ask, 'Who was that white-haired man asking questions about the renovation?' Some of the workers refused to work here because of him. He never appeared as a wraith. It was always as a normal man."

There was one time he appeared to a journalist. It was not to give an interview but to help prevent tragedy. Susan struggled to recall the exact details, but memory of the main incident was sharp. "She was a writer for, I think, Bride Magazine. They were doing an article about weddings here. The next morning she came down and asked. 'Do you have a ghost here?' The answer, of course, was 'yes, why?'

"The writer continued, 'Last night in bed, a man appeared to me and said, "Do not let her go on the ledge."' We asked what he looked like. The journalist made a sketch of the man and he bore a striking resemblance to Thomas Rowe. No one thought any more of it until a few days later when her photographer was doing a layout with the writer and a model on the rooftop. The rooftop there is actually a patio for the penthouse. The photographer wanted the model to get up on the ledge and get a shot of her. When he said 'ledge,' bells went off in the writer's head. She stopped the shoot, and when they examined the ledge they found bits of crumbled mortar on top. Had the model stepped there she might have lost her balance and fallen."

Susan has had personal experiences with him. She has never seen him, but she still finds little things happening that are unexplainable. "They only seem to happen to me when I am really rushing around doing something for a guest. For instance, the elevators are slow in the building. Usually I stand there and twiddle my thumbs while I count as the light tells the floors, 10, 9, 8 and so on. But if someone has forgotten something and I am rushing to get it back to him, inevitably, the elevator door opens just as I approach. No buttons pushed! No waiting! It is just there when I need it."

One receptionist who had come from Pennsylvania was temporally staying in the hotel. She and her husband were on the beach, and she looked up and saw a man in a white linen suit and a Panama hat. She called to her husband, "Look, that looks like Panama Jack." Her husband didn't see the man. She just thought he must have disappeared behind the bushes and gave it no more thought until she was doing her orientation and spotted a picture of Thomas Rowe.

Thomas seems to be very protective of "his" hotel still. Once when a bride's mother was very upset and blaming the hotel for just about everything, she was raving at the florist in the hotel. Suddenly all the shelves in the refrigerators holding flower displays came crashing down. That not only silenced the lady but also sent her scuttling away.

Another place Thomas Rowe shows himself frequently is in the kitchen. Workers will suddenly see a face in one of the freezers, and then it will be gone as fast as it appeared.

Many people have reported seeing a man and woman in period clothing walking around near where the original fountain was. Is it possible that Thomas and Lucinda do in fact "share our timeless love?"

Tampa Theater

Something about theaters seems to attract hauntings. Tampa Theater is a natural for at least one good ghost story. Its history and architecture alone merit a visit, but there is more lurking in its dark recesses.

The theatre was built by architect John Eberson in 1926 and has been a Tampa landmark ever since. The elaborate movie house attracts more than 150,000 people annually and is on the National Register of Historic Places. As you sit in the massive theater awaiting the lowering of the lights for a performance, you are surrounded by the atmosphere of a Mediterranean garden. After the lights go down, the starlit sky sparkles above. It was the masterpiece of its day when it opened. It even had air conditioning, which drew many people just for that in summer.

In a different twist on the Phantom of The Opera, Tampa Theater is rumored to be haunted by the friendly ghost of Foster Finley. Foster was the theatre's projectionist for 25 years until his death in the late 1960s. He would not leave the place where he had spent most of his adult life and is still glimpsed by visitors and employees alike.

He always came to work dressed in a suit, tie and hat, and then changed in the dressing room. His nickname was "Fink." The new projectionist who replaced him did not last too long. According to Tara Schroeder, then marketing manager, the poor man would hear the door open and close, and no one would be there. At that time, the projectionist needed to switch from one projector to another one as the reels wound down. The toggle switch controlling this would be flipped before he could reach for it. The unnerved projectionist decided two projectionists in the small room was one too many, especially if the other one was dead. He quit.

Many of the theater employees heard keys rattling. On two occasions, different employees who were opening the theater heard keys rattling at the level above the concession stand. They heard a key being put into the door up there and said, "Good morning." They then went up to see who was there only to find themselves all alone in the theater.

A group of St. Petersburg Ghost investigators came to the theater. They brought all the latest equipment and one that is still considered controversial, dowsing rods. They tried to rule out any natural causes, for instance any wiring behind walls when the detectors went off. In some cases, the detectors would go off indicating energy at that spot. They would leave it and go back later and, if no energy was detected, ruled out wires since they would always be present. Tara relates, "At one place, I watched the meter go off, and the temperature gauge dropped way down. Since it was so dramatic, they got out the dowsing rods. These were used to ask questions. If they crossed, it indicated a 'yes.' They asked a few questions, and nothing happened. I decided I would have some fun so I asked, 'Can I ask some questions?' I asked about several incidents like, 'Were you here when the keys jingled?' I asked, 'Were you employed here?' The rods crossed to indicate 'yes.' I went through the decades to determine the time frame. When I asked, 'Were you employed here in the '50s?' it indicated 'Yes.'"

Was Fink letting Tara know he was there and active?

Falk Theater

Tampa Theater isn't the only haunted theater in the area. Not by a long shot! The Falk Theater has its departed actress, Betsy Snavely. Betsy hanged herself in a third floor dressing room sometime in the 1930s after her husband deserted her and ran off with a stagehand. The theater now belongs to the University, but Betsy is still seen and heard.

Lake Worth Playhouse

Another theater in the area that boasts a resident haunt is the Lake Worth Playhouse. The art deco-style theater began life in 1924 as the brainchild of brothers Clarence and Lucian Oakly. The brothers operated it as a combination movie palace and vaudeville theater until they ran into some hard times. Vaudeville declined. A hurricane took off the Spanish-style roof. Each time, the brothers coped. That is until June 30, 1931. Lucien blew out his brains on the back porch of his home. Incidentally, his insurance policy would have expired at midnight.

Exactly a year later, Clarence died suddenly.

After the brothers' deaths, strange incidents have been reported. The theater changed its name in 1953 to the Lake Worth Playhouse, but the shadowy residents continue to play tricks.

Toilet paper rolls will mysteriously be lined up in the lobby. Items as large as 5-gallon water coolers move around. Pictures of actors are turned to face the wall in the lobby. Footsteps echo from various places when there is no one in those places. One manager even reports hearing applause in the empty theater. Psychics have suggested exorcism, but the current owners refuse. They feel their ghost is friendly and happy in the theater. When the last staff member leaves, he or she never fails to say, "Good night, Mr. Oakley."

University of Tampa

If theaters always have a ghost story, colleges always have even more. Perhaps it is that the multitude of young, open-minded people are willing to recognize paranormal phenomenon while older people tend to explain them away. Whatever, universities all over have their favorite stories. The University of Tampa is no exception. In fact, considering the history and buildings of the campus, it would be unbelievable if there were no specters roaming the halls.

The building that houses the main hall of the university, Plant Hall, was once the Tampa Bay Hotel. A minaretted Moorish/Victorian castle straight out of Arabian Nights, it was built by Henry Plant to house the visitors he drew to Florida via his new railroad.

Henry Plant's hotel looks like something out of a Gothic novel. His life story reads likewise. A relatively poor boy who spurned an offer by his grandmother to attend Yale and, she hoped, become a clergyman, instead he ran away at the age of 18 and became captain's boy, deck hand, and man-of-all-work on a steamboat plying between New Haven and New York. He married well, Ellen Elizabeth Blackstone, the daughter of Connecticut State Senator James Blackstone, in 1842. When Ellen died in 1861, Henry had one surviving son, Morton Freeman Plant. Henry was not totally satisfied with the boy. Morton was more of a playboy than a businessman. He preferred sailing his yacht instead of sitting behind a desk.

Henry married again in 1873. Perhaps he believed at 53 he could have more sons, but that was not to be. When Henry died in 1899, Morton, then 47, was not present. He was sailing his yacht. The will must have been a shock to the second wife, Margaret Josephine Loughman, and Morton. In fact, there is a story that Henry changed his will shortly before his death. In the new will, Henry had left Margaret and Morton only $30,000 a year apiece and the remainder to a yet unborn great grandson.

Margaret and Morton banded together and contested the will. They won, and Henry's wishes were thwarted.

Is Plant the mysterious "Brown Man" seen roaming the second floor hall of Plant hall?

One female student had arrived early and was visiting with her father who worked as a postman in the campus mail room located in Plant Hall. She had stepped away from the post office and saw a man dressed in an old-fashioned three-piece brown suit on the second floor landing. When she called out to him to see if he needed help, he turned and she saw that his eyes were glowing. Naturally she fled to the safety of her father's post office.

Another student saw the same man sitting one morning near the landing drinking a cup of tea. When she approached, he disappeared. Security officers in Plant Hall have had encounters where things were moved from one place to another. In one case, a guard had a flashlight knocked from his hand by an invisible presence.

The "Brown Man" is not the only phantom in the college. What is now the science section was the servants' quarters when the building was a hotel. Students have reported hearing the wheels of serving carts and the sound of footsteps in a passageway between the science building and Plant Hall. Many students in the science building also tell of seeing a dark-skinned man in a wide straw hat and boots who is believed to be the spirit of a faithful caretaker who once tended the building's grounds.

Where the present student union stands is the location of the old hotel casino that burned down in 1941. Students around the cafeteria late at night claim to hear the sound of dice rolling.

Merle Kelce Library

It is understandable that the older parts of the school would have their ghosts, but how can one explain the University of Tampa's Merle Kelce Library haunting? You would think a library would be a strange place for a ghost with its rules about quiet, but this library is definitely different. First, it's just down the street from Plant Hall. Although the library is a stark modern building, it has its share of unexplained phenomena.

Kevin McGinn, a former Technical Assistant at the library, has had several unnerving experiences. The library is a relatively new building, but that doesn't stop the spirits associated with things that occurred there before the present structure from causing disturbances. During the heyday of the hotel, this area contained a casino. It had a floor that opened and disclosed a swimming pool in the daytime and at night was closed to create a dance floor. Many celebrities visited and performed here them.

However, she said that the one visual experience she had was with a former employer. "He was behind me at the circulation desk. I think he pinched me one time. I have never seen him since, but once when I was in the building with a friend after hours, we both had a strange experience. We had gone to a show, and I had brought her back here to show her something. We were leaning over my desk looking at the papers. We both looked up at the same time and decided to leave. Neither of us said anything inside, but when we got outside, she asked me, 'Did you feel someone pinch you?'"

The man in question as an employee who passed away in the seventies, Joe Figerota. He was only in his thirties when he dies. The library has a plaque on one of the pillars in his memory.

Kevin comes by her psychic senses naturally. She will tell you "My mother is a sensitive, and she has told me there are different types of energy here. Some good and some not so good. She has seen people in the stacks who appear as solid and you or I."

I asked if her mother had observed the clothing since that is one way to gauge the era the spirit might derive from. She said her mother had said one man was wearing a dark suit like those worn in the nineteenth century. This would coincide with the time the casino existed on this spot.

The library has some unusual objects in its collection. After all, how often do you find the ashes of a deceased benefactor in a library? Kevin looked upward and lowered her voice when she told of this. "There is a dark force here, too. It manifests itself mostly if you stay after hours. I don't stay after hours and work anymore. I had a terrible experience. The Special Collections is right up overhead." At that time, we heard a tapping that I was able to capture on my tape recorder.

Kevin shrugged it off as an everyday occurrence. "That's what they usually do. They know we're talking about them."

She continued to explain where she believed the "bad energy upstairs" emanated from. The ashes of a descendent of one of the founders of Ybor City are there on the orders of a physic councilor. They are in a marble urn. The widow had a good bit of money and the pseudo psychic may have been trying to get some of it. My mother says he should not be here. His spirit is restless. His wife was also supposed to be interred here, but she's buried somewhere else."

At this point, I was not sure I wanted to accept her invitation to see the urns. The room is usually closed to the public, but when we entered the deserted space surrounded by venerable old books, the feeling was similar to entering a mausoleum. The two urns stood next to one another and were the first thing anyone entering the room would see.

She descried her "terrible experience" in that room as the feeling of being enveloped by a "Psychic Force" a "disembodied evil" rather than a spirit of a departed person. "It was horrible! I felt an inhuman energy. Like one of the plagues of Egypt. Like when the death took the firstborn in a family."

Kevin also pointed out that there were also "good forces" in the room that seemed to try to counteract the evil. "Twice when I was working in here, I fell. Both times, I felt hands break my fall and lower me to the floor gently." She did not appear comfortable in the room and we left quickly.

The ladies' room on the first floor is also haunted. She stopped in one night after work to retrieve something. Her mother and nephew were with her. As the building was dark, her mother said she was going to stay downstairs near the circulation desk. Kevin and her nephew went upstairs to the employee lounge to get some soft drinks. Meanwhile, her mother went to the Ladies Room to wash her hands. While they were in the lounge, they received a frantic call from her mother, "She whispered, 'Get down here quick.' When we got to the first floor, she told us she heard singing in the Ladies Room: many voices, mostly female and singing an operatic aria. The temperature in the entire area was dropping noticeably, so we left quickly."

Other employees had strange experiences with that rest room. Two of them also heard the singing and a third just had a feeling of being watched when she was in the room.

Another explanation for the female singer is found in the story told by a former employee that a young woman committed suicide in the library. At that time the library was located in the current Student Services building. Perhaps the woman moved into the new building when the library moved there. The death is believed to have occurred shortly after the university was built in 1956.

She frequently saw a phantom woman in the stacks on the fourth floor near the special collections room after all the patrons had left the library.

Ybor City

Ybor City is a place no visitor to Tampa wants to miss. They come to see the museums reflecting the culture of another era. The nightlife and restaurants offer entertainment. Sometimes it is easy to forget that this hot spot for tourists was home for the thousands of emigrants who sought a better life in America at the turn of the century. Some still remain through the ages.

"To understand Ybor City, you must visit the clubs." At first I took Helen Tasin's statement to mean nightclubs. But Helen, a representative of Centro Ybor, explained. In Tampa's historic Ybor City, "the clubs" have a whole new meaning. They represent a unique system the immigrants devised to survive in America's melting pot. Not only survive but maintain their cultural identity.

Ybor City owes its existence to one man's dream. Don Vicente Martinez Ybor was a wealthy cigar factory owner in the latter part of the 19th century. He had moved his factories from Cuba to Key West because of labor unrest, but found a lack of transportation there a problem. Encouraged by Henry Plant's new rail line into Tampa, he brought his factories there. Other wealthy owners followed. The factory workers settled on the forty acres of Ybor City. Italians, Germans, Spanish, Jewish and other Europeans followed. Soon, a thriving European community had sprung up on Florida's West Coast.

But Ybor City differed greatly from other enclaves of immigrants. The social clubs were one feature that made Tampa's cultural soup appealing.

These "clubs" were the closest to our insurance policies that the immigrants had. As an immigrant in a foreign land, your life and culture revolved around the clubs from birth to death. For the nominal dues, you received a place to go to hear your native language spoken, an entertainment center, and hospitalization in sickness, health and burial insurance. Most important, the club dances and socials were a place your children would meet future spouses of "their own kind" thus-hopefully ensuring that your cultural heritage would not be abandoned by the second-generation immigrants.

Max Herman of Official Ybor City Ghost Tours introduced me to his "friend," Don Vicente Martinez de Ybor, the cigar entrepreneur who founded Ybor City in 1886. Of course, the "friend" is just a bronze statue, but without him, Ybor City would not exist. Ybor City is like a city within a city. It has some of the most haunted building in America. It's one of only three National Historic Landmark Districts in Florida. Max led me on a terrific ghost tour of Ybor City. The Official Ybor City Ghost Tour is so good it's ranked #1 ghost tour on US City Traveler. One thing that differentiates it from other tours is you go into some buildings, not just look from the outside. In addition, my guide told a lot of authentic Ybor City history.

We visited Centro Espanol, the Spanish Club. Now in Ybor City, clubs had a different meaning than a nightclub or a health club today, although in some ways they served both purposes. Ybor City was the "Cigar Capital of the World." Although Don Ybor brought many Cuban workers here to work his factory, many other immigrants came because here jobs were plentiful. The city was filled with Cubans, Spaniards, Romanian Jews, Sicilians, Italians, Germans, and more. Each immigrant mingled daily with other nationalities, but on Sundays and in evenings, they each had their own clubs. They paid about a quarter a week. This provided them with not only a place to socialize, dance, gamble, and enjoy entertainment, but also had a doctor on staff in case of illness. Think about that. A quarter a week for health care? Who wouldn't join for that alone?

Max told of the night in 1908 when a fire broke out in the Spanish Club. A group of 18 somewhat shady citizens was in one room. The mayor's assistant, head police chief, and members of the organized crime family were meeting there. They had pushed a large safe in front of the door, probably for privacy. When the fire exploded, they could not push the safe away. One of them even shot the safe trying to get out. All 18 perished. The safe, with its bullet hole, is still there in the lobby. Today, workers in the improv club next door and those in the Centro building hear screams coming from that room.

Another interesting spot with a history and a tragic love story is now a place called Cerealholic, a cross between a kid's slumber party upstairs and a speakeasy downstairs. However, at one time, it was a Catholic Church. I don't want to spoil the surprise if you take the tour, but it's here in the basement a tragic murder left a spirit behind. Max showed me a video of an apparition that happened there to one worker.

The most beautiful and most haunted stop was the Cuban Club named by The Travel Channel as one of its Top 10 Most Haunted Places in America. It is gorgeous. It also had something none of the other clubs had, a swimming pool. The pool was the scene of tragic drowning of a little eight-year-old boy. He still plays there. Visitors often bring him balls and toys.

The classic theater upstairs has its spirit resident as well. A talented young actor who experienced stage fright for his first play. His friends in the audience booed and left. He then repeated the play perfectly and ended by hanging himself on the stage.

One more interesting fact about the club has nothing to do with ghosts except the spirit of racial inequality that still haunts us. This Cuban club was officially for the white Cubans. There was another club for the Black Cubans. However, at night when much of the city was asleep, Black Cubans would come to this club and were welcomed like any other Cubans.

El Circulo Cbano as the Cuban Club, was called, has at least one immigrant that is still clinging to the old ways. Dr. Paul Dorsal, a professor of history at the University of South Florida, tells of a piano-playing inhabitant at the club. "Several visitors have actually seen the keys moving and heard music when no living player was present."

The piano is located in the old dance hall of the club. The player is believed to be a young man who was killed near the club. According to Dr. Dorsal, the player is believed to be a young man who was killed near the club. Others claim the spirits that roam the old club are the result of young women who died there as a result of botched procedures preformed by an illegal abortionist who refused to get help for his patients when he could not stem the bleeding. Their spirits still call out for aid.

Once when some workers were readying the hall for an engagement, they heard "Help me! Help me!" repeated over and over. Looking around they noticed one of the workers was not present. Thinking she might have gotten locked in one of the rooms and needed help, they went looking for her. Finally in desperation they called her cell phone. When she answered, she told them she had not yet arrived at work and was just pulling into the lot. Who had called for help? To this day, no one has figured that out.

James Joyce Pub

The public buildings are not the only places to retain long-dead residents. Nor is the influx of immigrants looking for a better life totally over. One such immigrant is Shamus Hannigan, former manager of the pub.

The bar is up a dark flight of stairs. Within the James Joyce Pub, you might well be in the heart of old Erin. The only windows are to the front of the narrow building, causing dark shadows throughout. The rich old wood of the long bar adds to the feeling of twilight even at midday. But the bar was not always just a good place to escape South Florida's heat and enjoy a cool drink. It was once a home with a prosperous family and children.

When Shamus tore out walls and remodeled, there was one feature he could not uproot. He has learned she was a nanny around 1928. For some reason, the unhappy woman hanged herself in what is now the bathroom. Some patrons have seen her in a mirror near the back of the bar. Although she has never appeared to him, Shamus has still had encounters with her. "One night, I was here on my own, and I was cleaning the place. I took all the ashtrays off the tables, put them on the bar to wipe the tables and then put them back. I must have missed some of the tables because when I came in next morning, all the ashtrays were sitting on the stools. I was the only one with keys, so no one else could have come in and done it."

When he told some of his friends, they just didn't believe him. He said they told him, "'You're full of it!' I kept trying to tell them it had happened when suddenly that light"- he pointed to a spotlight aimed at "The Irish Republic" -- "went off. Now that's a halogen light. When they blow, they blow. They don't come back on. That one came back on. It wasn't the electricity or anything. Now those guys won't go in the bathroom unless three of them go in together."

Perhaps the nanny did not like her efforts to maintain a clean environment disparaged. As Shamus pointed out, "She looks after the place. She is a good spirit. Now every night when we leave, we salute her."

The spirit still harbors some jealousy toward other females. When there is live music, she never bothers the male musicians but often plays tricks on the female ones by playing with their sound system. Maybe it's a form of revenge. Perhaps in life, she lost her lover to another woman, driving her to suicide.

The bar has about 50 beers on tap, as well as 30 Irish whiskeys, and lots of other spirits. They're a seven times winner in *Tampa Bay Times* "Ultimate Bar of the Year" award.

Chef Trey Taylor's Jamison Burger won "Best Burger" at Burger Showdown, an annual event at Curtis Hixon Waterfront Park. He blends tender ground beef with Jamison's whiskey and special seasonings.

Columbia Restaurant

Columbia Restaurant is reported to have any ghosts, but I was unable to find any specifice. Considering its fascinating history it must have a few resident spirits. In 1905, a young Cuban immigrant named Casimiro Hernandez, Sr. opened a small 60-seat corner cafe in Ybor City where he sold Cuban coffee and his special type of sandwiches to the cigar factory workers. Responsible legends claim Casimiro invented the Cuban Sandwich. Each part of the sandwich represents the nationality that settled in Ybor City. The ham came from the Spanish, Sicilians contributed salami, the Cubans the roast pork, the Germans and Jews brought the tradition of the Swiss cheese, pickle and mustard. All placed on Cuban bread, which is pressed to melt the cheese and heat the other ingredients. The tradition continues to this day.

The Cuban bread is a tradition of its own. They invented it in Tampa at La Joven Francesca bakery. Francisco Ferlita, a Cuban-Spanish-Italian immigrant, opened the bakery in 1896 and it operated until the 1960s. The Ybor City Museum State Park is housed in the former bakery and has a display showing its oven and much more about Ybor City. Do visit the museum before or after you dine at Columbia Restaurant.

Safety Harbor Spa

A little way down the beach is a wondrous haven of peace and tranquility called Safety Harbor. Since prerecorded history, this magic spot has been a Mecca for those seeking the healing powers of its springs.

Hernando de Soto in 1539 was the first European to sample the curative powers of the springs. He thought he had discovered what Ponce De Leon had missed: the Fountain of Youth. He named them Esperito Santo Springs (Springs of the Holy Spirit). The native Americans had already known of the curative powers of the springs for thousands of years.

Through the late 1800s and early 1900s, a series of entrepreneurs tried to exploit the springs, but it was not until 1945 that Dr. Salem Baranoff bought the sanatorium and springs and provided overnight accommodations for spa guests. It's guest list read like a Who's Who of the world's rich and famous, The Great Houdini, department store moguls F.W. Grant and Russ Kresgeand their contemporaries came in droves.

When you visit Safety Harbor, you find so much more than the spa that has made it famous. You find a quaint Florida town. It's Main Street boasts unique shops and art galleries. In its small city square, musicians perform beneath the Victorian style gazebo. You can find any type of food you want from the fast food with flair served at the little Whistle Stop café-try the fried green tomatoes there- to the health conscious yet delicious Spa food.

If are very observant, you may find more than meets the eye there as well. Former dining room manager, Tom Lamonica, decided to stay over at the spa one night because of an early morning schedule. He was cutting through the East Room to the kitchen to get some orange juice when suddenly all the lights came on. He called to the security guard that he believed turned them on, "Chuck?" then observed the Palm Lobby door opening slowly, all by itself. Chuck, the guard, was at the front desk the entire time.

He had no choice but to attribute the occurrences to Dr. Baranoff. Tom reported other run-ins with the departed former owner. He is very particular about the table settings. Salt shakers are always set to the right of the pepper. No matter who sets the tables, Tom religiously checks these details. However, on many occasions, he had checked and found everything set to his satisfaction, then returned to the room a few minutes later to find the salt shakers switched with the pepper. Knowing that Dr. Baranoff did not allow salt on the premises, he feels "Maybe he is trying to tell me something."

Other employees have had encounters of the strange kind. Night Manager John Vitucci, went into the kitchen to turn off the lights and on his return trip almost fell over a large room service tray that wasn't there minutes before.

Perhaps the prize for the most bizarre incident goes to Stephany McHale. Stephany noticed that every time she went into the Signature Shop, a large bronze dog had been moved to a different location. One day, as she passed a full three feet away from the dog, it suddenly lunged and struck her squarely on the knee. Stephany had the last laugh, though. She banished the dog to the History Hall for biting an employee.

Lisa Wilkins was cleaning late one night in the huge, tiled spa fitness center when the television in the Ladies Waiting Area came on full blast by itself. Lisa's comment, "I was outta there and back to the housekeeping office fast"

This is not the only experience Lisa had. She was cleaning in the Men's shower at night and heard a shower come on. When she went to investigate, there was no shower on and none of them were even damp. This time, Lisa had a witness. Another housekeeper was working with her and witnessed the entire episode.

The Baranoff Theater is one of the places most likely to experience strange phenomena. Many people have seen or heard "Dr. Baranoff" in it. One worker was stacking dishes to return to the kitchen when he heard a melody coming from the speakers. He glanced toward the sound booth to see who was playing around there. Instead of spotting a familiar co-worker, he saw an elderly, white-haired gentleman with hat and glasses. He had seen enough photos of the Spa founder to recognize him and got out of there fast.

In fact, more of the employees have seen the spirit of Dr. Baranoff than haven't. Many of the housekeepers are afraid to work in the Spa's Harbor House, Springs or Palm Buildings.

It isn't only workers who have seen or heard Dr. Baranoff. Mrs. Beth Myers, an elderly guest, visited the Spa several years ago. She was awakened one night in room 319 in the Springs Building by a tap on the shoulder. She later swore it was an apparition of Dr. Baranoff's long dead niece. The phantom told her, "Everything will be alright."

It was not alright, however. Mrs. Myers died shortly after returning home. Did the gentle warning help her prepare for the inevitable? Who knows?

Perhaps Dr. Baranoff and his staff are still looking after their guests.

Safety Harbor Museum of Regional History

If the spirits at the Spa are not enough for you, try visiting the Safety Harbor Museum of Regional History. The museum traces the history of the area's Native Americans who also enjoyed visiting "The Place Where Healing Waters Flow." Maybe some of them are still dipping in the crystal pools seeking eternal life. Or have at least some of the area residents found their "Eternal Life?"

Ghost Ships

Water is always conducive to spirits. Perhaps that is why one of Tampa's oldest reported haunting takes place on the water. It was recorded by an Army officer, George A. McCall, in a letter to his father, dated March 28,

1823. The incident occurred at Old Fort Brooke, which is now long destroyed. Col. George Brooke, who was the commanding officer, saw a fleet of five ships approaching. Believing it was General Winfield Scott coming to inspect the troops, he ordered the men to clean up and don clean uniforms. But when he looked again, the ships had disappeared into the mist. McCall explained the phenomena away as five approaching sandhill cranes, which had seemed as large as ships due to the mist. When the cranes saw the soldiers and their guns, they flew away.

Other soldiers believed they were witnessing a fleet of ghostly ships who had been waylaid by pirates, their crews all murdered.

The water is the background for another "ghostly legend," the annual Gasparilla festival in Tampa. It celebrates the exploits of Jose Gaspar, the "last of the buccaneers." Unfortunately, Jose Gaspar is a mythical character and never was a real person, so I guess he can't qualify as a ghost, but the festival is a load of fun anyway.

Busch Gardens

Of course, if you get tired of "ghost hunting," there is a lot of other attraction in the Tampa Bay area. Busch Gardens offers entertainment to please every age. They do have a ghost experience of sorts, a 4D interactive movie called Haunted Lighthouse.

Sea Cruses

Starship Dining Yacht, Captain Nemo's Pirate Cruses, Dauphin Cruises and countless deep sea fishing vessels are just waiting for the sailors in the family.

Sun and surf, shopping, sports, art, theater and just about anything you might desire can be found in the area.

Jacksonville and its Beaches

Casa Marina

The Casa Marina was built in 1925, the oldest inn in Jacksonville Beach. Through all the years, it still retains its Gilded Era charm. Perhaps it retains a few of its early inhabitants as well. Newspapers of the day touted it as the safest place to stay since they had a state-of-the-art fire sprinkler system. The building was the first fireproof building on the beach. The then 60-room hotel offered a living room filled with wicker furniture where their wealthy and powerful guests could relax, dine and dance the night away. Most of the rooms had an unobstructed ocean view. The Spanish Mediterranean style with its terra-cotta tile roof was reminiscent of many of Hollywood's most palatial homes.

When World War 11 struck, it was transformed into military housing. After the war, it went through various hands and degenerated from apartments into a boarded up derelict.

From 1987 to 1991, it remained forsaken. Then new owners, Allan and Mary Lou Brown, began renovating it back to its original splendor. They reopened it in April 2001. It been popular ever since and still retains the glamor of a bygone era.

When you dine at its restaurant today, you will be served by a cheerful staff. The food will be the freshest available prepared in an innovating and tempting way. You can order over 44 wines by the glass or bottle. You can choose mixed drinks crafted to perfection.

The menu is varied. Items like Seafood Crepes, Fried Goat Cheese Salad or Flounder Spanaki, (a flounder filet rolled around spinach, feta and parmesan cheese baked in a fylo pastry and topped with Dijon cream) are some of the more exotic fare served at the Casa Marina. If you are more of a conservative, you will be ecstatic over their Roasted Chicken or Grilled Rack of Lamb. For lunch, you can choose a lighter fare like soup, salad or sandwiches.

However, while your server serves your meal, keep a sharp lookout for another shadowy figure also bearing trays of food. You may catch a glimpse of a server from bygone times. The story goes that in the inn's heyday, formally dressed black servers tended to the lustrous patrons' needs.

One of these young men, perhaps hurrying to serve exacting customers, fell through one of the dining room's tall floor level windows and died on the pavement below. His spirit is believed to roam the kitchen and dining areas of the Casa Marina to this day. One restaurant employee who wishes to remain anonymous also claims that there is another spirit in the Casa Marina, a woman who was murdered in the building by her husband. This person states that there are hardly any member of the staff who have not experienced "something strange." She even said that one housekeeper was actually touched by the phantom and almost went into hysterics.

Florida Theatre

One of Jacksonville's most significant downtown structures is the Florida Theatre. It originally opened on April 8, 1927. It provided early movies and vaudeville acts. Then there were 15 lavish movie theaters. It was recently renovated. Today, it is the city's last remaining example of a 1920s-style movie palace.

But it has something more than interesting architecture. It still has one of the original technicians from the 1920s. He's dead, of course, but that doesn't stop Doc Crowther from continuing to monitor the theater's activities and look out for the current maintenance man.

Earliest reports of Doc began with some of the cleaning people who saw "something" in the projection booth many years ago. Since then he has been observed by many of the theatergoers and employees. He is usually found in the balcony. Lights go off and on without the benefit of human activity. The theater's ghost became so well-known that a local television station did a special on him several years ago. They brought in psychic Jill Cook-Richards to investigate. Ms. Cook-Richards definitely confirmed a presence there. She actually saw him. She reported that he wanted to be called "J" for "Joy" in the future.

The ghost has never been harmful and has instead been helpful on at least one occasion. Saundra Floyd, then director of rental operations, was leading a tour of school children through the theater. Some of them became mischievous and began playing with the projectors.

Ms. Floyd told them that the ghost does not want them to do that and he would become upset and turn the light off if they continued. The children were unconvinced, until the lights actually did go out in that area. The children immediately joined the group and began to behave. The amazed teacher asked, "How did you do that?"

She was even more amazed when she learned that Ms. Floyd was not the one who turned the lights out at all.

Haunted buildings

The theater is not the only haunted building downtown. One, 1887 Building, 501 West Bay Street, is now office space. It was originally the El Modelo Cigar Factory. After the factory shut down, it became a saloon and boarding house. It was while it was in this incarnation that the incident that triggered the haunting occurred.

In 1907 a Spanish-American War veteran was murdered by a blast to his chest fired from a sawed-off shotgun as he entered the front door of the bar. The door was located in the southeast corner of the building, and you can feel a cold spot in that place. Workers often refuse to work alone in that part of the building at night. The building is on the National Register of Historic Places.

Two other Bay Street buildings, the Blackstone Building, 233 E. Bay Street, and the Churchwell Building, 301-313 East Bay Street, also have resident spirits. Blackstone's spirit is said to mostly hang around suite 711. The Churchwell Building boasts a young female spirit wearing a copper-colored dress looking out the window.

The residence of Captain W. J. King also harbors a spirit. Captain King was a St. Johns River pilot. This one has been investigated and confirmed by the Duke University Parapsychology Department.

It's not only the buildings in Jacksonville that have unearthly residents. Stories abound of a haunting presence on the Dames Point Bridge. Some report that she is an African American woman who either fell or jumped to her death from the bridge. Others say she was Caucasian.

Museum of Science and History

On the south side of the river, you will find the Museum of Science and History. MOSH, as it is called, has offerings ranging from dinosaurs to a state of the art planetarium. It is basically three attractions in one. Whether your interest is in the nature and history of Jacksonville, the stars and space, or you want to take your kids to a hands-on museum that will help them understand things like electricity or optical illusions, this is the place. It is plannng move to the North side on Museum Row near the Fire Museum. The Fire Museum was moved in 2022 to the new location near the stadium and the USS Orleck, and is expected to open soon.

Steve Christian, who is the host of the Jacksonville-based television series "Local Haunts" and his team incvestigated the old station and heard a lot of EVP recordings. They captured what semed to be full conversations between themselves and two spirits. They also heard a voice saying "hang it up" possibly referring to fire fighting equipment. The station was originally operated by a team of African American firefighters.

USS Orleck

The Jacksonville Naval Museum's *USS Orleck* is Jacksonville's newest museum. It's a trip back into military history as the Orleck was built in 1945 and used as a floating artillery in the Korean War and in Vietnam. My guide, John, led me through the entire ship from navigation deck, dining galley, officers' and enlisted men's quarters, and even a torpedo launcher on deck. The scullery where men took dirty dishes and utensils to be washed. This job was usually one of the first jobs assigned to new recruits to inspire them to learn a trade. It's too soon to know if there are any spirits lingering.

The Stonewood Grill & Tavern

Restaurants often have their own ghosts. The Stonewood Grill & Tavern located on the south side near Baymeadows Road and San Jose Blvd. has a whopper and I don't mean a burger.

The disturbances began almost as soon as it opened. Lee Boyer, the operating partner, and his staff began hearing noises. One night the night manager had turned off all the burners and went outside. He heard a noise and rushed back in to find the burners turned back on. If that wasn't enough to spook him, when he looked back outside, a sign that had previously been lying on the ground was now standing on its edge with the posts sticking up in the air. Nothing was holding it up. It just stood there.

The site has never been a cemetery and no one had died violently there to Boyer's knowledge. However, the place next door, where Walgreens is today, used to be a rough and rowdy bar called Motorboat Mel's. Several people got knifed there, and the owner committed suicide in the building. Perhaps some of those wild spirits are still looking for a little excitement.

Kingsley Plantation

The high ground of a hammock with its moss-draped oaks is natural setting for a ghost. If you cross the river on the Mayport Ferry, a delightful experience in its own right, and drive north on A1A (Heckscher Drive), you will cross a series of barrier islands.

One of this area's magnificent old plantations is the Kingsley Plantation. It has a terrifying phantom, Old Red Eyes. He is believed to be the evil spirit of a slave who raped and murdered two young girls. Eventually he was caught and hanged from a huge oak tree near the driveway. He is most often seen as a blazing pair of red eyes in your rearview mirror as you drive away from the plantation at night. The plantation was built by Zephaniah Kingsley who married Anna Madgigine Jai, an African slave he had freed.

After his death, Anna managed the plantation. During the Civil War, she had to flee because of her ardent Unionist sentiments. The plantation grew Sea Island cotton and boasts the oldest remaining plantation house left in Florida. There are also reports of a man and woman seen at the plantation and at the site of some tabby ruins before you reach the plantation entrance. Perhaps they are Zephaniah and his beloved Anna.

Little and Big Talbot Island

If you continue on north, you will come to Little Talbot and Big Talbot Islands. Both have state parks on them and are great places for bird watching or just strolling the beaches.

There are many ghosts on this island. The entire island once belonged to the Christopher and Houston families. Spicer Christopher acquired the island in 1783 and raised cotton, indigo, horses and cattle. John Houston, called "Big John," married Spicer's daughter, Elizabeth Susannah, combining the two families into one even wealthier one.

When Elizabeth died, "Big John" married a relative of his first wife named Mary Braddock Greenwood. Many of these families intermarried, and many of them are buried in the cemetery now called just the Houston Cemetery. John McQueen, who was immortalized in Eugenia Price's Don Juan McQueen, also lived in the area for a time. The cemetery is reportedly haunted by the planters as well as their slaves.

The cemetery is on Houston Road. People have heard and tape-recorded the sound of dogs barking there. But when the tape is played back, the barking isn't on the tape, just the normal voices of the group. Unexplained mists and cold spots also occur there. Photographs often show orbs. The cemetery is very old, and some of the crypts are open, creating an eerie atmosphere.

The island also had a Timucuan burial site near the same area. It is down a trail that begins about 300 yards north of the rest area on the right. There you may hear moaning and again spot orbs. The temperature is always many degrees colder than the surrounding area.

Farther north on the island is an area called "The Bluffs." People camping or hiking there have sensed a feeling of evil, especially at night. If you go there, it is wise to not go alone. Phenomena reported include apparitions, barking as of large dogs, and strange voices.

Caution: Like any big metropolitan area, there are areas of Jacksonville that you will want to avoid at night. Use common sense and ask at your hotel about sections you may plan on visiting after sunset.

Cemeteries

People expect the residents of a cemetery to stay put but not so in some of Jacksonville's old cemeteries. Old City Cemetery near Springfield has at least two wraiths that have been seen through the years. One is of a murdered Black woman who is buried near the rear of the cemetery.

The other was the subject of a sensational "unsolved" crime. Louise Gato was a wealthy and beautiful 19-year-old woman. She was shot fatally as she entered her parents' home in Springfield on April 20, 1897. She regained consciousness long enough to sign an affidavit that the assailant was a former boyfriend, Edward George Pitzer.

Pitzer denied the charges and claimed he was visiting another woman at the time of the attack. The defense succeeded in having the signed statement thrown out as evidence. They claimed Miss Gato was not capable of making that determination.

A strange side story to the murder was that the detective investigating the case, William Gruber, was killed while investigating another case. He was found lying in the bushes with his skull crushed. A woman's blue belt and small white handkerchief were found nearby. Were the two killings related? No one ever found out. Both murders remain unsolved. But Louise is still seeking justice; she wanders around the cemetery to remind people of her unavenged murder.

Evergreen Cemetery, 4535 North Main Street, is Jacksonville's oldest operating cemetery. It covers about 70 acres and has about 70,000 burial sites. It was established in 1881 and was the "in" place to be buried in the early days of the city. Isaiah D. Hart, Jacksonville's founder, is there as are politicians, business leaders, paupers and prostitutes, a Confederate General, the rich and famous, as well as the poor and downtrodden. Some of those who are not resting in peace include a Woman in Violet, a man in Confederate uniform, and the spirit of a woman who is always seen near the "Ugly Angel" Tombstone.

Fort Caroline

Jacksonville has so many other thing to see. Fort Caroline is where Florida's history began. If Pedro Menendez hadn't defeated Jean Ribault, Jacksonville would be the nation's oldest city. Timucuan Preserve Visitor Center at Fort Caroline shows the tragic history of Fort Caroline's French Huguenot settlers and early Timucuan Native American influence.

Underground tunnels

You might be surprised to know Jacksonville has a secret underground. There're remnants of a system of tunnels from the days when Jacksonville was a major banking city. They were used to move money between city banks. Some are still accessible. There's a section between the BB&T Bank Building and the former Atlantic National Bank. There's an old bank vault with a Debold safe dating to the 1930s. The vault served as a bomb shelter during the Cold War years, AdLib Luxury Tours visits the tunnel.

Ritz Theater

The Art déco Style Ritz Theater, built in 1929, was the center of the thriving Black LaVilla Community. Today, it's still an operational live theater with an insightful museum. My favorite exhibit, James Weldon Johnson, who wrote the lyrics for "Lift Every Voice and Sing."

Cummer Museum of Art

Cummer Museum of Art will thrill you no matter what style you like, from Renaissance Italian to Remington Sculptures. There are three gardens with reflecting pools, fountains, sculptures, arbors, and a 200-plus-year-old oak. The gardens are on the National Register of Historic Places. You can visit for free Tuesday, 4 to 9 pm, Friday, 4 to 9 pm, and the first Saturday, 11 a.m. to 4 pm. On Saturday, the Riverside Arts Market down the block under the bridge is open.

Museum of Contemporary Art

Another art lovers' heaven is Museum of Contemporary Art (MOCA) with one of the largest contemporary art collections in the Southeast. It's across the street from James Weldon Johnson Park which usually has events going on. Sweet Pete's, the largest candy store in the state is across from the Park. You can watch candy being made or take candy-making classes. It has an on-site restaurant, Fizzies and Fare.

Jacksonville Arboretum & Botanical Gardens

For a peaceful spot to relax and unwind, visit the botanical gardens. It's 120 acres with a lake and creek where you can wander around seven natural trails. You can do just a short walk around the lake or spend hours hiking the entire area.

Jacksonville Zoo and Gardens

One of Jacksonville's premier attractions that has ghosts of a different kind is the Jacksonville Zoo and Gardens. Tucked away on the north side of Jacksonville, snuggled up against the Trout River, is one of the city's hidden jewels, the Jacksonville Zoo and Gardens. The zoo sprang from modest beginnings. It grew along with the city to become the exquisite 89-acre jewel it is today.

St. Augustine

Casa Monica

When you visit the Oldest City, a triumvirate of magnificent Victorian buildings stands out among the older Spanish styles: Flagler College, the Lightner Museum and the Casa Monica Hotel. These all reflect the influence of the one man who, next to the early founders of the city, contributed more than anyone to creating the St. Augustine of today.

The Hotel Ponce de Leon was Henry Flagler's first, and many say most magnificent, St. Augustine hotel. It now houses the campus of Flagler College. The Lightner Museum, just across King Street, was built as another of Flagler's magnificent hotels, The Alcazar.

However, just down the block stands a Moorish castle, complete with turrets and an unbelievably lavish interior that is St. Augustine's own haunted hotel, the Casa Monica. It was not built by Flagler. One of his cronies, Bostonian amateur architect Franklin W. Smith, built it. However the Casa Monica was tied to Flagler by complex threads of history from its beginning.

Flagler originally owned the land where it stands. It was the lot to which Flagler moved the 10-year-old Sunnyside Hotel that he had purchased for its site where he built his luxurious Ponce de Leon Hotel. Smith was one of the engineers who supervised the coquina concrete mixture for the Ponce de Leon Hotel. Never one to lose a penny on any deal, Flagler then sold the Sunnyside to Smith. The hotel could hold only 40 guests, so Flagler did not see it as serious competition for either the Ponce de Leon or his newest hotel, The Alcazar, just across the street.

However, Smith had more grandiose plans. He again moved the Sunnyside to a new location and built a grand 250-room hotel in its place. However, Smith lacked the resources that Flagler had and was not able to maintain the hotel. Flagler purchased it from Smith on April 20, 1888, and it too became a success.

In the 1960s it was converted the county courthouse, but in 1999, it reverted to its former glory and is once again the Casa Monica Hotel. Many people who have stayed there state they have heard voices, seen indents in the carpet as if someone is stepping on it and witnessed furniture shift positions inexplicably. Others have sighted a woman in green strolling around the hotel. Only thing strange about her, she's not actually there. Visitors have glimpsed a man through the outside windows of the Henry Flagler Suite when the room is known to be empty. Some workers have seen a distinguished-looking man in period clothing walking in the lobby only to vanish when approached. Henry Flagler never did allow anything to stand in the way of his wishes. Perhaps he wishes to enjoy the splendor of his old/new hotel.

Casa Monica's flagship dining room, 95 Cordova, and its Cobalt Lounge offer the ultimate dining experience in the oldest city with an eclectic blend of American, Asian, Mediterranean, Caribbean, and Moroccan influences.

Flagler College.

Flagler was a self-made millionaire, a partner of John D. Rockefeller. When his first wife, Mary Harkness, died, he married Ida Alice Shourds. Ida Alice was unstable, to say the least. She claimed the czar of Russia was coming to meet her. She swore if he confined her to an institution, she would haunt him forever. When she stabbed her doctor with her sewing scissors, Henry had her institutionalized in a cozy cottage behind the Ponce De Leon Hotel, today Flagler College. He settled $5 million for her care and wanted to wash his hands of her for good.

After neatly settling the problem of a homicidal maniac wife, Henry wanted to remarry. His choice for the third Mrs. Flagler was Mary Lily Kenan, an attractive lady 30-plus years his junior. However, the fly in the ointment was that both New York, where Henry maintained residency, and Florida, where he spent most of his time at this point, both forbade divorce from a mentally incapacitated person. Henry solved the problem by changing his residency to Florida, which was benefiting greatly from his entrepreneurial spirit. To farther sweeten the pot he made huge contributions to the winning political party. In 1901 the Florida legislature passed a law allowing divorce from mentally incapacitated persons. The law only remained on the books for 10 days before it was repealed, but Henry quickly divorced Ida Alice and married Mary Lily. Mary Lily won the marital sweepstakes. Henry died still married to her and left her the wealthiest woman in the country. In fact, she was the only woman in America wealthier than the Queen of England.

Flagler died in 1913 at the age of 93. His body was brought back on his railroad, Florida East Coast Railway, to lie in state at his beloved Ponce de

Leon Hotel. There is a legend that Flagler's spirit still remains in the hotel-turned-college. There are those who say the millionaire's spirit as well as others haunts the old building.

On the night his body was laid out in the hotel, a caretaker cleaning around the coffin was suddenly frightened by a burst of wind in the otherwise-calm weather. It blew open the doors of the hotel and slammed shut the coffin cover. The terrified man cowered nearby as he observed a swirling glowing mist rise from the coffin toward the roof and then descend to the floor. When he regained enough courage to creep near the coffin again, he observed the image of Flagler's face in the tile. Flagler is buried in the Florida city that first captured his heart in a mausoleum at Memorial Presbyterian Church across the street from the former Ponce de Leon Hotel. However, he may not rest in peace. Many people have claimed to see his face reflected in the tiles in his first grand Florida hotel, the Ponce de Leon, now Flagler College. Some have seen him in the halls of Flagler College. Others have seen the spirit of Ida Alice waltzing around the ballroom with her imaginary Russian czar. Gentlemen, how many of you would like to be doomed to spend eternity with the one wife you wanted to get rid of?

Ripley's Believe it or Not Museum

Henry Flagler wasn't the only one of the Robber Barons to live part of their life in St. Augustine. William G. Warden, a former partner of Flagler and Rockefeller, arrived in 1887 with the original intent of investing in Flagler's railroad. However, when Warden realized the difficulties in the undertaking, he changed his mind. Instead, he decided he would not put a penny in the railroad but would build a large home here and watch Flagler go broke!

The result was Historic Castle Warden. Today it's a Florida Historic Landmark and home to St. Augustine's Ripley's Believe It or Not Museum. You might not be surprised to learn that some things that go bump in the night in the majestic gray stone "castle" are even more unexplainable than Robert Ripley's oddities.

Lynda Stephens, who worked at the front desk, told me of some of the stranger-than-fiction happenings. "One night we were counting the admissions drawer. It came out $144.49 short. That got us all upset. So the manager said, 'Let's count the gift shop, then come back and maybe we can figure it out.' We counted the gift shop and it came out exactly $144.49 over. The two drawers never mingle. Never!"

Lynda also admitted to hearing many unusual noises in the old building. She was not comfortable being there late at night. There are reports that the spirit of a woman who died in a fire that swept the third and fourth floors still prowls the halls. The fire struck in 1944, and two women were trapped in the building. They wrapped themselves in wet towels to try to stave off the flames but still succumbed to the fumes. One of them, Betty Richerson, was found dead in a bathtub. One of the exhibits on that floor near the location where she was found has a mirror in the central area. People have claimed to see Betty's reflection in that mirror.

Old Jail

Of course, with all these prosperous law-abiding citizens, there had to be a place to stow the others, the lawbreakers. From 1891 on into the 1950s, that place was the Old Jail. It is one of the few surviving 19th century jails, and within its walls survives something else, the vigilant spirit of old Sheriff Perry, St. Johns County's 7-foot-tall first sheriff. Maybe Slim Jackson, one of the early deputies, is in there, too. Or it could even be a man hanged on the gallows still displayed out behind the Old Jail. Whoever it is has been heard by more than one visitor to the site. Visitors hear voices, sometimes male and sometimes female. In addition to prisoners of both sexes kept in different sections of the jail, the sheriff and his wife and family lived on the premises. Mrs. Perry cooked and served meals to the inmates in the jail dining room.

Jeff Reynolds from Ghost Tracker Radio and his crew went to the Old Jail. They heard the sound of ghostly banging on cell bars and murmurs of phantom prisoners.

Fort Matanzas

But when Flagler and his contemporaries arrived in St. Augustine, it was already an old city. In fact, when the Pilgrims finally landed at Plymouth Rock in 1620, St. Augustine was already a thriving settlement. It had a fort, a church, a hospital, shops and more than 100 houses. It has accumulated ghost tales for some four and a half centuries.

Fort Matanzas -- the back door to St. Augustine! Just 14 miles south of the nation's oldest city, where the Matanzas River touches the Atlantic, is the windswept estuary where the Spanish heritage of Florida was indelibly sealed in the blood of 245 murdered French prisoners. Here, in 1565, the inlet earned its name - Matanzas, Spanish for slaughter.

With such a bloody beginning, is it any wonder that the nation's oldest city is besieged with restless spirits?

The drama that ended at this mosquito-infested inlet that October day more than four centuries ago revolves around two reckless European explorers, Pedro Menendez de Aviles and Jean Ribault.

Pedro Menendez was a younger son of a minor Spanish nobleman. He had served his king since he was 15 and had been commissioned captain general and governor of Florida with an important injunction: explore and colonize the new land of Florida for Spain and drive out any settlers of other nations.

Meanwhile in France, Jean Ribault received his orders. Protect the French colony of Fort Caroline in Florida. Do not let Menendez encroach on it. He hurriedly set sail for Fort Caroline. He and Menendez were both able tacticians and wily fighters.

Ribault was a Huguenot, as were most of the French colonists. France was a country torn by war with Spain and civil strife between the Catholic majority and the Huguenot minority.

Both men arrived in Florida on August 28th. Ribault sailed directly to the sod-and-timber Fort Caroline on the St. Johns River near what is now Jacksonville.

Menendez landed near Cape Canaveral. He turned north and began seeking the French. On September 3rd, Menendez found a place with a good harbor. He called this place San Augustine. On September 5th, the two men made first contact, Menendez on his "San Pelayo" and Ribault on his flagship "Trinity." A few shots were fired, and the French slipped away. The Spaniards gave chase but were outdistanced quickly. Menendez returned to his colony site and on September 8th, he officially founded the colony of San Augustine. Realizing the vulnerability of his two big galleons that could not come across the shallow bar in the harbor, Menendez sent them back to Santo Domingo on September 10th.

Ribault sailed in pursuit of the vessels. Fate intervened in the form of a typical Florida hurricane, blowing the French fleet before it with a vengeance. Menendez, realizing that the storm would prevent Ribault's return to Fort Caroline in time, marched his men overland through swamps and swollen streams in the storm to Fort Caroline. He captured it without the loss of a single Spaniard. Of the 240 Frenchmen, Menendez's men killed 132. A few escaped, but the victory was overwhelming. Menendez returned to San Augustine, believing if Ribault had survived the storm, he would attack the settlement while the main body of soldiers was away.

Meanwhile, weary and waterlogged, two separate groups of shipwrecked Frenchmen were slowly making their way back toward Fort Caroline. When Menendez heard this, he began moving south with between 50 and 70 men until he reached the south end of Anastasia Island. There, at a small inlet, he encountered the first contingent of 126 Frenchmen. Already dispirited by the shipwreck and the weather, they surrendered to him. The prisoners were fed and bound. They were then led down the beach a little ways and, except for 15 Catholics, were massacared.

On October 12th, Ribault and 350 remaining Frenchmen arrived at the inlet. Menendez ordered him to surrender. About half of the Frenchmen decided to take to the woods rather than trust Menendez to show mercy. The remaining 150 surrendered. All but 16 were slaughtered in the already bloody marsh. France had forever lost her chance in Florida, and the population of New World ghosts was dramatically increased. Many people have claimed to see apparitions of bloody French soldiers plodding in the marsh.

Today, this area is administered by the National Park Service. It is called Fort Matanzas National Monument in honor of the fort the Spanish built there in 1742. The fort is built of native coquina to replace the earlier wooden watchtower the Spanish constructed to protect them from English invasion. It is small but easily defended since it is located on tiny Rattlesnake Island and is accessible only by water. During its occupation, it usually housed 7 to 10 enlisted men, one junior officer and five cannon. Today, a permanent stairway replaces the wooden ladder used by the soldiers in the daytime and drawn up every night. A shuttle ferry runs between the fort and the Anastasia Island portion of the park from 9 to 5 daily except Christmas.

The park includes both Rattlesnake Island and part of Anastasia Island. The Anastasia side houses a visitor center with a small museum and a boardwalk nature trail. The trail winds through scrub and woodland that appear untouched since those fateful days in 1565. It abounds with birds and small wildlife. At places, patches of colorful wild flowers decorate the sandy soil. A small wooden sign commemorates the spot where the slaughter occurred. The boardwalk breaks through the palmetto at the river's edge where you can see both the fort and the inlet to the ocean. Today, small motorboats and modern sailboats ply the waters that were once the domain of the heavy Spanish Galleons.

The park is free and open daily except Christmas. It also has a picnic area and an ocean beach access. Of the First Coast's many tourists, only a small portion find the way here. Those who do are well-rewarded. They get a chance to see for themselves a turning point in the beginnings of European culture in the New World. As is true with many National Monuments, the federal government does not encourage "ghost stories," but, after you learn the history, would you care to spend the night here? Whatever the reason, the park is closed to visitors after dark, but even as twilight shadows lengthen, you cannot help but feel specters of the many souls who met their untimely end at the very spot even named for slaughter.

Prince of Peace Church

In spite of their ruthless battle practices, the Spanish were a very religious people, so one of the first things they did upon landing in St. Augustine was hear Mass offered by the ship's chaplain, Father Lopez.

This Mass was celebrated at the site of the Great Cross on the grounds of the Mission de Nombre de Dios. The stainless steel cross was erected in 1965 to commemorate the mission's 400th anniversary. It towers 208 feet and can be seen for miles out to sea at night.

At the very front of the grounds, you will see the Prince of Peace Church. It is the newest of the shrines on this ancient site. Built in 1965, it commemorates 400 years of the Catholic faith in the New World and was dedicated to world peace. On December 1, 2002, a strange event occurred at the church. At around 1 p.m., Jill Valley, her mother-in-law and her two children were decorating the altar. Jill was leaning on a pew when she heard a sound "like tiny pebbles dropping on the pew." Then the sound accelerated "like a truckload of sand being dumped."

Suddenly tiles from the floor began flying into the air, some as high as eye level. The Valleys fled the scene as if pursued by demons. Jill Valley stated, "It was the weirdest thing that any one of us had ever seen."

Explanations of why the phenomena occurred ran the gauntlet from scientific to superstitious. None ever really made sense. Eric Johnson, the director of the Nombre de Dios Mission, speculated that it could have been cold-induced contractions of the church's coquina walls or concrete floor. Yet he admitted there was no cracking in the walls or windows, just the floor tiles.

The elder Mrs. Valley speculated that it might have been because she was Presbyterian. Not too likely that whatever caused it cared what denomination the witnesses were.

Another explanation offered and just as quickly refuted is that it was a sinkhole. Sinkholes would have caused things to sink. In this case, the tiles flew upward.

Mr. Johnson was quick to point out that he wasn't blaming anything supernatural. It had to be something that could be "explained by science and physics."

When the same sort of thing happened in two properties managed by Tom Rivers, a local realtor, he had a different explanation. "It's a ghost that throws things around," he said. "This one likes to move floors."

Contractors and engineers in each of the three cases could find no evidence of any problems with the structures. So maybe Tom Rivers is right about his "Floor Poltergeist."

Oldest House

Some of the real estate in St. Augustine has been accumulating psychic energy for centuries. The oldest house in the city is the González-Alvarez House. A Spanish soldier, Tomás González, built it for his family around 1702. Church records document that one of the children died there in 1727. Perhaps it is the child who haunts the home. Perhaps it is a spirit of someone who stayed there at a later time. No one knows for sure, but many people will agree "something" outside the normal is there.

This building is one of the most studied homes in America because it is so well documented. A national historic landmark, the house has a history of continuous occupancy from its construction on into the 20th century. It is one of the favorite house-museums in St. Augustine and a must-see for any fan of Eugenia Price who immortalized it in her novel, Maria.

St Francis Inn

Just around the corner from St. Augustine's Oldest House stands the St. Francis Inn, the city's oldest inn. It was built by Gaspar Garciaon on a lot granted to him by the King of Spain in 1791.

Since he was a sergeant and would not normally have been able to afford the magnificent thick-walled fortress-style home, the fact that he was in charge of construction of the public buildings for the government might explain his living so far above his means. He had access to the best building materials and tools available in his day.

St. Francis Inn has two permanent residents, Lily and her lover. Lily was a beautiful slave girl who worked in the home in the 1800s. A young British soldier lodged in the house. The two fell hopelessly in love and had clandestine trysts in her room.

Since the property was built after the British occupation of the area, the affair probably took place during the ownership of Thomas Henry Dummett, retired colonel of Britain's Royal Marines, or his daughter, Anna. She was the one who converted the family home into a lodging establishment in 1845. She raised 10 nieces and nephews in the inn, children of three of her deceased sisters. Since she was a staunch Confederate during the war and a slave owner, this is the most-likely timeframe for the doomed love affair.

The young soldier was probably one of Anna's nephews. The affair was discovered when Lily became pregnant. The family was able to end the affair but not Lily's love. Rather than live without her lover, she hanged herself in the attic room where she and the soldier had met. It is now named Lily's Room and one of the most popular rooms in the inn.

Many people have reported seeing Lily. They usually see her from the back. She is known for playing around with the female guests' makeup and jewelry, perhaps since she had no such amenities of her own. Guests, especially in Lily's room, often tell of being touched or gently kissed at night while in their beds. Psychics who investigated the inn found lipsticks they deliberately left on a dresser unmoved while other lipsticks from the investigators' private bags mysteriously moved to other places. They did not see Lily but recorded disturbances and sounds in "her" room. They did see a slightly built Hispanic male and an older man dressed in a tri-cornered hat. No one has any explanation for these apparitions.

Bev Lonergan, who worked at the St. Francis, told me of an unusual experience. She was working the front desk on the night shift. "I got off at 10:30 one night and was sitting downstairs figuring out the books. I felt the hair on the back of my neck and arms start to stand up as if I had received a fright. When I looked up there was the soldier! He was short and was wearing a bright red uniform coat with brass buttons, just leaning against the wall with his arms folded. He was looking straight at me and smiling. Then he was gone." She got out of there fast and left the books for the next day.

Bev also says she has frequently glimpsed Lily but always from the back as the phantom girl hurries away from her. She hopes "one day Lily will trust me enough to show her face."

Castillo de San Marcos

As Spain secured its hold on this part of the New World, a main fort guarding the colony became necessary. The Queen of Spain decreed the building of Castillo de San Marcos. This was in 1672. At that time, the Spanish had captured a young English pirate named Andrew Ranson. Since pirates had sacked and burned the city and plundered the supply shops, feelings ran high about the penalty that should be exacted. Ranson was sentenced to be garroted. The executioner, not having an official garrote available, used a makeshift one. He drilled a hole at neck height in a straight palm tree. On the day of the execution, the pirate was marched to the tree, a rope inserted through the hole and encircling his neck. Behind the tree, the executioner placed a stick through the loop of the makeshift noose and began to turn it. In preparation for death, Ranson took out a rosary from his pocket and began to pray. The priest in the audience noted the rosary and wondered what a Protestant Englishman was doing praying a Catholic Rosary. No sooner had the pirate begun his prayer, than the stick used to twist the rope broke. Ranson fell to the ground, and the priest grabbed him and led him into the cathedral. He believed God spared the young man's life for a reason.

In those days a church was on sacred ground and no one could be taken from it, so Ranson was safe for the moment. He was badly rope-burned, however, and needed someone to treat the sores. The priest asked a young girl in the congregation, the executioner's 14-year-old daughter, to tend to the prisoner.

Within a short time, the girl and the pirate were in love, to her father's shame. He decided to find out more about the pirate who had captured his daughter's heart.

He discovered that Andrew Ranson had been a stonemason before seeking a life on the high seas. Since the city needed a good stonecutter to build the proposed fort, and since his daughter was adamant about her love for the pirate, the executioner struck a deal for the young man. He would gain a pardon for him and all his crew if they would build the fort. If Ranson did a good job of it and wanted to remain, the executioner would give him his daughter's hand.

Obviously, Andrew Ranson did a wonderful job. The fort's unique building material, coquina, a type of shell-stone quarried from Anastasia Island, absorbed cannon blast rather than crumbling. Perhaps it is for this reason that the fort had never been conquered. It changed hands may times but always by treaty. Although it belonged to the British, the United States and the Confederacy, it is the original Spanish construction and influence that remains strongest. But people in the area are reminded of its English connection by the many "Ransons" still in the area. Yes, the pirate did remain and marry the executioner's daughter.

Perhaps some other Spanish influences lurk around the fort as well. The old fort has rumors of restless spirits from the days of Florida's Spanish domination who still roam its dank tunnels to this day. One tale of illicit love and jealous rage may explain the rumors of a strange glow and a perfume aroma that persist within the walls of the fort. Colonel Garcia Marti had a beautiful young wife. Perhaps she was neglected as the colonel went about his duties, or maybe she just grew bored in this tiny colonial town. Whatever the reason, she began a clandestine affair with her husband's assistant, Captain Manuel Abela. The story goes that the colonel found out and murdered both of them, tossing the bodies into a shallow grave in one of the deepest dungeons. Later, bones of man and woman were found in the dungeon.

Another tragedy of history that may have created a residual haunting at the fort is the story of the Seminole imprisonment there. Osceola and a group of Seminoles were imprisoned there during the Seminole War. Osceola was treacherously captured when he approached the whites under a flag of truce. Failing to honor the truce, the soldiers seized the chief and imprisoned him in the old fort. Twenty of the Seminoles starved themselves until they could twist their bodies through the narrow bars of their cells, but Osceola remained behind. Perhaps the fact that he was sick with malaria was the reason, or perhaps he just wanted to shame his captors for their foul actions. He was later moved from the fort to a different prison, but legends remain of his specter. His face is said to be seen on the walls of the fort on dark nights.

Casa Blanca Inn

The bayfront of St. Augustine abounds in exquisite homes that have been converted to bed and breakfasts or restaurants. One of the many beautiful homes built during the Victorian period is the Casa Blanca Inn. The Mediterranean Revival home on the bayfront was built by an Irish couple in 1914. The gentleman wanted to watch the sunrise from the porches. However, both of them were quite fond of "the creature" and frequently had rowdy parties there. One day, the husband died.

The young widow was left with the large home but no money. She decided to turn it into a boarding house. She began throwing parties with rum flowing generously. She charged well for these parties and began to prosper.

Then a disastrous thing happened, the Volsted Act. Her parties would come to an end if she didn't do something. Being an enterprising lady, she befriended a group of rumrunners. One became her lover. Their ship would enter the bayfront, dock and stay a while with the merry widow.

All ointments are destined to have a few flies, however. These particular flies were the G-men sent to St. Augustine when the government learned it was a hotbed of rumrunners. This didn't faze the widow too much. Instead, she met the agents at the train and invited them to her boarding house. That way she could keep an eye on them. When they were in town, she would keep her widow's walk dark. But when they were away on other business, she would wave a lantern from the highest part of the widow's walk to let her lover know it was safe to come on in.

After prohibition was repealed, her fickle lover no longer came to call. Rumor says she still waved a lantern from the widow's walks until her dying day to no avail.

Even death seems not to have extinguished her lantern. Neighbors and sailors in the inlet claim to often see the ghostly lantern shedding its light across the waterfront. Some have even seen a dark shadowy figure in the widow's walk at night.

Obviously, the lady still feels that this is her "boarding house." One guest staying at the inn took some pictures. In one of them, she caught her own reflection in the mirror with her camera. Even though she was alone when she took the picture, standing right behind her in the photograph was a lady dressed in period clothing with a lantern in her hand.

There appears to be another resident still remaining in the inn from Victorian times. In those days, gentlemen would retire to the back porch to smoke their cigars. Today this "smoking porch" is an elegant bedroom. A female guest awoke one night to find a man sitting on the side of the bed smoking. When she awoke and saw him, he told her to "go back to sleep, everything is okay."

Casa de La Paz

Just next door to the Casa Blanca is a Mediterranean Revival style mansion that was once the Casa de La Paz Bed and Breakfast.

It was built just one year after its haunted neighbor. Its resident spirit is a lady named Mabel. Mabel came to St. Augustine for her health with her husband in the early 1900s, and they stayed at the inn. Her husband must have gotten tired of a sickly wife and left the inn one day and never came back. Well, as well-bred Victorian ladies did not travel alone those days, Mabel just stayed on at the inn waiting for his return. He never came back, and Mabel never left.

In the past guests at the inn report seeing her dressed in a long traveling dress with a broad-brimmed hat and holding a small tapestry bag in her hand. She walked down the stairs, stops at the bottom of the landing and then returns upstairs. Other guests told of hearing a timid knock at their door and a voice whispering, "Is it time to go yet?" When they opened the door, no one is there.

Peace and Plenty Inn

Another of Flagler's cohorts built himself a home in St. Augustine while he worked on the construction of the railroad and also on the Bridge of Lions. Walter Decker built what is now the Peace and Plenty Inn on Cedar Street around 1890.

In the ensuing century, the stately home fell into disrepair. Then in 1996, Court and Glena Terrell took on the task of restoring it to its former glory. They half jokingly say, "We have the scares to prove it!" Their remodeling was chronicled on the Home and Garden television show If Walls Could Talk. Glen da has since passed awsy but I recalteh story she told.

Their two sons, Clay and Casey, had an unearthly experience in the parlor. Clay says, "Casey was calling our dog, Dallas, and as he called, I heard a mocking female voice in the parlor repeating Casey's call, 'Dallas, Dallas.' This happened when we were remodeling it. Dallas appeared confused and shaken by the echoing voice. She is usually a bold dog but was completely cowered and went running to Casey as if she was frightened."

Penny Farthing Inn

Just next door at the Penny Farthing Inn, a similar-style building also constructed by Mr. Decker, even stranger events are still taking place. Ghost Victor turns on lights and televisions. He is a party-type ghost and likes a good time. Guests have frequently thought there was a party going on in the parlor.

Once he turned the television on in a guest's room during the night. The husband and wife each thought the other one had done it.

Victor also "talked" to the former proprietor, Connie Goodwin-Schwartz. When she was undecided what she wants to do he will mentally suggest, "Why don't you change the drapes?" or whatever ever he feels she should do.

The Penny Farthing Inn is also home to a ghostly yellow cat, Copper Penny, who belonged to a former owner. The cat died of old age under the house long ago, but Connie frequently feels him rub against her legs and pat her with his paw. A guest once saw and heard him crying in his room. When he got up to let the cat out, it disappeared.

Harry's Restaurant

St. Augustine transferred into British hands in 1763. During the transfer, many families were uprooted. The customs and religions of the two countries were too far apart for many of the Spanish families to remain under British domination. One case gave rise to a restless spirit who still remains in her ancient home.

The home was built in 1750 and was the dwelling place of the DePorres family. There were nine children, the youngest a fiery beauty named Catalina.

The DePorres family departed for Cuba when the colony was ceded to England. Catalina grew into womanhood and married while in Cuba, but she always yearned for her childhood home.

Her chance came when the Spanish returned to Florida in 1783. She must have been a headstrong woman because she persuaded both her husband and the new Spanish governor that this home on 46 Avenida Mencndez was where she belonged. Indeed, she felt so at home there she still resides on the property.

The original home was burned in 1877, but Catalina must still have been working her will. It was rebuilt to resemble the original home.

It has been a series of restaurants in modern times. Once it was named in her honor, Catalina's Gardens. Today it is Harry's Seafood Bar and Grill. But Catalina is still throwing her weight around.

Bill Boyd, a former manager at Harry's, recounts his experience with Catalina. He was putting up curtains in the old part of the building. He felt as if someone was in the room, but no one was there. After he got the curtains up, he turned to gather up the tools and leave. The curtains, rod and all, were yanked off the wall and tossed across the room. Perhaps Catalina did not like the color or style.

Catalina seems to have been joined by a mysterious man in black. While Catalina is seen and felt most frequently in the upstairs part, the man dressed in black from head to foot and sporting an old-fashioned black hat is seen downstairs, often near the fireplace. He will stare at women diners. If they complain to the management, the man will disappear before the manager can arrive on the scene.

Perhaps it is the man who caused the disturbance that another former manager, Linda, experienced with the burglar alarm going off repeatedly. When the police arrived, no one was there and there was no sign of a break in. Finally, when they entered the building after one of the false alarms, she and police observed the lights above the bar swinging for no apparent reason.

Cemeteries

The importance placed on religions in St. Augustine created another opportunity for spirits to be restless. There were two cemeteries in the old days in the city, Huguenot and Catholic. Both have reported sightings of restless spirits.

Tolomoto Cemetery is the Catholic one. It was the site of the Tolomoto Indian burial ground. A guide on the Ghost Tour, tells of an experience there. "I was guiding a group of fourth graders. I had my back to the cemetery and was telling a story to the kids. They began to fidget and finally broke and ran to their bus. When we calmed them down, they all told the same story. They saw a young boy about 5 years old dressed in knee pants and a white linen shirt. He came up from one of the graves and drifted up into the branches of an old oak tree where he sat and made faces at the children."

She felt they must have been telling the truth because "I don't see how 30 fourth graders could have made up identical stories on the spot. Even if they sat around in class and made up what they were going to say, how could they have known the tree and the grave were going to be right where each of them described? Another guide also had a similar experience with a group of girl scouts."

Not knowing the child's name, the guides gave him the nickname of "Nicolas." Upon investigation, Shannon found that there had been a little boy buried there. His gravestone is a little short stone with the name "James P. Morgan" and the dates make him 5 years and 10 days old. For that reason, she believes that must be the boy the children saw.

The cemetery also has had reports of other ghosts. A Franciscan Missionary, Father Corpa, was killed by a Native American on that spot and is said to roam there at night.

There is a lady in black haunting the cemetery as well. She seeks Colonel Smith. She was married but fell in love with the handsome colonel at a ball given in his honor. She succumbed to a fever she contracted right after the ball. Her weeping family, according to her family tradition, carried her to the cemetery in a chair. As they approached the cemetery, a thorn from an overhanging tree pricked her cheek, and blood flowed. Colonel Smith saw the cut and called out that she was alive, and the family rushed her home to nurse back to health.

She lived for another six years but never regained her health or her beauty. Then she once more fell victim to the raging fever. Again, she appeared to die. This time her husband, who had lost interest in his no longer young and beautiful wife, made sure she was not carried anywhere near the tree. She was buried in the family tomb. There are those who claim she did not die and still searches for Colonel Joseph Smith to once more rescue her from the grave where she has lain since 1829.

Just down the block from the cemetery, the city's oldest drug store was built right on top of the grave of Chief Tolomoto. After the store was built, they tried moving the stone out of the way and all sorts of strange things happened. They put the stone back and all was quiet again. So to this day,

Chief Tolomoto's grave is still marked by the stone in the old drugstore which is now Potter's wax Museum, America's oldest wax museum.

Just outside the city gates at the Huguenot Cemetery, the most-sighted spirit is that of Judge Stickney. John Stickney was what was commonly called a "carpetbagger." He came to St. Augustine after the Civil War with his three daughters. He was a lawyer who was appointed judge. When he died of typhoid fever, he was buried there under a stately oak tree.

His good friend, John Long in Washington, D.C., had agreed that if anything happened to the judge, he would raise the three daughters like his own children. So after the good judge died, the girls went to live in Washington with their adoptive father. Twenty-one years later, after John Long had also died and was interred in Washington, the girls agreed it would be a good thing if their real father could be moved to lie beside their adopted one in Washington.

So they hired a gravedigger named Wells to disinter their father so he could be moved to Washington. Gravedigger Wells finally got the coffin out of the ground. But the carriage had not arrived to pick up the body, so old man Wells decided to lie down in the shadow of the big oak and take a nap while he waited.

As he slept, two intoxicated rogues who had perhaps felt the judge's justice during his lifetime spotted the body. The answer to how their next binge would be financed was solved. They forced open the judge's mouth and pried out his gold teeth.

Perhaps this is why many people have sighted the judge, dressed in a tall hat and long cape, walking bent over, as if he's looking for his teeth?

The judge may even have been caught on videotape during one of his late-night walks. The ghost tour guide told of an encounter she didn't even know she'd had. "A friend's brother was on my tour one night. The brother videotaped it. When the friend was watching the video, she asked her brother, 'Was anyone behind me that night in the cemetery?' 'No,' he answered. 'There is now,' she replied. Sure enough in the background of the tape, there a dark figure of a man in top hat and cape is walking toward the visitor center. Had to be John Stickney!"

City Gates

Just across from the cemetery are the City Gates. In early days of the settlement, these gates were closed at dark, and nothing got them opened before dawn. One of the gatekeepers had a daughter, Elizabeth. Elizabeth's ambition was to grow up and become a gatekeeper herself. Her wish was not to be. She died in a yellow fever epidemic. However, on dark nights many people have seen a young girl wrapped in a white sheet at the city gates waving to people entering the city. Could it be that Elizabeth has achieved in death what was denied her in life?

Spanish Military Hospital

During the second Spanish period in St. Augustine history, had you been a sick or injured soldier you would have been treated at the Spanish Military Hospital. You can tour the museum that is part of this hospital, but parts of the place are forbidden to the public. They are reserved for the departed souls of those who died in the old hospital long ago. The curator, Diana Lane, started Ancient City Ghost tour that does an after-hours tour of the building.

One of the workers actually videotaped a door opening and closing by itself. It has an old-time latch that must be manipulated to open. You can hear the latch open, and there is no one on the other side.

The hospital functioned from 1784 to 1821 and was built on the first Spanish period's graveyard in what had been an Indian burial ground when the settlers arrived. When the city installed new sewer lines several years ago, they found both Spanish bones and Native American ones. They just laid the pipe and covered it, trying not to disturb the graves any more than necessary.

While the Ghost Trackers were present, a garden stake, about 6 feet long and bent at the end like a shepherd's staff that could be used as a plant hanger, levitated. It was in the corner with boxes in front of it. It rose up, catapulted up and over the boxes, and landed at their feet. Diane Lane and the crew of the show all saw it happen.

During another of their investigations, a coke can began walking down a perfectly flat bench. No one was near it. An English high school class was in with them on tour doing a workshop for a class paper, but no one thought to take a picture.

During one tour a woman was mentally thinking, "Is there a spirit here?"

The following day, her husband saw some writing on her back. It appeared to be backwards and upside down, so he had her stand with her back to a mirror and was able to read the writing. It said simply, "yes." The owner, Diane, said she thought she saw something but couldn't be sure. It had faded out somewhat by then. The lady in question has since had the spirits follow her home as things are still happening to her. A good reason you should not try to interact with any entities you may encounter.

Historic Section

So many of St. Augustine's restaurants, museums, and bed and breakfasts have ghost stories, it's a good idea to ask the staff. You will get enough stories to fill a book.

Start your visit with a walk down St. George Street. You can spend hours poking into all the unique shops and museums there. Don't miss the Oldest Schoolhouse. When you hit the City Gates, stop in at the Milltop. It's a St. Augustine tradition.

Another Old Spanish building that has its ghostly tales is O. C. White's. It was constructed in 1791 by Don Miguel Ysnardy, a merchant ship owner, military official and building contractor. He also was the builder of the St. Augustine Cathedral. At one time it was used as a hotel, but in the 1800s the home was bought by Mrs. Margaret S. Worth, the widow of Major General William J. Worth, a Revolutionary War hero.

Kerry Sullivan worked at O. C. White's. He told of working near the bar one day and smelling a strong odor of urine and sweat. He remarked, "I mentioned to another worker, somebody needs to clean around the bar. It smells awful.' The other guy replied, 'It's just the ghost.' I went back there and sniffed. The odor was gone. This happened many times while I worked there. Apparently, the original owner, an older lady, was not too careful with personal hygiene. Folks say she still hangs around the bar." Could it be Mrs. Worth?

There is so much to see, it's a good idea to take one of the tour trams. You can get off at any stop and reboard the same day as long as you don't lose your sticker. And do take one of the ghost tours.

Lighthouse

When the U.S. acquired North Florida in 1821, St. Augustine was the leading port of new territory and needed a harbor light to protect increased shipping. There was a small, three-story tower that may have been used for a beacon by the Spanish. They placed a temporary light atop this tower and planned to strengthen and outfit it with new lights and lens.

However, a government inspector sent to check out the tower felt it would be more practical to build a new one. The new tower rose 73 feet.

There have been women keepers as well as men. The first official woman keeper was Mrs. J. Andreau. She maintained the old lighthouse in the late 1850s, succeeding her husband who fell to his death while painting the tower. Perhaps his are the footsteps still heard on the stairs of the new lighthouse today. Many workers have also glimpsed a male figure ascending the stairs in the lighthouse.

One worker, who preferred not to be identified, told of going into the lighthouse one day when no one else was in it and noticing a rank smell. "It was like cigar smoke and bad body odor."

She then became aware of a muffled conversation. She could not make out any words but said, "It was a man and woman and they had a teasing tone in their voices, like maybe they were a little bit mad at one another."

The old lighthouse lighted the harbor until extinguished by the Confederate Army during the Civil War. Re-lit in 1867, it was increasingly threatened by erosion, prompting the construction of a new lighthouse on Anastasia Island. The old tower finally succumbed to the relentless tides in 1880.

The new lighthouse was lit for the first time on October 15, 1874. The building was not completed without tragic costs. It took its toll in human life. Three young girls were drowned during construction, Mary and Eliza Pittee, the daughters of the construction supervisor, and an unknown African-American girl. To this day, visitors and staff alike have glimpsed these girls near the building.

In spite of the harsh and difficult nature of the job, a keeper's pay was notoriously low. By the late 1800s, a keeper earned less than $600 per year and the assistant keeper, half that amount. The St. Augustine keeper's position was a coveted one, perhaps partly since it was less-isolated than many lighthouses and partly because the keeper's quarters were one of the best in the South.

The keeper's house, completed in 1876, was a two-story brick duplex, with a basement, which was quite unusual in Florida. It was split down the middle, each side mirroring the other. Each had two rooms downstairs, the kitchen and eating area and the parlor. There were two bedrooms upstairs. In 1885 two summer kitchens were added in back of the house. Indoor plumbing came in 1907, and a small bathroom was squeezed between the bedrooms for both the keeper and the assistant. Water was supplied by means of roof gutters flowing into cisterns in the basement. The lighthouse didn't get electricity until 1936.

The keepers served faithfully, the only interruptions in service being during the Civil War and again during World War II. President Roosevelt ordered the light dimmed because German Submarines would lie in wait for American vessels, which would be silhouetted by the lighthouse beacon and thus made an easy target for the German torpedoes. 1955 brought automation to the lighthouse and eliminated the need for a keeper.

The house was rented for a while and then began to fall into disrepair. It was considered surplus government property. Finally came the most devastating blow, an early morning fire in the abandoned building. Dawn arose on a burned-out hulk. Little remained of the once-gracious home but the blackened walls and some of the foundation. It was hinted that the fire might have been arson but never proven. Could it have been started by one of the ghost children playing with matches?

The Junior League of St. Augustine began the Lighthouse Project to restore the two buildings. They purchased the house and grounds for $29,000 and signed a 99-year lease with the Coast Guard for the lighthouse. They have done a painstakingly accurate job of restoration. Then in 2003, the buildings were turned over to the city of St. Augustine to maintain.

Today, the keeper's house is a museum housing lighthouse memorabilia. The parlor and kitchen/eating area of one side have been recreated. The other side is devoted to a souvenir shop. The upstairs that once housed the bedrooms is now a large ballroom, which can be rented for weddings or parties. One side of the basement houses museum displays. The other side contains a small viewing room with a video presentation about the history of the lighthouse. It is here that workers frequently sense a man's presence. Some have even seen him.

It is not just downstairs that strange things happen in the keeper's house either. The gift shop is located upstairs on the first floor. Many of the workers here have had unexplainable occurrences. Tina Guillotte closed one night. She set the alarm and went home. She also was the opening person the next day. When she went in, she sensed something was wrong, but she didn't realize what at first. Then as she stood at the register and counted money, it hit her. "All of the books in the store had been turned face down. I knew they had not been like that when I left. I was the last one out last night and first one in that morning."

Tina feels like it is one of the little girls since the incidents seem like a playful child's pranks. Another worker opened one morning to find all the disposable cameras and film piled in a stack like building blocks on the counter.

It is not just during the night that these things happen. Another worker, Pam Troll, was getting ready to close. Two other workers, Chris and Judy, were also present and saw the same things. She had counted the cash register and shut down the drawer. "I'm standing over by the counter. The cash register drawer popped open. Then a few minutes later, some little toys called Puddle Jumpers, one jumped off the counter. It was too far to have just fallen out. It went about seven feet, way too far to fall. We also have this little thing that when someone walks by it, the seagulls go around in a circle and plays music. We have some in back. Judy was on the other side of the stockroom. For no reason it went off. Someone had walked past it, but none of us were near it."

Pam also stated that all last summer workers would see someone go into the stockroom and when they went in after them, no one would be there.

I took the ghost tour and while I didn't see anything there was a eeiri feelign around us. They guide you through the lighthouse, keepers house, and the grounds. It's well worth it.

Greenbriar Light

One of the most persistent and widespread tales of hauntings involves lights. St Johns County has its own Greenbriar Road Light. Drivers on this road just inside the St. Johns County line have seen what appears to be a single headlight behind. It will follow cars for miles but is not really there. The story is that a motorcyclist was killed in an accident. His head was severed from his body. The light is believed to be that headless cyclist.

There are so many other -places to see in St Augustine that may not have ghosts but are still worth seeing.

St. Augustine Alligator Farm

The St. Augustine Alligator Farm is one of the oldest continuously operated attractions of its kind in Florida. The practice of luring visitors into a small museum or roadside souvenir shop with an alligator display began in the 1890s. At the turn of the century, the owners of a small tram that transported visitors from the mainland and Flagler's tourist hotels to the beach recognized northerner's fascination with the reptiles and began the South Beach Alligator Farm and Museum of Marine Curiosities.

It moved to its present location in 1920 and has been a major attraction in the area ever since. In 1992 it was listed on the National Register of Historic Places. It is also an accredited zoo.

Today, it offers much more than reptiles. It has a large collection of mammals and an exhibit that developed almost accidentally when the owners added more swamp land and a boardwalk to the alligator exhibit. Wading birds had always frequented the zoo, but with the expansion it became a full rookery for egrets, herons and other wading birds.

And while it doesn't have any ghosts we know of, it does have a great exhibit of albino alligators from Louisiana.

Medieval Torture Museum

This one's not a good place to take a budding serial killer but for visitors seeking knowledge, The Medieval Torture Museum is fascinating. The museum is filled with some unusual devices people in earlier times used to punish those they disliked. One look at the Spanish Boot and you'll stop complaining about your shoes being too tight. Those who told tales about their neighbors got to tangle with the Gossipers Violin. And the rack, the drunkard's barrel, and hundreds of other ways once used to maim, hurt, and kill are displayed here. It's interactive to a point. You can touch and handle the instruments. You just can't use them on an enemy.

In the other half of the building there's a partner museum, Micro Masterpieces Art Gallery. It is filled with tiny art you can barely see with the naked eye. Portraits of castles, buildings, famous people, and a train engine are done in microscope size. Look at them with the naked eye and you see a tiny blur; peep into the microscopes and the amazing details jump out at you.

Lincolnville Museum And Cultural Center

The Lincolnville Museum and Cultural Center first opened as the Excelsior Museum and Cultural Center in 2005 in a former Black high school in Lincolnville. It changed to its current name in 2012. One exhibit, in particular, a section of the original Woolworth counter where high school students staged a sit-in shortly before President Johnson signed the Civil Rights Bill, really moved me.

Fort Mose

Before the days of the Underground Railroad escaping slaves headed south to the welcoming Spanish Colony of San Agustín. Here, in 1738, the first free community of former slaves was established called Gracia Real de Santa Teresa de Mose or Fort Mose and was the northernmost defense line of St. Augustine. Any runaway who agreed to become a Catholic and all able-bodied males family members would join the militia were accepted. Today, it's Fort Mose State Park.

You will find interpretive signage and a museum that explains the history of the park as well as the usual hiking, kayaking, and picnicking. Through the year, there are several reenactments of events that happened here. In June, there's the reenactment of the Battle of Bloody Mose. The battle occurred during an obscure war between Britain and Spain known as the War of Jenkins' Ear and proved the worth of the colony to the Spaniards. In the fall, Harvest Time at Fort Mose celebrates the first harvest at Fort Mose where you can sample various food probably cooked here that first year. Throughout the year you find reenactors inhabiting the park who will explain its history.

Lightner Museum

At the same time, Flagler built another hotel across the street, The Alcazar. The Alcazar sported a casino, Turkish and Russian baths, a gymnasium, and a grand ball room as well as other amenities the super rich would appreciate like an indoor swimming pool, which you can still visit today.

Otto Lightner purchased the building and filled it with his collection of rare and unusual things. It is Lightner Museum today and still filled with the rare and unusual. It's filled with fantastic treasures from glassware to a huge stuffed lion. The glassware collection is literally priceless.

Villa Zorayda

This architectural gem was built by another of Flagler's contemporaries and sometimes partner, Franklin Smith, who built the Casa Monica Hotel. This was Smith's winter home. If you ever wanted to visit the Alhambra in Spain, you can save the airfare and come here instead. Smith modeled his home on the famed Alhambra. Since it only had one other owner after Smith, much of the contents are original to the home. Imagine what good taste and unlimited money could do and you get an idea of the scope of Villa Zorayda.

Crooked River Lighthouse

Gibson Inn

Fort Clinch

Palace Saloon

Lobby at Don Cesar

Spanish Club

Henry Plant Museum

Urns

Captain Mayhem at Pirate and Treasure Museum

Firing cannon at Fountain of Youth

Kingsley Plantation

Fort Matanzas

Chapter 3 Georgia

St. Marys

Riverview Hotel

St. Marys is one of the fastest growing small towns in Georgia, thanks to the Kings Bay Trident Submarine Base located there. In fact, Money Magazine voted it the "Number 1 Small Town in America" in 1996. It's still the kind of quaint little town you love to visit and hate to leave. In fact, some of its residents have refused to leave for more than a century. We're talking disembodied residents.

The Riverview Hotel is a St Marys' landmark. It was built as a hotel in 1916 on the banks of the St. Marys River. The waterfront location and old-fashioned charm never cease to calm and relax my cares away whenever I visit. In the 1920s, Miss Sally Brandon must have also fallen under the spell of the inn. She bought it and along with her sisters, Miss Semora and Miss Ethel, made the inn a popular stopping place for visitors from all over. One of their most-famous guests was Roy Crane, a cartoonist. He, too, succumbed to the charm of the old inn and the quaint town. He developed the comic strip, "Wash Tubbs," based on the town and its railcar while staying at the Riverview. The waterfront restaurant, Trolleys, commemorates the cartoon.

It remained in the family until 2019 when innkeepers Jerry and Gaila Brandon, sold it to new owners, Bert Guy and CB Yadav, who are retaining the same friendly atmosphere. In spite of his busy schedule several years ago, Jerry told me his experiences with the inn.

Jerry grew up in the hotel and told me of one strange episode concerning a guest in room nine, Red Myers. Mr. Myers stayed there during the time he was working at the bag factory. One day, a friend came looking for him. The desk clerk let this friend into Red's room to wait, and the visitor fell asleep. He awoke when he felt someone pulling on his leg. He jumped up and found no one there. He rushed downstairs believing Red was playing a trick on him and asked a group of people downstairs, "Did you see Red come out here?"

They assured him they had not. Further, they informed him, "Red has gone to Douglas for the weekend."

Upon discussing it with Red, his friend found that the same thing had happened to Red on several occasions.

Jerry informed me he had not seen anything personally, but "my sister, who is not a believer in the supernatural, swears she saw an apparition. It happened in the '50s when the hotel was not operating. The family still lived here but didn't use the upstairs. She and her friend were in the second-floor hallway and clearly saw what appeared to be the figure of a man. It scared her so bad she wouldn't go up there for a couple of weeks. No one ever saw the man again."

The Riverview also has a restaurant, Seagle's, with great steaks and seafood and a quiet little bar. It's across from the ferry landing to Cumberland Island, one of Georgia's most haunted islands.

Orange Hall

One of the most-commanding buildings in the historic downtown area is Orange Hall. This magnificent Greek Revival mansion served as the Welcome Center as well as a house museum demonstrating life in the Antebellum South. I had driven past it many times, but when I finally entered it a few years ago, I felt as if I had stepped into the home of a friend. It was the home of Reverend Horace Pratt -- his portrait hung over the mantel in the upstairs parlor -- and his second wife, Isabel Drysdale. The family atmosphere was pervasive. I felt comfortable. The house was a gift from his first wife's family. This first wife, Jane Wood, died in 1829 after only six years of marriage. The distraught pastor mourned for three years. Eventually he married one of Jane's friends. When their first child was born, there was no question of her name. She was called Jane. This told something of the character of the second wife, Isobel. She had to be a sweet, generous person to carry this child, go through labor and then name her in loving memory of her predecessor.

Jane grew into a delightful and inquisitive child. Standing in her room, I could almost sense her presence. The room just shouts of a happy, curious child spirit. It was only natural when a shipload of Arcadians heading for Louisiana docked at St. Marys that Jane dashed off to view the unusual occurrence. Sadly, the Arcadian ship carried an invisible passenger, Yellow Fever. The beautiful child sickened and died.

Her spirit was too vibrant to be quelled by death. Modern-day visitors reported spotting a pretty child strolling up the walk or playing in Jane's bright airy second-floor bedroom overlooking the front lawn. There is only one entryway open, the stairway leading from the basement into the living quarters, an attendant was always on duty and would have noticed any child who entered the building. However, the child was seen when the attendant has not admitted any little girl fitting the description. It is temporarily closed due to age and hurrricane damage and is undergoing restoration.

St. Marys Submarine Museum

Another unique museum is located there. The St. Marys Submarine Museum is on Osborne Street, the main street in the historic section. You enter the converted movie theater, step past a sailor lounging in the corner and catch a fascinating glimpse of life aboard a submarine. Be sure to peek at the town through the periscope, which extends through the roof.

Cumberland Island

Another lodging option for the courageous souls is Cumberland Island. I say this is an option for only fearless hardy souls for two reasons: One is you must take the ferry over with all your camping equipment and set up your camp in a totally primitive albeit beautifully wooded camping area, and two, the island is reputed to abound in ghosts.

For the less prinitive visitor, one of the Carnegie mansions originally existing on the island, Greyfield is an inn and is best remembered as the site of the J.F.K. Jr./Caroline Bessette wedding reception. It is an elegant, if expensive, way to enjoy the island. Greyfield was a wedding gift from Lucy Carnegie to their daughter Margaret.

Cumberland Island nestles close to the mainland at the southernmost tip of Georgia. It's a place of rare natural beauty. Although it has been inhabited for more than 4,000 years, man has trod lightly here on this, the largest of Georgia's barrier islands. Camped among the moss-shrouded trees, where there is no electricity, few cars and little technological development, it is easy to visualize spectral shapes within the mists.

In some areas you will notice the grass has been grazed as neatly as if trimmed by a mower. The park-like effect is the result of the feral horses and wild deer that feed under the stately oaks. Throngs of other wildlife also inhabit the island. Bright flashes of red, blue and yellow dart among the branches as the island birds announce their presence with bursts of song. Deep in the forest, small rain-fed ponds glisten in the sun. Occasionally, just the eyeballs of a lone alligator break the surface. On the eastern side, the forests are thick with undergrowth. The Saw Palmetto intertwines with vines and grasses to form an almost impenetrable barrier to anyone striving to reach the dunes just beyond.

Jennifer Bjork, former National Park Service resource specialist, explained about one of the island's most environmentally important events. At night, sea turtles lumber ashore to lay eggs in some 200 nests. The tiny reptiles hatch in 60 days, and, guided by instinct, they rush home to sea.

I spent one night camping among the moss-dripping oaks and could sense a presence of some sort on the island. Perhaps it is just its turbulent history. Perhaps something else really roams the pristine island at night.

Spanish explorers visited Cumberland Island in the mid-1500s. They met the Quale, a branch of the Timucuan tribe of Native American who had inhabited the island for thousands of years. When the Spanish departed, they left their Arabian and Barb horses to fend for themselves on the island. With no natural predators, the horses thrived.

Shortly after the Revolutionary War, General Nathaniel Greene purchased land on the island to build a home for his family. Greene planned the home on the site of an old hunting camp belonging to General Oglethorpe. The General died before it could be built. His wife, Catherine, constructed the elegant four-story mansion and named it "Dungeness." Catherine lived in Dungeness with her second husband, Phineas Miller, and her children. The house was left unfinished because an old family superstition predicted disaster should Dungeness ever be completed. But even that attempt to thwart disaster failed. The family remained at Dungeness until the Civil War drove them away. The elegant home survived the war but was burned during reconstruction. Afterwards, human activity on the island diminished, and the feral horses interbred with those abandoned by planters.

In 1882 Thomas Carnegie acquired most of the island. America had entered the "gilded age," and new money flowed freely. Jekyll Island, a few miles north, became the summer playground of the nation's wealthy, but Thomas and brother Andrew, despite their sizable fortunes, were not invited because of their Scots ancestry.

In 1884 Thomas answered the snub with a Scottish castle on Cumberland Island. In defiance of the old superstition surrounding the original house, he built the magnificent turreted mansion on the site of the old Dungeness ruins and called his new home by the same name. Thomas, with his wife Lucy and their nine children, made the new Dungeness the social center of the area. Thomas, like Nathaniel Greene, did not have long to enjoy his mansion. He died in 1886. Lucy continued using Dungeness as a seasonal home. Over time, Lucy divided the surrounding acres among her children as they married. Gradually, the magnificent showplace fell into disrepair. A fire ravaged the castle in 1959, leaving only a skeleton standing. The horses, their gene pool increased by the Carnegies' fancy saddle horses, now graze on the once-manicured lawns of Dungeness.

Some say that the sprit you are most likely to see while camping originated from this era. Thomas Hutchinson was hired to design a golf course for the Carnegies. He was killed shortly afterwards while riding his horse beneath a low-hanging branch after leaving a boisterous party at the mansion. Many partygoers reported that he fled in anger after a dispute with his host; others claimed he was merely going to fetch more spirits to liven the party. Whichever the case, he was riding recklessly across the island when he hit the low-hanging branch. His body lay for several days on the lonely beach before he was discovered. Staff and visitors sight him frequently.

Plum Orchard, which resembles a smaller version of The White House, also still stands. Plum Orchard was a wedding gift from the Carnegies to the oldest son, George, and his bride, Margaret. It's a magnificent 30-room Classical Revival style by Boston architectural firm Peabody and Stearns who built most of the Carnegie family homes on the island.

After George died in 1921, his widow sold the furniture and abandoned the house. The youngest Carnegie, Nancy, moved into Plum Orchard. There are many artifacts left by Nancy Carnegie and her second husband, Doctor Marius Johnston. The home had running water and electricity before it was available in most other places. There's a swimming pool and squash court inside the home.

The current resident is the spirit of a troubled lady of the evening, prefers it that way. Many staff members have heard the dumbwaiter rising and returning in the empty house. Some have experienced the smell of fresh tobacco smoke and heard footsteps in the mansion. Many people have seen a woman in red in the servants' quarters. It is believed a prostitute died on the island while "visiting" Plum Orchard. She is reputedly buried in the Stafford Cemetery. Caretakers have seen her trying to leave the cemetery.

The original Stafford was the home of William and Gertrude Ely Carnegie. It burned to the ground in the late 1890s. The couple then lived in the little tabby house that is still standing. (Tabby is a building material made from sand, lime, oyster shell, and water.) Gertrude died in 1906, and William became severely depressed. He later married his nurse, Betty. Betty, too, abandoned him by committing suicide shortly afterwards. Today, family members report that Gertrude's presence is felt in the Stafford House and even more so in the tabby house. Guests there reported jewelry moved and shades rolling up by themselves. A family member once saw Gertrude's apparition there. A woman in white also is frequently seen around the old carriage house.

The Carnegies later deeded their land to the National Park Service. Some homes there are still private property, but the bulk of the island is preserved in a natural state. When the Carnegies gave the land to the Park Service, one stipulation was that, to preserve the island's natural character, no bridge could be built from the mainland.

Today, Cumberland Island offers a nature lovers' paradise with miles of hiking trails, dirt roads and sandy beaches. Fortunately, water and restrooms are available.

Land and Legacy Tours depart from Sea Camp Dock and are the best way to visit the south end of the island. Remember, the island is 18 miles long. You can bring a bike or rent one at the dock, but that is a long way to pedal. If you want to see the north end of the island, take this tour. Not only does the six-hour-tour take you through many buildings including Plum Orchard, but your guide gives a detailed history of each place along the route. Frequently, you will stop to see the feral horses on this end of the island and the other wildlife, like turkeys, deer, and armadillos. According to Mike, our guide, there are three separate herds on the island, the south end one around Dungeness Ruins, a herd near Stafford Plantation site, and one near The Settlement.

Stafford Plantation ties into Carnegie history but predates it. Robert Stafford is an interesting character. He was the largest plantation owner on Cumberland Island and needed slaves. However, he disapproved of slavery and treated his slaves differently. They could earn money after completing plantation duties. Stafford encouraged them to save the money and insisted they learn basic reading, writing, and arithmetic. He had a church and a hospital for the slaves. He had two mixed race families, both of which he provided with large trust funds. One of his daughters, Nancy, became one of the first African American doctors.

His plantation was purchased from his heirs by Lucy Carnegie and gifted to her eldest son, William, upon his marriage to Margaret Ely. January 5, 1900, a fire destroyed the original Stafford mansion. A year later, William built another house similar to the original on the site. He turned portions of the original cotton field into a nine-hole golf course. You will visit the cemetery where Stafford, his mother, and sister are buried. The golf course is now overgrown and all that remains of the slave quarters cannot be seen, as they are on the same private land as the home currently owned by the Rockefellers.

After the Civil War ended, Stafford's freed slaves migrated farther north on the island and lived in what they called The Settlement. Union Soldiers returned home and told of the pleasant southern winters. That created a market for several hotels on the north end of the island. Hotel developers saw the already-in-place African Americans as an excellent source of hired help, both in building the hotels and staffing the finished resorts. They sold the residents lots for $11, where they could build houses. The Great Depression ended the hotels. African American residents left for jobs on the mainland.

Today very few buildings remain at The Settlement. There is the African American Church where JFK, Jr. was married. Kennedy and the Fergusons, owners of Greyfield Inn, were friends for years and he choose this location for privacy. Mitty and his sister, Janet Ferguson, helped plan and keep the wedding secret. The church and one other building are open for visits.

The other open building was the home of Beulah Alberty, daughter of one of the original homeowners. Beulah was a college-educated schoolteacher. She returned to The Settlement and helped the community with legal matters, started a school for the children, and became known as the Mayor of The Settlement. Her house is unfurnished but has photos and restrooms but no drinkable water.

Next to the church, there is an old red house. It is dilapidated and not safe to enter. It possibly belonged to Beulah's uncle, Rogers Alberty.

The other standing house here is labeled with a large banner stating "Wildcumberland.org" and belongs to Carol Ruckdeschel, a self-taught biologist who opposed the island tours, feral horses, and much of the visitor use of the island. Do not trespass on her property. Carol does not welcome visitors and in the past, shot and killed a supposedly violent ex-boyfriend at this cottage. There are bound to be a few unknown spirits roaming the southern part of the island.

It's impossible to overrate the charm and mystic of this island where there are few cars and only 300 people a day are permitted. Feral horses, wildlife, history. And multiple spirits claim Cumberland as their own.

Riverview Park

The Riverview Park is located just next to the ferry dock and boat launch. It boasts lots of white gazebos and attractive landscaping and is a great spot to enjoy the view.

Crooked River State Park

For campers, Crooked River State Park is four miles away on the banks of the St. Marys River. The park accommodates anything from tents to the largest RV. The park offers great fishing and a boat launch. It also has cabin rentals. In certain times of the year, you will want to be well-provided with bug repellent as it occasionally has a gnat and mosquito problem.

McIntosh Sugar Mill

Between Crookeed River State Park and the city, visit the ruins of the old McIntosh Sugar Mill built in 1825. Some people believe the ruins are that of an old mission built long before the sugar mill. Whatever it is, the moss-draped trees and wooded surroundings allow your imagination to supply the site with spirits of long-deceased inhabitants.

Jekyll Island

Jekyll Island

The barrier islands of Georgia's southern coast are called the Golden Islands for many reasons. The golden sun rises from the depth of the wave-crested blue sea and bathes their sandy beaches. Here, too, was where the early Spanish Conquistadors sought the legendary gold promised by the original Creek inhabitants of these isles. Legends of the pirate Blackbeard's gold supposedly buried there is one more reason for the sobriquet. Of the three major islands, Jekyll boasts the most golden heritage.

The Creeks were the first to cherish this golden isle. They had no concept of "ownership." They and the land were one. The murky Marshes of Glynn was their home for hundreds of years. They shared it in harmony with the animals. The deer, raccoon, possum, pheasant, wild turkey, and alligator inhabited the land with them and provided all the necessities of life.

The creatures of the sea also provided food and tools. Then in the late 1500s, a new breed of man arrived on the island. The Spanish were seeking treasure of a different kind. They wanted gold. However, they recognized the richness of the land and established a mission to convert the Indians and claim the land for Spain. Their enjoyment of the island was short-lived.

In 1680, the British attacked the island, destroying the mission and driving off both the Spanish and the Indians. Major William Horton, one of Oglethorpe's officers and later successor as commander of the military force in Georgia, built the first English residence on Jekyll in 1736. The gray tabby walls still stand near the northern end of the island on the marsh side. When I gaze at these ancient ruins, I am amazed that so much still stands of the original structure. These ruins bear witness to the durability of the material.

After the Revolution, Christophe Poulain du Bignon purchased Jekyll. He enlarged the Horton house and used it for his residence until 1825. The du Bignons were the leaders of the area's plantation families until the Civil War put an end to that lifestyle.

Across the street from the Horton house stands the du Bignon Family Cemetery, its weathered tombstones silent sentinels to the five generations of du Bignons who cultivated the island plantation until 1886 when John Eugene du Bignon sold the island to a group of millionaires searching for a playground.

With the sale to the Jekyll Island Club, the island entered a new era of prosperity. Its 100 members were rumored to control a seventh of the wealth of this country among them. Men like Rockefeller, Morgan, Astor and Gould built "cottages" here for their families' winter home. These 12-to-20-room mansions contained every convenience money could buy.

The piece de la resistance of Millionaires' Row is the Clubhouse. Its turret stands head and shoulders above the other structures on the island. There you can bask in the luxury that once was accorded only the millionaires and their chosen guests. You can spend the night, or as many nights as you can afford, being pampered in the Victorian elegance of the clubhouse. The richest and most powerful men on earth called this hotel home once so perhaps it's only natural that they refuse to let even death persuade them to depart its splendor. Could that be a Vanderbuilt or a Morgan at the next table? Once they sat there being served by their skilled staff of the finest chefs imported from the best restaurants in New York. More likely the one rich and powerful personage I might spot could be Samuel Spencer, president of the Southern Railroad Company. Samuel insisted the Wall Street Journal be delivered to his room. For years it was his ritual to drink a cup of coffee while scanning the paper. In 1906 he was killed instantly in a train accident. Since then, club members and hotel guests who occupied Spencer's room have found copies of their newspaper disturbed, moved or folded in their absence. Coffee cups have been mysteriously poured or drunk when guests returned. Or possibly I might share the space with General Lloyd Aspinwall. He was to be the club's first president; however, he died a year before the club opened. Perhaps he won't leave the premises because he resents the fact that he never achieved the expected office in life. His figure has been seen strolling along the veranda as if he belonged there. Perhaps he does. As I sit there sipping a cup of tea, I can easily imagine the general peering over my shoulder, shaking his head and murmuring to himself, "What is our fine club coming to that this unescorted woman dares sit in here as if she was one of us?"

In front of the clubhouse you can play croquet on a lawn as plush as a green carpet, splash in the sparkling pool, or just loll in one of the many wicker rockers adorning the hotel veranda. Just in the mood for a snack or a drink? Try Cafe Solterra or the Lobby Bar. If the bar in there looks familiar, that's because an exact replica was used in the movie "The Legend of Bagger Vance."

Golfers can play on one of four club courses. Three 18-hole courses (Oleander, Indian Mound, and Pine Lakes) are located inland on the island. The historic Great Dunes 9-hole course, whose links were originally laid in 1910, is located next to the ocean. This course contains part of the original course where J. P. Morgan once tipped his caddy a nickel.

Historic Village

When I open the door of Sans Souci, now a part of the hotel complex but originally built in 1896 for members of the hunting club, I always sniff the air for a whiff of fine cigar smoke. One member, J. Pierpont Morgan, liked to sit out on the porch of his third-story apartment in the early morning hours, watch the river and smoke a cigar. Guests rising early can still smell his cigar smoke. I guess I have just never arrived early enough.

The Crane Cottage upstairs is now used for the Jekyll Island Authority offices, but the first floor is open to the public. The Courtyard at Crane Cottage is now one of the complex's fine restaurants.

The cottage was built in the Renaissance Revival style, many of its features copied from 16th-century Italian Villas. From its double-door arched entry to its red tile roof, it speaks of elegant simplicity. You can visualize Richard Crane's family sedately dining at the massive mahogany table, one of the children perhaps fingering the carved rungs of his chair, waiting to be allowed to go and play in the huge enclosed courtyard while his parents observed from the arched walkway or perhaps the upper veranda. One thing is sure: The fidgeting child would never have to wait his turn to use the bathroom. Mr. Crane was the owner of the Crane Company, an international plumbing fixture company that was first to produce colored plumbing fixtures. His home boasted 20 rooms and 17 bathrooms.

Indian Mound, originally built for Gorden Mckay and later purchased by William Rockefeller, displays the extravagant opulence of the Victorian age. A three-story shingle structure, it has a vine-covered wrap around porch and large bay windows on each floor. One of the first-floor bays is a massive semicircle of glass looking out over the Jekyll River. Its 25 rooms are furnished luxuriously. It has a stained-glass window on the stair landing, a dumbwaiter, a cedar-lined walk-in safe, and taps for hot and cold salt water in the master bath. It proudly displays countless antiques and art objects. The Goodyear Cottage now serves as a center for creative arts, housing the Jekyll Island Arts Association and is open to the public at no charge. The Moss Cottage, a two-story green cypress shingle dwelling with a roofed porch that runs the length of the house, was once owned by George Macy, the owner of A & P. It is open for tours Wednesday through Sunday, 10 to 2.

You can tour the du Bignon House, Indian Mound and Mistletoe Cottage by taking the tram tours. The tours depart daily from the Museum Visitor's Center, which is housed in the former stable. The Museum presents an informative film about the history of the island to 1930. It also has artifacts, pictures, and memorabilia of that era. Even if you don't plan on spending the tram tour fare, the museum and film deserve your attention.

Along with the millionairs homes, there are many other buildings worthy of a visit. The Faith Chapel was the site of most of the island's religious functions. As you sit in the chapel beneath its two stained-glass windows -- the western one is a signed Tiffany -- imagine yourself a guest at a 1920s wedding. Marcullus Dodge, heir to the Remington fortune, is marrying Geraldine Rockefeller. The union is rumored to make them the richest couple in the world. The chapel is open daily from 2 to 4. The Gould casino, although not restored, is interesting just for its sheer size. Jay Gould's son, Edwin, who lived at Chichota Cottage, built it around 1913. Originally there was another building that has been lost, but the one still standing once housed tennis courts, lockers and showers. The powerhouse, now Santa's Christmas Shoppe, is a delight any time of year. The Cottage, now a bookstore, has many books about the island as well as other topics.

Marinas

The marina, located in the historical district, was where the famous yachts once anchored. Today it is the site of a restaurant, the Latitude 31, and is the boarding point of the water taxi, which operates several tours and trips to St. Simons.

Another marina is located south of the historic district. Here you can dine or just sip a cool drink overlooking the Jekyll River at SeaJay's. Both marinas provide docking. The Jekyll Harbor provides hookups for long-term docking. Kayaking and canoeing provide another popular way to enjoy the marsh.

Campground

If you're a camper, the Jekyll Island Campground is located on the north end of the island and can provide you with everything from primitive to full hookup. The campers' store is staffed by friendly personnel and has bike rentals. Incidentally, bikes are a great way to navigate the island. The 20 miles of paved bike trails wander through places you can't reach by car.

The Wanderer

It was during the era just before the Civil War that an event occurred that would live forever in the annals of infamy. It was on a stormy night in 1858, long after importing of slaves was made illegal, that the Wanderer landed on Jekyll's shore. The ill-fated ship carried the last cargo of slaves ever brought from Africa.

To this day, when the night is dark and the thunder rolls, people claim to see the glimmer of ghostly fires amid the sheltering trees where so many years ago they were lit to dry the huddled cargo and crew of the Wanderer. While camping, I came out late one night. Although I heard and saw nothing out the ordinary, the hair on the back of my neck rose when the moon went behind a cloud. No longer curious, I quickly returned to my car and hurried back to the shelter of my nice modern camper.

Other Attractions

The island also has a water park, miniature golf, numerous picnic areas, and horseback riding. If the ocean isn't enough for your water fun, Summer Waves Splash Zone is another alternative.

Just next to the water park, the University of Georgia operates the Tidelands Nature Center. Here you can enjoy hands-on marine environmental science programs for both the general public and school groups. Drop in to meet some of the island's native flora and fauna.

Jekyll Island is a unique state park. Homes once a symbol of status and privilege are now open to tour. Although they differ in style, they all have one thing in common: They reflect the feel of the gilded era when people flaunted their wealth. If you wish to pretend you're rich and famous, Jekyll Island is the place to do it. Be sure to keep an eye peeled for distinguished-looking guests that may be dressed a bit more formally than the average visitor. You may be catching a glimpse of the death-styles of the rich and famous from another era.

Americus, Plains, and Andersonville

Windsor Hotel

One of Georgia's best-kept secrets is hidden away in the small town of Americus. While most Americans are not aware of this Victorian hotel's charms, local residents are charmed by the Windsor Hotel.

The Windsor originally opened to fanfare and a great ball on June 16, 1892. Over the years, the hotel's popularity declined and the building went on the auction block. In September 5, 1899, Charles A. Fricker bought the Windsor and attempted to rekindle its former glory. In spite of major renovations, it declined and was finally operated as an apartment house. When even that failed to maintain the huge building, it was destined for the wrecking ball.

The bankrupt hotel came into the possession of the City of Americus, and the hotel reopened on September 20, 1991, after considerable restoration to return the elderly dowager to her youthful beauty. Finally, the historic hotel was on its way back to its rightful place, a property that can hold its own among the great hotels of the world.

The original golden oak woodwork in the lobby was refinished, as was the original pink-and-gray marble floor. The mirror on the back wall of the lobby dates back to before the Civil War. The mahogany phone booth, one of the highlights of the lobby, is authentic although not original to the hotel. The clock on the second-floor lobby is the only original furnishing. It came from the Windsor jewelry shop. It's been restored and is on permanent loan from Sumter Historic Trust.

The Roosevelt Boardroom has been nicknamed the "Lucky Room" because of the successful political campaigns began there. President Roosevelt and President Carter used it for their meetings.

Through the years, the Windsor played host to the famous and the infamous: John L. Sullivan, former heavy-weight boxing champion; Congressman William Jennings Bryan; three-time Democratic presidential nominee, the governor of New York and soon-to-be President Franklin D. Roosevelt and even, Al Capone, who posted an armed guard at the foot of the stairs. Lindbergh played pool there. President and Rosalynn Carter are frequent visitors and have a suite named for them in the turret. Jessica Tandy, who stayed there during the filming of one of her movies, also has a room named for her.

The Windsor has a few secrets of her own. Her stately halls are roamed by the ghost of a former housekeeper and her daughter. The lady was head housekeeper there in the 1920s and was thrown down an elevator shaft. Both the housekeeper and her daughter still may be glimpsed by the unwary. They are not malevolent. The mother appears to be looking out for "her" guests. The little girl is playful. Ida Robinson, who worked there can attest to that. She recalled walking down the hall on the third floor around 1 a.m. one morning with a tray in her hands when she spotted the mischievous child pass her in the hallway and then disappear. "It was very scary." Ms. Robinson told me.

Ida also told of "someone" filling up a salad bowl in the kitchen when she left the room to answer a phone call once. She also has seen pots and pans fly across the kitchen.

In August 2005, Turner South sent a crew to tape scenes at the Windsor Hotel for a show called *Blue Ribbon Specials*. I had the honor of being invited to the taping since my book *Georgia's Ghostly Getaways* retells the story of the Windsor's ghost.

The staff made me welcome and put me in a room near where some of the sightings took place. Unfortunately, I didn't see any ghosts. I did see first-hand what tremendous work goes into filming a show like this.

The day was fraught with mishaps for both the camera crew and me. For me. The disaster of the day was my car's breaking a belt and stranding me just a few blocks from the hotel. By the time the car was finally on its way to a "car hospital" for cars injured in the line of duty, I was free to devote my attention to the hotel and the taping. Kris Lawsen, the show's producer, had heard about my book and planned to interview me that evening, Meanwhile, I learned the TV camera had also broken and could not be fixed. (Could the ghosts have been responsible for all the breakdowns?) They had sent part of the crew, cameramen Dave Dawson and Kevin Maggiore, out to a local tech school to get a camera they could use for the filming. So they were already way behind schedule.

I was supposed to do my thing at 5 p.m., but since I was staying overnight they asked if I minded being pushed back to 8 p.m. Okay, that gave me a chance to follow the crew around and see what filming was like.

They filmed lots of people, including Roy Parker, who had been in charge of the heating and cooling installation when it was last renovated. He offered much more than information on the mechanical systems of the hotel. "I first saw the Windsor with my grandmom," he stated. "She would take me into town, and we would stop at the Windsor."

Even then he was impressed. Later, in high school, crashing parties at the Windsor was a fun thing to do for his friends and himself.

The current State Senator George Hooks talked of his recollections of the Windsor. He told of having "ballroom dancing lessons at the Windsor when I was in about sixth grade. It was the most useless thing I have ever learned. I never used it in later life."

Senator Hooks also encapsulated what most people who have visited the Windsor feel about the grand old hotel. He is glad the Windsor was not torn down to build a parking lot because "we have lost too much during the '50s and '60s in the Deep South. The Windsor is a link to our past and a bridge to our future. It represents the best of the South that came out of reconstruction."

One of the cutest things was when they were interviewing Senator Hooks on the second-floor balcony. The senator was in the middle of a great sound bite about why he was so glad the hotel had not been torn down when a truck passed below and hit its horn, blasting out *Dixie* loud and clear. They re-shot that scene. I think they should have left it in.

The scene they filmed the most was a re-enactment of the dining room manager seeing the ghost of the little girl. Ida Robinson played herself in the scene very well.

Mary Frances Thomas, a precocious redhead with aspirations of being an actress, portrayed the girl's ghost and stole the show. Judging by her vivacity and talent, she has a good chance at achieving her ambitions.

She added to the ghost lore with a few accounts of her own while waiting our respective turns before the camera. Mary Frances recounted, "There are two other spirits at the Windsor Hotel. One is a young woman who was decapitated by her boyfriend at the hotel. She still roams the halls, most likely hunting her head or her awful boyfriend."

The other spirit, who according to Mary Francis, "everyone knows about," was one of the original construction workers of the hotel, Floyd, who later worked as an elevator operator there when it first opened. He died by falling down the elevator shaft. The hotel bar, Floyd's, is named in his honor.

Rylander Theater

Just down the street from the hotel stands the Rylander Theatre. For decades after it closed in 1951, it sat hidden behind a row of offices. Just a few old timers remembered its existence, those who had visited it in its glory days when it featured the Ziegfield Follies or World War I sharpshooter Sgt. Alvin York. But until the fall of 1999, only the termites graced the stage. The moths and perhaps the restless spirits of former actors were the only ones occupying the costume vaults.

The owner of the local Ford dealership, who saw silent movies in 1919 when he visited New York City, built the Rylander. He decided Americus should have this luxury. Two years later in 1921, the Rylander opened. It boasted a stage and dressing rooms for live shows as well. It closed when the company running it opened a new movie theater elsewhere in town.

Today the Rylander has been completely restored to its former glory. It features live performances, the finest in family entertainment, national touring companies, 1928 Moller Organ concerts, movies, corporate meeting services and community theatre. Partnerships with Georgia Southwestern State University, Sumter Players and the Americus Sumter County Arts Council offer diverse opportunities for the community.

Much of the new has been added, but whenever possible the original craftsmanship was restored. Of course, the spirit is still there and lets its presence be felt occasionally with a flicker of lights or a cold spot in an otherwise warm theater.

Fish Home

Americus is filled with Victorian homes. Many of them may have their own restless spirit. However, even if they don't, viewing these lovely buildings reminds us of a time when homes were built for beauty rather than convenience and economy. The spirit of a more elegant era lives on in Americus. On the northeast side of Americus, drive past a restored antebellum home. Built around 1852 for Colonel George Fish and his wife, Martha Hansell Fish, today it is a private home. The owners did major restoration on the old home, moved it from Oglethorpe to its present location in 1969. However, the move and the restoration did not dislodge the presence of Col. Fish. An associate, John Holsenback, murdered him in the

Macon County Courthouse. Although the murderer was brought to justice and hanged, Col. Fish still remains in his former home.

Lee Bell Bridge

Another spot in Americus where it is rumored you might have an otherworldly encounter is at the bridge on Lee Bell Road. The apparition of a little girl has been seen and heard walking across the bridge. Perhaps it related to a murder by the bridge. Leigh Bell, a 15-year-old cheerleader, and the daughter of the Americus city manager Leland Bell, was last seen on the evening of June 6, 1979. On the early afternoon Friday, June 8, her body was discovered in Muckalee Creek under some branches. The murder had never been solved.

Downtown Plains

The excitement of the movement that transformed "Jimmy who?" to President Jimmy Carter still lurks in the streets of the small rural town of Plains. Feel the spirit of The Jimmy Carter National Historic Site, his residence, boyhood home, high school, the railroad depot that served as campaign headquarters, and the National Preservation District that protects the heritage of a town where America's longest lived president claimed as his hometown.

The SAM Shortline Excursion Train with its scenic 1949 vintage railcars carry visitors from Cordele to Plains, Americus and Archer, a tiny hamlet just outside Plains where Carter's boyhood home is located. The farm that Jimmy Carter grew up on is an unpretentious rural slice of Americana, with its rural farmhouse, country store, blacksmith shop and even an outhouse.

On the way to visit the Boyhood Farm Site, you will pass a very different residence of the former first family. This crumbling Federal Style home, known as the Rylander House, sheltered the Carter family from 1956 to 1961. The house was built by Matthew Rylander in the mid-1850s. According to Fred Boyles, a national park employee who oversaw the Andersonville site and was temporarily in charge of the Carter house as well, the house "is believed to be the oldest house in Sumter County. It predates the Civil War." He also said there is no secret to the fact that it is supposed to be haunted. "It is labeled on the NPS map as 'Haunted House.' Jimmy Carter refers to the house in his book, Why Not the Best? In spite of this, the Carters loved the house and tried to buy it, but the owner would not sell."

Although the Carters knew of its reputation before they moved in, the spooky stories were reinforced almost at once. In an article in the Examiner, "Mrs. Carter said that one night they were startled by the sound of a loud crash coming from the front room. 'We waited a bit, then the whole family trooped in together, thinking a window had fallen shut. But the window was still wide open.'"

Union soldiers occupied the house during the Civil War, and it is their spirits that are supposed to haunt the dwelling. The house, built in the 1850s by African Americans enslaved to Matthew Rylander, had already frightened generations when Jimmy and Rosalynn Carter rented it from 1956 to 1961. "I don't know when I first heard it was haunted," Rosalynn Carter told a reporter. "Over the years, there were many bizarre occurrences, but one story I remember was that a light in the attic window was a candle kept burning by a lady so soldiers would know where to hide during the Civil War."

Besides the soldiers, there are other spirits present. There is a small white dog that vanishes mysteriously when anyone tries to pet him. There is also a woman in a long white gown. She appears to be weeping. The ghostly activities seem to center on the living room. Adding to the mystery, there is a small room hidden in the space between the attic and the ceiling. Jack, the oldest of the Carter children, found several loose bricks in the hearth of the attic fireplace and discovered the room. It was furnished with only a ladder. Could some tragedy have happened in this secret room that triggering the strange events in the antebellum mansion? Plains Better Hometown Program purchased the property in 2008, to restore and maintain it.

A great time to visit the area is for the annual September Peanut Festival. The historic Drama "If These Sidewalks Could Talk," is built on the memories of Plains' residents as they watched "their" Jimmy make history when he became the 39th president. The play is new and fresh each year, but the overall theme remains the same. Just as the Americus/Plains area is growing and vibrant, it still remains a stronghold of rural and small town Georgia.

Andersonville

If any place deserves to be haunted, the site of the infamous Confederate prison at Andersonville is the spot. Andersonville's very name conjured up horror during the Civil War. Today, it spreads a message of hope. During the 14 months the prison functioned as Camp Sumter, 45,000 Union soldiers were imprisoned there. Of that number, 13,000 died from starvation, disease, unsanitary conditions, or exposure to a bitter winter cold. Conditions were so bad there that one prisoner, Sgt. David Kennedy, described it as "this hell on earth where it takes seven of its occupants to make a shadow."

The Commander there was Captain Henry Wirz. He was the only Confederate officer hanged for war crimes. His malevolent presence is rumored to still haunt the site. Wirz was not a natural-born Southerner. He was a Swiss imigrant who had joined the fourth Louisiana Infantry. Assigned as commander of Camp Sumter in March of 1864, he was placed in an untenable position. The war was taking its toll on the South's resources. Sherman's march to the sea had left behind a blazing trail of destruction. There was no food to feed the citizens. Soldiers lived on what they could forage off the land, which was little.

The Union blockade had cut off all supplies to the South including medicine and anesthetics. The situation would have eased if the prisoners could have been swapped for Confederate prisoners languishing in Northern prison camps, however United States Secretary of War, Edwin M. Stanton, had forbade that in an effort to strike the final blow to the Confederacy. He felt the exchanged prisoners would return to fight for the South, thereby prolonging the war.

The prison had been built early in 1864. It consisted of little more than a 15-foot-high stockade enclosing about 16 ½ acres. In June, that was enlarged to enclose 26.5 acres. Sentry boxes, called pigeon roosts, by the prisoners were built every 30 feet along the wall. About 19 feet within the wall was the "deadline." Any prisoner who entered this space was shot. The only water in the camp was a tiny stream that meandered through the stockade. The stream was used for all the prisoners' sanitation needs as well as cooking and drinking. Naturally disease was rampant. Shelter consisted of what the prisoners themselves could fashion from their limited resources. As is usually the case in situations like this, bullies arose within the prison. A group of the dregs of the Union prisoners preyed on their weaker compatriots. Led by Willie Collins, these renegades called themselves "The Raiders." They stole what little other prisoners had and often killed other prisoners. Finally the prisoners informed Wirz. He allowed the prisoners themselves to try and convict several of "The Raiders." Six of the outlaws were hung from a makeshift gallows inside the stockade to the cheers of the prisoners. Collins went to his death defiant and cursing his accusers. The graves of the raiders are located near the front of the cemetery. This is not a spot where I would choose to be late at night. There are those who say Collins and some of his raiders still remain within the walls of Andersonville Prison.

Wirz was charged with the responsibility for their care. Had he been a saint, he would have been able to accomplish little under these conditions. At the end of the war, horrified Federal officers brought Wirz to trial as a war criminal. He was accused of conspiracy to "murder in violation of the laws of war." There was no conspiracy, but the conditions so horrified the Northerners that Wirz was convicted and hanged. The United Daughters of the Confederacy have since tried to clear his name, claiming he was just a scapegoat. They have erected a monument to Capt. Wirz in the town of Andersonville. Perhaps Wirz's spirit is still bound to the prison in the hope of making people understand that there was nothing he could have done to change the conditions that created the horror of Andersonville Prison.

In spite of the impossibility of the situation, there was one man who tried to ease the pain of the wretched prisoners trapped in this hellhole. If you are strolling on the prison grounds and come upon a little man dressed in ragged black carrying an umbrella, you may be face to face with the prison chaplain, Father Whelan. Whelan was the only chaplain who could endure the conditions at the prison. Although he was a Southerner, he ministered to Protestant as well as Catholic prisoners. He begged the archdiocese to send help, food and medicine. Other priests came but could not stand the conditions and left. There was no money to send. Father Whelan used what little money he had to buy flour and had bread baked in nearby Macon, which he took to the starving men in the compound. By the time the war ended, 45,000 men had passed through Andersonville's gates almost 13,000 died there , the largest number of any Civil War prison camp.

Those who died were transported to the "Dead House," a small building made of tree branches just outside the South Gate, until interment in the prison cemetery.

Perhaps the suffering of so many helpless souls caused psychic energy to emanate from the site even as early as August 9, 1864. A strange -- some say miraculous -- event occurred then. As the prisoners huddled in a fierce summer rainstorm, a spring burst forth from the ground. Because of the unsanitary conditions of the stream in the camp, fresh water was one of the most pressing needs of the prisoners. Many had even tried to dig wells to no avail.

Today, it is a national historic site and houses the National Prisoner of War Museum as well as the Andersonville National Cemetery. The National Prisoner of War Museum honors all Americans who suffered imprisonment for their country. The exhibits are graphic. A moving film depicting interviews with former POWs gives a deeper understanding of what it is like to be a prisoner.

Town of Andersonville

The little town of Andersonville offers a yearly fair in October. As you stroll the streets of the tiny Civil War Village, you are apt to meet Abraham Lincoln, Robert E. Lee and other personages of the time. Music, dancing and re-enactments are among the entertainment. The heart of the village is the Depot Museum housing memorabilia of the time.

Be sure to visit the old log church just west of town and the Pioneer Farm at the north end of the village.

If you plan to visit in October, accommodations are filled to overflowing so plan ahead. Andersonville RV Campground is convenient and reasonably priced. It is comfortable but not fancy. It does offer both RV and tent camping. A Place Away Bed and Breakfast is also near the village for non-campers. There are some chain motels outside town or you can stay in Americus, which is just a few miles away.

Andersonville is a part of our American heritage and should be seen by every man, woman and child to understand the terrible cost of war.

Macon

The 1842 Inn

Macon can truly be called the city of "White Columns and Cherry Blossoms." It was founded in 1823, and one of its most beautiful white columns, the 1842 Inn, was built less than two decades later.

Its history and the city's are intertwined. Judge John Gresham built the gracious Greek-revival home as his family residence. A successful cotton broker, he served two non-consecutive terms as mayor of Macon. Gresham was very proud of his stately mansion, with its stately columns, shady veranda and lush magnolia trees. It was and still is the perfect Southern image of hospitality. So proud was he that he refused to part with it after death. Many claim he still inhabits the master suite.

Mayor Gresham will not harm you. He is a very gracious host. He and his home have played host to many famous people over the years. Jefferson Davis, the president of the Confederacy, stayed there in 1865 as he fled south to avoid capture.

The Gresham family was not the only one to leave its mark on the Inn. They owned it until the early 1900s, when B.F. Adams purchased it for his family's residence. The Adamses adding two side porches and additional columns, and replaced the flooring with parquet flooring.

It was around the same time that the Victorian cottage located across the courtyard from the main house was built in the neighboring Vineville area. The cottage was moved to its current location in the early 1980s and is now part of the inn. It features 12-foot ceilings, original heart-of-pine flooring, and a wide front porch. Including the cottage, the inn offers a total of 19 rooms.

Each room is named for some prominent person or place that has a connection to Macon. Georgia Belle, Dogwood and Magnolia rooms pay homage to the South's favorite flowers, both literally and figuratively. Of course, Jefferson Davis has a namesake room. The Cotton Merchant's room is named for B.F. Adams; it's no surprise to find rooms named in honor of Sidney Lanier, Georgia's most famous poet, and William Bartram, the naturalist who traveled though Georgia. What is unusual in this bastion of Southern heritage is to find a room (it's actually not a sleeping room but a public parlor) named in honor of William Howard Taft. The reason? Taft stayed here in 1909 shortly after his election.

The home was used as an apartment building from about 1930 to the early 1980s, when it was purchased and made into an inn by 10 Macon couples.

Fort Hawkins

Macon's history began even before the city's founding when President Thomas Jefferson commissioned the building of Fort Hawkins. A settlement grew up around the fort that grew into the town called New Town, whose citizens later laid out the city of Macon on the western side of the Ocmulgee River.

The old fort saw action during the War of 1812 and later served as an important barracks and repository for supplies as well as a center for trade with the local Creek Indians. By the time of the Civil War, it was only a ruin, but the city's volunteer army crossed the river to succeed twice in repelling Federal raids near the old fort. Perhaps even then, Macon's guardian angel protected the city. It is believed a mysterious presence still patrols the watchtowers of the old fort. Residents have seen the spectral sentry by the light of a full moon as he patrols high on the top watchtower of the reconstructed fort's blockhouse.

Ocmulgee Mounds National Historical Park. t

American settlers were not the first people to have encounters with the supernatural. Huge earthen mounds guarded by the spirit dogs of these ancient inhabitants are all that is left at the nearby Ocmulgee National Monument of an ancient Mississippian settlement dating back to around 900 AD. Actually these people displaced an earlier group of nomads and started a farming culture on the banks of the river. Several mounds and a reconstructed earth lodge offer a glimpse into a way of life that stretches back into prehistory. The earliest mention of ghosts in the area dates to 1775 when a trader, James Adair, recorded tales of ghostly Indians at dawn in his diary.

I took a candlelight tour of the mounds, and though I did not see any sprits, I could feel the presence of countless others who had trod this sacred ground before me. It's not only phantom humans that are seen here. Many staff and visitors to the Mounds see and hear ghost dogs. The wolf-like animals howl pitifully at night, but toward dawn the cries become joyful. Indian legends claim the dogs are souls of the people buried there. Another Indian legend claims the black dog is a spirit left to guard the sacred place.

Other spirits are not always related to the native people of the area. Sylvia Flowers, a former master ranger at the site, told me of employees hearing a child laugh in the building, but when they searched, no child was ever found. One visitor at a Cherry Blossom Lantern Light Tour reported seeing a Confederate Solider in the mists. Many people have reported seeing a small white dog that disappears when you approach.

Perhaps these souls are holdovers from a later time. During the War Between the States, Samuel Dunlap's plantation stood there. It's not known if he had any children, but he did have a small white dog.

Cannonball House

It was during the Battle of Dunlap Hill that the now-famous cannonball came to be lodged in Judge Asa Holt's residence, known as the Cannonball House. The Greek-revival home and rear two-story kitchen house of hand-molded brick was built in 1853 by Judge Holt. The rear building is one of the few such structures surviving today. The upper level served as quarters for the house servants while the bottom floor was a kitchen.

The infamous cannonball was fired by Union cavalry forces under Gen. George Stoneman from where the mounds are located. The ball first struck the sand walkway, nipped one of the columns left on the gallery and entered the parlor just over a window. It landed and left a dent in the hall floor but failed to explode. Macon was fortunate! This was the only damage to Macon when Sherman's army came to call. Many people credit Fort Hawkins' ghostly guardian for protecting the city.

The home and rear kitchen building are now open as a historic house museum and Civil War museum. The Cannonball House staff has more on their hands than just managing a house museum. They have to keep their resident spirit happy as well. Whenever there is a party planned there, hosts are careful to invite Miss Elizabeth. If she feels slighted, she is sure to make her presence felt.

Hay House

Interestingly enough the cannonball was never meant for Holt's house. The artillery men were trying to destroy the home owned by William Butler Johnston (the Hay House), who was the treasurer of the Confederacy.

Built in 1860, the Hay House had such amenities as hot and cold running water, walk-in closets, and its own heating and cooling system long before the White House did.

The Hay House is owned by the Georgia Trust for Historic Preservation and is open to the public as a museum. Although the official statement is "There are no ghost in Hay House," there have been too many sightings and strange phenomena to keep its phantoms secret. The sightings began in 1980 when the 18,000-square-foot palace was undergoing extensive renovation.

Johnston made his fortune in insurance, real estate and banking. His young wife, Annie, called Hay House "her fairy palace." She really did not want to leave and probably never did. During the renovations, the family butler, Chester Davis, saw Annie, dressed in period clothing and inspecting the work. Other members of the staff saw her as well. A psychic who came to the house detected the presence of Annie and believed she was concerned about the renovations. Annie has not been seen since the renovation. Davis also glimpsed other former residents of the house. He sighted Judge William H. Felton, the home's second owner, and his daughter-in-law, Luisa. He hesitated to mention any of the apparitions for fear people would doubt his sanity. However, when other staff members mentioned similar sightings, he came forward with his story.

Woodruff House

Woodruff House is a Greek-revival mansion currently owned by Mercer University. Because of its Doric columns and triglyph frieze, it resembles the Parthenon. Previously named Overlook Mansion, it sits atop Coleman Hill with a commanding view of downtown. The house has sheltered many of the rich and famous in its time. It was built by cotton baron Jerry Cowles and later served as the residence of Reconstruction Military Governor General James Wilson, who "captured" Macon several weeks after the war ended.

The otherworldly occurrences began when the second owner, Colonel Joseph Bond, was killed by his former overseer, Lucius Brown, in 1859. They argued over the mistreatment of one of Bond's servants.

When the Robert W. Woodruff Foundation donated $1 million to Mercer University in 1993 to renovate the mansion, the college renamed it Woodruff House in his honor. During the renovation, Pat Wood of the Mercer police force was assigned to protect the house from vandals. She encountered strong feelings of hostility when she entered the house and became convinced Col. Bond was upset at strangers in "his" house. She began the practice of speaking to him and explaining her presence and the plans for the house.

Gradually she sensed a lessening of the hostility. When the alarm system was installed, her presence was no longer necessary. However, the alarm began to go off several times a night. There was no mechanical or electrical reason, so once again Wood explained to the colonel what was happening. After that the alarm functioned properly. The lights would flicker, though no electrical problem could be found. The portrait of Henrietta, Bond's wife, would repeatedly turn itself to face the wall. A rug would be pulled from under a table. In the upper floors, a baby could be heard crying from the attic. A psychic visiting the building claimed to sense a presence there. On other occasions, a visitor in the house saw a man dressed in Civil War-era clothing, and a security guard reported seeing the Colonel several times. The guard also saw a female presence wearing a long black dress in the home. Henrietta perhaps?

The home is not open for public tours.

Back Door Theater

A guard has seen the same woman in Willingham Chapel, another Mercer property on the University's main campus several blocks away. Willingham Chapel houses the College's Back Door Theater. Drama students blame mysterious happenings on an unseen entity they call "Oscar." But even before the theater was installed in the chapel basement, there were rumors of unexplained occurrences. Students in the early 1900s claim to have sighted the spirit of a Confederate soldier who was killed there in the 1860s. Some just seem to attract ethereal spirits. Theaters are one of those places.

Grand Opera House

Perhaps old actors continue to believe "The play's the thing." The Grand Lady of Mulberry, Macon's Grand Opera House certainly lives up to a theater's expected level of haunting. Built in 1884, it once claimed the largest stage south of the Mason-Dixon Line. You can still catch a performance there even though it has been leased to Mercer University. The Season at the Grand features professional productions, but many local performances are held there as well. The theater suffered a decline with the era of movies and then television. It was destined to become another high-rise parking lot when it was rescued through the efforts of Supporters of the Grand Old Opera House in 1967.

It was Macon's first building to appear on the National Register of Historic Places. The theater experiences regular poltergeist activity. Some of this is blamed on "Randy." Randall Widner, the managing director, committed suicide there in 1971. Since then whoever opens the Grand Opera House always greets Randall as if he were there - and perhaps he is. But the strange events predate Randy. In 1937, the Macon Telegraph reported a night watchman, J. D. Jones, claimed to see a woman in a long white gown floating across the stage. Many others have reported footsteps and cold spots in the theater. So catch a performance when you visit Macon. You may get more than you bargained for.

Douglass Theatre

The newest -- it was built in 1921-- of Macon's trio of supernaturally inhabited theaters is Douglass Theater. The Douglass is one of the few historical theaters built, designed, owned and operated by an African-American. Charles Douglass was a man ahead of his time. His theater offered patrons the opportunity to see three or four short films on its golden screen and traveling vaudeville performers. During its heyday, it hosted the likes of Duke Ellington, Ma Rainey, Little Richard, Otis Redding and James Brown. Then in 1972, the theatre closed its doors.

But the dream didn't die there. It reopened in 1997 after a more than $3 million facelift. Shortly after reopening, many strange events occurred regularly. Lights would mysteriously dim and brighten repeatedly, projectors and curtains began unusual malfunctions. The staff has come to believe the dynamic personality of Charles Douglass is proud of his newly reopened theater and is trying to communicate. The theater now shows films, laser shows and stage performances, and boasts one of the finest sound systems in Georgia.

Tubman African American Museum

When Richard Keil, then-pastor of the Saint Peter Claver Catholic Church, began the purchase of vacant 8,500-square-foot warehouse and former nightclub in downtown Macon in 1981, no one dreamed that this was the start of downtown's number one attraction. However, until September 1996 when it was slightly upstaged by its neighbor, the Georgia Music Hall of Fame, the Tubman Museum drew more visitors than any other downtown Macon museum. However, the Tubman is still going but the Music Hall of Fame is no more.

The unimpressive warehouse purchased by Father Keil to begin his dream of a museum dedicated to African-American History was never adequate to showcasing such an immense treasure trove. The Tubman museum moved to larger quarters. The new museum boast 49,000 square feet. It is now in the last stages of completion and is expected to open in 2009. It is crowned with an elliptical copper dome, reminiscent of a ceremonial headdress, the stucco finish will be is made of edo, a naturally occurring clay from West Africa, and the brickwork is set in intricate and contrasting patterns to resemble traditional African and African-American basket and textile weave designs.

The exhibits make it a unique attraction, from military heroes such as Crispus Attucks, the first Black to die in the American Revolution, and Rodney Davis, Macon's only Medal of Honor recipient, to entertainment greats such as Otis Redding and blind singer-guitar player Rev. Pearly Brown. Rev. Brown performed at Carnegie Hall and became the first Black entertainer to perform at the Grand Ole Opry. The museum has a lot of Macon's music history. There is an entire section where I sat entranced watching a video about Otis Redding. There is a section devoted to Little Richard including a colorful pair of boots he wore. After seeing so many of the exhibits that had once been in the now defunct Georgia Music Hall of Fame

The Museum of Arts and Science and Planetarium

The Museum of Arts and Science and Planetarium allows you to view a 40-million-year-old whale skeleton found near Macon, view art exhibits and interact with exhibits. From Nutty, the Prevost Squirrel native to the rainforest of Borneo, Sumatra, and Malaysia to the Mark Smith Planetarium, this tried and true Macon attraction is fun and educational.

Capricorn Studio

Although Macon was already a star in the music constellation with Otis Redding's Soul Music and Little Richard's Rock and Roll, it was Capricorn Studio that flamed like a blazing meteor through the musical sky with the Allman Brothers Band and the birth of Southern Rock. Like a meteor, its life was short. Loss of two of the Allman Brothers Band in motorcycle accidents within a year, an economic recession, and new genres like punk ended Capricorn's success. By the 1980s it was gone as a musical force. Last time I visited Macon a few years ago, it was just a group of huddled decaying buildings destined for the wrecker.

Today, Mercer College has revived Capricorn. Downstairs, you can tour their brand-new working studio completed in 2019. It's an active recording studio. Across the lobby is the original studio where musicians like the Allman Brothers Band, James Brown, Lynyrd Skynyrd, Marshal Tucker Band, Wet Willie, and Charlie Daniels recorded in the 1970s. I could feel the old vibes there. I refrained from singing "Sweet Home Alabama" here in Georgia. There is a small museum on the second floor. It has a digital collection of all the old albums that made the original Capricorn Studio unforgettable.

The Big House

The Allman Brothers Band created a new genre, Southern Rock. It was a mix of Rock and Roll, Country, Jazz, and Blues. The Big House was where they and some of their friends lived while they were creating this music. It was their home from 1970 to 1973. The three-story house is filled with their personal possessions, albums, instruments, scraps of paper where they wrote songs. There is a painting of the band next to their many gold records.

The Allman Brothers Band were a big influence in electing one of their fans president. One of my favorite exhibits is one showing Jimmy Carter wearing the band's tee shirt with "Win, Lose, or Draw" on it. Under he is quoted, "I don't intend to lose."

Some spirits still inhabit the house. There are many accounts by former residents and workers of an apparition at the Big House. Kristin and Kirk West owned the house before it became a museum, . Kristin once saw a face of " a young female ghost hovering over her bed. When she asked who it was, the apparation replied, "this was my daddy's house." Linda Oakley who lived in the Big House wiht her husband and baby also told Kristine about seeing a apparition. Kirsten said. "She was very aware of it and so were anyone associated with the Allman Brothers."

Richard Brent, Director of Collections is another who has experienced strange occurances. He said, "On a handful of occasions it's been really noisy; I've heard footsteps a lot." he said.

Rock Candy Tour

The Rock Candy Tour is a great way to see places related to music in Macon. Rex Dooley was my guide on the Rock Candy Tour. He took me to all the places related to music in Macon. Many were little out-of-the-way spots with a big significance like the Downtown Grill, hidden away in an alley. It used to be Le Bistro when Capricorn Records Vice President Frank Fente opened it in 1973. Rex said, "Mick Jagger sent his personal chef to cook for the opening night."

It played host to many famous people like Andy Warhol, President Jimmy Carter and the Allman Brothers Band. It is famed in music history as the place Gregg Allman proposed to Cher.

The Tic Toc Restaurant where Little Richard worked as a busboy had a fire and is now closed down. We passed by and I was saddened to see the broken glass and damages.

My tour touched on the Otis Redding Foundation and Douglass Theater. Rock Candy Tours offers a variety of different tours, even a ghost tour. I'm not sure if those folks get to see the ghost of dead rock stars but it might be a fun tour.

Georgia Sports Hall of Fame

Sports fans are not forgotten in Macon either. The state-of-the-art Georgia Sports Hall of Fame opened on April 24, 1999. This Macon museum allows participation, not just appreciation. Your tour begins with a fast-paced video introducing you to the world of Georgia sports in a 205-seat theater modeled after a ballpark stadium. When the cheers die away, you emerge into a colorful display of jerseys and banners. The museum merges interactive activities such as an interactive wheelchair race, or you can sit in the sportscaster's chair and make the call for one of sports history's great moments. A riveting display is Bill Elliott's red NASCAR car, featured prominently on the second floor. No way could it have been driven to that spot. The museum's publicity director told me the secret. "It was hoisted and maneuvered through an opening on the second floor where a huge, curved window had been removed to allow the car's access."

I tried out the interactive NASCAR exhibit. I buckled into my car. The screen told me I was in a race against 27 other drivers. The sights and sounds on my screen were so convincing I found myself cringing when I "scraped" my "car" fenders against the "fence." I found out I was never meant to be a race car driver. Better stick to writing.

Lake Tobesofkee Recreation Area

Lake Tobesofkee Recreation Area provides three parks and 1,800 acres of freshwater fun. It offers fishing, boating, picnicking, tennis and swimming. Two of the parks, Arrowhead and Claystone, offer camping along the lake's 35 miles of shore. It's a great place to park the RV or set up a tent and just chill.

Cherry Blossom Festival

Macon's biggest festival revolves around the Yoshino Cherry Tree. This tree produces no fruit. Its sole purpose in life is to create beauty. Each year, in early spring, the trees drape the city of Macon in a blanket of pearly pink blossoms. The residents are so intoxicated with nature's blushing masterpiece they want to share it with the world. In 1983 they decided to wrap the city with pink bows, put together a plethora of varied and fun activities, invite artists and crafters, and throw a terrific city-wide block party. The first International Cherry Blossom Festival was born.

The festival traces its roots to the late William Fickling who began propagating the trees and sharing them with the community. As a result of his generosity, some 280,000 Yoshino Cherry Trees burst into bloom all over Macon's parks and neighborhoods in mid-March. The city is transformed into a fragrant pink bower earning it the title "Cherry Blossom Capital of the World."

Rose Hill Cemetery

Rose Hill Cemetery founded in 1840 on 65 acres of land adjourning the Ocmulgee River is Macon's oldest and larges cemetery. It is also reputed to be one of the most-haunted. There are more than 600 Confederate graves, along with the graves of three Georgia governors, 31 mayors, and several senators/congressmen. The murdered members of the Woolfolk family repose here in the Forest Hill Ridge section.

Duane Allman and Berry Oakley of the Allman Brothers who died just a little more than a year apart -- both in motorcycle crashes -- are interred here. In their hippie days, the band lived just across the street from the cemetery and strolled its hills and valleys often enough that two of their of their songs, "Little Martha" and "In Memory of Elizabeth Reed," bear titles taken from gravestones in Rose Hill Cemetery.

An angel monument is reputed to appear to turn and stare at visitors, and unnatural sounds are sometimes heard in the cemetery.

A great way to get around downtown Macon is via MITSI, a Trolley that operates downtown Monday through Saturday. It offers three packaged tour options: House museums, interactive downtown museums, and combo – all three include trolley transportation and admission into the attractions, and are good for up to 12 months until all included attractions are visited. You catch her at the Visitors Center.

The Visitors Center had moved into new digs. It is now in the totally refurnished former Trailways Bus Station at 450 Martin Luther King Jr. Boulevard promoting "The Song and Soul of The South" with enticing exhibits and displays, and a 900-square-foot theater that offers a great film about Macon.

Massee Lane Gardens

I visited Massee Lane Gardens in nearby Fort Valley. It was a a riot of color and greenery. It's been the home of the American Camellia Society since 1968. Besides the Formal Camellia Garden there is a Japanese Garden with a pond and tiny waterfall and an Environmental Garden and Pavilion perched on the edge of a small lake.

After you have absorbed nature's outdoor offerings, visit the museum building housing the largest public collection of Boehm Porcelains in the country.

Lane Southern Orchards

Lane is the largest grower of peaches in the state. Whatever else you enjoy from the Peachtree café's menu, you have got to get one of their fabulous homemade peach ice cream cones and kick back in one of the porch rockers to enjoy that "right from the orchard taste." During peach-picking season, they offer self-guided tours.

Warner Robins Museum of Aviation

The Museum of Aviation is the second-largest of the Air Force museums. Here I found more than 100 aircraft and missiles dating from a replica of an 1896 glider to modern aircraft like the F-15 fighter and B-1B bomber and four buildings housing everything from, The U-2 Spy Plane to Heritage Building's Windows to a Distant Past, exploring the culture of Georgia's indigenous people.

Hangar One, which opened in 1991, includes a 5,000-square-foot exhibit on the contributions of Black Americans in aviation: "America's Black Eagles--The Tuskegee Pioneers...and Beyond," the largest Tuskegee Airmen exhibit in the United States.

Another popular exhibit is the God is my Co-Pilot: The Robert L. Scott Jr. Story about Brigadier General Scott, a native of Macon, Georgia. The exhibit traces his early attempts at flying, a self-propelled glider that he launched from a third-story Macon home rooftop, to his heroism as a Flying Tiger in WW II. The museum is home to the Georgia Aviation Hall of Fame, which honors the achievements of 75 of Georgia's greatest aviation aces.

The latest project is the construction of a new 60,000-foot World War II Exhibit Hangar to honor veterans. Some of the exhibits the new addition will offer are: Maintenance at Robins AFB, 507th Parachute Infantry Regiment: Airpower and the Invasion of Normandy, the Air Wars in Europe and the Pacific, Training in the Southeast and the Home Front. Best of all, this great museum is free and it's opened daily from 9 to 5. A café, gift shop and picnic area are also available

The Swanson

For dinner, I decided to try a newer restaurant housed in a historic building in the heart of downtown Perry, just minutes from Macon. The restaurant is a charming eatery with dining in three rooms. It maintains its historic character with its pine floors, high ceilings, and tall wavy-glass windows. It may have an additional perk, a resident spirit.

The earliest building here was a livery stable constructed by Mr. Bennett around 1790; then a three-room house was added to the property in 1880 by former Mayor Cox of Perry. Mr. Swanson added additional rooms in the 1920s. His daughter, Norrine Swanson Jones, lived the home from the 1920s until just before her death. Ms. Swanson played both the organ and the piano for several downtown churches and was very active in community plays. A staunch believer in education, she established Perry's first kindergarten in this building in the late 1930s. Since her death, there have been stories that she still remains in her beloved home.

Michael and Kim Sheridan moved back to Kim's hometown of Perry and fell in love with the old house. Kim told me, "We knew we wanted to open a restaurant but had no experience, so we just jumped in and began to learn as we went along."

Judging by the food and service, they learned well. I had the fried green tomatoes for an appetizer. It was tasty, the batter crunchy and the tomato inside juicy and tangy. For my dinner choice, I just had to go Southern and try the fried chicken. It too was perfectly fried. The outside was crunchy and the inside tender.

Evergreen Cemetery

That evening the Perry High School Drama club was conducting "A Ramble Through Evergreen Cemetery." The student/re-enactors were good. They really brought those stories to life. The cemetary still offers tours in October.

The story that grabbed me most was the story told at a grave of a man whose nephew was a mass murderer. I had never heard of Thomas Woolfolk before, but I could not forget him after this. Although the murderer himself was buried in Orange Hill Cemetery in Hawkinsville about 18 miles away, the story had ties to both Perry and Macon.

Tom was born near Macon on June 18, 1860, to Richard F. and Susan M. Woolfolk, Bibb County cotton planters. Tom never knew his mother as she died soon after his birth, and Tom was sent to stay with his aunt, Fannie Moore, his mother's sister. Fanny raised the boy until 1867. In 1866 Tom's father remarried and requested that the boy be sent home to live with his father and new stepmother, Mattie H. Woolfolk. From the first, Tom hated his stepmother; as his six stepsiblings were born, he grew to hate them as well.

When Tom went to Athens in March and June 1887 to visit Aunt Fannie, she was terribly worried. She realized that his mental condition had deteriorated; he was irrational, paranoid and carried a gun, but she never foresaw the terrible tragedy that was to follow.

Tom returned to his father's home. In the early morning hours of Aug. 6, 1887, nine persons -- his father, Richard F. Woolfolk; his stepmother Mattie H; their six children, Richard F. Jr., 20; Pearl, 17; Annie, 10; Rosebud, 7; Charlie, 5; baby Mattie, 18 months old; and a relative of his stepmother visiting from Americus, 84-year old Temperance West -- were all found in pools of blood, hacked to death with a short-handled ax that belonged to Tom Woolfolk. The ax was later found in one of the murder rooms. The only person in the house at the time not slain was Tom Woolfolk. He rushed to a neighbor's and claimed that his father's family had been murdered and that he had narrowly escaped by jumping out a window and seeking help.

He rushed back to the house before anyone arrived and claimed he had heard the unknown killers fleeing out the back door just ahead of him. He then took the time to wash and clean himself and toss his blood-spattered garments in a well.

Crowds rushed to the scene, and the coroner's inquest was held on the premises. The evidence was overwhelming. Tom was arrested and taken to jail. Newspapers from all over the country put the murders on their front pages. It was called "one of the most heinous crimes committed in this or any other state," "the bloodiest, blackest, chapter in Georgia criminal history," "the most shocking murder ever committed in Georgia," "without parallel in the criminal history of the South if not the world," "the bloodiest tragedy in the annals of crime," and "the most ferocious and harrowing crime ever recorded in the annals of civilization."

Tom Woolfolk was recognized around the county as "the most notorious criminal of modern times." Tom was only tried on one count of murder, his father's. Although the evidence was circumstantial, it was very conclusive. At his trial in the Superior Court of Bibb County December 1887, the jury found Tom guilty of murder and sentenced him to death. However, because spectators at the trial had been allowed to vilify the accused in the courtroom, the Georgia Supreme Court overturned the verdict and granted him a new trial.

Tom was granted a change of venue and his second trial took place in Perry in the Superior Court of Houston County. This second trial also resulted in a guilty verdict, and Tom was again sentenced to hang. This time there was no reprieve. On Wednesday, Oct. 29, 1890, Tom Woolfolk met his destiny in Perry before a crowd of 10,000 people.

The execution took place where all public executions did in Houston County, the valley where Big Indian Creek joins the Fanny Gresham Branch. It did not go well; the rope slipped and instead of a clean break, Tom choked to death slowly for almost 15 minutes.

Those who went expecting a death's door confession instead heard him profess his innocence. Just a few years later, Georgia banned public executions. Tom at the age of 27 left behind a divorced wife, Georgia Byrd Woolfolk, nine dead relatives, sisters who felt an injustice was committed, relatives of his stepmother who blamed him, and an unsolved mystery that has been swept under the carpet of history.

Tom's sisters, Floride and Lillie, as well as his aunt, Fanny Crane, continued to maintain Tom's innocence. His defense lawyer, John Cobb Rutherford, believed so strongly in Tom's innocence that he ruined his health in defending Tom and died at age 45 just five months after his client was hanged.

In later years, many of the townspeople came to believe Tom could not have committed the murders. Suspicion fell on a local black man named Jack. There is even a story in Perry about a man who was tried and executed later for a very similar crime elsewhere. In his possession was a letter indicating he had meant to kill Tom but "I really fixed him anyway."

When you visit Perry, it is likely you will drive across the very spot on the Dr. A. C. Hendrick Memorial Bridge, which spans the valley at the place where Main Street meets Gen. Courtney Hodges. Does Tom's angry spirit still hover near his last earthly memory? I never visited the spot under that bridge. If you are braver than I, perhaps you will one night.

Peaches to the Beaches Yard Sale

On a much lighter note, one event you will want to check out if you are in this area during the second Friday and Saturday in March is the Peaches to Beaches Yard Sale. It's an annual event stretching over 200 miles along Hwy 341 from Barnesville, GA to Brunswick GA.

Warm Springs and Pine Mountain

Warm Springs Hotel
Before the white man settled in this part of Georgia, Native Americans visited the warm mineral springs. They thought of them as a sacred place, a place of healing. Later these healing waters drew settlers. In 1832 David Rose began the first "resort area" in Warm Springs. It became a popular summer resort. Later, in 1893, Charles Davis built a 300-room Victorian called Meriwether Inn. The inn had all the latest amenities and, of course, the main draw, the 88-degree springs flowing from the hillside of Pine Mountain.

In 1907, Hotel Warm Springs was built on the site of the oldest building in the town. Incorporated in 1893, the town was first named Bullochville. As the automobile became the preferred means of travel, the town fell into a decline and was almost abandoned.

The hotel changed hands and at one time was named Tuscawilla Hotel after a Creek princess. The owner at that time, Mr. Butts, was so enthralled with the name, he also named his oldest daughter Tuscawilla. The name is still part of the hotel history and lore, and lives on in the ice cream parlor known as the Tuscawilla Soda Shop, once frequented by President Roosevelt.

It was former President Franklin Delano Roosevelt who again brought the visitors thronging back when, in 1924, he visited the town's naturally heated mineral springs as treatment for his polio-related paralysis. He advocated the name change to Warm Springs to promote the healing mineral springs.

When he became president, the hotel hosted such guests as the King and Queen of Spain, the Queen of Mexico, President Sergio Osmena of the Philippines, Bette Davis, FDR's secret service men, the press, and a host of other import VIPs.

The hotel has been the scene of a gruesome double murder. The murders occurred when the hotel was owned by the Thompson family. Mr. and Mrs. Thompson and their five children lived in the hotel. To bolster the family income during these lean times, Mr. Thompson did deliveries from one train to another and sometimes delivered parcels arriving by train to families living outside town. For this reason, he always carried a gun.

At the same time, he leased a pharmacy in the hotel to a pharmacist, Mr. Bulloch. Bulloch was a somewhat rowdy character. He liked to indulge in loud late-night poker games in a room he kept at the hotel. He also had a "fancy" lady he kept there. He often got violent with the woman, slapped her and locked her in the room when the mood struck him.

Thompson had repeatedly warned Bulloch that this kind of behavior would not be tolerated in his inn. Things came to a head one day in 1915. Thompson had just returned from delivering some packages. He was tired, hot and wanted to eat lunch and relax. His wife, very pregnant with their sixth child, met him as he came in and told him that Bulloch was up to his old ways again. Bulloch had slapped his woman and locked her in the room. When Mrs. Thompson had told him that he could not do that, Bulloch had turned on her with threatening words.

This was more than Thompson was going to tolerate. He approached Bulloch and told him he could keep his pharmacy in the hotel but the woman had to go and he would no longer be allowed to maintain a room in the hotel. That settled, Thompson went into the lunchroom to eat.

Bulloch went to his drawer in the pharmacy and took out his gun. He followed Thompson into the dining room and shot him. Thompson's niece tried to prop her wounded uncle up. Thompson then drew his own gun and shot and killed Bulloch on the spot. Thomson died a few days later.

You would think after such a dramatic double murder either Bulloch or Thompson would still be haunting the hotel. Strangely enough, the ghosts at Hotel Warm Springs seem to have nothing to do with either victim. Gerri has never seen anythng strange.

Once she was leading a woman up the stairs to her room when the woman began to shake her shoulders rapidly. Fearing that the woman was having an attack or something, she asked, "what's wrong?"

The woman grabbed her and said, "Don't you feel it?"

Gerri replied that the only thing she felt was the woman's hand grabbing her. The woman proceeded to tell her, "I'm psychic. There are ghosts in the hotel."

The next day, the woman was telling other guests about the ghost. "I felt him in the hall."

When they asked how she knew it was a man, the woman replied, "I could smell his cologne."

When two different guests at different times told her of seeing children's ghosts, she began to think there must be something here. One family saw the children standing at the end of the bathtub in their room. The other saw them playing in the hall.

One night when Gerri had gone to a wedding and returned to the hotel to meet another wedding party who was going to be staying at the hotel, she saw a guest sitting on the porch waiting for her return. The wedding group pulled up right about the same time, so the man just waited until she finished checking them in. Then he approached her and told her he wanted to ask her something but didn't want to ask in front of the guests she was checking in. She assumed he was going to complain, but that was not what he had on his mind.

He told her while he was sitting on the porch; he saw an apparition moving across the yard wearing a long white gown. He wanted to know if she could think of any event that might have triggered such a spirit.

At first she could not, but then she remembered. When she had first bought the hotel, the family who owned it had brought the wife's mother to stay with them after her father had died. The mother was grief-stricken and would not be comforted. She refused to eat and just stayed in her room in her nightgown. Finally one night, the distraught woman decided she did not want to live now that her husband was gone. She had taken her own life by jumping from a third-story window.

Gerri also says people are always saying they hear things. She has heard lots of things, too. She tried to dismiss them as the natural noises an old building makes. Funny thing is when she hears odd noises and goes to investigate, she never finds the source of the noise but often finds things that need to be done. "It's almost like they are looking after the hotel and me," she said. "Like one time I kept hearing a 'thump thump,' and I started to look for something rubbing against something else that had worked loose. I never found anything like that, but I did find a lit candle burning in a small holder in one of the rooms that was supposed to be cleaned and closed up. After I put out that candle, I never heard that noise again."

Yes, the wonderful old building has its resident spirits who want it to be cared for so they will always have a home.

It took Gerri a while to realize that, however. She has owned the hotel for over 30 years. Naturally in a historic building you are always fixing things. The first time anyone approached her about "ghosts," she was doing some stenciling on the front door. Three couples came in and one of the men asked, "Ya got any haints here?"

Not in the best of moods she replied, "If I saw a 'haint' here, I'd slap a paint brush in his hand and put him to work."

Little White House

Once FDR discovered Warm Springs, he wanted and needed his own cottage there away from the hustle and bustle of politics. He built the modest home that came to be known as The Little White House while still governor of New York just a year before being inaugurated as president. This is the modest cottage where he developed his "New Deal." Here, he was able to escape into the charm of this small Southern town where he took refuge from the pressures of leading a nation during the worst war the world has ever known. It was here that he died on April 12, 1945. He left behind a legacy in which any world leader could take pride.

The home and its grounds are now a Georgia State Park and Museum. It was here, while posing for a portrait on April 12, 1945, that FDR suffered a stroke and died a short while later. Today, the "Unfinished Portrait" and many other pieces of Roosevelt memorabilia are housed in the museum dedicated to his memory. Standing in the dim room staring at the portrait, I could feel why he always came back here in times of stress. Perhaps even his soul still abides here in this home he so loved.

Franklin Delano Roosevelt State Park

FDR State Park separates Warm Springs from Pine Mountain with a peaceful drive that combines history with outdoors activities. Spectacular waterfalls and unusual rock outcroppings await you at this 10,000-acre park. Perhaps the most famous spot in the park is Dowdell's Knob, a picnic area FDR liked frequent. Recently, the first statue of the president wearing his leg braces was unveiled there. Dowdell's Knob is also interesting for another reason. It has a phantom that has appeared there for many years. The story goes that there was an old man, possibly a descendent of the original Dowdells, who lived there for years. The old man was feeble and blind and somewhat of a hermit. Invading Union soldiers killed him and threw his body off the cliff. He still roams the area.

In more modern times a young man was murdered and his beheaded body was found there. Perhaps his spirit has joined that of the old man who haunts this peaceful spot.

Pine Mountain Wild Animal Safari

For spirited fun of a different kind, tour The Pine Mountain Wild Animal Safari. It is filled with more earthly adventures. Here animals from every continent roam freely. You are the one encased in your car or the zebra-striped bus that transverses the domain of these wild creatures. Perhaps an ostrich or a llama will stick its nose into your window hoping for a handout. We had several that tried to almost get in the car with us. Or maybe a tiny fawn will stop beside your car and gaze in curiosity at you.

Callaway Gardens

Cason and Virginia Callaway dreamed of building the prettiest garden since the Garden of Eden. In May of 1952 their dream became reality when the gates of Callaway Gardens swung open for the first time.

For over a half-century, they have provided visitors with a glimpse of heaven right here on earth. From the blooming Azalea Bowl, the world's largest, to Sibley Horticultural Center, a five-acre conservatory featuring some of the most colorful plants in existence, to the Day Butterfly Center, aflutter with jewel toned "flying flowers" and darting hummingbirds, to the native wildlife, deer, raccoons, birds and others, all protected by the lush growth, the Garden is a photographer's paradise. The newest creature to inhabit the gardens is the American eagle. When you glimpse this majestic bird in flight, you will understand why they are a national treasure as well as our national bird.

Bulloch House Restaurant

When it came time to eat, I had to try the Bulloch House Restaurant; boy, was I happy with it. More food than anyone can eat, it's buffet style and delicious. The original restaurant was in a house built in 1892 by Mr. Bulloch (not the killer at the hotel) who believed every bird should have a home. During his lifetime, he built hundreds of birdhouses. Current owners Peter and Sandy Lampert purchased the Bulloch House in March 2011 and carried on the tradition of serving the best in Southern food. Tragedy struck, on June 10, 2015, lightning struck the Bulloch House, starting a fire which destroyed the building. The owners would not let the tradition die and the restaurant found a new home downtown on Broad Street in a building that was originally a mercantile and later the Victorian Tea Room. It's even older than the Bulloch House.

Part of the old house remains in the reclaimed wood for tables and uncovering original brick. Peter and Sandy expanded their gift shop into one of Bullochville's original buildings, now called Fireflies Gift Boutique. In the rear of the gift shop, they have added a second smaller eatery, the Lightnin' Bugs Café & Bakery that serves coffee, delicious baked goods and a lunch menu. The Bulloch House Restaurant stands as a testament to the important role that the Bullochs played in the history of Warm Springs.

The downtown area is so small it is fun to walk off your food there and visit some of the unique shops in the village. Whether it's natural beauty, historic sites or outdoor activities, this area will please everybody.

Adairsville and Northeast corner of Georgia

Barnsley Gardens Resort

The two most common sources of ghost stories are lost love or murder. Barnsley Gardens includes both – a love too strong for death to destroy and fratricide resulting from two strong-willed brothers' battle of wills to possess the magnificent estate. It has spirits that have been recorded through the decades. It has stately ruins that bear witness to Southern history's most turbulent times. The resort boasts a garden over a century and a half old planted by a spirit who still lingers to care for it. The floorboards of the old ruin have a bloodstain that will not wipe out. The story is poignant and tragic.

Yet I almost didn't include the resort. It's hard to classify. It's not a bed and breakfast or an inn. It is a hotel only nominally in that it functions as a fine hotel even though the "rooms" are located in replicas of old English Cottages. The grounds, garden, several of the buildings and, towering over it all, the ruins are over a century old while the "rooms" are new construction built to mimic a Victorian English village. So when you visit and say "I wouldn't call this a hotel," you could be right. However, whatever you call it, you will have to call it "wonderful."

One visit convinced me this is a treasure that could not be omitted from this book.

The Barnsley story, as well as the history of Adairsville, begins with Godfrey Barnsley, an Englishman who moved to Savannah as a penniless youth of 18. There he made his fortune as a cotton broker. There, too, he met the love of his life, Julia Scarborough, the daughter of a wealthy merchant and shipbuilder. He and Julia were married on Christmas Eve 1828. They soon began a family and by 1841 had six children. On the surface, it looked like a fairy tale life. But the fates were lying in wait.

By 1841, Julia's health was in decline. Godfrey decided to move his family to the healthier climate of north Georgia. His discriminating eye was caught by a beautiful parcel of land in the small village of Adairsville.

In particular, an acorn-shaped hill on the 10,000 acres was his choice of the perfect place to build his beloved Julia a home worthy of their love.

An old Indian shaman who worked for him warned Godfrey not to build on this particular site; he told him the site was sacred to the Cherokee and anyone who tried to live there would be cursed. But Godfrey was a sophisticated man and ignored the old Indian. He began the construction of his beautiful mansion there. He chose an Italian Villa style with 24 rooms. There would be hot and cold running water, unheard of in his day. The marble for the mantel and the tiles for the verandas were imported. Everything was to be the finest workmanship money could buy. He designed the gardens in the style of Andrew Jackson Downing and filled it with every kind of rose he could find. His Julia deserved the best.

Fickle fortune who had smiled on Godfrey for so long now turned away. His infant son died. Before the home could be completed, Julia passed away. Devastated, Godfrey lost all desire for the home that had been his passion. He threw himself into his business and on his infrequent trips home, he sat among the untended roses in the garden he had hoped to share with his beloved.

Then in a letter that is preserved by the estate, he told of "seeing" Julia in the garden. She spoke gently to him and told him it was her wish that he get on with his life and finish the home she was so proud of as a legacy for their children.

Godfrey was imbued with new spirit. Work began again on the mansion. But fate continued to withhold her favor. His oldest daughter, Anna, married and left to live in England. The second daughter died in the house in 1858. Then the Civil War began. Godfrey's fortune was in the cotton he brokered, and that was no longer sellable. It rotted in New Orleans warehouses. In 1862 his oldest son, Howard, who had become a ship's captain, was killed by Chinese pirates while sailing in the Orient. Barnsley's other two sons, George and Lucian, had enlisted in the Confederate military. His daughter, Julia, had married Confederate Army Captain James Peter Baltzelle who had insisted his wife seek refuge in Savannah.

Still Godfrey was obsessed with finishing the castle. He accumulated art and furnishings from Europe for his home. When the War finally came to Woodlands, Union troops found Godfrey alone with his treasures and his still-incomplete mansion. The day was May 18, 1864. A friend of Godfrey,

Colonel Robert G. Earle of the Second Alabama Light Cavalry, rode to Woodlands to warn Barnsley of Sherman's troops' approach and was shot down within sight of the house. He was buried there at Woodlands and still remains in the garden perhaps in spirit as well.

Charles Wright Willis, 103rd Illinois infantry, wrote this account of the event in his book Army Life of an Illinois Soldier:

May 18, 1864. Our cavalry had a sharp fight here this p.m. and on one of the gravel walks in the beautiful garden lies a Rebel colonel, shot in five places. He must have been a noble-looking man; looks 50 years old, and has fine form and features. Think his name is Irwin. There must be a hundred varieties of the rose in bloom here and the most splendid specimens of cactus.

The Federal officer commanding the troops, Gen. McPherson, forbade looting of the unfinished mansion but his orders were blatantly disregarded. Godfrey's costly furnishings were destroyed; an Italian statuary was smashed in a search for hidden gold; what could not be consumed or carried away, was broken and smashed.

By the end of the war, Godfrey was almost destroyed financially. He moved to New Orleans to try and salvage something of his brokerage.

George and Lucian refused to sign the oath of allegiance to the Union and emigrated to South America where their descendants live to this day. Godfrey left his son-in-law, James Baltzelle, and daughter Julia to manage Woodlands. Julia was a strong woman who some say Margaret Mitchell modeled her famous Scarlett after. She led the servants out into the fields and woods and searched out wild edible plants to keep them from starvation.

Baltzelle started a timber business but was killed in 1868 by a falling tree. Julia and her young daughter fled to New Orleans to join Godfrey. Julia later met and married a German ship captain named Charles Henry Von Schwartz.

After Godfrey died a broken man in 1873, Julia returned his body to Woodlands where her new husband also died.

Adelaide grew up at Woodlands and married a chemist named A. A. Saylor. Saylor too fell prey to the Barnsley curse and died while their two sons, Harry and Preston, were very young.

Times grew very dark for the young family. A tornado in 1906 destroyed the roof of the main house and forced the Saylors to take refuge in the only intact part of the home, the kitchen wing.

The two boys grew very different as they matured. Preston used his body to earn a living and became a nationally known boxer under the name K. O. Dugan.

Harry became somewhat of a schemer and got involved with a group of men who wished to divide up Woodlands and sell it to developers. Harry had remained at home while Preston traveled to rings around the country. The brothers fought bitterly over what was best for them and their mother. Harry, influenced by his cronies, induced their mother to sign a mortgage on Woodlands. He also had Preston committed to an insane asylum supposedly because he had become unbalanced due to blows to his head suffered in the ring.

The power struggle came to a head in 1935 when Preston, finally released from the asylum, shot and killed Harry in the small kitchen wing where he and Adelaide still lived. Preston chased his brother down and kept firing until Harry fell and died in his mother's arms. The bloodstain is still there permanently embedded in the dark wood of the floor. Many say Harry's spirit is still there as well.

Preston turned himself in and was sent to prison. The governor who knew much of the circumstances surrounding the murder pardoned Preston after he had served less than seven years, but it was too late for Woodlands.

Adelaide had struggled valiantly to keep the mortgage paid, but when she died in 1942 the estate and what she had not sold piecemeal of its furnishings were sold at auction for a fraction of their value. Preston did not get out of prison until a few months later, and by then all was gone. The property was used for farming and the once magnificent home left to the encroaching kudzu.

It would seem that Godfrey's dream was finished. But fate again turned her head and smiled. In 1988, Prince Hubertus Fugger and his wife Princess Alexandra, Bavaria, purchased Woodlands, which was now called Barnsley Gardens. Clent Coker, a neighbor who had grown up obsessed with the Barnsley story and was unwilling to see such a historic treasure lost, went to the prince and told him of the history behind the ruins. The prince agreed that the estate had to be restored and its history honored.

Between them, that has been done. Clent continued the research he began a boy, interviewing the elderly residents of Woodlands and preserving the Barnsley's story in his book, *Barnsley Gardens at Woodlands: The Illustrious Dream*. He was the historian for Barnsley Gardens until his passing in 2022.

The Prince brought in gardeners to salvage the gardens and restore them to their former glory. He build cottages to match the historic feel of the old castle and turned the ruins into a showplace.

Present management does not play up the supernatural elements of their resort, yet they cannot deny them. Stories of apparitions dot the long Barnsley history and persist today around the ruins. Godfrey's statements about seeing and even speaking with his dead wife in the gardens are well-documented by his letters. He was not the only one to report seeing Julia there. Julia Barnsley Saylor, her granddaughter, also told of having seen her grandmother in the gardens so frequently that she came to view it as natural. Mrs. Saylor had another paranormal experience that she documented. The night her Uncle George died in Brazil, he appeared to her at Woodlands.

Would Godfrey's life been different if he had heeded the words of that old Indian and built his home in any other spot than that acorn-shaped hill? Like a Greek tragedy, the one decision made with hubris shapes the inevitable future.

The Rice House

How the Rice House came to be at Barnsley Gardens is an interesting story. It started life in 1854 as a log farmhouse in Rome, Georgia, home of Fleming Rice and his family. It survived a Civil war battle in 1864. The bullet holes still scar the front exterior wall.

During Barnsley Garden's ownership by Prince Fugger, Clent Coker told the prince about the historic building that was doomed to destruction. Instead of letting it meet its fate, the prince bought it, had it cut in sections, loaded on trucks and moved the few miles to Barnsley Gardens in 1994. There it was restored and now houses the fine dining facility of the resort. It is a nice balance for the other larger restaurant at Barnsley Gardens, Woodlands Grill. Rice House serves contemporary Southern dishes and is only open two nights a week, whercas Woodlands is more of a steakhouse and is open seven days.

Rice House does have one thing most other restaurants don't offer. Visitors have reported hearing doors opening and closing and a man in a suit and top hat has been seen occasionally. He is reported to just sit and stare, then disappear.

Booth Western Art Museum

In Cartersville, you can explore the West without ever leaving the South. From exhibits by the artists that explored the real life early west to depictions of the Hollywood version of the wild and woolly West, you will find them here in Georgia's second-largest museum. There are also sections devoted to the Presidents and the Civil War. There is a theater for showing the museum-related film "The American West" as well as other films, a reference library for Western American art, culture and history, Civil War history, United States presidential history, and local history related to the art collections.

It's also lots of fun to ride the glass elevator operated with real weights – one of only two in the country. If you meet Jim Dunham, ask him to show his artistry with a gun. When we visited, he put on a faster-than-lightning exhibit of fancy gun handling. In fact, Jim taught many of Hollywood's fastest-guns-in the-West how to perfect that fast draw. If you search the credits in many westerns, he will be listed.

New Echota State Historic Site

Today, New Echota near Calhoun is a ghost town. No one lives there anymore. It's just one of many Georgia State Parks. But once, it was a vibrant community, the capital of the proud Cherokee nation. By 1825, the Cherokees had established a form of government that was modeled after the United States government. This was the site of their Supreme court, a council house, a town square and perhaps most importantly, The Phoenix, the only native American newspaper printed in a native language. This was the seat of government for a highly civilized, literate people.

By 1835, New Echota was abandoned, its citizens imprisoned and then banished to the wilds of Oklahoma. More than 4,000 men, women and children died before the Cherokee reached their barren new home.

A few hundred managed to evade the Georgia Militia and remained hiding in the woods. These few comprise the ancestors of the Eastern Band of Cherokees living in North Carolina today. The reason behind this tale of man's inhumanity to man is simple: greed. Gold had been discovered on the Indian lands. The state of Georgia wanted it. Andrew Jackson was president, and he hated all Indians. In spite of the fact that Cherokees had fought under him in the Creek War, he wanted them removed at all costs. Indeed, one Cherokee, Junaluska, had saved Jackson's life at the Battle of Horseshoe Bend. Jackson proved to be a hero with feet of clay. When Junaluska sought an audience with Jackson after the removal act was signed, Jackson refused to see the man. Junaluska told the press, "If I knew then what I know now, history would have been different."

Even in the face of the Supreme Court's upholding the Cherokee claim to their land, Jackson plotted removal of the same people he had once promised, "You shall remain in your ancient land as long as the grass grows and the water runs."

The Trail of Tears is a red stain of infamy on the history of a people who had pledged "liberty and justice for all."

Not all white men upheld the persecution of an innocent people. Samuel Worcester was a minister who had come to New Echota not only to preach the gospel but also to help in the establishment of the Cherokee newspaper. The Cherokees called him "The Messenger." As Georgia Governor Gilmer pushed harder for Indian removal, he passed laws prohibiting whites from living on Indian land without obtaining a license from the state. Worcester and several other ministers not only refused to get the license but also met at New Echota to sign a resolution against it as undermining the authority of the Cherokee Nation, which had been upheld by Chief Justice John Marshall of the Supreme Court.

Governor Gilmer had Worcester arrested and imprisoned. The Supreme Court upheld the signers, but the governor continued to hold them prisoner. When Worcester was released the following year, he left for Oklahoma to prepare for the relocation of the Cherokee nation.

Today, Samuel Worcester's home stands far to the back of the historic site. It is a place troubled by the evil that occurred around it. There are tales that a Cherokee was murdered in the house in the 1830s. Even without that act of violence, the crimes perpetrated against the Cherokees on this site could account for the troubled feeling one experiences within the house. Whatever the reasons, newspaper accounts as far back as 1889 report ghostly manifestations in the simple two-story white farmhouse.

Although the death of the Indian is only rumored, two deaths are proven. In the 1900s, the house was used as an apartment house. Two card players got into a dispute over the fairness of a game of chance and killed one another in the downstairs area of the house.

Visitors have heard dragging chains and disembodied footsteps and seen the unearthly figure of a short thin man. One park employee told me that people frequently report seeing ghostly images in or near the house. The uneasy feeling you will experience within the house is completely at odds with the furnishings of a typical rural Georgia home in the early 19th century. A loom and other weaving implements, an old fashioned cook stove and other everyday items attest to the fact that this was once a happy home shared by Samuel and Ann Worcester before greed and betrayal left its aura on the lonely house.

As you wander the site, many of the buildings are steeped in an aura of melancholy even though no one has reported seeing or hearing any unearthly beings. So much treachery and evil occurred here.

The reconstructed Phoenix Office is a highlight of the restored city. The Cherokee Phoenix began in 1828 as a means of uniting the Cherokee Nation by keeping the far-flung people informed of the latest happenings and laws. The editor, Elias Boudinot, eventually came to be a member of the "Treaty" party led by Major Ridge and his son John. The "Treaty" party felt the tribe's only hope of survival as a nation was to accede to Georgia's demands and move to Oklahoma. Principal Chief John Ross opposed removal.

The paper ran out of funds and ceased operation in 1834. When John Ross attempted to move the press in the dead of night to a safer location in Tennessee, the Georgia militia and Elias' brother, Stand Watie, captured the press, stomped the soft lead type into the red Georgia clay and burned the original building. They had effectively silenced the voice of the Cherokee Nation.

As you peer into the tiny office, the importance of freedom of the press comes to mind. Remember it was only three years after the destruction of the Phoenix that the Cherokee people were rounded up, herded into stockades for five months, then marched over a thousand miles in the dead of winter with inadequate food and clothing prodded onward by men inflamed with racial hatred.

The means to remove the Native Americans came about when Boudinot, Ridge and his son, John, signed the Treaty of New Echota in December 1835. Major Ridge stated after he signed the treaty, "I have just signed my death warrant."

Indeed that was true. Within six months, the three men were brutally slain by fellow Cherokees. The crime of selling tribal land without the permission of the Supreme Council was ruled treason, punishable by death.

Perhaps there is another ghost that stalks this tiny place, the spirit of the slain Cherokee Nation.

Etowah Indian Sites

Just off I-75 near Cartersville are the remains of an ancient culture. On this 54-acre site are all that remains of what was once a thriving village: six earthen mounds, a plaza, village area, borrow pits and a defensive ditch.

More than 500 years ago, Native Americans performed elaborate religious ceremonies atop a 63-foot flat-topped earthen knoll. They buried their priest/chiefs in handmade costumes accompanied by items they would need in their after-lives. The Etowah Mounds, now a Georgia State Park, is the most intact Mississippian Culture site in the southeastern United States.

Even though only 9 percent of this site has been excavated, we are learning a lot about the people who came before us. The park is open Tuesday through Saturday during normal daylight hours and on Sunday afternoons. The state also offers candlelight tours of the mounds at certain times of year. That would be a wonderful way to search for the spirits that must be still lingering in this sacred spot.

Chieftains Museum

Another native American site in the area is located in Rome. The Chieftains Museum tells the story of Major Ridge, the leader and principle signer of the Treaty of New Echota. Ridge struggled to adapt to the white man's ways while still remaining true to his Cherokee heritage, an impossible task in his time.

The main building in the museum complex, Ridge's family home, was originally a two-story dogtrot-style log cabin that was added to as the family became more prosperous. Today, it is a National Historic Landmark. It's located on the banks of the Oostanaula River, where Ridge and his family were ferryboat masters, store operators and slave-owning planters. The museum contains exhibits describing Ridge's life and some of the history of the Cherokee people.

Berry College

Martha Berry was born in 1865 into a well-to-do family and was well educated. At a very young age, she realized that not all children received the kind of education she did. In fact, she was appalled to discover that many poor children did not even learn to read the Bible.

She was sitting on the steps of a small log cabin built as a playhouse one Sunday reading a Bible. Some of the local children came by, and she began reading them some Bible stories. The children had never heard anything like this, and when she invited them back next week, she told them to bring their brothers and sisters. The next week the children returned with not only brothers and sisters but "babies and dogs."

Her little cabin became a "beehive of humanity." This was actually the birth of Berry College. She began driving to three different locations in the area to teach the mountain children. In 1902 she opened her first school, the Boys Industrial School. In 1909 that first school was followed by the Martha Berry School for Girls. Today, Berry College has grown to a 28,000-acre campus, the largest campus in the nation. Attendance averages more than 1,800 undergraduates.

Along with being a remarkable university, Berry College has become one of northwest Georgia's most popular tourist attractions. Art connoisseurs are drawn to the Martha Berry Musuem to view the fine collection of art there.

Nature lovers are estatic about the gardens, Sundial Garden, Goldfish Garden, Sunken Garden and Formal Garden as well as the Wildflower Meadow and two nature trails, Fernery Nature Trial and Hillside Trail. They have to visit the Catfish Pond and Bridal Walk.

History buffs enjoy touring Oak Hill, the mansion where Berry grew up. The Greek Revival mansion is furnished as it was when Martha Berry lived in it and managed her rapidly growing school. There are many other historical buildings on the campus.

Martha Freeman was Berry's beloved servant aand companion throughout her life. Freeman's home is preserved as it was during her lifetime. It was constructed as a schoolhouse for the Berry children and later converted as a home for "Aunt Martha."

The original cabin, the Roosevelt Cabin, now a museum dedicated to Martha Berry, an old mill house, a carriage house with several of the vintage automobiles presented to Martha Berry by her friend Henry Ford, and several old churches are a history lover's fantasy.

Practically the entire campus is a ghost hunter's dream. One of the kindest spirits found on the campus is Martha Freeman. Rebecca Roberts, our guide, told me about the experiences of students who stayed in Martha Freeman's cabin. "Instead of installing a security, we relied on students to protect Oak Hill, and many of the girls who stayed in this cabin swore they felt someone sit on the side of their bed or tuck them in, but when they looked, there was no one there."

One of the most common stories that recurs about Berry College is of a little boy. I spoke to a former student of the college, and she recalled an experience in the office when she saw a small boy approach her and then disappear. The child was dressed in rough clothing as a mountain child might have worn in the late 19th century. Rebecca also confirmed that there have been several instances of students witnessing the sighting of this little boy.

The ruins and cemetery of the old Mountain Springs Church are another spot where strange things occur. People have claimed to hear music from the church and footsteps and crying from the graveyard.

There is a wooded road that runs between the main campus of Berry College and the new mountain campus. Before the mountain campus was built, this was a popular spot for students to go at night to neck. There is a legend on campus that one couple had made use of the seclusion for a bit of heavy petting back in the 1940s.

Afterwards, the couple argued, and the girl demanded to get out and walk home. Angry, the boy let her out and drove off. After driving just a little ways he cooled off and returned to find his girlfriend. In his haste, he felt the car strike something and believed it was a deer. But when he got out the car to check, he found he had struck and killed his girlfriend. The story goes that if you go to the spot on the road where the girl was killed and say, "Green lady, green lady, green lady," a pale green light will appear in the trees.

Another legend about a dead student revolves around the tower between two girls' dorms in the Ford area, East and West Mary. The story relates that a student at Berry hanged herself in the tower and the body was not discovered for days. Although the door is kept locked nowadays, if you stand outside it you can feel an unearthly cold seeping through and if you continue to stand outside it you can hear her crying just as she did before taking her life.

Another phantom is more cheerful; he is usually seen by the old water-mill and is dressed in a costume from the mid-19th century. He just walks around and may glare at you but not say anything. He then disappears when you look back at him. Fortunately, Berry College has been around for more than a century and is not going to disappear, so make it a stop on your next Georgia visit.

Plum Orchard

African American Church at south end of Cumberland Island

Feral horse grazing in front of Dungeness Ruins

Jekyll Island Club

Cherokee Cottage

Horton House ruins

Windsor Hotel

Carter headquarters in Plains

Michigan Monument at Andersonville

1842 Inn

Cannonball House

Hay House

Guide, Suzanne, leading cemetery tour

The Big House

Ocmulgee Mound

Warm Springs Hotel

The Little White House

Vann's Tavern at New Echota

Ruins at Barnsley Gardens

Chapter 4 Kentucky

Harrodsburg

Shaker Village of Pleasant Hill

Long ago and far away, a simple peace-loving people were searching for a place they could live in harmony with nature and their fellow man. In 1779, a few of their number had sailed from their homeland in search of a place to settle. Many settled in New York and founded a colony there. In 1805 some of the group moved down into Kentucky. They found a beautiful land of rolling hills and streams. The soil was rich. They put down roots in a rural area they called Pleasant Hill. It might be a bit on the western edge of southeast but the place is too good to miss.

Mostly things were peaceful in spite of a few disputes with their neighbors. That was to be expected. After all, they had such radical beliefs: racial equality, gender equality, land held in common by the entire community and, strangest of all, celibacy. They also believed the veil between life and death was gossamer thin and that the dead could and did often communicate with the living.

In the 19th century, the idea of a woman making decisions in business and all aspects of life was unheard of. So, too, the idea of a black man and a white man considering themselves equal. Yes, many of the ideas of the United Society of Believers in Christ's Second Appearing are strange even today. At first people mocked them and called them "Shakers," but as they saw the craftsmanship of their buildings and furniture, the good stewardship of their farmers and the honest dealing of the group as a whole, they were left alone to work their land, build their homes and furniture, and live their life.

The Shakers came by their beliefs through the teachings of Ann Lee who was born in Manchester, England, on February 29, 1736. She was a member of the group called the Shaking Quakers. While she was imprisoned for trying to spread these beliefs, she had a vision that she was the second coming of Christ, and when she was released, she founded the new religion in 1772. She taught her followers that God was a dual personage, male and female, rather than the masculine-oriented traditional belief of all-male trinity.

They interpreted the passage in Genesis that stated, "So God created man in his own image, in the image of God created he him; male and female, created he them." to mean that both man and woman were in God's image; therefore, God was both male and female, father and mother. They did believe Jesus was the first coming of the messiah, but, unlike traditional Christians, they believed the second coming had already occurred with a female incarnation, Ann Lee, based on her vision. Thus they felt we were living in the last millennium, and since all humans were brothers and sisters, they should not marry as they felt the world as we knew it was ending. There was no longer a need to procreate. Instead they believed people should live communally as one family of brothers and sisters.

The Shakers did not isolate themselves from the outside world. They welcomed visitors and maintained a tavern. However, only trustees conducted business with the outside world. The Shakers practiced scientific farming and introduced new strains of sheep, hogs and cattle. They invented the flat broom and clothespins. They were highly respected for their packaged garden seeds and preserves.

By the latter part of the 19th century, the industrial revolution and changing lifestyles caused a decline in the Shakers. The last Pleasant Hill Shaker died in 1923. Their village passed into private hands and was called Shakertown. The people and their beliefs were almost forgotten. The beautiful buildings they had raised were being used as gas stations, auto parts stores and worse. There was no protection for the finely crafted old buildings; they could have been torn down and replaced with McDonald's or even subdivisions at will.

Then in 1961, a non-profit corporation was formed to restore the old village and offer a historic teaching facility for the public to learn about this little-known historic and religious phenomena. Today, they preserve and interpret 34 buildings. The Inn at Shaker Village is spread out between 15 of the restored buildings. You can put yourself in the heart of this unique community for a day trip or, if you really want to experience the feeling of their simple lifestyle, for several days. Along with the Inn, there is a restaurant that serves mouthwatering traditional Shaker and Kentucky classics. If you only have room for one dish, have some of the corn pudding. The beautifully crafted Trustee's Office Building is now the dining hall. You can't help but be awestruck by the craftsmanship of its graceful twin staircase.

The Meeting Hall is especially interesting both for its architecture and the music and dancing that did -- and still does, thanks to interpreters -- happen there. I had the good fortune to be there when one interpreter, Phillip Mulhall, was performing some of the Shaker songs. That man has a beautiful voice; he makes the simple music live again.

Craft shops will offer you a chance to own a peace of this almost lost heritage. The cookbooks tempted me, as did many of the handcrafted items. For the animal lover, don't miss the barnyard animals. I spoke with Billy Pruitt. His official title when I visited was "Ag Interpreter," but he said he is actually the "animal's slave." He showed me the baby goats and other barnyard inhabitants. While we spoke, one of the tiny goats and a huge tom turkey had a slight disagreement. It was so cute to see that little goat butt the big turkey with his tiny nubs of horns. The turkey retaliated with flying feathers and pecking beak. Naturally no one was really hurt, just a few ruffled feathers. Throughout the village, you will find interpreters working on the crafts and everyday life tasks the Shakers performed. It is so easy to slip back in time even if only in imagination.

When I visited, I spent the night in a pleasant room in West Family Dwelling. The room was furnished with simple yet beautiful Shaker reproduction furniture. A large living room area was to the rear of the building. I could imagine many of the Shakers gathered in that room on a cool evening, discussing the latest crops or perhaps the newest baby goats. Just beyond was the game room and kitchen, which still had the old baking oven built into the wall. It was so easy to feel in touch with the spirits of these simple people who once created these buildings as a part of the "new heaven on earth" that was so much a part of their lives.

Time has proven that these spirits do remain behind to communicate with those of us who visit their former homes. Not surprising considering their beliefs.

Not only are the original Shakers commonly found returning to help modern-day visitors and workers at their old home place, there is at least one example of modern-day spirits visiting at Pleasant Hill. I spoke to

Susan Hughes, then education specialist for the village. She told me about Mary Leigh, an interpreter totally devoted to Shaker Village, who died several years ago. On the anniversary of her death, at the same hour, everybody in the hall where she had worked was overwhelmed with the scent of lilacs for about 45 minutes. No lilacs are grown on site as the Shakers did not grow flowers except those that could be used for medicinal purposes. Lilacs are not one of those.

Susan explained, "It was not just me; about seven people in all smelled it, some almost to the point of nausea. We all looked at one another and knew it was her. We just said, 'we miss you, Mary Leigh, and wish you well.' The following year it happened but not as strong or as long, and the next year, nothing."

The experiences are many and varied. One person was working in the herb garden and heard her name called and looked up and saw a white apparition.

Not only workers but also guests are subject to these experiences. During an Elderhostel weekend, one lady told Susan of feeling someone trying to get into bed with her. Her husband was on her other side and three nights in a row, she felt this person trying to get into the bed next to her. Finally, on the third night, she just said "I know this is your bed, but I am sleeping in it tonight. Please find somewhere else to sleep." She was not disturbed anymore.

Another person had a similar experience. A group had gone to Shaker Village for an overnight stay. One woman, Lois, had retired early. She had just turned out the lights when she felt someone pulling her foot out of the bed. She turned out the lights and saw a woman dressed in Shaker clothes and wearing a bonnet.

Lois demanded to know what this strange woman was doing standing in the room. The apparition stated, "You are in my bed." Lois just told her "Lady, I'm tired and I'm staying right here." The woman just turned and walked right through the wall of the room. Lois slept peacefully for the rest of the night.

Susan informed me that none of these happenings are unusual for Shaker Village. "At least twice a week someone here reports a paranormal experience. Even if half of these were imagination, there is still reason to believe there is something here. Another common phenomena is rocking chairs that rock by themselves for no reason."

Susan is not the only one who seems to take these phenomena for granted. One of the housekeepers I spoke with has had an experience in the West Family Sisters building. Amanda Stamper said she was cleaning the room, and "suddenly the television came on for no reason." She had not been touching it or even close to it. The experience did leave her spooked, but she still enjoys her job there.

Some of the odd occurrences include the sound of voices raised in song, audible footsteps when no one is present, appearances of people dressed in Shaker-style clothing, and even spirits helping living persons with every-day tasks.

One of the most amazing experiences happened to a former employee while he was practicing singing in the Meeting Hall. He began to sing descending notes and suddenly a shimmering form materialized on the benches at the sisters' side of the room. He felt cold chills and rushed out of the building.

Later when he was relating his experience to the music instructor at the Village, he received a possible explanation for the phenomenon. The instructor, Randy, told him he had been singing the "Angel Shout," a series of descending notes used to call Shakers to meeting. Needless to say, he never sang those notes in the meeting hall again.

Old Fort Harrod State Park

When the Shakers arrived in Pleasant Valley, the nearby town of Harrodsburg was already more than 30 years old. James Harrod had established this frontier settlement, the oldest permanent settlement west of the Alleghenies, in 1774. Today, you can relive the experiences of the early settlers at Old Fort Harrod State Park.

It offers an Earliest Settlers Cabin with many artifacts from the beginnings of the town. Among the other reconstructed buildings at the fort are many cabins of noted residents, the fires schoolhouse, the pioneer cemetery, The Mansion Museum and the Lincoln Marriage Temple,

The cabin where Abraham Lincoln's parents were married on June 12, 1806, was moved here from the original site near Springfield, Kentucky. In October, they host haunted house events.

Perryville

Perryville Battlefield State Historic Site

During the war, Kentucky's hopes of staying neutral were dashed. As a slaveholding state that chose not to leave the Union, it was suspect by both sides. Fighting was fierce in Kentucky, and this area saw the carnage of war firsthand with the Battle of Perryville on October 8, 1862. The Confederates were defeated, and Harrodsburg was placed under Federal martial law for the remainder of the Civil War.

The battle of Perryville is reenacted annually on the weekend of the anniversary.

A "Ghost Walk" at the Perryville Battlefield State Historic Site is now part of the Civil War battle re-enactment. Visitors will hear from re-enactors portraying soldiers and civilians talking about what it was like in Perryville on Oct. 8, 1862, after the largest Civil War battle in Kentucky. The battle resulted in more than 7,000 casualties, so it is not unexpected that along with the living re-enactors, people have reported hearing and seeing souls who have remained on the battlefield where they lost their lives some 145 years ago. Sounds of horses and fighting still are heard in the wee hours. Even the area around the battlefield has had its share of experiences.

Karen Wheeler, who had a store on Merchants' Row in Perryville, describes seeing a Confederate soldier when she was a child living in a house along one of the main roads leading to the battlefield. She and her brother were playing upstairs and heard footsteps on the stairs leading from the downstairs entrance. At first she thought it was her father, but when she looked, she beheld the form of a Confederate soldier. He was wearing a full uniform and disappeared when she screamed.

Karen had another encounter in the store on Merchants' Row one night. She was hanging a mirror and heard footsteps behind her. When she looked in the mirror, she saw a shadowy gray figure. She turned around and no one was there, but she heard footsteps departing. She tried to be brave and continue hanging the display items. When she next turned to hang a picture, she again heard the footsteps. She decided it was time to go home. Another time, she had strung a display of wreaths and returned the next day to find the wreaths strewn over the floor. The building her store is located in was an opera house in antebellum days.

The county is well aware of the importance of its history. They have begun restoration of Merchants' Row, one of the only surviving 19th-century mercantile districts in the nation.

Taylor County

Tebbs Bend Battlefield

In nearby Taylor County, another Civil War battlefield is remembered in a 10-stop driving tour. The battle of Tebbs Bend occurred on July 4, 1863, incidentally the same day Vicksburg surrendered to union forces in Mississippi.

Confederate General John Hunt Morgan's forces attempted to cross the Green River near a spot called Tebbs Bend. Although the Confederates greatly outnumbered the Union troops and had four pieces of artillery, eight attempts to breach the Union lines failed.

When I spoke with Marilyn Clark, a local historian, she told me that just recently a picture was unearthed that showed a fort located on the battlefield. Prior to finding the old picture, no one even knew a fort had been there.

Due to the bloody fighting there, ghost hunters may discover interesting phenomena all along the battlefield.

Jacob Hiestand House

Another historic home believed to be haunted in Taylor County is the Jacob Hiestand House. It is a fine example of Federal architecture that was built in 1823 by German immigrants. It is only one of fewer than a dozen stone houses in Kentucky. It is open to the public as a house museum. When you visit, beware the house is rumored to be haunted by Jacob Hiestand and his family.

Green River Lake

Green River Lake

For a change of pace, drive out to Green River Lake. It's a Corps of Engineers Lake with several great resorts for fun on the water. Emerald Isles has a marina, restaurant and condos on the lake. Another resort is Holmes Bend, which offers houseboat rentals and cabins as well as swimming, fishing and any other water fun.

I stayed in a cozy cabin overlooking the lake at Holmes Bend. Some of our group stayed at Emerald Isles condos, so I got to see both. The condos are more upscale and offer wi-fi, but the cabins are more private. Both are great bases from which to explore the area.

I got to see the lake up close and personal in a houseboat, thanks to David Butler, the marina's owner. I was impressed with the pristine shores of the lake and the lack of busy traffic as we glided along the clear waters.

For breakfast or a quick lunch, the marina offers limited dining at reasonable prices.

Greensburg

Greensburg Courthouse

Purely by accident I discovered a treasure. We were headed to lunch and parked the car. There on the corner was one of the most charming little buildings I ever saw. I asked and found out it was a historic treasure: the oldest courthouse west of the Alleghenies.

The two-story building is only 34 by 40 feet, composed of irregularly cut local limestone. The stone was quarried and laid by a local mason, Thomas "Stone-Hammer" Metcalfe. He had served in the War of 1812 and later became the 10th governor of Kentucky. The courses are fairly straight even though the blocks are of different widths, creating a pattern similar to Flemish bond brickwork.

The building was remodeled in 1869 by closing a balcony to add an additional upstairs room. A wooden floor was laid over the original flagstone floor and a new bell was added in 1879. Other than that it looks like it must have back in 1804 when it was first built.

Perhaps the most famous attorney who practiced here was Andrew Jackson, who passed through on his way to Washington. He also stayed at what was Allan's Inn next door. The inn is currently under renovation to open as a museum in the future. The Jane Todd Crawford Library is housed on the second floor of the courthouse.

The courthouse was in use until 1931, but locals will tell you that there are still ghostly attorneys and judges presiding over spectral cases. There have been reports of courtroom activity, talking and footsteps.

Another possible spirit there may be that of a man named Jack Thomson who died violently in the courthouse in 1895. Thomson was an immigrant from Scotland whose body was found at the foot of the stairs going from the first floor to the basement. Custodian John L. Smith found Jack's body.Invetagation showed that his neck was broken and his head had been severely battered. There was no further inquiry into the death because it was presumed that Thomson's neck was broken by the fall down the steps. The body was taken to the Greensburg Furniture Co. That business also made caskets so Jack was hurried to his grave. But what about the severe battering of the head? Was Thompson beaten and then thrown down the steps? Perhaps his spirit wants justice done and his killer found.

It's well known that animals seem to be more sensitive to spirits. Some of the worker on night shifts, brought their dogs to work with them. , In at least two cases, while the owners heard nothing, the dogs seemed to sense something and the hair on the back of their necks stood up and they growled. Each time was when they were walking up the steps from the basement. Another worker felt something behind him but when he looked no one was there. This was also on those stairs.

Shaker building at Pleasant Valley

Greensburg Courthouse

Print of Battle of Perrysville

Chapter 5 Louisiana

New Orleans

Hotel Monteleone

We all thrill to stories of penniless emigrants sailing into New York Harbor under the shadow of the Stature of Liberty and then making their fortunes in the land of the free. In the 1800s, New Orleans was also one of the main ports of entry for those seeking the American dream. Not all were poor and desperate. One of those travelers was a successful Sicilian shoe manufacturer and minor nobleman, Antonio Monteleone. Already prosperous in Italy, he decided to come to America in search of greater things. In 1886 he bought the Commercial Hotel, a 64-room hotel on Royal Street and Iberville in the heart of the French Quarter.

It has hosted many celebrities. Writers with troubled souls seemed especially drawn to the Monteleone: William Faulkner, Tennessee Williams, Truman Capote and Ernest Hemingway. Capote claims to have been born at the Monteleone. Technically, he was delivered at a New Orleans hospital, but his parents did reside in the hotel when he was born. Williams immortalized the hotel in his The Rose Tattoo. Because of its strong literary heritage, Friends of Libraries USA designated the hotel a Literary Landmark.

As might be expected in a hotel with such a rich history, the Hotel Monteleone claims its share of otherworldly souls who like the place too well to let a little thing like their deaths make them check out of this spooktacular place. Its spirit residents are verified by the International Society for Paranormal Research (ISPR). They confirmed at least a dozen resident spirits particularly on the 14th floor (actually the 13th, but the hotel skips the number 13 on its elevator). Not unusual for a hotel this old. Also it had been occupied by Union forces and used as a hospital during the Civil War, another reason to suspect paranormal activity. So I was expecting something really unique when I checked into this gracious old hotel. I wasn't disappointed.

Now, New Orleans is my birthplace. I grew up roaming the narrow French Quarter streets and visiting many of the museums. But like most residents of a city, I never stayed in any of its hotels. So my impressions of the Monteleone were probably similar to any other visitor's even though I had passed its facade many times during my resident years.

The hotel is quite European in style as befitting a city as cosmopolitan as New Orleans. Not just in the lobby but throughout. I love its many luxury touches like marble baths and a rooftop pool that serves as a relaxing haven by day and transforms into a romantic oasis at night. I enjoyed the luxury of the pool area but would have loved to spot its resident ghost, a young lady who made a suicide pact with her boyfriend at the poolside and then took her life before she had time to regret her rash decision. She was confirmed by ISPR, when it investigated the hotel in March 2003. The young lady is seen frequently, but her boyfriend isn't. Maybe he chickened out after she died.

One of the furnishings that grabbed my attention was a hand-carved mahogany clock set right in the middle of the lobby. At the time I didn't know its history. It just was striking. I later found out it was created by Toledano, Wagan and Bernard in New Orleans and sculpted by Antonio Puccio in 1909. Rumor states that Mr. Puccio was so impressed with his creation that his spirit is still glimpsed working on it in the wee hours. Perhaps he is still hard at work, or perhaps the rumor was started by patrons leaving the Monteleone's nearby signature bar.

This bar is one of the most unique in the city, perhaps the world. It is the Carousel Bar just off the lobby. It slowly revolves (one revolution per 15 minutes) as you sip one (or more) of its innovative cocktails amid its inviting splendor. It features a 24-seat revolving bar that was installed in 1949. Unlike on most carousels, patrons sit on stools featuring painted circus scenes instead of on carved horses. The bartenders must crawl over the bar to go to work.

I preferred to sit at one of the cozy tables as I joined my brother Jerry and nephews Dane and Kevin downing a few of the cocktails for which the Carousel Bar is world famous. My choice is the Goody. Don't let the name fool you. It consists of 1 ounce each dark rum, light rum and Orgeat, 2-ounces orange juice and 1-ounce pineapple juice and packs a sneaky punch. The Carousel has been voted best bar in New Orleans by National Geographic.

Since the Carousel Bar is credited with inventing many of the favorite drinks, like Ramos Gin Fizz and the Southern Comfort, it is always a big part of the annual Tales of the Cocktail Tour. The tour offers a chance to mingle with mixologists, authors and others interested in the history and culture of the cocktail.

Earlier, a lounge called the Swan Room was located just off the main bar. Liberace was the first performer to play the piano here. Other greats like Nelson Eddie and Marie McDonald played there as well.

In its over half a century history, the Carousel has gathered some devoted fans. None is more loyal than Ms. Kilda LaFortune. She always stopped by the Carousel each evening after work for more than 30 years. Her daughter, Ms. La Fortune Forrester, was a Champagne Dancer in the Swan room. Ms. LaFortune died in 2000, and after the wake her daughter brought her mother's urn to the Carousel bar for one last ride. I have often wondered if I knew La Fortune Forrester by sight, as she was a former Arthur Murray dance instructor in the early '60s. I also was a dance instructor for Arthur Murray in New Orleans at about the same time. Life provides some strange coincidences.

The Carousel may be the best-known of the hotel's facilities, but it is not the only one. The Hunt Room is the place to have dinner and Le Cafe is famous for its breakfast at the hotel. LeCafe is also one of the psychic hotspots. For years the paranormal activity, doors opening and closing, was attributed to a draft, though no one could find the source. During the recent investigation by ISPR, psychics captured on film evidence to show that the mysterious opening is caused by the spirits of two former employees. One is a former maintenance worker who prefers the doors open as they did when the room now occupied by Le Cafe served its older function as a maintenance area. The other entity is a butler or waiter who comes and goes through the paranormally opened doors. These are not the only faithful employees to remain at their posts from the afterlife. During the ISPR investigation, a middle-aged male spirit identified himself to investigators as "Red," a former engineer.

One Monteleone employee had a personal experience with the spirits that inhabit the old hotel. Cleatter Landry was working the concierge desk when it happened. "As most people know, the concierge desk is located in the center of the lobby by the grandfather clock, and not far from the Café. The hours of the Café are 6:30 a.m. until 2 p.m. At 2 p.m. sharp the Café is locked for the night, but occasionally the doors would fly open about 7 p.m. Sometimes I would wait awhile before I asked someone to close the doors, thinking that the banquets crew was hosting an event."

Cleatter explained that this wasn't just an isolated event. "One night when the doors opened up, I asked the bellman to close the doors, and he did. The next day they opened again. I got up to close the doors and asked the wait staff in the Hunt Room Grill if they opened the doors and they replied, no. My thoughts were we must have a ghost.

Years ago, we had a cashier and a waitress who passed away within the same year. The two individuals had worked here at the Monteleone for many years, so my guess is their spirits are with us."

The Monteleone was one of the few hotels to remain solvent during the years of the Great Depression. In fact, there are records of employees giving the formerly wealthy patrons money to return home. One such guest did not choose to return to face bankruptcy. John Wagner identified himself to ISPR investigators as "Solemn John." He had migrated from Tennessee to New Orleans where he conducted business deals. Many of his deals fell apart, and during the depression years, this was an irrevocable ticket to poverty. His last bad deal was the end of the line for "Solemn John." He committed suicide when he could not face the consequences. He appeared to the ISPR team sporting a light-colored, lightweight summer suit popular among well-dressed gentlemen of his era.

The hotel has also played host to many of the world's rich and famous, from movie stars to heads-of-state to flamboyant Louisiana politicians. Both Huey P. Long and Earl K. Long stayed under its elegant roof. Huey's favorite prank was having himself paged so as to appear important. Former Governor Edwin Edwards hid out there after death threats when he defeated former Ku Klux Klan leader David Duke in the election.

One of the best-documented paranormal activities is the sighting of Maurice. Phyllis Paulsen, a successful financial planner from California, was staying at the hotel on the 14th floor in room 1462. Her account of what happened is eloquent. "I was just relaxing in bed one morning when I looked up to see a young boy about three years old walk by the foot of my bed," she vividly recalls. "Since he had come from the sitting room, I immediately got up to see if the door was open and to check if a parent may have followed him into the room. My husband had just left for a meeting, and I thought he may not have closed the door all the way." The door was securely closed. "It didn't take me long to realize that I had seen a ghost," she continues. "He was a friendly little fellow wearing a striped shirt. One moment he was there and the next he was gone."

Ms. Paulsen had since returned to the hotel twice and requested the same room in the hope of renewing her acquaintance with the boy, but so far Maurice only made the one appearance to her. However, he has been seen and heard by numerous other guests and employees over the years.

His story goes like this: Maurice was the son of Josephine and Jacques Begere who had visited New Orleans in the late 19th century to attend an opera in the famous French Opera House. Maurice was left with his nanny while the couple went off to the opera. When they returned to the hotel after the opera, the horses bolted at a loud noise and Jacques was thrown from the buggy, killing him instantly. Josephine died within a year of a broken heart. Legend states the ghost of young Maurice, although he did not die in the hotel but presumably returned home and grew up elsewhere, sometimes roams the halls searching for his parents particularly on the 14th floor near the room where they stayed. Perhaps he returned after death to the most traumatic place in his life.

Maurice is not the only child spirit seen at the Monteleone. While ISPR was researching the hotel, they discovered another young wraith. The spirit told the psychic that although he was older at the time of his death, he enjoyed manifesting as a 10 year old because he liked to play hide and seek with another young spirit. Could Maurice be the companion he frolics with?

One other phantom uncovered by the researchers at the hotel is known as "Poor Helen." Apparently Helen had fallen from the roof and died at the hotel in the past. She was not aware she was dead. Daena Smoller, a psychic medium skilled at channeling, was able to free her spirit and let her move on. Incidentally, this encounter is caught on tape.

While I was staying at the hotel, I struck up a conversation in the elevator with another guest who had had an unusual experience just the night before. Carolyn and her daughter, Katy, were sharing a room. Just before going to bed, Katy had placed her cell phone on her night table at the head of her bed, but when she awoke next morning, the phone had moved to the foot of her bed. Neither Carolyn or Katy had moved it from the table, and no one else had been in the room. No living being anyway.

Whether you visit the Monteleone in hope of spotting a disembodied spirit or just because it is a magnificent hotel, it will be a delightful experience. Antonio's small hotel has grown from its 64-room beginning to become the Four Diamond-rated 600-room landmark that dominates the 200 block of Rue Royal. It is also recognized as one of the Big Easy's premier hotels. Since Antonio's first venture into the hospitality business, four generations of Monteleones have loved and cherished Antonio's dream. In a day of chains, it is a single entity. In a time of corporations, it is still family-owned. The same pride that caused Antonio to journey across the ocean to find a dream remains true today under his ancestor William Monteleone. Like New Orleans itself, the Monteleone has remained true to its roots and is unlike any other hotel anywhere.

Bourbon Orleans

Of all the historic hotels in New Orleans, Bourbon Orleans is one of the most interesting. It has a unique history and a few spirits of the past that still remain. I had the pleasure of staying there on a press trip recently and so enjoyed the decor, atmosphere and comfort.

The hotel is conveniently located on Orleans St. between Bourbon and Royal. Accommodations range from roomy guest rooms with either two double or queen beds or one kind. Their pillow-top mattresses are an instant invitation to dreamland or a perfect perch to watch the 42" flat-screen TVs. There is also a comfy couch to relax on. Rooms have a wet bar with complementary coffee or tea. Plantation shutters and a Plantation Style wide bladed ceiling fan give the feeling of old New Orleans.

If you want to move up, literally, try a Bourbon Balcony on the third floor of the hotel. You'll have a two level floor plan, with a spacious living room and large wet bar downstairs. You can step through French doors onto you own private balcony overlooking Bourbon street. The loft features a cozy queen bedroom. You will have the same amenities as the rooms. There is a heated saltwater pool nestled in a cozy French Quarter courtyard just off the lobby. You can dine or have a cocktail without leaving the hotel. The hotel's fine dining restaurant, Roux on Orleans, serves up a tasty menu of Creole cuisine.

Wandering around the lobby or public areas of the hotel you can feel the history reaching out to tell its tale from the profane to the profound. This was originally the site of Salle d'Orleans, one of the places where wealthy Creole planters would visit to dance with and often enter into plaïsage agreements with gorgeous young quadroon women.

Among the Free People of Color in New Orleans during the first half of the 19th century, a placee was respected as having a "left-handed marriage."

The ballroom was adjacent to and connected by a balcony to Theatre D' Orleans, New Orleans most famous opera house. Must have been very convenient when there was an opera and a Quadroon Ball going on at the same time. Young blades could accompany their white family to the opera and during intermission slip over to view the African American beauties dancing at the ballroom. The ballroom, also known as Orleans Ballroom, was used for variety of other elite functions as well. It was chosen as the site for a gala to entertain the Marquis de Lafayette when he visited in 1825. In 1828 the Government House burned and the State Legislature met in this ballroom. From 1852 until 1881 the First District Court held sessions there. In 1866, the theater portion of the building burned to the ground but the ballroom was spared.

It was in 1881 that the building entered its "profound era." It was purchased by the Sisters of the Holy Family. This was the first female-led African-American religious order in the country, founded in 1842 by Henriette DeLille, Juliette Gaudin and Josephine Charles, all Free Women of Color. Although New Orleans is best known of its Saints dressed in black and gold jerseys and tossing a football, Henriette DeLille is in the canonization process of the Catholic Church. If she is canonized, she will be the first female native-born African American saint.

New Orleans was the site of a Civil War battle from April 25–May 1, 1862 when Union forces invaded the city by way of the Mississippi River. (see Civil War Trails) Wounded soldiers were often nursed in convents by nuns. The Holy Family Convent probably saw its share of dead young soldiers the nuns could not save. That would explain the sighting of a Confederate soldier roaming the hallways of the Bourbon Orleans.

Whether you are looking for just luxurious quarters close to the heart of the Crescent City or a step back into history, I strongly recommend the Bourbon Orleans. I first visited the ballroom in the late 1950s. The former ballroom was then a chapel and open to the public on Good Friday and my mother, a staunch Catholic, insisted we "make the nine churches," a New Orleans tradition of walking between nine churches in honor of the crucifixion of Jesus. Even as a child, I was struck by the beauty and fair complexion of these nuns. My mother then told me the story of the old ballroom and explained why so many of these nuns were so light-complexioned. It was an experience I have never forgotten.

The nuns remained in residence until the 1960s when they moved to the East Gentilly section. When the Bourbon Orleans Hotel acquired the property in 1964, they were very careful to preserve the original faï¿½ade and old ballroom. Grand functions, weddings, carnival balls and other events, are still held beneath the Orleans Ballroom's crystal chandeliers.

As might be expected with such a checkered history, there are many spirits still roaming the building. One of the specters is a ghostly quadroon girl who is sometimes glimpsed dancing in the glow of the ballroom's crystal chandeliers. Another female soul sometimes seen in Room 644 of the hotel is dressed in a nun's habit. she is believed to be the spirit of a Holy Family nun who took her own life.

During the years of the nun's tenure, they maintained a orphanage and school for Black children, St. Mary's Academy, in the building. During the yellow fever epidemic of 1905, some of the orphans contracted the disease and died in the building. It is said their spirits still play in the lobby and kitchens. Workers have seen table cloths move as if someone brushed against them. Glasses unexplainably clink together as if in a mock toast. Some of the staff have felt their shirt tails or aprons pulled when no one is there. Tinkles of childish laughter is sometimes heard. A few have even glimpsed a little girl playing with her ball in the corridor.

Court of Two Sisters

In New Orleans, food is considered a deity and food preparation a mystical experience. To say the least, the art of fine dining has been taken to a new high in the Big Easy. At no place is this more true than at the Court of Two Sisters. I experienced one of its Jazz Brunches and have to agree this place is first-rate even in a city known for its over-the-top dining.

When you step through the huge double doors leading to the largest restaurant courtyard in New Orleans, you are transported to a different realm. It would be so easy to believe you stepped back to the late 1800s and were visiting the home and notions shop of two aristocratic Creole sisters, Emma and Bertha Camors. With just a bit more imagination, you might feel you had stepped back even farther into the home of Sieur Etienne de Perier, royal governor of colonial Louisiana between 1726 and 1733. The history of this upscale eatery is impressive, but the present-day food and service live up to the legendary past. The premises served as home to these and many other historical personages before finding a niche as a fine-dining establishment.

Drop in any day and sample the famous Jazz Buffet. More than 80 items, many unique to New Orleans cuisine, fill the buffet boat. If this isn't enough, you can order specials, such as their own version of Eggs Benedict that never fails to please. The quality and quantity of the food will guarantee you will linger for a leisurely meal, but the icing on the cake is the trio of jazz musicians who add to the ambience.

Whether you dine indoors in one of the three dining rooms or in the courtyard letting the tinkling fountains compete with the soul-stirring music, you will know you are in New Orleans. Only here could history, music and food combine into such a perfect package.

When you dine in New Orleans, you expect wonderful food, cosmopolitan atmosphere and great service, but the Court of Two Sisters had something most restaurants don't have, its resident specter. Two actually, the sisters, Emma and Bertha, could not be separated in life and remain together in death as well. Born two years apart in 1858 and 1860, respectively, they remained united all their life throughout marriages, widowhood and the reversals of fortune that caused them to open their popular notions shop. It appears they refuse to let death separate them, either. They died within two months of one another in the winter of 1944 and are buried in St. Louis Cemetery number 3. However, they are often seen in their former notions shop, AKA Court of Two Sisters. Naturally, they are sharing a table.

Brennan's

In a city with the haunting traditions of New Orleans, it is not surprising that many restaurants are haunted. Brennan's is another New Orleans tradition. My fond memories of this superb eatery are mainly of breakfast. My own high school Senior Breakfast was held at Brennan's, and I have never forgotten the elegant feast. Breakfast at Brennan's is unlike breakfast anywhere else.

The superb food is only a part of the reason. The other had to do with a mysterious portrait hanging in the Red Room upstairs. The portrait is of Monsieur LeFleur, one of the residents of the building when it was a graceful home. When you dine there, observe the portrait. At first glance, it appears to be a well-dressed 18th-century French aristocrat who posed with a pleasant smile on his lips. However, as you continue to stare, the smile fades and becomes a knowing smirk. There is good reason for his unpleasant transformation. In life, he was considered a respected man until the day he went out and arranged for three funerals. He then went home, murdered his wife and son and then hanged himself from the very chandelier you are dining under. It is believed that he suffered financial reverses and could not face life in a "reduced" status. Workers in the room have often spotted his misty figure.

He is not alone. The spirits of at least three former employees still reside there. The oldest residing worker may be a slave named Percy, who worked as a caretaker. Then there is Chef Paul Blange. Chef Paul created two of Brennan's signature dishes, Eggs Hussarde and Bananas Foster, and when he died, he was laid to rest with a menu, knife and fork on his chest. Naturally, he is most often found in the kitchen overseeing present-day staff.

The third ghost is that of Herman Funk, a former wine master who frequents the wine cellar and often makes a clinking noise on a bottle to indicate to a waiter the "correct" wine choice for a customer.

The restaurant was originally the first bank in the territory after the Louisiana Purchase. It was also home to Paul Morphy after his family moved from the Charters Street home until his death. (You'll read more about him under the Beauregard-Keyes House.)

Café du Monte

As a girl, one of my favorite haunts in the Quarter was Cafe du Monde, located in the French Market at 1039 Decatur Street. I loved to order the hot beignets covered with powered sugar and, as I am one of the only people from New Orleans who doesn't drink coffee, chocolate milk. My friends and I would laughingly blow across the beignets to spray our comrades with the sugar. The real fun was if someone was unwise enough to wear a dark color. The sugar would really stand out then.

We would sit and stare at Jackson Square and make up stories about the passersby. Perhaps that artist lugging his easel and paints toward the Square would one day be a famous artist. Maybe that odd-looking woman with the turban was a distant relative of Marie Laveau. Nowhere else on earth offers such rich people-watching as New Orleans' French Quarter, and the Café du Monte lets you savor a unique treat while you do so.

For coffee drinkers, beware. New Orleans is known for its coffee and chicory. The brew is strong enough to dissolve a spoon if you leave it in too long. The beignets are light airy square donuts that can be consumed by the dozens if you let yourself. The coffee shop stays open 24 hours a day, 7 days a week. It does close for Christmas and very close hurricane encounters. It was opened in 1862, so it is steeped in history, and its walls ooze tales of past grandeur and ghost stories. One favorite is of the Ghost Waiter who takes your order and then never returns. Personally, I often wonder if it is a handy excuse for a waiter who forgot to turn the order in, but go and find out for yourself. With or without the ghost, the Café du Monde is a tasty treat.

Jackson Square and its surrounding buildings

A great way to work off the beignets is to stroll around Jackson Square. It's a favorite haunt of artists and musicians. The square and its adjourning buildings comprise the most famous, and most haunted, area in the Crescent City.

The Place d' Armes, as it was originally named, was designed by Audrien de Pauger in 1721 as a military parade grounds and site for public hangings. Public hangings? Yes, hangings were conducted in front of huge audiences then. So no wonder the square has its share of spirits. It was renamed Jackson Square in 1856 to honor Andrew Jackson, the hero of the Battle of New Orleans in the War of 1812.

St. Louis Cathedral was built around 1794 and named for a former king of France; this is the oldest cathedral in the United States. It's actually the third church built on this site. The first was destroyed by a hurricane in 1722 and the second by a fire in 1788. Its triple spires are perhaps the most-photographed landmark in the city.

The cathedral's best-known spirit is Friar Antonio de Sedella, who came to New Orleans around 1774. In his early years, he was a fierce and vindictive man who tried to bring the inquisition to New Orleans, but as he grew older, he changed and mellowed. Perhaps he regretted his harsh ways. As pastor of the parish, he was much-loved and affectionately called Pere Antoine. He is reputed to have baptized and preformed the wedding of Marie Laveau. During his life, he worked to help the free women of color in New Orleans. Perhaps he is still ministering to his parishioners.

Worshippers at Midnight Mass often spot him standing to the left side of the main altar, holding a candle. His Capuchin robe makes him very noticeable next to the modern robes worn by the archbishop and other priests.

He is not the only pastor to remain behind in the cathedral. Pere Dagobert was a Capuchin monk who became pastor of St. Louis Church in 1745. At the time France ceded New Orleans to Spain in 1764, a revolt erupted. By March of 1766, the first Spanish governor, Don Antonio de Ulloa, had arrived in New Orleans. The French revolutionaries continued to work against the new governor and overthrow the Spanish. These plotters were some of the city's elite and influential citizens.

In November 1768 they seemed to succeed, and the Spanish governor fled to Havana. Naturally, Spain could not allow this to continue. They sent a Spanish fleet of 24 ships to New Orleans under the command of Don Alejandro O'Reilly, an Irish expatriate, to crush the rebellion and destroy its leaders.

On October 24, 1769, five of the rebel leaders were executed by firing squad. The sixth, a man named Villere, had been bayoneted and had died earlier. The rebellion was crushed, but a stranger tale arose.

After the revolutionaries were executed, O'Reilly refused to allow them to be buried. The corpses were left to rot in the square, and the bodies were placed under the watchful eye of the Spanish garrison.

Pere Dagobert would not permit this to continue. He summoned their families to the cathedral in the dead of night and held a funeral mass and then, in the typical New Orleans down-pouring rain, he led the funeral procession to the men's final resting place in St. Louis Cemetery No. 1. To this day, no one has figured out how Dagobert managed to steal the bodies from under the watchful eyes of the Spanish soldiers. However, especially on rainy nights, the little friar is heard chanting the Kyrie Eleison in the cathedral.

Perhaps the ghost you would think least likely to be found in a Catholic cathedral is Marie Laveau. You would be wrong. Marie has been seen, clad in a flowing white dress, her head wrapped in the tignon free women of color were compelled to wear in her era, kneeling and praying quietly at the cathedral's high altar. She is most often seen in the early morning hours and at sundown, perhaps honoring the tradition of her time of both morning and evening devotions. It is not so strange when you realize Voodoo was a mixture of both African religions and Catholicism.

Another very unlikely female spirit is said to haunt the cathedral. She is none other than Madam LaLaurie; mistress of the ill-famed LaLaurie house on Royal Street. Rumors abounded of Delphine LaLaurie's cruelty and savage temper. Neighbors saw her chase a slave girl with a whip onto an upper balcony of the home and ultimately cause her to leap to her death in the street below. When a fire ravaged the LaLaurie mansion, her abuse could no longer be hidden. Mutilated and tortured slaves were discovered. She and her husband had to flee Louisiana for their lives. The story of the mansion and its slave ghosts is so well-known it needs no repeating, but the fact of Madam LaLaurie's spirit being seen in the cathedral is cause for speculation. Is she is looking for forgiveness for her heinous crimes? Perhaps that is why she is often seen loitering near the confessionals.

The bell in the cathedral tower has always been special. In the days before 911 and even phones, church bells were the system used to warn people of disaster. The cathedral bell was no exception. But when the fire of March 21, 1788, broke out at the home of Vincente Jose Nunez on Chartres Street, it was already the early morning hours of Good Friday. Catholic tradition states no bells shall be tolled on this holy day, so the bell of the then-Church of St Louis had been carefully wrapped in cloth the night before to prevent any accidental tolling.

On learning of the fire, the good priest rushed to the tower and ripped the wrappings asunder, but it was too late. The Good Friday Fire destroyed much of the city, including the church itself and adjourning Cabildo.

The new church, now elevated to a cathedral, was completed in December 1794. Ironically a few days before, another huge fire devastated the city, but this time the church was spared. It wasn't until 1819 that its central tower and present bell were added. A renowned architect, Benjamin Henry Latrobe, was commissioned to build it. The city also commissioned New Orleans clockmaker Jean Delachaux to install a clock and bell. Delachaux traveled to Paris, France, where he purchased a beautiful bronze bell from the same foundry that had made the Notre Dame bells. He also purchased a Swiss clock for the tower.

The tower was completed in 1820, but Latrobe did not live to see his masterpiece finished. He died in September of that year in a yellow fever epidemic. The bell was blessed at a high mass conducted by Pere Antoine and christened "Victoire." It and the clock were installed as the builder lay on his deathbed. His was one of the first funerals for which the great bell tolled. But it seemed the builder was reluctant to abandon his project. Workers putting finishing touches on the tower reported their tools moved mysteriously, strange sounds and the great bell tolling softly for no apparent reason. Delachaux reported a presence while he was in the tower checking on the clock. To this day, Latrobe's presence is felt in the tower.

Delachaux lived for many more years, but after his death people began reporting seeing a man in 19th-century clothing standing in the tower with a pocketwatch in his hand as if he were checking the time of the clock. And if you listen closely on a Good Friday morning before dawn, sometimes you may hear echoes of the warning bell even though no one is ringing Victoire.

A recent phenomenon occurred when Katrina struck. The cathedral suffered only minor damage; however, in the rear garden there is large statue of Jesus. The garden has several giant oak and magnolia trees, some of which are more than 150 years old. Two of these trees and much shrubbery were blown down around the statue during the storm, but the only damage to the statue was the loss of a finger and thumb from the left hand. Parishioners believe Jesus flicked the storm eastward and spared the city even greater devastation. The archbishop had declared that those digits would not be repaired until the city itself is mended.

The organ in the back loft seems to draw the misty figure of a woman, dressed in a dark, flowing dress in the Empire style of the mid-1800s. She is believed to be the spirit of Aimee Brusle. She was the daughter of a prominent New Orleanian Camille Brusle, who had escaped from the Haiti slave uprisings of the 1790s. The beautiful Creole had her pick of suitors, so many were shocked when she chose Edward Gottschalk, a Jewish northerner 13 years her senior who refused to convert to Catholicism.

She was soon disillusioned in her marriage. Her husband continued to keep his quadroon mistress and spent many hours away from home. To drive her further into depression, she lost a child to yellow fever and then her 8-year-old son, Louis Moreau Gottschalk, who was destined to become a famous pianist, was sent to Europe to study piano. She spent more and more of her time in the cathedral loft playing the organ, so it is no surprise that she still lingers there these many years.

Both alleys on the side of the cathedral, Pirates Alley and Pier Antoini Alley, have their own stories. Pirates Alley is known as the haunt of the Pirate Lafitte. (Yes, you may see him all over the Crescent city.)

Today, a popular tradition is being married in Pirates Alley. This stems from the legend of the first wedding preformed there. The story goes that a young English pirate who sailed with Jean Lafitte fell in love with a Catholic Creole daughter of a prominent family. Naturally her family would not countenance a wedding to a protestant pirate. So they met in secret. Finally just before he was to join his leader in fighting in the Battle of New Orleans, he learned his love was pregnant. Seeking to do the right thing, they sought out a clergyman to marry them. No Catholic priest would do the deed. They eventually found a protestant minister who was currently jailed in the Cabildo who agreed to perform the ceremony. The problem was his jailers would only let him out of his cell as far as a small window that opened on the alley. That was where the young couple was married. No one knows the fate of the young newlyweds. Perhaps he was killed in the ensuing battle and she lived out her days with her family in the View Carre. Perhaps he survived and they fled to Galveston with Lafitte. Whatever, their spirits are said to frequent Pirates Alley.

Pere Antoine Alley is where you are most likely to run into the spirit of Pere Antoine as he strolls and reads his prayers. If you encounter him, the common belief is you will be immersed in a feeling of peace. My husband, Martin, encountered the phantom priest as a small child. Martin used to shine shoes in many of the Quarter bars to earn spending money at a very young age. He was about 10 when he met Pere Antoine and has never forgotten that night. He was returning home after dark and took a shortcut through Pere Antoine Alley. While he was in the midst of the dark alley, he glimpsed a shadowy figure in the alley with him. Since he had lived all his life in the area and knew many people around there, he peered closer to see if it was someone he knew. Then the figure disappeared. He told me, "I never used that alley again after dark, after that night. I always used the other one."

The Cabildo (circa 1799) was the seat of government during New Orleans' Spanish period. It was named for the council (Cabildo) that met there. As a museum of not only New Orleans but also Louisiana history, it is superb and should not be missed. For you ghost hunters, there is one story I was able to track down. It relates to a notorious murder. As you have already figured out, the Mafia has played a big part in New Orleans history from the days of the first Sicilian immigrants.

The event that seems to have triggered the spooky happenings was the killing of Arthur Guerin, who was shot by Deputy James D. Houston. Guerin, who was evidently a 19th-century version of a hitman, had gunned down David Hennessy, a policeman involved in attempting a Mafia cleanup. Houston shot Guerin either in or just outside an upstairs courtroom in the Cabildo, which was then being used as a courthouse. In later years, many more people including Hennessy's son, also a policeman, were killed in the same mafia power struggle. Since that day, there is a gate in the patio of the building that opens on its own accord at night.

Other buildings

Presbytere (circa 1797) doesn't have any ghostly myths I could find, but it is a great place to view the history of Mardi Gras.

The Baroness Micaela Pontalba is the person responsible for the transformation of the square from a military training field and gallows to the lovely public park Jackson Square is today. In 1852 she completed her Pontalba Apartments along one side of the square. She was perhaps the wealthiest woman in New Orleans at that time, and if she wanted a lovely park next to her expensive apartments, well, that is what she got. Both Upper and Lower Pontalba buildings are preserved, and some parts are open for tours. The Upper Pontalba Building is said to be haunted by the ghost of singer Jenny Lind who lived in it for a time. It is said music can be heard coming from the windows of the old building.

La Petite Theater adjacent to Jackson Square is the oldest continuously run theater in the county. It was started by the Creoles in 1800 as a special performing arts center. Naturally it has several resident spirits.

Catherine dates from the early 1900s. An older producer promised her top billing if she became his lover. Unfortunately, she was not a very talented actress and not a success as a leading lady. Her producer friend moved on, and she was replaced by a more-talented actress. Catherine was upset, to say the least. On opening night, she hanged herself from the catwalk in front of the stage, so the only thing people would remember of the play's opening night was her suicide. Today, she is still seen wandering in the theater. She usually is seen by the audience who frequently ask the cast what a hanging figure has to do with the current play.

Another actress often seen in the theater is Caroline. Caroline fell to her death from a balcony where she rendezvoused with her lover between acts. She is seen wearing the costume for the play she was appearing in the night she died, a white wedding dress. Caroline is very helpful to actors searching through the costumes for a particular item. If they can't find it, they just ask Caroline to look while they take a break. When they return, the item is usually in plain view.

Two male phantoms are also spotted in the theater: the Captain, who only manifest at rehearsals, and Sigmund, a former stagehand who is accused of damaging sets mysteriously.

Children are also often seen in the theater. Workmen who were brought in to renovate the theater refused to work there when their tools were moved around, and they saw children running all around the place.

Old Mint

The Old Mint on the edge of the French Quarter was the only mint to produce American and Confederate coinage. The mint was built in 1835 and used continually first by the United States and then for a short time by the Confederacy as a mint.

After the Civil War, control passed back to the Federal government and it resumed minting coinage for the United States until 1909. It was the only southern mint to reopen after the war.

Downstairs, the exhibits show the tools and techniques used to produce coins.

On the second floor, there is a great music exhibit very in keeping with the Satchmo Fest devoted to New Orleans jazz greats. Fats Domino's piano and Louis Armstrong's cornet were the highlights for me. I was and am still a fan of both.

New Orleans Historic Voodoo Museum

The New Orleans Historic Voodoo Museum is a great place to learn more about the religion as well as the life and times of Marie. It was founded by Charles M. Gandolfo in June of 1972. Charles passed away February 28th, 2001 (Mardi Gras Day). He was one of the most knowledgeable and interesting men I have ever met. Although he held two college degrees and was also a hairdresser and an artist, his interest in Voodoo led him to found the museum to help others understand the history and meaning behind this misunderstood religion. Anyone who beholds Charles' portrait of Marie Laveau cannot help but realize his deep feelings on the subject. His feelings were a natural outgrowth of hearing his grandmother's story about how his ancestors came to the United States from Haiti in 1802 after the slave uprisings. Their family plantation was burned to the ground and their lives saved by a close friend who was a Voodoo Mambo The high priest smuggled them out in barrels and placed them on a ship en route to New Orleans.

His museum today is in the capable hands of his younger brother, Jerry Gandolfo. Jerry tells me the museum suffered from Katrina but is still up and running on Dumaine St. between Royal and Bourbon Streets in the French Quarter. They offer tours, readings and most of all education about Voodoo. The museum also doubles as a working church for believers.

New Orleans Pharmacy Museum

For those who did not want to be seen mingling with the voodoo priestess, potions were obtainable in other ways. Many pharmacists sold them. New Orleans is the site of the oldest licensed pharmacy in the United States. It's located at 514 Chartres Street where Louis Joseph Duffulo, Jr., opened his shop in 1823. Duffulo later sold the business to Joseph Dupas, a Civil War physician and apothecary. Dupas was feared by slaves who believed he used the pregnant slaves for devilish experiments. Dupas died in 1867 from syphilis.

His spirit is believed to remain tied to the building where he carried out his experiments. He favors the stairway to the second floor. People climbing those stairs report being pushed from behind, Some people have even mysteriously felt sick when in the museum but it passes as soon as they leave the premises. Pregnant women seem to be affected most by the evil pharmacist's presence.

The museum is interesting enough to risk a little discomfort. Remember if you do feel ill, all you need to do is leave the building and it will pass.

Beauregard-Keyes House

From a very young age, I was interested in sites related to the Civil War, ghost stories, old houses and books. The boxy yellow house on Chartres St. just across from St. Mary's Italian Church fit the bill on all counts. It was built in 1826 by successful auctioneer Joseph Le Carpentier who reputedly gained his wealth by selling the pirate Jean Lafitte's ill-gotten booty.

The style is what is known as a "raised cottage" this translates to a much more magnificent structure than that sounds. It is a large columned home with a huge hall that runs the length of the building having large rooms on either side. One designer described it as "an architectural puzzle -- not quite French and not quite American." Perhaps the ill-gotten money used to build it put some type of curse on the house. It passed down through a multitude of hands, often with a scandal or mystery involved.

Le Carpentier's daughter, Thelcide, and her husband, Alonzo Morphy, were the next owners. Their son, Paul Morphy, was a chess prodigy. Besting some of the greatest players of the era while he was still a child. As an adult, he easily conquered all American and European challengers and won international fame. Then suddenly he retired from chess and lived in seclusion in New Orleans. Rumors of madness abounded. He was known to chase down passersby and threaten them with a knife and for a time was committed to the state asylum in Mandeville. Although he only lived there as a child, Paul Morphy's troubled spirit is often reported in the house. He is usually seen as a child playing chess with his grandfather.

Swiss Consul John A. Merle bought the house from the Le Carpentiers. It was his wife, Anais Philippon Merle, who added the garden. When they returned to Swissland, some other Creoles, named Andry bought the house then sold it to an Italian grocer. Dominique Lanata, who bought it for a rental.

It was during his ownership the home was rented to P.G.T. Beauregard, who lived in the house twice. Once for a short while as a honeymoon home when he married Caroline Deslonde on May 28, 1860, and then from 1865 to 1868 while re-establishing himself in business after the Civil War and rising to the post of president of the New Orleans, Jackson and Great Northern Railroad. Today, the Beauregard chamber still contains furnishings used by Beauregard.

Of course, his ghost is the best-known one seen in the home. There are two stories: one of the reenactment of the Battle of Shiloh and the other of a lively ball with people in antebellum dress dancing and laughing.

The battle ghosts are said to be a horrifying scene with cannon fire and dead bodies all around. This was the first story I heard as a young child but it has been discounted as just a tall tale. Beauregard was a brilliant leader in battle. He was the man in command when the first shots were fired a t Fort Sumter. However, when he let his Confederate troops into battle at Shiloh it was a devastating defeat.

The other ghostly scene, the phantom ball, is more likely. Who would want to relive the worst moment in their lives? In fact, the ball that people witness may well be his wedding party. At that point in his life, he was superintendent of construction for the New Orleans Custom House, happy and respected. His assistant was my great-great-grandfather, John Roy, who mentioned his boss's wedding in his diary.

In 1904, the house was sold to a Sicilian, Corrado Giacona. Giacona was nominally a wine merchant. It was during his ownership that another tragedy occurred. He may have been involved with the early Mafia, then called the Black Hand for the symbol of a handprint in black ink left to frighten those who dared defy these early godfathers. A gun battle on the rear porch in 1908 ended with three of the Giacona's rivals dead and a fourth wounded. Some members of the family were arrested but later released for lack of evidence. After that, the family made the home into a veritable fortress until 1925 when they sold the home to Antonio Mannino. He was an importer and wanted to build a macaroni factory on the site. Fortunately, he was thwarted in that plan. Some of the home's specters seem to date to that incident as people have reported sounds of a gun battle on that porch. (An interesting item regarding the fact that both of the Italian families' interests related to food: A series of later murders in New Orleans have never been solved; all victims were Italian grocers and their families. They were called the Axe Man Murders.)

The house then passed into the ownership of Gen. Allison Owen, a prominent New Orleans architect and editor of *Architectural Art and Its Allies*. He was the one who stopped its destruction at the hands of Mannino. He then sold it to Beauregard House Inc., a group of women who wished to preserve the historic building. They protected the house by using it for weddings, parties and various other functions until 1944.

It was then that writer Francis Parkinson Keyes fell under its spell. She loved the gracious home with its historic past and wanted to restore it to its former glory. She first rented and later bought it.

Keyes was a prolific author. Of the 50 novels she wrote, many were penned on Chartres Street during her 25-year residency.

Two of her books relate to the house and its former residents. *The Chess Players* is a semi-fictional account of the life of Paul Morphy, and *Madame Castel's Lodger* chronicles Beauregard's return to the house after the war. The group she began, the Keyes Foundation, operates the house museum today. Her apartment in the home is preserved with many of her possessions including her fan collection.

One of the spirits sighted in the home is related to Ms. Keyes' era. At the time of her death in 1970, her pet was a small Cocker Spaniel named Lucky. He followed his beloved owner in death after just a few days. Visitors to her apartment have spotted him. Perhaps he had an invitation to remain in spirit from Caroline, a cat long known to haunt the home and believed to have been one of Beauregard's children's pets.

New Orleans Cities of The Dead

New Orleans cemeteries are unlike any others in the country. There, people are buried in raised graves because of the city's low sea level. Often the graves are ornate tombs, so viewing them all in neat rows is like looking at a city in miniature; thus, cities of the dead.

Perhaps the most famous of these strange "cities" is St. Louis Cemetery No. 1. It is the resting place of one of the city's most-legendary dark figures. I use the terms "resting place" and "one" loosely as there is some dispute about these facts. Not the fact that Marie Laveau, High Priestess of Voodoo, is interred in that cemetery. Oh no, she is there. But does she "rest?" Many say not. As for "one," well, aside from New Orleanians, most people don't know it but there were at least two Marie Laveaus.

Her story began when Marie was born in New Orleans between 1794 and 1801, the daughter of a white master and an African slave woman. She was a freed woman, not a slave. It was only natural that she had been initiated into her mother's religion at an early age. It was equally natural that she would have been baptized a Catholic. Marie was reputed to have strong powers. Perhaps she did or perhaps her strong powerful physique and handsome mulatto features combined with the air of mystery she wore like her ever-present tignon helped foster the image of a powerful Mamba.

The power elite in New Orleans tried to stamp out Voodoo at the same time they tried to use it for their own ends. It is only natural that white slave owners everywhere would fear this dark religion. "Dark" not necessarily in its beliefs -- it is basically a religion of good although there were some who did use it for evil -- but "dark" in the fact it was a unifying force among the slaves. It was one of the few reminders of their homelands. As frightened captives, they had been shackled, dragged from their homelands all across Africa, brought to a strange new land, bought and sold as if they were cattle and forcibly baptized into a Christian religion that had no relevance to their lives.

Powerless to choose otherwise, they combined aspects of their own religions with the new faith that had been foisted upon them. Originally, Voodoo, or Vodun as it called in Haiti, was a religion of the African people. Today, many white practitioners worship Dambella, Vodou's chief god, along with the descendants of those African slaves.

I learned a lot about the religion from a now-deceased friend who was a practitioner. Charles Gandolfo, founder of Historic Voodoo Museum, explained that the Vodou religion was based on beseeching gods or lesser deities for favors. Most often those favors related to everyday needs like a good harvest or a spell of good weather when fishing boats departed. Also personal things would be asked. These requests were much like the Christian rituals of Blessing the Fleets or simply prayers and services for a desired purpose.

Marie gained in stature among her followers in New Orleans as years passed. She had entered into a common-law marriage with Christophe Glapion, her second husband, and had several children by him. Since he was white, although he passed for a free man of color to be accepted as Marie's husband, they could not legally marry. The eldest child was a daughter whom she also named Marie Laveau. Perhaps part of her influence stemmed from the fact she and her daughter, Marie, were hairdressers by trade. She worked on the hair of the wives of the richest and most powerful men in the city. Women chatted freely in front of their hairdresser, so she must have gleaned some interesting information as she plied her daytime trade. She was respected and feared in 19th-century New Orleans. She led her followers in rites around huge bonfires at Bayou St. John near Lake Pontchatrain and wielded enormous power.

White petitioners also visited her in secret to beg charms to gain a lover they desired or best a rival. She reportedly was able to exert strong influence on police and high-placed politicians. She was a knowledgeable herbalist and far ahead of many doctors of her era when it came to healing patients.

One fact that helped maintain her power was she never appeared to age. People who had known her in the early 1800s swore she looked the same decades later. It wasn't until much later that people realized it was her daughter, not the original Marie, who had assumed her mother's role and continued the practices long after Marie Laveau the elder's death in 1881. The agelessness as well as the power she wielded caused the legend to be larger than life. In fact, Charles M. Gandolfo, in his book *Marie Laveau of New Orleans*, states: "Some believe that Marie had a mysterious birth, in the sense that she may have come from the spirits or as an envoy from the Saints." However, a plaque on her supposed tomb placed by the Catholic Church refers to her as "this notorious 'voodoo queen.'" Mr. Gandolfo states that the "Marie Laveau" practicing as late as 1919 could have been another Marie: possibly her granddaughter.

Both Marie senior and her daughter are interred in two separate tombs in St. Louis No. 1. Some say the elder Marie is not actually in the tomb that bears her name but in an unmarked grave in St. Louis No. 2 instead. Where the granddaughter or that possible third "Marie" may lie is anyone's guess. Wherever Marie senior lies, both she and her daughter have been seen rising up and leading their phantom followers in midnight bonfire rituals near Bayou Saint John. She has also been seen in St. Louis Cathedral.

Should you wish a favor, the faithful still leave offerings at Marie Laveau's tomb asking her intersession. Sometimes she is sighted around her former home on St. Ann Street, and sometimes she just prowls around the streets. There are those who say she assumes the form of a large snake, crow or black cat. If you spot Marie's ghost in its former human shape, you can easily tell which Marie it is. The elder will be wearing a tignon, a seven-knotted handkerchief on her head. One word of caution: New Orleans cemeteries are a dangerous place to prowl around alone. Always go in a group and be alert to your surroundings.

The Old Absinthe House and Lafitte's Blacksmith Shop

If you want to see Louisiana.s most famed pirate, famed pirate, Jean Lafitte is reputed to haunt many spots in New Orleans. The Old Absinthe House, located at 240 Bourbon St. at the corner of Bienville, has been a fixture in the French Quarter for more than 200 years. It was a popular late nightspot for New Orleans' well-to-do and fun-loving partygoers of the 1800s. The copper-colored wooden bar and its antique fixtures were a favorite place for those who imbibed the deadly green drink that the bar is named for.

Jean Lafitte, Louis Moreau Gottschalk, Andrew Jackson, "The Beast" Benjamin Butler, and even Voodoo Queen Marie Laveau all would have passed through the doors of the Old Absinthe House in life and are still glimpsed here today.

They and a pantheon of other lesser-known specters amuse themselves and baffle bartenders and visitors by moving bottles and glasses around behind the bar, moving chairs back and forth, and opening and closing the bar doors.

Jean Lafitte is particularly linked to the place as it was reputed he had built a series of tunnels between it and his blacksmith shop just down the street and the Old Mint on the fringes of the quarter on Esplanade Ave. eventually leading him and his men to the river embankment and a means of smuggling booty to and from the Mississippi River.

Lafitte's Blacksmith's Shop, at 941 Bourbon St., looks ready to fall down any minute. It looked that way when I was a kid and probably when my grandmother was a toddler. It's packed with history -- and ghosts. This was the Lafitte brothers' front,, the business that gave them respectability. It was a grand cover for their real business of pirating and smuggling.

Rumors abound that his treasure is buried somewhere on the premises. Many patrons have claimed to have seen a scowling gentleman twirling his mustaches and fingering his sword who disappears when he sees he is being observed.

A mirror in the upstairs area is reportedly possessed by a female phantom, perhaps one of the buccaneer's many ladyloves. In the downstairs bar, there is a fireplace grate that visitors have sworn had two glowing red eyes peering out at them. It is rumored that some of Lafitte's gold was hidden somewhere in the chimney, and it is haunted by the spirit of the pirate Lafitte killed and ordered to protect the treasure for all eternity.

Audubon Zoo

Believe it or not there are some attractions in New Orleans worth seeing that do not have a resident ghost. After a hectic day dealing with humans, what's better than a zoo? Well, that's easy, a zoo plus an aquarium and insectarium It's even better if you throw in an IMAX theater. The New Orleans Audubon Nature Institute, Inc., offers all that and more.

The Zoo, like all of New Orleans, took a hit with Hurricane Katrina, but it has bounced back and made a full recovery. Sure there are a few scars and gaps, but in all it is a wonderful experience for child and adult alike. Today, it is one of the country's top-ranked zoos.

What a difference from the days when my brothers and I used to beg our parents to take us to see the much-smaller range of animals penned in tiny cages at the Audubon Zoo. This time as I viewed the zoo, with my brother, sister-in-law and nieces, I could not help but marvel at the changes. Today, the much greater number and variety of exotic guests there have the equivalent of five-star accommodations. Habitats resembling their home turf with lots of room to roam make a modern visit to the Audubon Zoo a pleasure for both the visitor and the inhabitants. Along with the animals from around the world, the area is awash in the color and texture of the lush gardens that form the Zoo's backdrop.

The Aquarium of the Americas and Insectarium

The Aquarium features a lot of aquatic and some non-aquatic wildlife from all over the world.

One of the attractions that impressed me most was the white alligators. Having been married to a Cajun for more years than I like to remember, I know about lots of the Cajun superstitions. One is that white animals are considered good luck. Being in the aquarium gaurantees them a longer life since they probably wouldn't have survived long in the wild as their white coloring would cause them to be easily spotted and eaten by other animals that prey on tiny 'gator hatchlings.

Just across the street is the insectarium in what was once the old custom house. I visited but did not see any spirits just lots of insects including my least favorite, the roach.

Considering the history the old custom house witnessed as a cannon factory during the Civil War, there must be some spirits still around unless the insects scared them all off. The tickets for the aquarium also include the insectarium.

IMAX Theater

Rounding out the "Big Three" of the Audubon's attractions is the IMAX Theater. I know you have all been to an IMAX, but this one is special. It is one of only six in the world with a spectacular flat screen, single projection, IMAX 3D and high-definition capabilities.

The IMAX opened in 1995 and, with the exception of down-time caused by Hurricane Katrina, has been entertaining visitors ever since.

Chalmette Battlefield

Just about seven miles out of New Orleans in St. Bernard Parish is the site of one of the country's most-famous battles. It was a battle that never should have been fought. Its aftermath launched a president and created a legend. The Battle of New Orleans has been the subject of story and song ever since. Andrew Jackson and Jean Lafitte's pact fired the imagination. Pirate and patriot joined in love of their country and her defense. In fact, the war was over for 10 days when the battle was fought. Jackson was probably mostly concerned about his reputation and gaining a stunning victory. Lafitte was interested in the pardon that would save his neck from being stretched by a vengeful Governor Claiborne. The story goes that Lafitte and Claiborne's young second wife were having a steaming affair under the governor's nose. But who am I to ruin a batch of great legends with a few facts.

This was the third and final thrust of the war of 1812. It began in late December when 36-year-old British Major General Sir Edward M. Pakenham at the head of 10,000 seasoned British troops arrived by way of Lake Borgne to threaten the port of New Orleans. The city's capture would have put Britain in control of the main seaport on the Mississippi and would have left the U.S. unable to continue its westward expansion.

In defense of the city, there were only about 5,000 militia and volunteer soldiers, which included Jean Lafitte's Baratarian corsairs. Ambitious Major General Andrew Jackson would take all the help he could get and not question motives. On December 23 Jackson attacked near Chalmette Plantation taking the British off-guard. The day was a rousing victory for the young United States and made Jackson the "Hero of New Orleans."

Frequently visitors to the battlefield report sounds of battle, gunshots, cannon fire and ghostly voices shouting. Some have even seen a headless British soldier wandering the area.

Transportation

One caution: If you are planning on renting a car on your trip, if at all possible wait until you leave New Orleans to rent it. Parking costs in the quarter will be more than $20 per night, and getting a car out of a parking garage to go anywhere can be a very slow and difficult procedure.

The bright side is New Orleans has great public transportation. The Canal Streetcar runs up and down Canal, the main street, from the river to way uptown. The river streetcar will get you anywhere along the riverfront in the Quarter. Public buses run on good schedules, and a weekly pass can be purchased very inexpensively.

You can get pretty much anywhere you want to go in the city this way. In the Quarter, everything is just a short walk. Even getting from the aquarium, on Canal Street near the river, to the zoo, way uptown past the Garden District, can be accomplished by a reasonably priced steamboat ride. Plus you get the advantage of enjoying the scenery instead of watching out for traffic.

One trip visitors make now for fun that was strictly business when I lived on the Algiers side of the river is riding the Algiers Ferry across the river. If you want to get up close and personal with Old Man River, this is a cheap way to do it.

In this charmed city, even the buses and streetcars have their own ghosts. In the old days when I was growing up, my dad worked for NOPSI (New Orleans Public Service, Inc.). First he was a streetcar operator (for non-New Orleanians that is a trolley car), then transferred to the buses. They were huge air-stream type monsters that made a lot of noise and were strictly utilitarian. Today, New Orleans has rolling works of art for buses.

The army green streetcars of my day are now reincarnated in bright red bodies with yellow trim that invoke a more colorful era.

It was a pair of these old buses, one labeled "Desire" and one "Cemeteries," lumbering along Franklin Avenue that inspired Tennessee William to write *Streetcar Named Desire*. (Yes, that is a fact. I personally remember routes by those names. But they never had a streetcar called Desire.)

There are those who have had modern-day encounters with the long-defunct silver buses. Drivers have crashed trying to avoid hitting phantom buses that burst into their path out of nowhere and disappeared as rapidly. Early morning passengers have approached their bus stops and observed one of the old buses idling with its light on and motor running. Open doors invite an unwary passenger to enter the empty interior, but don't do it. These are not of our dimension. Witnesses have seen this phenomenon only to observe the unoccupied and apparently driverless bus pull away from the curb and disappear forever.

New Orleans is a city of excesses. Fun and fantasy are no exception. Like everything else here, it does have more than its share of paranormal phenomena.

St. Louis Cathedral

Historic Voodoo Museum

Beauregard-Keys House courtyard

St. Roch Cemetery

Satchmo Festival by Old Mint

Our host at Antoine's points to an area spirits have been seen

New Orleans Canal Streetcar

Chapter 6 Mississippi

Natchez

Natchez was a city born of the river. Its very existence came about because of its proximity to the "Old Man River." Inhabited by the last great mound builders in America who built the Grand Village of the Natchez, today it is preserved as a national historic site.

Then in the 1690s, the French, realizing that whoever controlled the river controlled the entire continent, established Fort Rosalie on the bluff overlooking the river at the place we call Natchez today. They were followed by the English (1763), the Spanish (1779), and finally the Americans (1797). To each of these ethnic groups, it was always the River that made Natchez such a prized piece of real estate.

When cotton became king in Mississippi prior to the War Between the States, Natchez was at its zenith. Again the river can be credited. Planters all over the delta switched from tobacco and indigo to the more profitable cotton. They developed vast holdings there, but the inland delta was low and swampy. The plantations were miles apart with no easy access for socializing. Natchez became the sun about which the wealthiest planters revolved. They built graceful homes there and remained for much of the year, visiting the overseer-run plantations when necessary. Natchez became the glittering social hub rivaled only by New Orleans. In the 1800s Natchez had a larger percentage of millionaires than any other American city

Naturally, the War Between the States changed Natchez forever, but because of its river location and port facilities, it recovered much better than the rest of the south.

Dunleith Bed and Breakfast

For all you Gone With the Wind fans, Dunleith is as close as you come to Tara. The house is build with a columned porch totally surrounding the stately mansion. Dunleith started life as Routhland, built by Job Routh for his family in the late 1700s. The home passed on to their daughter, Mary Madelaide Ellis, a widow at only 15. Mary and her second husband,

Charles Dahlgren, whom she married in the 1840s, lived there until 1855 when a fire destroyed the home.

Charles then built the beautiful mansion that stands today for his young wife. Sadly Mary died only three years later, and Charles sold the house to a Scotsman, Alfred Vidal Davis. Davis renamed the house Dunleith.

Joseph Carpenter acquired the home in 1886. He had three daughters, and they followed the old tradition of engraving their names in the windowpanes with their engagement rings. Look for these mementos of an earlier era.

There are rumors of at least two resident spirits in the fine mansion. One is Mary, the tragic young wife who died after only living in the mansion for three years. She is often heard playing her harp.

The other phantom is a middle-aged slave called Bessie. Bessie was the head housekeeper, and she loved the fine mansion as if it were her own. A travel writer, Jessica Maxwell, was visiting Dunleith recently and had this to say about the spirit she glimpsed: "She was handsome and broad-boned, and had the endearing habit of standing with her arms folded across her waist. Her silvered hair was parted down the center and pulled sideways into an elegant coiffure, and she wore a shawl fastened in front with a brooch." She later identified Bessie's photo with the help of the tour guide.

Another African-American who left a mark on Mississippi and the country as a whole had a connection to Dunleith. John Roy Lynch spent most of his boyhood there as a slave until freedom came with the fall of the Confederacy.

John Roy Lynch was born on September 8, 1947, near Vidalia, Louisiana, to a slave mother, Catherine White, and an Irish father, Patrick. Patrick had planned to free Catherine and his son, but he died before he could do so. On his deathbed, he entrusted a friend with that task, but the friend instead sold Catherine and her son to the owners of Dunleith.

After the war, he learned photography and ran a successful business in Natchez. Although he had only four months of formal education, he educated himself by reading late into the night. Seizing the opportunity for African-Americans to finally hold political office, he became a Justice of the Peace. He then successfully ran for Mississippi state representative. He was only 26 when he was elected to the U. S. House of Representatives.

He later served in the army during the Spanish American War. He died at the age of 92 and is buried in Arlington National Cemetery.

Dunleith is now an elegant bed and breakfast inn and hosts a fine dining restaurant, the Castle, on site.

Natchez Under-the-Hill

Natchez in the old days was really two cities. Natchez was the beautiful antebellum city where planters and businessmen lived in the lap of luxury. Natchez Under the Hill is often remembered as the place where Jim Bowie fought his famous duel.

Actually, the duel was fought on a sandbar a little north of Natchez, and it originally wasn't Jim Bowie's duel. He was the second for a man named Samuel Levi Wells, III. Wells and Dr. Thomas Maddox were the principals. The seconds were there to insure that the rules of order were carried out. Boy, did they fail at that!

Dueling in that era was a spectator sport, and about 16 men had gathered to watch, including Wells' supporters, Major George McWhorter and General Samuel Cuny. Supporting Maddox were his "seconds," Major Norris Wright, Colonel Robert Crain, and brothers Carey and Alfred Blanchard.

The principals fired and missed. Perhaps the spectators wanted to see more bloodshed. As the crack of the pistols' fire ended, Robert Crain fired at Samuel Cuny. When Cuny fell, Bowie fired at Crain. Then Norris fired at Bowie, wounding him in the chest. Undeterred, Bowie drew his knife and began to chase down Wright. The Blanchard brothers and Wright wounded Bowie in several places, but still he continued to fight. He slashed Alfred Blanchard's arm and sliced Wright in the chest. The Blanchard brothers fled, firing a second shot at Bowie as they ran.

Thus it was that Jim Bowie earned his title as the greatest knife fighter in the country.

This was typical as Natchez Under the Hill was where the rough element congregated. This was the first place where sailors just off a ship headed to look for a good time. One Confederate soldier just back from fighting had heard all the rumors of the ladies at one particular brothel located here. The young man had been a good soldier and a good son. His mother had told him of opening a restaurant in Natchez, and he had sent her a large part of his salary to help her keep the business going. He felt he deserved a little fun before returning to help his mom run the business, so he decided to stop for a short fling first.

He could not have known what awaited him when he opened the door to the most-notorious brothel in Natchez Under the Hill. Imagine his surprise when the painted lady that approached him decked out in a very revealing outfit was none other than his own dear mother. Overcome with shock and shame, he drew his military revolver and shot her to death on the spot.

Today, that early brothel has evolved through many incarnations. It has been a bar, a warehouse and a grocery before becoming the present-day Under-The-Hill-Saloon. Mom's ghost is still reputed to walk the floor late at night, perhaps still in shock that her own darling son would murder his mother.

I have also heard this story about a restaurant which was once located where the Isle of Capri Riverboat is docked today, but Patti Jenkins at the Eola told me it was the Under the Hill Saloon that was the true location. Perhaps the original brothel included both locations.

Other phantoms you may meet Under the Hill are Joseph Hare or his mistress. Hare was one of the outlaws who roamed the Natchez Trace. He claimed to have seen a phantom white horse and other specters on the Trace. He fell in love with a lady of questionable virtue who lived Under the Hill. He showered his mistress with jewelry he had stolen from travelers in an attempt to buy her faithfulness. Still, old habits die hard, and the lady reverted back to her old ways. Infuriated, Hare stripped off her clothes and loaded her body with all the jewels he had given her, then threw her into the Mississippi River. The weight of the jewels drew her into the muddy depths. And she drowned. Eventually, the law caught up with him and he paid the ultimate price at the end of the hangman's rope. He is still roaming the area laughing at some unseen joke. The lady also roams the riverbank at night.

Another outlaw might still be found there as well. John Murrel was an early con man that plied his trade in the local saloons. He would steal a slave and sell him over and over again. Then when the slave became too well-known for his trick to work, he would kill that slave and acquire another one, sell and resell. Eventually, he was apprehended and lynched. Murrel as well as the spirits of his slaves are sometimes seen

Some even older spirits are also reported there. One is a man in military uniform who is believed to be an American soldier who sold secrets to the Spanish when they were in control of the territory. Others are Spanish soldiers who still roam the old street near the river.

Perhaps it is the jingle of slots and the lure of easy money from the Isle of Capri Casino that draws these spirits. Aside from the hope of winning a pile of coins, the riverboat casino is a great place for dinner. I ate at the buffet my first night in Natchez and thoroughly enjoyed it. Unfortunately, I didn't leave with any more loot than I boarded with. Still, it was fun feeding those slots. Just like the idea of a ghost encounter, you never know when it will hit.

Kings Tavern

Even the glittering city of Natchez on the bluff itself began as a somewhat rough outpost. What is believed to be the oldest building in Natchez -- possibly in the entire state of Mississippi -- was originally a combination fortress and stopping point for the Natchez Trace travelers.

It was constructed during the Spanish occupation around 1789 by Ricardo King. He used ship timbers, brick and native cypress to build the strong three-story building.

But tragedy made its mark on the old tavern also. During King's ownership a dark deed occurred that still reverberates there today. Ricardo was enamored with a 16-year-old barmaid, Madelaide. Eventually, his wife found out about the affair. She would not tolerate a rival. So one day during a period when construction was going on in the tavern, the young girl disappeared.

Perhaps Ricardo searched for his mistress, but he never found her. The authorities there were sketchy at best, so no one ever questioned Mrs. King about the disappearance. But strange things began to happen at the tavern. Dishes would move on their own, shadows would be seen when there was no person to cast them. Cold spots would be felt by patrons.

During the time Ricardo King and his wife ran the tavern, it was on the frontier. There are still bullet holes embedded in the walls bearing testimony to its wild past. It also played host to some notable figures: Andrew Jackson and Aaron Burr were among the travelers seeking its shelter. Some were not so civilized or harmless. Outlaws roamed the deserted Trace killing and robbing travelers. Two of the most infamous were Micajah

Harpe and Wiley Harpe, AKA Big Harpe and Little Harpe. These may well have been the first American serial killers. They were big brutal men with not an ounce of human feelings. They killed indiscriminately as much for the pleasure of killing as for robbery of their victims. Few who met either Harpe along the Trace lived to tell about it. It was during one of their forays into Natchez that another tragedy struck King's Tavern.

Big Harpe was staying incognito at the tavern for a night, and a baby continued to cry in the great room. Irate, Harpe threw the child against a brick wall and killed him, then fled.

Ricardo sold the tavern in 1817. It continued as a tavern owned by the Postlewaite family for several generations.

Finally its age made the building dangerous. A new owner in the 1930s decided to renovate. It was then that the mystery of Madelaide's disappearance was solved. When workers took out the old brick in the downstairs fireplace to re-point the mortar, they made a grisly discovery. Three skeletons were discovered inside the wall. Two were unknown male remains, but the third was the bones of a young girl of about 16. Madelaide had been found at last. She had not deserted her lover. The murder weapon was also found within the wall. It was a small jeweled dagger such as a woman might use. Did Mrs. King dispose of her rival with the knife?

Who the two men were is not known. Perhaps she paid two ruffians to dispatch the girl and then decided they could not reveal her secret if she also killed them. Or maybe they were just two innocent witnesses to her crime.

Madelaide is not the only spirit you might find at the tavern today. Many visitors have heard a baby crying when none was present. Two male figures are also often seen. One is wearing a red hat, and the other seems to be an Indian.

Rosalie

Like Natchez, there have been two "Rosalies." The French settlers placed their fort high on the bluff overlooking the river when they settled present-day Natchez in 1716. They called it Rosalie after the Duchess de Pontchatrain.

At first relations between the French settlers and the Natchez Tribe were cordial, but that soon decayed and became open warfare. After skirmishes on both sides, the Natchez attacked the fort and massacred more than 250

French in November 1729. The French retaliated and almost exterminated the Natchez.

In 2000, an archeological dig uncovered the remains of a French cemetery on the grounds. They excavated about 25 graves and estimated that there were at least 10 or 15 more.

I leave it to your imagination as to whether there are any restless spirits on this site.

The present Rosalie is a stately federal-style mansion built by Peter Little between 1820 and 1823. Peter had moved to Natchez from Pittsburgh in the 1780s. He developed a steam circular saw and made his fortune from the vast timberlands across the river in Louisiana. He had Rosalie built for his wife, Eliza Lowe. His brother-in-law, James Griffin, was the architect and used local cypress and imported mahogany, which he cut in his own sawmill.

Peter neglected one thing: He failed to make a will. So when he died in 1857, Rosalie was auctioned off and sold to the Wilson family. Mrs. Wilson and her adopted daughter, Fannie, traveled to Europe to acquire furniture. She brought back 20 pieces of John Henry Belter Rosewood furniture.

During the Union occupation of Natchez, General Grant used Rosalie as his headquarters. He ordered the more-fragile furniture placed in the attic for protection. The only room damaged by the soldiers was the dining room which they used as a kitchen and mess hall. There is a historic table in one of the upstairs rooms of the mansion. This is the table where Grant signed the order consenting to General Sherman's March to the Sea.

The Mississippi Daughters of the American Revolution purchased the home from the Wilson descendants in 1938 and maintain it as a house museum.

Stanton Hall

Frederick Stanton immigrated to Natchez in 1815 from Ireland at the age of 21. By 1857 he was one of the richest men in Natchez thanks to his cotton brokerage business. He hired a local architect, Thomas Rose, to build the most-opulent home in Natchez to display that wealth.

Today, the home still displays the taste and fortune of Fredrick Stanton. The hinges and doorknobs are plated with silver, the art is museum-quality, and the woodwork is hand-carved. Something else from the past remains in this home, the owner. The shadowy form of Fredrick Stanton has been seen in the garden and on the stairs.

The Carriage House Restaurant is located behind the house museum and is a great place to enjoy a relaxing meal.

Longwood

Doctor Haller Nutt had big dreams. He dreamed of owning the most-magnificent original home in Natchez. In 1860 that was indeed a huge dream as Natchez already boasted some of the finest homes in the state if not the entire country.

But Dr. Nutt would not let anything stand in the way of his vision. He loved his beautiful wife, Julia, and wanted to make her the chatelaine everyone else in Natchez would envy. Julia had often talked about her friend Mary Williams' home, Longwood, and how much she loved the place. Nutt decided to surprise Julia by buying Longwood for her. She was thrilled, but the home soon became too small for their growing family. He decided to build an grander Longwood.

He hired the finest Philadelphia architect he could find, a man named Samuel Sloan, and commissioned a six-story castle with octagonal sides and an onion-shaped dome atop a huge cupola. It was to be constructed of the finest brick and imported marble and furnished with the best European furnishings.

Unfortunately, the country was poised on the brink of a disastrous war that was even bigger than Dr. Nutt's dream. Nutt was an ardent Unionist and did not believe the war would really happen. If it did, he perhaps felt his Northern sentiments would protect his fortune. He was wrong.

Northern workers just laid down their tools and abandoned the home in mid-construction at the start of the war. Union blockaders captured his European imports. The Confederate forces burned a large part of his cotton to keep it out of Union hands, and Federal forces confiscated what was left of more than a million dollars worth of cotton. Nutt attempted to go to Vicksburg and appeal to General Grant but was forced to turn back due to inclement weather. Haller and Julia cowered in the first floor of his unfinished home, the only part complete. The doctor contracted pneumonia and died a sad and broken man. Julia and their eight children continued to live in the unfinished building.

Eventually, the home was donated to the Pilgrimage Garden Club which now maintains it. But within, it remains the same as on that fateful day in 1861, unfinished.

Other things remain the same also. Dr. Nutt and Julia still roam the building and grounds. The doctor seems to prefer the garden, while Julie is more often seen in the house. Groundskeepers have seen a man in period clothing prowling around the garden. He also seems to want the tour guides to present accurate information. One guide noted that every time she made a mistake, the lights would blink in just the room where she was.

A housekeeper reported seeing Julia dressed in a hoop skirt. When the worker approached the figure, it disappeared right in front of her eyes. One witness saw a woman dressed in 19th-century clothing standing on the stairs. He believed she was a docent until he saw a picture of Julia Nutt and realized that was whom he had seen.

The scariest encounter was by Louise Burns, who was the resident director; she awoke one night to find her head lifted from her pillow by an unseen hand. She naturally was frightened but quickly realized she had to decide if Dr. Nutt could frighten her away. She decided he would not and instantly was released from the unseen grip.

Magnolia Hall

Perhaps you are wondering what was the last great mansion completed before the war made this lifestyle gone with the wind. That would be Magnolia Hall. In Natchez, it's hard to say which one of these gorgeous Southern castles is "the best," but this one is definitely in the running.

Thomas Henderson was a successful planter and merchant. He was well-respected in his church and community and wanted a home to reflect his status. In order to construct Magnolia Hall, he moved another property he owned off its lot. Pleasant Hill was no slouch of a house in its own right, but it had to move to make way for Henderson's dream house.

The house was damaged by shelling from the Federal gunboat Essex when the Union troops captured Natchez. A cannonball landed in the kitchen. Natchez, unlike Vicksburg just down the river, surrendered almost immediately. Life there would never be the same. However, Henderson was not destined to take part in post-war life. He suffered a stroke and died shortly before the end of the war. Magnolia Hall is considered one of the three best examples of Greek-revival homes in Natchez. The downstairs is furnished much as it was in Mr. Henderson's day. Upstairs houses a fun costume-and-doll museum. I had a blast pretending to be a Southern belle. Imagine trying a hoop shirt over your jeans.

With such a fabulous lodging place, it may come as no surprise that Thomas never left. He is reported to still be found in the downstairs bedroom he occupied after his stroke. You might say he leaves a definite impression. When the house manager suspected the maids of leaving an indentation in the bed, she decided she would make the bed herself. Sure enough no sooner had she smoothed the bedding up nice and taut, there was an indentation just where Mr. Henderson would have lain.

Eventually, a paranormal group was invited in to investigate. On visiting the bedroom one of the group asked, "Did anyone die in here?" The group had not been told any of the house's history. During the investigation, they heard shutters that should have been secured hitting the side of the house and a piano begin to play loudly by itself, and witnessed lights in the parlor flipping off and on.

One investigator sat on the bed and played a guitar to try and get Henderson's attention while another member videotaped him. He must have succeeded because when the videotape was played back, there was a bright purple light above throughout the entire tape.

The paranormal activities there prompted the filming of a Turner South Blue Ribbon episode. During the filming, the production crew witnessed the impression in the bed purportedly made by Thomas Henderson and heard a ghost-tracking device beep repeatedly.

Ghosts of Goat Castle

Often a ghost story springs up because of a strange or brutal murder. One of the strangest murders in history occurred in Natchez in August 1932. It involved a stranger cast of characters than you would expect in a Stephen King novel. It all began with Jane Surget Merrill, who preferred the nickname Jennie.

Jennie was born in 1864 to a pro-Union family in Natchez. Her father retained his wealth after the war due to his friendship with Grant. When Grant became president, Ayres P. Merrill was appointed ambassador to Belgium. Jennie was raised in the lap of luxury. She traveled in Europe with her father; she even was introduced to Queen Victoria.

After her father died in 1883 in Natchez, she lost the family home of Elms Court by failing to pay the mortgage even though she had plenty of money. For a time she moved from home to home including a stay at beautiful antique-filled Glenwood with her neighbors, Richard Dana and his mother. Then in 1904, she used part of her quarter-million-dollar inheritance to purchase Glenburnie, a lovely plantation home near the subdivision now called "Glenwood."

She was a beautiful young woman and a popular member of Natchez high society, and it was logical to assume she would marry soon. The reason she didn't had to do with her cousin, Duncan Minor.

Duncan traced his linage back to a Spanish governor of the Louisiana territory. His family also had managed to retain their wealth, and he was raised in a privileged environment. Speculation was rife that Jennie and Duncan would wed, but the announcement never came. People believed that was because of Duncan's mother. Duncan lived with his mother, and Mrs. Minor did not think it proper for cousins to marry. They continued to be seen together and appeared the best of friends. Often they were accompanied to parties by another couple: Richard Dana, her neighbor, usually called Dick, and Octavia, his girlfriend.

Dick's father was a respected minister and well-regarded in Natchez. Dick was born in 1871 just two years before his father died. He was raised by his mother until she too passed away in 1885. Dick attended Vanderbilt College and studied music. He dream was to be a concert pianist. He knew Jennie all his life. Their homes were less than a quarter mile apart.

Dick's dreams of fame were dashed when a window sash fell on his hand, causing injuries that diminished his skill at the piano. He was heartbroken, and his behavior became erratic. The one bright spot in his life was his love for Octavia.

Octavia Dockery had been born in Arkansas in 1865 at the Lamartine Plantation. Unlike the Merrills or the Minors, the Dockerys lost their home as a result of the Civil War. Her father had served in the Confederate army as a Brigadier General. In 1877 Octavia's family moved to New York, and their fortunes improved there. Octavia was sent to Comstock School for Young Ladies. When her mother died in the 1880s, her older sister, Nydia, met and married a Mississippi planter, and Octavia accompanied them back to Natchez. She was a stunning redhead and immediately became popular in Natchez society. She was considered very forward as she was the first woman in Natchez to ride astride instead of using the proper sidesaddle. She began to gain a name for herself as a poet. She and Dick became a pair. Together they gave recitals where he played the piano and she did poetry readings. When Nydia died in 1893, Octavia moved in with Dick at Glenwood.

At some point around this time, the friendship between the quartet fell apart. No one knows the reason, but they no longer were seen together at parties or other events. In fact at the same time, Jennie began to become somewhat of a recluse. No one but Duncan was ever invited to Glenburnie. He came to call on her each day at dusk riding his horse and stayed the night; in the morning he returned home to his mother's home. Even after his mother's death, this strange situation continued.

Jennie's eccentricity showed in other ways, too. Although she had plenty of money, she refused to modernize her home and continued to become more isolated from society. She refused to enter stores, instead tooting the horn of her Packard for shopkeepers to come out and wait on her. However, her financial condition moved ever upward. She was shrewd enough to withdraw her money before the stock market crash and lived in a prosperous if outdated manner at Glenburnie. Duncan also became increasingly isolated, refusing to speak to people and maintaining the strange nightly visits to Jennie and early morning returns to his own home.

Meanwhile, unable to earn a living with his piano playing, Dick let his home, Glenwood, become more shabby and run down. Dick himself became increasingly out of touch with reality. He refused to shave and ran around the woods in dirty clothes with uncombed hair and a scraggly beard. In an effort to earn some money, Octavia began raising goats and chickens. As the animals' numbers increased, so did the irritation from their neighbor and former friend.

Jennie persuaded Duncan to bid on the long-overdue taxes on Glenwood so she could evict Dick and Octavia. He did so, but they had not counted on Octavia's cleverness. Octavia had Dick declared mentally incompetent and herself appointed caretaker. In Mississippi, it was impossible to evict a person who was not competent, so Dick and Octavia remained; the goats remained; the situation remained the same and Jennie became more frustrated and odd.

The feud exploded on numerous occasions. Jennie frequently filed legal complaints about the Glenwood animals on her property, and when the law failed to stop the intrusions, she took the law into her own hands.

One day, when some of Dick's goats began lunching on Jennie's rosebushes, she shot and killed at least one of the animals. Dick filed charges with the county, but the case was decided in Jennie's favor. It was rumored that Dick and Octavia swore to get revenge. But by 1932, the case had been mostly forgotten. Jennie and Duncan continued their reclusive nocturnal meetings. Dick and Octavia's goats continued their grazing.

Then on that August evening, when Duncan rode his horse to visit Jennie, he found her missing and blood all over the veranda. When the police searched the grounds, they found the bullet-ridden body of the old lady in a thicket about 100 yards from the house. She was dressed in a pale blue dress and had been shot in the head and chest by a 32-caliber gun.

Although Duncan was her sole heir, he was never a suspect. Everyone's thoughts turned to Dick and Octavia. They were immediately arrested and held for 10 days.

During that time, newspapers and authorities saw the filth and ruins at Glenwood for the first time. People began calling it "The Goat Castle." Priceless antiques had rotted and stood in the midst of animal droppings and the dust and debris of decades of neglect. Rare books had become worm-eaten and tumbled out of mahogany shelves. Manuscripts that had belonged to Robert E. Lee and Jefferson Davis had been nibbled on by goats in the library. The couple no longer slept in any of the old four-poster beds but on mats tossed on the fetid floors of their respective rooms. The scene and characters were reminiscent of a Faulkner novel.

For a few days, authorities believed they had their killers. There was motive, the longstanding feud, opportunity, the proximity of the houses, and means; a 32-caliber handgun was a common weapon easily available. To cinch the matter, a bloody handprint believed to have been Dick's deformed hand was found in Jennie's living room. The two prisoners loudly proclaimed their innocence. They claimed to have heard the sounds of a quarrel and gunfire from Glenburnie during the evening of the murder.

What finally cleared Dick and Octavia was the shooting of a man called George Pearls by Pine Bluff, Arkansas, police. Pearls had been threatening the officer with a 32-caliber handgun, and it was known that he had recently been in Natchez. When the Arkansas police notified the Natchez authorities and allowed them to examine the gun and papers of George Pearls, the trail led to a rooming house owner named Emily Burns.

Burns finally confessed that she and Pearls had gone to Glenburnie to try and get a loan from Jennie. When Jennie, angry at their intrusion into her home, pulled her gun to force them out, Pearls had shot and killed her. Interestingly enough, Pearls also had a deformed hand, which could have left the bloody print.

Emily was convicted as an accomplice but only spent less than eight years in prison. Gov. Paul B. Johnson, Sr., pardoned her in 1940. Many people in the area wondered if Emily's story and later pardon was too pat.

Ever clever at making her way, Octavia managed to turn the situation into a profit for her and Dick. She convinced him to clean up and shave. They then began offering tours of the Goat Castle grounds for 25 cents or of the house for an additional 25 cents. Octavia escorted the "guests" as she carried a goat under her arm and told tales of the plantation's heyday while Dick played on a borrowed piano. At night after tourists had departed, Dick was often heard at the piano trying to regain the skill he had known before his injury, but it was impossible. In his frustration, he banged the keys louder and louder. Some hearers said he played loudly enough to "wake the dead." And perhaps he did.

He died in 1948 and Octavia a few months later. Her tombstone reads simply "Octavia Dockery, 1865, April 22, 1949. Mistress of Goat Castle."

Strangely enough, in death as in life, she remains not far from Jennie's tomb in the Natchez City Cemetery. But does any of the group remain at rest? Perhaps Duncan does, but as for the other three former friends, not likely.

After Octavia's death, cousins inherited the Goat Castle and had it torn down in the '50s. By that time it had become a wooded ruin inhabited only by animals and unfit for rehabilitation. The land around was sold off for the present subdivision, leaving only the beautifully restored Glenburnie and eerie sounds and strange sights in the night.

The screams of a ghostly Jennie as she seeks vengeance had begun earlier as Dick pounded his piano, but now she is accompanied by glimpses of a phantom Octavia, sometimes clad in a ragged calico gown and sometimes seen in a lovely Paris creation from an earlier, happier era. And over it all is heard the faint tinkle of a piano played mournfully into the night.

Glenburnie is now a private home but is often open on the Pilgrimage tour of homes.

Johnson House

It was not only the rich planters and their descendants who left their mark on Natchez. William Johnson was one such man. Born into slavery in 1809, he was freed by his owner/father at about the age of 11. He learned barbering and set up a shop and a bathhouse. As he became more successful, he began making loans and investing in real estate. Both increased his wealth.

One problem that might have caused trouble for a lesser man was collecting bad debts from white men. Even freed men could not take a white man to court in Mississippi, so Johnson used a simpler method to recoup his bad debts. When a white man did not pay, Johnson merely sold the note to another white man who could take the debtor into court. He married Ann Battle, and they had 10 children. He was murdered over a land dispute in 1851.

He kept a dairy of his life that offers a glimpse into his life as a freed man. Incidentally, he was a slaveholder himself, owning 16 slaves. His home is part of the Natchez National Historical Park, which also includes Fort Rosalie (not open to the public) and Melrose near Natchez Trace.

The William Johnson Home consists of the three-story brick house he built on his mother-in-law's lot in 1840 after the original home, along with much of downtown Natchez, was destroyed by a tornado. The family would have lived on the upper floors while the first floor was rented out for commercial use. The site also includes the adjourning McCallum House and a two-story dependency, which probably contained the kitchen and dining room downstairs and the servants' quarters above. There is also a kitchen garden, pigpen and chicken coop as the home would have been in Johnson's day.

Natchez Museum of African-American History and Culture

The Natchez Museum of African-American History and Culture, located just next door to the former Eola Hotel, chronicles the rich history and culture of African-Americans in the southern United States.

The Grand Village of the Natchez

Long before either white or black man set foot in the state of Mississippi, the Natchez ruled in pomp and ceremony. They held sway in the area from 700 to 1730 AD. As I left Natchez for Vicksburg, I visited the site.

The culture and civilization of these people is apparent by the artifacts they left behind. You cannot help but be impressed by their culture. They were farmers, not hunters and gatherers, and lived in permanent huts. Each family had its own land and grew corn, beans and squash, which they supplemented with fish, game and wild plants.

The society was matrilineal. The Great Sun was the ruler, and he inherited his position through his mother's line. His brother was the Great Serpent. The people built great flat-topped ceremonial mounds. Society was divided rigidly into nobles and commoners.

Two of the mounds have been reconstructed: The great Sun's Mound and the Temple Mound. At one time a structure stood atop the Temple mound. A perpetual sacred fire was once kept alight for years, possibly centuries, within it.

A reconstructed hut gave me a real feeling of how these people lived so long ago. I left with a sad heart. These people who had such a rich culture are -- although a tribe of the Natchez still exists -- lost to us forever. Just remnants of their past glory can still be glimpsed there and maybe a few spirits.

Natchez Trace

I continued on toward Vicksburg. I decided to take a portion of the Natchez Trace instead of the swifter Highway 61. I was well-rewarded. The Trace has its roots in prehistory. It began as an animal trail, probably made by buffalo, then used by pre-historic people. When the French and Spanish settled in the area, it was already a well-established pathway for Choctaw, Chickasaw and Natchez hunters. It served the "Kaintucks" well as a road home after they poled their flatboats down the Mississippi, sold them for lumber and then had to walk back.

By then it was the haunt of many outlaws who preyed on helpless travelers. Even the hardened outlaws claimed to see many strange things on the trace, and the travelers went in fear of both natural and supernatural enemies. Yet, by the early 1800s, this was the "superhighway" of the Southwestern United States. Until the coming of the steamboat, this was the best route between Natchez and Nashville, Tennessee. The early trace was dotted with "stands" or inns that provided convenient stopping places for weary travelers. They were spaced about 10 miles apart. A few of theses old way stations have been preserved. One such is Mount Locust. It's at the

15.5-mile point and is a great way to experience what it was like to travel on the Trace two centuries ago.

All over the trace, you will find remnants of its past history. You will find the ruins of one of the earliest women's colleges in Mississippi, Elizabeth Female Academy, where elegant Southern young ladies, including Varina Davis, were educated. Ironically, Jefferson Davis attended Jefferson College, a preparatory and higher education facility for young Southern gentlemen. Traces of earlier inhabitants await you at Emerald Mound, built by the precursors of the Natchez People around 1400 A.D.

Just a short distance along the Trace, at the 8.7-mile marker, I pulled over and got out of the car. This was my first chance to see what the Trace looked like in its heyday. Although I was just a short distance from the road and my car, it was as if I were deep inside a primeval forest. The trace itself was a worn indentation several feet lower than the rest of the landscape. It was narrow by modern standards, certainly not wide enough for two cars to have passed. But for foot traffic, horsemen and wagons bouncing along the rutted byway, it was much easier than making their way through matted forests. The roadway floor was covered in fallen leaves that muted even my lonely footsteps. The trees growing along the sides curved outward then upward, giving them a twisted appearance. Roots were exposed along the sloping walls of the hollowed pathway. Dappled sunlight drifted lazily through the interwoven branches overhead. I felt as if I were the sole human within hundreds of miles. I fully understood how this ancient pathway gave rise to the many ghost stories.

One of the more-common stories is of travelers seeing one or more white spirit horses. Some believed that the sight of these horses foretold their own death.

The most gruesome specter sighted on the Trace is of one of its most notorious outlaws, Big Harpe. Harpe was hanged and his head sliced from his body and left in a tree fork on the Trace as a warning to his brother and the other outlaws That roamed there. Many people have reported seeing a burly headless man carrying a bleached skull in his hands. Another story is that an old Indian medicine woman took the skull and ground it into powder she used to cure fits.

Witch Dance is another place on the Trace that has a paranormal story about its beginnings. It's located farther up near the 230-mile mark well past where I turned off for Vicksburg, but the story is worth telling for those of you who might want to continue up the Trace farther.

According to Kathryn Tucker Windham, in *13 Mississippi Ghosts and Jeffrey*, she considers it one of the most-haunted places in Mississippi. Witch Dance is a place where patches of dead barren earth are surrounded by verdant grass and woodland. The earliest natives recount that nothing ever grew in these spots. The reason being that in earliest times, witches danced here and where there feet touched the earth, they scorched it so badly nothing could ever grow from that day until the end of time. The Natchez feared this place for its magic and avoided it.

It continued to baffle the early land pirates of the Trace. Some feared it while others boasted they were tougher than the old magic of the place.

One of the other outlaws, Joseph Hare, was always respectful of Witch Dance. A few years later, Hare was making a getaway after robbing a traveler; he saw a white horse just ahead of him on the Trace. As he drew near, the animal vanished before his eyes. He never forgot the incident and recounted the story just before his death in 1818.

Another legend tells that the Paleolithic people, who settled the area near Witch Dance, were descendants of the Mexican Toltecs who traveled here with the bones of their ancestors. According to their ancient myths, they were led in their travels by a medicine stick and a white dog. Each night as they set up camp, they implanted the stick in the ground, and in the morning it would be pointing in the direction they would take. The dog led them to food along the way. When they reached this spot, they believed they were meant to settle, and there they built mounds and buried the bones of their ancestors.

Even farther along on the Trace, you come to a marker, "A short walk on the old Trace takes you to the graves of 13 unknown Confederate soldiers." The rangers will tell you no more about these isolated graves. Perhaps the soldiers still remain to roam the Trace watching for the invading Yankees.

One spirit believed to still frequent this part of the Trace is that of an Indian scout who followed the Confederates. The Confederates caught and executed the scout. Travelers have reported strange lights and noises there at night. Southern Paranormal Investigations Research and Education group checked out the area and got some strange readings on their equipment. Perhaps the scout is still doing his job.

There is one other of the early bandits possibly hanging around still. It is rumored that John Murrell's treasure is buried on the Trace. It can be safely assumed his malevolent sprit guards his ill-gotten wealth even from the depths of hell.

Melrose Mansion

Just a short distance out of Natchez, I found the Melrose mansion. From first glimpse, I knew there were some restless spirits there. I am not really sensitive, but every now and then I can feel something. This was one of those times.

Melrose is part of the Natchez Historical Park. It is a massive Greek-revival structure. Four huge Doric columns rise to the roof and frame a front entry and second-story porch. The proportions are perfect. It is of red brick and built with all the conveniences money could buy in that time. The rear also has two columned porches and a separate entryway for the slaves that allowed them to come and go without being seen by the family or guests relaxing on the porch. The grounds also include the outbuildings as they were in the home's heyday: the dependencies that housed the kitchen, livestock, carriages, and slaves. There are vegetable gardens and fruit orchards. The rose gardens and the magnolia tree that was planted so the owner's wife would see it from her bedroom window when she awoke still stand. The front lawn rolls on seemingly forever, giving the place an English-manor look.

The exterior of Melrose is striking, but to feel the force of this magnificent home, the interior tour is needed. Because the home was sold with most of its original furnishings the few times it changed hands, it is totally authentic.

This is the creation of the McMurrans. John McMurran came to Natchez from Pennsylvania to partner in a law firm with his friend John Quitman. He prospered and bought cotton plantations to supplement his law earnings. In January of 1831, he married Mary Louise Turner, the daughter of an influential Mississippi State Supreme Court Justice. In October, Mary Louise gave birth to their first child, a daughter they named Mary Elizabeth. Mary Elizabeth died as an infant. They then had a son, John, Jr., in

1833 and a second daughter in 1835. Strangely, they named the second girl Mary Elizabeth also, as if tempting fate.

Fate was kind to them for a time, however. John's law firm and cotton plantations prospered. John ordered construction on a magnificent home set on just over 100 acres in 1841. It was more than eight years in construction, but in 1849 when they moved in they must have felt it was worth the wait.

For a time, life was good. John, Jr., married Alice Austin in 1856. Mary Elizabeth married Farar Conner the next year. John fathered two children, Caroline and Alice. Mary Elizabeth had two also, a son and a daughter.

Then in 1861, the war that would change life at Melrose forever began. Their fortune declined. Mary Elizabeth contracted spinal meningitis and died on the parlor couch at Melrose.

Two of the grandchildren also died during this period, and the McMurrans decided to sell Melrose and move into town. Just after that, Mr. McMurran was killed in a steamboat explosion on the river.

Elizabeth and George Malin Davis purchased the Melrose estate from the McMurrans in 1865. It is believed that the Davis' Natchez home Choctaw had been ravaged by Union soldiers who occupied it during the war.

They left their mark on Melrose with two significant items. One is a marble table that has an interesting design of inlaid birds. The story goes that the Yankees plucked out the semiprecious stones used for the birds' eyes.

The other is sadder, a Victorian funerary portrait of their young daughter, Frances, hangs in Melrose. The guide pointed it out and mentioned, "That is not a sleeping child."

One other death occurred at Melrose. In 1883 their other daughter, Julia, left behind a 6-year-old son, George Kelly. Apparently George Davis had also died by this time and Elizabeth had moved from Melrose and raised young George in New York. Melrose, beautiful but tragic, was left in the care of two former Davis family slaves, Alice Sims and Jane Johnson. The home was closed until the beginning of the 20th century.

I asked the National Park ranger who led the tour about any paranormal activities observed in the house. Naturally, he responded "No. Nothing like that has ever been reported."

I believe a federal employee would still say that if confronted by an apparition who manifested in front of a tour of hundreds. But this was one of those times I knew there was some spirit still guarding the magnificent mansion. It felt like a female, so my guess is Mary Elizabeth since her happiest memories must have been in this house. She was married there and stayed there when she was convalescing after childbirth. She died there in such a time of turmoil. But it could have been Julia, who also left behind a young child or even Francis who never lived in the house but has her portrait in a place of honor there. Perhaps either Alice Sims or Jane Johnson is still taking care of the place.

When you go visit, see if your feelings are similar. Maybe one of you who are more sensitive may even see or sense which restless spirit still abides in the beautiful mansion at the edge of the Trace.

Windsor Ruins

Sometimes, I feel that houses have souls, too. If this is true, the Windsor Ruins is its own ghost. Today what stands is a metaphor for the old South. Literally gone with the wind or, in this case, in a blaze of fire left what was once one of the most beautiful antebellum mansions in Mississippi, just a pile of charred ruins. Oh, but what a pile of ruins. What catches your eye most is the 23 remaining Corinthian columns that still stand. The first thought on seeing Windsor is that General Sherman had passed this way. Wrong! It was not a dastardly Yankee torch that destroyed this Southern symbol but the carelessness of an invited guest.

Of course, it does have its War of Northern Aggression story. General Grant did make use of the mansion during the conflict, as did its Confederate defenders.

The new year of 1862 must have looked rosy to Smith Coffee Daniell. He was married to the woman of his choice, his cousin, Catherine Freeland. She had just given birth to his third child, his second son and namesake. His plantation covered more than 26 thousand acres. Their new home, Windsor, was almost completed.

The Greek revival mansion had cost him $175,000 (about $3.5 million in today's money) it stood four stories tall with 29 pillars, 45 feet tall, made of bricks manufactured on site by his own slaves and covered with mortar and plaster, supporting the galleries. Within were 25 rooms, each having its own fireplace. The indoor bathrooms were supplied with water from an attic tank. It was a work of art for which he had imported skilled tradesman from New England to supplement his own slave labor. The fourth floor had an observation tower from which he could watch the river.

Yet in just a few short months, all was changed. Smith only lived a few months in his mansion on the hill. He died in it at the age of 34. The war that would make this lifestyle obsolete swirled around Windsor. Confederate troops used the observation tower to spy on the Federal forces and to send signals to the command post across the river in Louisiana.

When Port Gibson fell in May 1863, Windsor became useful to the Union forces as a hospital and again observation point. That fact, coupled with the charm and graciousness of its widowed mistress, Catherine, saved it from Yankee torches.

It continued on as a social gathering place and home to Smith's family until February 17, 1890, when a careless guest tossed a lighted cigarette into a pile of wood chips. The family had gone into town for supplies for a party and arrived home to see the home in flames already too far gone to be saved.

Mark Twain was a guest in the home and described it in his *Life on The Mississippi*. The ruins have been the backdrop of several movies, among them *Raintree County* starring Elizabeth Taylor, Montgomery Cliff and Lee Marvin, and *Mississippi Burning* starring Alec Baldwin.

The lonely columns stand stark against the Mississippi sky, alone by day but at night, who knows what specters arise from the nearby cemetery, begun by Smith's ancestors atop what was already an Indian burial mound.

Is it any wonder that this countryside feels inhabited by phantoms who lived and died in this turbulent place?

Port Gibson and Grand Gulf Military Monument

I was afraid I had accidentally gone too far down (up? It gets confusing as the mile markers begin at Natchez, the southern terminus of the Trace instead of Nashville, the northern end) the Trace when I passed Port Gibson. I'm still not sure just what road I was on, but eventually I found myself on 61 heading toward Vicksburg. I kept seeing signs for "Grand Gulf Military Monument" and decided to see what was there. Boy, was that a good decision.

Hope Joyner, a sprightly senior citizen who manned the cash register in the museum at the Grand Gulf State Park when I visited, informed me about this fabulous place I had never heard of.

The battle of Grand Gulf was part of Grant's strategy to take Vicksburg. It was one of those strange situations where even though the South was victorious in the battle to hold Grand Gulf, General Grant still came out the winner. After realizing that Grand Gulf was too heavily fortified to capture, he changed his strategy and instead captured nearby Port Gibson, leaving the Rebel forces at Grand Gulf outflanked. The Confederates had no choice but to abandon the fortifications, leaving Grant's route to Vicksburg open.

The South suffered just a few casualties at Grand Gulf. Some of the casualties occurred due to a faulty cannon. One of the 20-Pound Parrott guns burst and killed two men outright. It mortally wounded one other and wounded seven other soldiers in varying degrees.

The other casualties were a direct result of enemy fire from the gunboats trying to pass the fortifications. One of these casualties was Colonel William Wade, General Bowen's chief of artillery. According to a young soldier from Missouri, William L. Truman who served in the 1st Missouri Light Artillery, CSA, and kept a dairy recounting the events of the war, Wade was a colorful and well-liked officer.

"Capt. Wade went to Richmond about Dec. 15th, 1862, and returned with his commission, a Col. of Artillery. He wore his new suit of Confederate gray, trimmed in red and as he is a small man, the trimming seems to be overdone and makes him look too flashy and vain. He is naturally proud, and as he walked about with his flashy suit, we could not keep from chuckling to ourselves, at his ludicrous appearance, and we called him, among ourselves, the 'Red Woodpecker.' But soon we became used to his suit and nothing more was said about it. He had it on when killed, and was perhaps buried in it."

Later in the memoirs, Truman describes Wade's death at Grand Gulf on April 18, 1863.

"The enemy attacked us early and they did their best for more than one hour to silence our guns, came close down to us and were repeatedly struck by our balls. They withdrew without receiving much damage, so far as we could see, but our loss in the death of our beloved Col. Wade is indeed sad, and all of our Missouri soldiers feel his loss. He was a noted personage, and I believe every Missouri soldier knew him where-ever they saw him. He was very popular with the officers and privates, and was honored for his merit and brave soldierly qualities. About the last shell the enemy fired, bursted right in our midst, a piece struck Col. Wade just above his forehead, at the edge of his hair and carried away a piece of his skull, without breaking his brain, but leaving it exposed. He was standing very near me and as he fell, I sprang to his assistance; as I knelt by him and he looked me in the eyes and smiled, he moved his lips several times, and tried so hard to tell me something. His eyes gently and slowly closed and with the smile still on his face, he passed from earth, into the presence of God."

When I found the Memoir and read this passage, it made something Ms. Joyner told me much more understandable.

In talking about the battlefield and what had transpired there, Ms. Joyner told me she had felt a "presence" many times as she went about her daily duties. "I feel sure it is Colonel Wade," she said. "He seems to be trying to communicate." She placed a pencil lying flat on a clipboard and showed me. "When I put a pencil on a clipboard like this, no matter how flat it is lying, it will roll in a certain way. Mind you, it's only certain pencils and never a pen."

Put her experience together with Truman's statement in his memoirs that the Colonel was moving his lips and trying to say something as he died. It makes sense that perhaps Colonel Wade is still trying to communicate whatever it was he tried to say to William Truman over a century ago. Remember they did not have ballpoint pens then, but he would have been familiar with pencils.

Ms Joyner told me she often heard noises, and the doors and windows would rattle when there was no wind to cause it. Perhaps another way he tries to communicate.

Nearby Port Gibson was once a thriving community. It was the third city incorporated in the state and had the state's first library.

During the Civil War it was crucial to Grant's strategy to take Vicksburg from the South. When he could not vanquish Grand Gulf, he successfully attacked Port Gibson. Fortunately he did not destroy it. He is reputed to have said, "Port Gibson is too beautiful to burn."

Today, it's a quaint little town that has much of its historic past on display. Its many churches are well worth a visit. One in particular is interesting for its steeple. Instead of having the traditional cross, it has a gilded hand with the index finger point up to heaven. The present minister claims it is because the original pastor was known to make that heavenly gesture frequently. Another unique feature of this church is the beautiful old gasoliers that once graced the famous steamboat Robert E. Lee.

The local bed and breakfast is the Bernheimer House. It was built in 1901 and has some of the most fabulous stained glass mosaics you will ever see. When Loren and Nancy Ouart bought the old home, someone had actually painted over the mosaics. They have been painstakingly restoring them ever since.

The battle site is preserved just outside town on Old Rodney Road at Point Lookout. It began at the A. K. Shaifer House. The house is not open to the public at this time.

It's hard to leave Port Gibson. It is really a page out of time. But now I needed to turn my attention toward Vicksburg.

Vicksburg

Cedar Grove

Cedar Grove is a buff-colored Greek revival-style home. Galleries and columns grace both front and back. I approached it with my rolling suitcase bumping along the brick path from the back parking lot and circling the swimming pool. It felt warm and welcoming. Nothing like what you expect in a haunted house. Yet the history of this Vicksburg home is a series of fabulous highs and devastating lows. It survived Vicksburg's darkest hours and has the scars to prove it. This cheerful sunny façade is home to many souls who have lived through both personal and national tragedies.

Cedar Grove was never a working plantation; rather it was a showplace; a gift from a loving husband to his young bride. It is an elaborate token of a love story that stood the test of time and remains a marker in Vicksburg's turbulent history.

John Alexander Klein had moved to Vicksburg from Virginia a young man of 24. He was a jeweler by trade and did well in his new hometown. He diversified his earnings and grew wealthy very quickly as he had a finger in many pies: cotton plantations, sawmills, railroads, banking and investment property. In 1838 he was well-respected in Vicksburg and felt he lacked only one asset: a wife.

When he met Elizabeth Bartley Day, a beautiful young Ohio girl visiting nearby relatives in 1838, he knew he had found the one for him. The fact that Elizabeth was only 12 years of age did not deter him. He was a patient man. In 1840 he began construction of Cedar Grove with the intention of gifting his bride-to-be with the most magnificent home in the city. The home was set on eight acres of land, which he had landscaped in elegant style. One of the high points was his 9-foot-deep catfish pond; today it houses darting goldfish. The back yard was a grove of 25 cedar trees, thus the name.

By 1842, the central part of the home was completed and, at 16, Elizabeth was deemed old enough to marry her 30-year-old suitor. He presented her with the gracious home and took her on a year-long honeymoon trip to

Europe, where they searched out the rarest of furnishings for the mansion on the bluff. Money was no object.

The newlyweds returned by way of New Orleans and contracted Prudent Mallard, one of the best furniture builders in the country, to make several pieces of furniture for Cedar Grove. They also brought some treasures from Europe: gold leaf mirrors which are dusted with 24 caret gold, Italian marble fireplaces, Paris window treatments, French Empire gasoliers which burned carbide and water, creating the equivalent of today's natural gas, and one of the most innovative and expensive treasures, Bohemian glass to place above the exterior doorways. It reflects the sunlight to help with insulation; it appears black when viewed from outside and red from within and is mixed with 24-carat gold.

The Kleins began their family, which would eventually number 10 children, and the fairy tale ended and real life stepped in. Of the 10 children Elizabeth bore, only six grew to adulthood. Then there was that worst of Southern ghost makers, the War Between the States.

The siege of Vicksburg found Elizabeth pregnant with her last child. She was six months along, huge and terrified – the house had already been struck by more than 40 cannon balls, one of which is still embedded in the floor of John's Smoking Parlor -- when the opportunity to get to safety presented itself. General Sherman was related to Elizabeth; an uncle by marriage. He offered to transport Elizabeth, her mother and children back East until the war was over if he could use Cedar Grove as a hospital. Elisabeth agreed and thus saved her home from the torch.

The downstairs portion of the present-day Library Suite was the original wine cellar for the home, and, because of its cool temperature, it was used as the morgue during the time the home was a Union hospital. This suite is haunted by many spirits. Many guests note a smell of decay here as if the bodies are still making their presence felt. Others have heard the sound of men marching. But the departed Union soldiers are not the only specters here. Ninety percent of the books in the bookcase are original to John and Elizabeth. Two books, *How to be a Lady in Modern Society*, a favorite of Elizabeth's, and *Notes on Law,* one of John's favorites, are frequently rearranged in the bookshelf by some unearthly presence. Tour guides will frequently attempt to show them and find they have been moved from their normal places.

This is not the only place where you might encounter John or Elizabeth. They still seem to inhabit much of the house, as do the spirits of several of their children. The master bedroom, called the Grant Room as the general stayed in this room for one day after the siege of Vicksburg, is on the first floor near the foot of the stairs, with the adjourning room to the front of the house, now the Bay Room, acting as the nursery. It was in these two rooms that three of the Klein children died. They can be heard playing nearby still. One spirit that is seen occasionally is a young girl bouncing her ball up and down the front stairs between the first and second floor.

Their youngest child met a horrible fate. Born during the siege just months after General Sherman had moved Elizabeth to safety, the grateful mother named him William Tecumseh Sherman Klein. Horrified neighbors swore any child bearing the name of the most-hated general in the history of warfare would be cursed. But Willie grew to young manhood as an intelligent and handsome boy. He was 16 and had just returned from a hunting trip with a friend when disaster struck. He and a friend rested under a magnolia tree in the back yard then, but when his friend tried to get up from the ground, he accidentally discharged his gun. The bullet slammed into young Willie's chest. The wounded boy tried unsuccessfully to seek help by climbing the black iron staircase but only made it part of the way up and fell dead at the foot of the stairs. Guests still hear the footsteps and the thump mostly in the middle of the day.

John's presence is sometimes seen in his original smoking parlor. Many people have smelled cigar smoke in there. More impressive is the story of the employee who was cleaning the room and felt someone standing behind her. When she looked into the pier mirror in front of her, she saw the reflection of a man, but when she turned around, no one was there. Others have had a similar experience.

The back porch, now the Wicker Room, looks out on John's catfish pond. This was also the scene of a terrible tragedy. A small child was playing one day and fell into the pond and drowned. His body was not found until hours later floating in the water. One employee was leaving the office one evening and heard a child scream followed by a loud splash. When she checked the fountain, she found nothing there. At least nothing she could see with mortal eyes.

This room also served as the functional "front" of the house. It was here that carriages dropped off guests for the lavish balls. The carriages then proceeded to the Carriage House just across from it to stable the horses. Guests who stay in the Carriage House suites often hear horses whinnying and stamping their hooves.

The room that parapsychologists agree has the most activity is the ballroom. The cause of this activity occurred many years later after the home had been sold out of the family. The third owners of Cedar Grove were Doctor Podesta and his family. They loved to entertain with fancy balls. Unfortunately one of their daughters was mentally handicapped. To avoid embarrassment, they locked the girl in her room when they were entertaining. During one lavish ball, the daughter escaped from her room. She somehow got a gun and went into the ballroom. There, in front of the shocked guests, she pulled the trigger and ended her unhappy life. It is said that she appears in the ballroom on the anniversary of her death.

I stayed in the Bonnie Blue Room on the second floor and enjoyed it immensely. I had a great view, and the huge old-fashioned bed was comfortable. No bumps in the night awoke me. The inn is so welcoming, and the breakfast in the dining room downstairs is first-rate.

Duff Green Mansion

In 1856 Duff Green built a beautiful new home for his bride, Mary Lake. He built the mansion as a place of enjoyment and entertainment; however, when the war came to Vicksburg with a vengeance in 1863, the home was right in the line of fire. It was struck with cannonballs several times. The Greens decided on the best way they knew to try and preserve their home: They donated it to the Union forces to be used as a hospital.

The Greens moved into two caves they had dug in the backyard while the house was in enemy hands. It was there that Mary gave birth to a son whom she named William Siege Green.

The Union medical staff moved into the home. They treated the Union wounded on the top floor and Confederate wounded on the main floor. The kitchen on the bottom floor was converted to an operating room. Stories tell of amputated limbs piled up several feet high there as hundreds of soldiers were operated on. Many did not survive the treatment.

Today, many visitors to the home note a medicinal smell in this area, and guests staying in the Dixie Room, also located downstairs, have awakened at night to find a one-legged Confederate soldier sitting in the rocker.

After the war, the Federals used the mansion for recuperation of soldiers until they were well enough to travel home. These wounded soldiers lived in the mansion until 1866. Perhaps it is one of these invalid residents who featured in one of the best-documented sightings in the state.

Harry Sharp, who owned the mansion then, showed me the photograph, which caught "someone" not of this earth. He explained how it was taken. "A crime scene investigator was taking random pictures outside. In one he happened to get a shot of the (mansion's) front door. When the print came back, there was a figure of a man in dark clothing right at the door."

Naturally, the investigator was shaken, as when he had shot the picture, no one was visible anywhere near the door. The photograph looks to be of a man wearing a military uniform coat. I was stunned. It would appear one of the soldiers who had recuperated here as a temporary resident has decided to make it his permanent home. Sharp since sold the inn to Harley Halpin and her husband, Rick. They continue the tradition of a gracious southern inn. The "soldier" is still in residence.

When the Greens moved back into the home, they remained there raising their family until Duff died in 1880. Mary then sold it to the Peatross family, who remained there until 1910. They sold to Fannie Vick Willis Johnston, a great-granddaughter of Vicksburg's founder, Rev. Newet Vick. She lived in the mansion until her new home, Oak Hall, now known as the Stained Glass Manor, was completed around 1913. That has a few ghost of its own as well.

Another reminder of those dark wartime days is on the floor at the base of the stairs. Harry showed me the dark spot made by the blood of a soldier who was waiting his turn in the operating room but died before he could be helped. The stains will not come out, no matter how many times the wood is cleaned.

After Mrs. Johnson moved out, the home had a number of uses. It then was used as a Salvation Army home until 1985 when it was bought by the Sharps and restored to its former splendor and opened as a bed and breakfast. In spite of – or because of - the ghostly phenomena, it is one of Vicksburg's most popular.

Harry told me of one of his employees who had lived in the home when it was run by the Salvation Army. She says she sees the same phantom woman, one-legged soldier and child she saw as a child. They never frighten her; instead she feels protected.

Harry said he has seen Mary out of the corner of his eye. She was a pretty blond woman dressed in a long flowing dress. Interestingly, Harry is a descendant of Robert E. Lee and an avid Civil War buff. Naturally, he seems to fit right in with the ambiance of the house.

I spoke with Harry's son, David, while there. He told me of one incident when he heard what he thought was his father coming in. He began talking to him, then looked up and saw no one was there. Maybe it was just no one he could see.

The Vick in Vicksburg

Vicksburg was founded on the site of a community called Walnut hills. A Methodist preacher called Newet Vick planned to establish a town there, but he and his wife died within minutes of each other of yellow fever in 1819.

His sons proceeded with the planned city, and Vicksburg was later incorporated in 1826 and named in Newet Vick's honor. Ever since that time, the name "Vick" had been a lingering part of the city's history. There are two main homes associated with the Vick family, Stained Glass Manor, which was built as Oak Hall by Fannie Vick Willis Johnston, Newet's great-granddaughter, and the Martha Vick House, called "the Last Vick House in Vicksburg," built for the unmarried daughter of Vicksburg's founder, Newet Vick. The home was built in 1830, has been restored and is now open for tours. I'm not sure why it is called the "last," as the Stained Glass Manor was built in 1902 and is actually the real last Vick home built in Vicksburg. Nonetheless, the Martha Vick Home is worth a tour.

So is Stained Glass Manor. Aside from its architecture -- it was designed by George Washington Maher, Frank Lloyd Wright's teacher, who perhaps surpassed his famous pupil with this home -- it has an interesting ghost story. One of the first things you notice when you tour the home is the 36 original stained-glass panels that give the home its name. The architecture is mission-style, and it's massive. The furnishings are exquisite and the staircase gorgeous. There is nothing shy about this beauty.

Likewise, the presences in the home don't hesitate to make themselves known to visitors and residents alike. It gets lots of visitors, as it is a bed and breakfast. Many of the visitors report similar happenings.

There are two phantoms that recur. One is believed to be Fanny herself. The other is the reason they both still remain in this home.

According to Shirley Smollen, the current mistress of the manor, Fanny had a friend with a child who was handicapped -- either crippled or mentally handicapped. Believing they were doing what was best since the child would never be able to help himself, Fanny may have helped her friend suffocate the boy in the attic.

Fanny is frequently seen in what was her bedroom or around the house, and the boy has been seen in the attic. He most often is seen by other boys around his age. One youngster surprised his parents by telling them that he had been playing with "the young boy in the attic." Of course, there was no one staying in the attic at the time. At least not any corporeal child.

Sheffield Carriage Tour

I found one great way to begin a tour of Vicksburg was on the carriage tour. My driver was fairly well-informed and gave me a great overview of the historical district. It certainly spared my legs from extra walking up and down those hills. Besides, there is nothing like riding in an elegant carriage to get into a historical mood. One of the most important buildings that loom over Vicksburg is the Old Courthouse Museum. I viewed it in the distance and resolved it was my first stop after disembarking the carriage.

Courthouse

The Old Courthouse Museum stands on one of Vicksburg's highest hills on land donated by the city's founding family, the Vicks. It has been visited over the years by many famous people, including Presidents Ulysses S. Grant, William McKinley, Theodore Roosevelt and Dwight D. Eisenhower. It was the place one local plantation owner launched the career that would take him to triumph and despair: Jefferson Davis now has an exhibit in the courthouse with whitch he was so familiar.

In fact, the courthouse is brimming with artifacts recalling historic events. One little-known trial points out a common misconception that there were no Black Confederate soldiers. Holt Collier, a black Confederate veteran, who was accused of murdering a white Union officer, was tried there. Holt was acquitted and went on to an illustrious career in his chosen field, bear hunting. In fact, he was the hunt master that led the famous hunt for President Teddy Roosevelt from which the teddy bear got its name. One fact about Holt is important: He served as a Confederate soldier and did not go as a body-servant to Colonel Hinds, his former master.

Marlene and April of the GHG Ghost Hunters, a group from northwest Florida, visited the courthouse and found some anomalies. There were lots of orbs and an unpleasant smell that seemed to come and go in an instant. One of the researchers experienced a feeling of being pushed.

While I was at the courthouse I met Gordon Cotton, at the time he had been curator for 27-plus years and probably knew more of the museum's history than anyone alive. He told me about the courthouse's role in the siege. He explained that since it was so high it made an excellent target for Union artillery and was hit by a mortar, killing two Confederate soldiers. Then they decided what to do to protect the courthouse. They placed all the Union prisoners on the top floor and sent word of the move to the Union forces. The courthouse was not bombarded again.

It was here that General Grant and John Pemberton, the Confederate commander, rode their horses from Pemberton's headquarters and climbed the steps to watch the changing of the flags when Vicksburg was formally surrendered July 4, 1863.

Incidentally, Vicksburg never celebrated July fourth after that until 1947 when General Dwight D. Eisenhower visited the city.

McRaven

McRaven is considered one of the most well-documented haunted houses in the country, so, naturally, it was one of places on my "must see" list. I was greeted by a genial guide. Leonard Fuller told me he had been doing tours at McRaven for more than 14 years. He was quite willing to talk about the house's famed ghosts. "Yes, they are here. We have no control over them whatever. They just come and go at will," he said.

He told about one tour he did. "This little boy kept running off and his mother kept trying to get him to stay with the tour, and he said 'Mother, all I want to do is go play with that little redheaded boy.' Thing is, no little redheaded boy has lived here in the past hundred years. That was one of the Murray boys."

Apparently there are a lot of young spirits at McRaven. Leonard told of another experience. "A research group took pictures in one room got the image of a young lady in a 1900s dress. They also got a picture of something else. When the Murray family lived here, they had a hobbyhorse. When Leyland (Leyland French, present owner) bought the house, he gave the horse to the museum in Jackson. That horse hasn't been here since 1986 and the little girl long before that."

The group was happy with the results of the investigation. "They said that there was more activity here than any other house they had ever been in." Leonard said. "We are considered the third most-haunted house in the United States by their records."

Leonard experienced one incident firsthand. "It was when my mother was sick and I was staying up a lot. I was here at the house with another tour guide, a young woman who was always joking around. She was doing a tour, and I was resting in a rocking chair. I put my hands over my eyes, not sleeping, just resting my eyes, and first thing I know I'm down on the floor. I thought it was the other guide playing a trick, but then I heard her upstairs talking to her tour. First thing, she couldn't have gotten back up there that quick, and second if she had run up and down those stairs, she wouldn't have energy to say a word."

Most incidences have been good or at least neutral, but there was one unpleasant incident. Leonard said the current owner, Leyland French, had a disturbing encounter while cleaning the dining room floor one evening.

"He was down on the floor on his hands and knees, and something shoved him down till it broke his glasses on his face. After that incident, Mr. French brought in an Episcopal priest who came through with holy water to ward off the evil spirits."

During his time at McRaven, Leonard has seen nine of the reported dozen ghosts. "They are just like you and I when you look at them, but then they fade out and disappear," he said.

McRaven House is called Vicksburg's time capsule because it was built in three different times. Each section is preserved to showcase the time it represents.

It was first built in 1796 and expanded twice (1836 and 1839). Then Vicksburg was still called Walnut Hills and was just a frontier settlement. The oldest part of the house is the back section and includes first owner Andrew Glass's bedroom and some of the original furniture. Glass earned his living as a highwayman. He worked under the protection of the Spanish who were in power in Vicksburg at that time. He, his wife and his band of raiders would prey on travelers on the Natchez Trace, which was controlled by the French. After a raid, he would slip back to Vicksburg and Spanish protection. He was finally killed by his wife, who slit his throat.

Another activity that could be responsible for some of its resident spirits is that it served as a way station for the Cherokee as they were forced on the Trail of Tears. Then in 1836 things became more respectable at McRaven.

Sheriff Stephen Howard bought the old home and added a "modern" addition to it for his pregnant young wife, Mary Elizabeth. He built in front of the original section and had it constructed in the Empire style. Unfortunately Mary Elizabeth got very little usage out of her new home. She died in childbirth in the lovely new middle bedroom that same year. She was only 15.

She is the most-commonly seen spirit. Leonard said she is very playful and likes to turn the lights off and on during tours. Mostly she is seen in or near the middle bedroom where she died. Leonard believes she may be looking for her baby. Her shawl is often felt to grow warm to the touch when handled.

Interestingly, the baby survived. The distraught sheriff brought his tiny daughter to people in Yahoo County, MS, to care for. The child never returned to McRaven and in turn had a daughter of her own.

This granddaughter of Mary Elizabeth lived and died in Lexington, MS. Before her death she left a trunk with mementos and relics from her mother with a neighbor. She described a man who would come to pick up that trunk in the future. In 1963 the Bradway family were the first owners to open the home for tours and were researching the history of the home; they sent a man to Lexington looking for information about the Howard granddaughter. He located the house that had been her last residence and spoke with the neighbor who told him the woman he was asking about had left a trunk "for him."

The researcher replied that wasn't possible, as he had just been hired to investigate. The neighbor replied, "She described you to a 'T.' Wait, and I will get you the trunk."

The next owner was John H. Bobb. He was the one who added the front Greek-revival section in 1849 and owned the home during the siege of Vicksburg. According to Leonard, he was the first civilian casualty after the surrender of Vicksburg. He owned a brickyard in Vicksburg at the time and was remodeling since the home had been damaged in the nearby battle. He came home and found several Union soldiers in his newly planted rose garden pulling up the bushes. He threw a brick, slightly injuring one of the men. Since Vicksburg was under martial law at the time, this was a serious offense, so Mr. Bobb felt he needed to explain.

He went to General Slocum's headquarters and told Slocum what had happened. The general promised Bobb he was not in any trouble for defending his home and that the soldiers would not bother him again. However, as he was returning home, the soldiers had been lying in wait and attacked and killed Bobb.

Leonard told of a group of re-enactors who were doing an event at McRaven and saw Mr. Bobb walking back and forth where the old garden was for about two hours before he disappeared.

Although Bobb was the first death at McRaven after the surrender, there is another tale of vengeance and death regarding the mansion.

After Vicksburg surrendered, one of the officers left behind to administer the affairs of the fallen city was Colonel James H. Wilson, acting as provost-marshal. One of his aides was a young man who had previously lived in Vicksburg, Captain McPherson. The captain's knowledge of the ways and customs of the Southern city were invaluable to Wilson, and a strong friendship developed between the two officers.

When McPherson failed to report for duty one day, Wilson was concerned. He ordered a search of the entire city to no avail. That night McPherson appeared to the colonel and told him of his murder by some of the Confederate sympathizers. He did not want vengeance; he just wanted to let his commander and friend know his fate. Since that day, he is one of the many specters to be seen at McRaven.

Belle of the Bends

When 19-year-old Kate Wilson married Murray F. Smith on April 13, 1874, they built their Italianate Revival home on a bluff overlooking the Mississippi River. It was completed in 1876. Today it is called Belle of the Bends, after the Belle of the Bends steamboat. Kate's family owned an ice business in Vicksburg. Considering the lack of refrigeration and the heat in Mississippi, you can see why that would have been a very successful occupation in the 1800s. Murray went on to become a Mississippi state senator.

The mansion is located on Klein Street very near Cedar Grove. Kate died on June 10, 1912, and the home was sold to a jeweler from New Orleans that same year.

The jeweler in turn sold it in 1919 to the Belowe family. And therein lies the beginning of its ghost story. George Belowe loved his home and never wanted to sell it. He felt it should always be on display, so he planned to leave it as a house museum on his death.

But in 1990 Wally and Josephine Pratt fell under the home's charm. Josephine begged George to sell, promising she would open it as a bed and breakfast so it would always be available to visitors. George agreed and sold it to them.

In 2004 after operating the Bed and Breakfast successfully the Pratts sold it to Dan and Mary Ahern Lee, also to be used as a bed and breakfast.

I visited Mary and Dan and discussed history with them. Mary told me that about two weeks after they bought the home and just before they reopened it to guests, Mary decided to try out some of the rooms and see if they were as comfortable as she wished them to be. "We were living on the third floor, the attic,

"I was downstairs at 1:38 a.m. and was in one of the rooms, and I heard footsteps on the stairs. At first I thought this is just an old house. I heard the steps again very distinctly. I ran upstairs and woke up Dan. I told him, 'There is someone in the house; we need to go through the house.' Of course, we didn't find anyone."

A few days later, she saw the former owner and told her about her experience. Mary was stunned at Jo's reply. "She said, 'That would be George, your ghost.' I said, 'Come on, Jo, I don't believe in ghosts.'"

Jo's response did not set Mary's mind at rest. Jo told her, "I didn't either, but let me tell you what happened to me." When she had owned the house, she was arranging the room for guests. She put a bouquet of flowers on the mantel. Jo was the only one home at the time. She went out, and when she returned to the room, the flowers had been moved to the other side of the mantel and turned so all the greenery was facing out.

Mary continued," I still didn't believe in ghosts, but since then I have had the same sort of thing happen over and over. I will be down in the kitchen fixing breakfast, and I will have a guest come in and ask, 'Do you have a ghost?' I reply, 'Why do you ask?' and they tell me a variety of things. Several have felt someone touch their cheek. Others have felt someone sit down on the bed. I have had four different people at different times of the year describe a small man standing near the window. They all describe him exactly the same. Some other people have seen a man on the other side of the room. These people do not know each other. I'm changing my mind about believing in ghosts."

Mary's husband, Dan, has had his own encounter with ghosts. He explained, "I was in the kitchen making lunch. Mary was out running errands. I heard her come in, and I yelled, 'Hey, I'm here in the kitchen.' There was no response, so I figured she had not heard me. These walls are thick. I heard another noise, so I stuck my head out into the hall where she had to hear me and called to her. Still no response. I looked and no one was there. Mary had not returned.

"That was early when we had only been here about three months. About a year later, I came in from the yard to use the restroom and heard someone walk all the way down the hall. I just thought it was a guest. I came out, and again no one was there. Mary wasn't home, and no vehicles were either in front or back."

Mary has also had some strange experiences in the dining room. The place setting at the foot of the table will be missing a piece of silverware when no one has been in the room but her, and she knows she had put it on the table. "It's always the same place setting," she relayed.

Anchuca

Still another Vicksburg mansion with a legend was built in 1837 by Richard Archer. It was named Anchuca. Richard had five daughters he guarded fiercely. One, however, was his favorite. She looked so much like him that her nickname was "Archie." She devastated her doting father when she fell in love with a plantation overseer. Richard forbade the marriage and sent the young man away. Archie became a recluse to the extent of refusing to even eat at the same table with her father. She even refused to sit down for her meals. Instead, she ate each evening at the fireplace mantel.

Her spirit is seen as a young woman wearing a long brown dress standing at her favorite eating spot, the mantle.

It was here that Jefferson Davis made his last public addresses to the citizens of Vicksburg. Davis' brother, Joseph Emory Davis, lived here until his death in 1870.

Walnut Hills

After all my touring, I had worked up a huge appetite. Luckily my guide, Pat Strange, took me to just the spot to fill the bill not to mention the gnawing hole in my middle: Walnut Hills.

Walnut Hills was the original name of Vicksburg before 1819. Walnut Hills, the restaurant, has only been around since 1995. What it lacks in history, it makes up historical recipes from the heart of Dixie. You will find fried chicken and fried catfish, naturally. However, they step out past the traditional with items like an exquisite pork loin with molasses, apple cider and sage.

You can sit at private tables or choose the "round Table" and join fellow travelers in your feast. Either way, the food can't be beat.

I chose the fried pork chops. Yeah, like I really need fried food to help insure that I could not zip up my jeans! At least I passed (regretfully) on the batter-dipped french fries and had the equally delicious baked potato. Of course, I heaped it with sour cream.

Vicksburg Battlefield

Undoubtedly the biggest draw for visitors to Vicksburg is the Battlefield Park. Vicksburg was critical to both sides from the beginning of the war. Until the Union could control the entire river to Cairo, Illinois, it could not prevent the South from supplying its own armies. Whoever controlled Vicksburg controlled the river.

Vicksburg was called the "Gibraltar of the Confederacy." It stood on a bluff guarding the river and was protected by heavy artillery on the bluff and a ring of forts that protected it by land. The key players in this drama were Union General Grant who attempted first to attack the city and then laid siege to compel the surrender, and General Sherman who attempted to take Vicksburg from the south. The chief Confederate here was General John Pemberton, who repulsed the original attacks but could not withstand the long siege.

This was a battle site where not only soldiers were casualties but civilians. The bombardment forced the residents to take shelter in caves. The bombardment was not the biggest killer, however; starvation and disease were the main culprits. The Union forces fouled all the streams flowing into the city and prevented any provisions from reaching the desperate people. By the end of the siege, rats were being sold to those lucky enough to get them at the butcher shops.

The battlefield is considered very haunted, as are most places where this many lives were cut down suddenly in their prime. Reports of cannon fire, unusual fogs, whispers and the smell of gunpowder have all been experienced. Phantom soldiers have been glimpsed among the trees.

The fogs are the most common. There were two different episodes I discovered of people seeing them. One man was visiting an area where some of the heaviest fighting had taken place, and suddenly a portion of the area was engulfed by a low fog that only stood about a foot off the ground.

Another man witnessed a similar occurrence. It was around twilight, and he was in the park for his regular run. He came to the cemetery and saw an eerie fog. It was about a foot above the ground and came up to the middle of most of the gravestones. It only was in that portion of the park; nothing but the graves were engulfed. The cemetery was designated for only Union soldiers. So be sure and visit the National Cemetery. No telling what you might see. If you should see a phantom Confederate soldier there, it's because somehow two Confederates slipped in and are buried there: Ruben White from Texas and Charles Brantly from Arkansas.

Vicksburg's, fall followed by Port Hutson nearby in Louisiana, gave the North full control of the Mississippi River. The Confederacy was sliced in half. The Vicksburg battlefield includes 1,330 monuments and markers, a 16-mile tour road, a restored Union ironclad called the Cairo, the Shirley House -- the only surviving structure in the battlefield -- and a National Cemetery.

Strange things happen in a battle, especially one as fierce as Vicksburg. One of those is the story of Union Maj. Gustavus Lightfoot. He had been saving some expensive cigars for a really special occasion. Just before the battle, he broke open the cigars and passed them around to his comrades saying, "I won't be needing these anymore." Sure enough, he was killed in the next battle.

Battles of this magnitude often leave behind stories of heroism above and beyond. One such story is that of 13-year-old Orion P. Howe, a young drummer and fife player for Company C, 55th Illinois Infantry. Orion was severely wounded in the leg, but he refused to leave the field. Instead, he would crawl up and down the hill to report when his battalion needed more ammunition. He was awarded the Congressional Medal of Honor for his bravery in the field.

The Illinois monument recognizes Orion along with all of its fighting men – and woman. That's right. There was a woman enlisted in the Illinois infantry.

Private Albert D. J. Cashier mustered out with the remainder of the regiment on August 17, 1865, after serving for three years and 11 days in the ranks. But Albert had a secret. "He" was a "she."Even after the war ended, "he" lived as man. Cashier joined the Grand Army of the Republic, the largest organization of Union veterans. When Cashier applied for a pension in 1899, "he" was examined by three surgeons to determine "his" eligibility for a veteran's pension.

It wasn't until 1911, almost 50 years after Vicksburg, that Cashier was struck by an automobile. The doctor who was summoned to examine the old soldier noted a broken leg. Just in case there were other unknown injuries, he further examined Cashier. Imagine his surprise when he discovered that Cashier was a woman but, after listening to the old soldier's pleas, agreed to maintain her secret.

But things did not continue as "he" wished. Just three months later, the old veteran was forced to move into the Soldiers' and Sailors' Home in Quincy, Illinois. Even as "his' health deteriorated, Cashier attempted to continue the male identity. "He" was successful for only three more years when a mental condition led to confinement in an insane asylum at Watertown, Illinois. There she was finally compelled to wear female attire and live the life of a woman. In death, Cashier was partially allowed to revert to the male role. "His" tombstone reads "Albert D. J. Cashier, Co. G, 95 ILL Inf Civil War, Born : Jennie Hodgers, In Clogher Head, Ireland 1843 – 1915."

Pennsylvania's Monument is simple compared to some. It is a granite shaft at the back of an elliptical platform with a flight of three steps. It has five bronze medallions portraying the five unit commanders who fought here. It drew a lot of attention when someone noticed the faces in the medallions "weeping." Apparently, it was not real flesh and blood tears they were shedding but a dripping of the condensation from dew.

One of the most-interesting legends concerns the Wisconsin Monument. It's a granite column that stands 122 feet in height. A bronze statue of an eagle sits atop it. That eagle was Old Abe, the 8th Wisconsin Company C's mascot. He was mean and went through several handlers as he had a habit of biting them until they passed the ornery bird on to another hapless caretaker. Nonetheless, the Company C boys loved him so much they were called the "Eagle Regiment." The Confederates hated him and called him "the Yankee Buzzard." They tried to shoot him but only wounded him once. When the war ended, he was given a place of honor in Madison at the state capitol building. There was a fire, and he died from smoke inhalation, but they had him stuffed and put back in the capitol. Then another fire devoured the tough old bird, but he is honored with a bronze eagle monument in Madison to this day. Legend says you might see his spirit circling the battlefield still.

The battlefield park has the only monument dedicated to African Americans in any national military park. It was erected on 2-14-2004 by the state of Mississippi and honors the units that fought at Milligans Bend across the river in Louisiana. The monument consists of three bronze figures on a base of black African granite. Two of the figures are black Union soldiers, the third a common field hand. The field hand and one soldier support the second soldier between them. That soldier is wounded to represent the sacrifices made by African Americans on the battlefield during the Civil War. The field hand is looking back at a past of slavery, and the first soldier gazes toward a future of freedom.

Another monument with an interesting legend is that of General Grant. Grant is mounted on his horse, Kangaroo. He had three horses he used there. One was called Cincinnati. The other was a small horse he stole from Jefferson Davis' brother's plantation. He named that horse "Jeff Davis." The story is that when the park was open 24 hours, you could come in at night and visit General Grant, and he would tip his hat and look at you.

Be sure to visit the U.S.S. Cairo display, the only such vessel currently restored. It was a Union ironclad that was sunk in the Yazoo River by a torpedo. It went down in 1862 and was raised in 1964.

Sweet Olive

Considering the importance of the river on Vicksburg, what better way to view the city than from a boat? The *Sweet Olive* offered me the perfect opportunity. Not only did it cruise the river along the banks of Vicksburg, it also provided a running narrative of the city's history. The captain was knowledgeable and offered a sometimes-humorous twist to the events that shaped history. I took the sunset cruise, but there are earlier choices especially on Saturday. It's an hour and a quarter of beauty and entertainment. While you are waiting for the boat, visit the city's murals. They depict critical points in the city's history. Currently there are more than 20, and plans are in the works to have at least 35.

Casinos

After all that serious history, a frivolous evening on the casino boats beckoned to me. I tried out two of the four, *Isle of Capri* and *Ameristar*, and enjoyed a great buffet for dinner. Didn't win any cash, however.

As I stood looking from the deck of the floating gaming boat, my thoughts were drawn to the river and its impact on this fabulous town. It was the river that brought it into being in the first place. It was the river that made it so important an objective in that long-ago war. As I gazed at the moonlight reflecting on the water, I couldn't help but wish I could travel back in time and see Vicksburg as it was in 1863. Perhaps what I had seen today was as close as any mortal could come to reliving history.

Longwood

Rosalie

Dunleith

King's Tavern

Vicksburg Courthouse Museum

Walnut Hills Restaurant

Illinois Monument at Vicksburg Battlefield

Battlefield

Chapter 7 North Carolina

Fayetteville

Radison Prince Charles Hotel

If any one city in the South could be called America's Home Guard, surely it is Fayetteville, North Carolina. Settled in 1739 by Scottish immigrants, it played a pivotal role in every America war. From its very inception, the military tradition is deeply rooted in its soul. It began life as two separate towns near the mouth of the Cape Fear River, Campbellton, named for a providence in Scotland, and Cross Creek. The two were joined by an act of Congress in 1783. Today Fayetteville is best known as the home of Fort Bragg.

Perhaps its military history has a direct connection to all the restless spirits found in the area. Before many of the other American Colonies had considered separation from their mother country, a group of 55 Fayetteville patriots met at what is now called Liberty Point on June 20, 1775, and signed the "Liberty Point Resolves," which declared them independent from England and pledged to fight until the end was accomplished. You can visit the site, a small triangular park at the intersection of Bow and Person streets.

Naturally, there were those who chose loyalty to the crown. Flora MacDonald, the Scottish heroine credited with saving the life of Bonnie Prince Charles, was the foremost loyalist and rallied her husband and his followers as they paraded within sight of Liberty Point in 1730.

Today, downtown Fayetteville has preserved four designated historic districts: Downtown Historic District, Haymount Historic District, Liberty Point National Register District and Market House Square National Register District.

When the brand new Prince Charles Hotel arose to its magnificent eight stories in 1925, the city was already well-seasoned. The hotel was an architectural work of art with its Palladian windows and doors; marble floors and staircases; and soaring columns and pilasters. It looked like an Italian palazzo. It was near the railway depot, which was the main means of travel in this time period. In spite of its glamour and glitz, it was not a commercial success at the time and ran into financial difficulties. It was foreclosed on and sold at a public auction in 1929, a scant four years after it opened.

Its European style kept it afloat until it again hit financial snags. This time it had deteriorated so badly that the city condemned it in 1979. It was foreclosed on again in 1990, and the owners filed for bankruptcy. It had known the best and the worst life could offer and still stands like a beacon: a symbol of the city's history.

It was finally purchased by the Radison company, and although it is called Radison Prince Charles Hotel, it seems to only rent apartments on a longer term. They renovated it but I am sure they couldn't evict the spirits that linger. I stayed in it in its actual hotel days. If you are not planning on a long term visit, you could stil do a walk-thru.

I was not sure what to expect when I went to visit the Prince Charles. When I walked through the doorway, I felt I had stepped into the past. Soaring ceiling and gleaming dark wood set off the front desk and doors, and an elaborate chandelier that must weigh a ton illuminated the lobby. There were original doors and a majestic old elevator, although the elevator was for show and did not work.

It does have a few residents who like it so well they just won't leave. One of them may stay because she had no other place to go. Her name was Charlotte, and she was there for her wedding not long after the hotel opened, but she found her groom in bed with one of her bridesmaids. She knew she would never be happy married to this philandering cur and jumped from the eighth floor to her death below.

I spoke to Jacqueline who worked the front desk then, and she told me that Charlotte is most active when there is a wedding going on in the hotel. Jacqueline told me of an experience she had when the elevator doors opened and she saw a shadowy mist inside. No one was in it: no one mortal anyway. This has happened to others as well. Two other staff members witnessed a similar incident just the night before I arrived. Charlotte is known to play tricks with the locks on the guestroom doors

Jacqueline said there are also people who have seen a soldier who had gotten hurt and later died in the mid-1900s.

Some of the most-interesting evidence of a spectral presence came from a trio of ghost hunters, Noah Ankney and two of his group, Shannon Jackson and Tom Kuntz, from Fayetteville Ghost Hunters Society.

They had gone to the hotel to conduct some research. The owner at first refused them, but they rented a room and then were free to roam about the place. Noah said the staff was very helpful.

When they first arrived, they heard a fire alarm go off and feared they would have to leave if there was really a fire. There was not; it was just one of the occurrences they observed.

First thing they did was take the elevator to the ballroom on the eighth floor; however, it wouldn't work normally. At first they could not get it to come when they punched the button. Then it seemed to go slower than normal. There was a wedding in progress, so they could observe unobtrusively. They did get some photographic evidence in room 701, which was where Charlotte had stayed while preparing for the wedding. Their EMF detector kept giving high readings, indicating some energy was present there

However, it was in room 401 that they got the most surprises. At that time that room was used for storage. In the 1930s it was a guestroom, and one night it was rented to the chief of police. He had arranged to meet some other people for dinner but did not show up for the meeting. When they went to his room and had an employee let them in, they were shocked. The chief lay in the bed wounded; it turned out to be fatally. He had been shot in the head with his own revolver. They rushed him to the hospital, but it was too late. His death had never been solved. Was it suicide or murder.

It was here that the investigators caught a strange voice on their EVP. An EVP converts magnetic signals into audible sound. In room 401 they caught a male voice yelling, "Get out." When they asked the presence for his name, they got "J" or "Jay."

They also took some pictures in room 401. Strangely enough when they were developed, there is a reflection in a window of a man wearing a long-sleeved shirt. All of the group was wearing short sleeved ones that night. They also got a picture of three strange faces reflected on a window. One was male, the other two not discernible.

The three faces could indicate the trio of ghosts in the hotel: Charlotte, the chief of police and the soldier. They also talked to a staff member who saw the soldier. He told them he watched as a man in uniform walked into an unoccupied room. When he checked the room, no one was there.

There was a lovely old-fashioned piano on the mezzanine. The trio was admiring it when suddenly it began to play by itself. In fact, it did it three times. No one was up there except them and it was about 2:30 in morning.

Interestingly enough, considering the historic nature of Fayetteville, it is surprising that none of the spirits at the hotel seem to have any historical significance. But that is okay since the town itself has enough history to make even the most avid history buff happy.

Market House

One of the most-striking and significant historical landmarks is the Market House. The original structure on the site was the State House. It was here in 1789 that North Carolina ratified the United States Constitution. In 1831 a devastating fire wiped out more than 600 structures including the State House.

In 1832 the present Market House was built. It is one of only a handful of buildings in America to use this town hall-market scheme that is common in England. It dominated the downtown landscape as it sits at the center of the town's main crossroads. The clock still chimes the hours, and the bell in the cupola still rings at 7:30 a.m. for breakfast, at 1 p.m. for dinner, at sundown, and at 9 p.m., which was once considered the curfew hour. The upstairs served as a base of government, while the lower unenclosed floor was a market for produce and meat markets, cotton peddlers and other goods.

It was here on March 11, 1865, that General Wade Hampton awaited General Sherman as the Union forces advanced into Fayetteville. An enemy soldier attempted to kill Hampton, but he returned fire and killed his assailant instead.

In the early days of automotive history, it was a rite of passage for high school boys to drive through the arches. The building was in use from 1832 to 1906 when the increasing automotive traffic made it impractical.

Today, the city is trying to repurpose the building to tell Black History more appropriately..

Independent Light Infantry Armory

Major Bruce Daws, the commanding officer of one of Fayetteville's most elite quasi-military organizations, the Fayetteville Independent Light

Infantry, took us on a tour of their Armory. The militia was formed in 1773 and remains the oldest Southern militia unit and the second-oldest in the entire country. The interesting thing about the unit is that all the volunteers had to outfit themselves. In times of war, these mostly agricultural men would willingly spend time away at battles. Their ancient regulations required that members must be gentlemen. Any member acting in a manner unbefitting a gentleman would be expelled.

The museum is filled with artifacts related to the military. Its most-interesting exhibit is the carriage used by the Marques de Lafayette when he visited Fayetteville. The museum is free and open by appointment only.

During the War Between the States, the militia was taken over by the Confederates. The state was slow to secede and did so only when President Lincoln demanded that it furnish a large number of troops to defend the union. When they threw in their lot with the Confederate states, they furnished more men than most of the other states. These soldiers fought so bravely that they earned the nickname "Tar Heels." It was a reference to the fact that when they dug in to fight, they held their positions as if they were stuck by tar on their heels.

Historical Complex

The Tar Heels had occasion to fight when Sherman embarked on his Carolina Campaign. There were two things in Fayetteville that Sherman wanted destroyed. The arsenal was something he would not tolerate operating since it was an ammunition and gun factory supplying the rebels. The other thing was more personal. Sherman wanted to burn the city's newspaper, The Fayetteville Observer. The Observer's editor, Edward Hale, was very outspoken about Sherman. He hated the man and reviled him in the pages of the paper. Sherman returned the feeling and wanted to obliterate the Observer and its troublesome editor.

The arsenal was originally a federal project. After War of 1812, Congress decide to build arsenals. It commissioned eight, but only six were actually funded. Of that number, five were for storage, and only this Fayetteville one was a factory. The year 1836 saw the cornerstone laid. Little work was done until 1842. Colonel Bradford was the man commissioned to manage the building and wanted the arsenal to be a showplace. He drastically overspent and rapidly ran out of money. The building was finally complete in 1856, but it was never fitted out with the necessary machinery.

When the militia took over the arsenal after secession, machinery was obtained from Harper's Ferry. The machinery and parts were used to make Fayetteville rifles. Even more important than the guns was the ammunition that was made here by women workers. One record shows that 60 woman produced 900,000 rounds of ammunition in three months.

Today the site contains three entities, combined to create the Museum of the Cape Fear Historical complex, which is a branch of the North Carolina Museum of History. The museum galleries of the complex opened in 1988. Inside the two floors of the museum I found everything from the Native American exhibits through the recent past, covering pirates and Scottish highlanders mingled with Confederate and Union Soldiers. One of the most-interesting exhibits is a Native American canoe from nearby Grays Creek that dates to about 600 AD.

The remains of the original arsenal are scattered throughout a 4½-acre site. Little is left standing, but there are outlines and even a ghost tower. No, it has no spirits; it is just a simulation of what the original tower may have looked like.

The third branch is the Poe House. This is a late-Victorian home built by the family of Edgar Allan Poe – no, he's not *the* Edgar Allan Poe. This Mr. Poe operated a brickyard and bought the land for his home when the government tried to recoup some of its original investment in the arsenal. The house dates to 1897. Poe and his wife, Josephine, raised eight children in the home.

When Sherman arrived in Fayetteville, he spent three days. Since he had no men to leave behind and hold the arsenal, he ordered his head engineering officer, incidentally also named Poe, Colonel Orlando M. Poe, to totally batter and burn the arsenal to the ground.

Just a few houses burned accidentally from the sparks of the burning arsenal. One man who had a home nearby and rented it to the arsenal laborers was Edward Monahan. He and Sherman were friends. They had fought together in Mexican War and so Sherman did not burn his house.

Cool Spring Tavern

Cool Spring Tavern is the oldest structure in the city. It was built in 1788. It got its name from Cool Spring, a natural spring that flows from the bank of Cross Creek beside the tavern. The spring was the public water source from the late 18th century until the early 20th century. The tavern, which once housed the delegates who ratified the U.S. Constitution for N.C., features double porches, a gabled roof and brick chimneys. It's built in the Federal style. The fire of 1831 came close but did not get the tavern. Unfortunately, it's not open to the public.

Heritage Square

Heritage Square includes three historic structures listed in the National Register of Historic Places: The Sanford House, built in 1800; the Oval Ballroom, a freestanding single room built in 1818; and the Baker-Haigh-Nimocks House, constructed in 1804. The trio is owned by the Fayetteville Women's Club.

John William Sanford, a cashier at the Fayetteville bank, purchased the Sanford House in 1823 when he married Margaret Halliday. Prior to that the downstairs served as the bank and John had rented the second floor. Visitors to the home will tell you it definitely has a ghostly presence. The spirit of a woman dressed in black is seen slowly moving up and down on the stairs.

The most-popular belief is that the Lady In Black is the sweetheart of a Civil War soldier. The soldier was killed and buried in the basement, maybe in the old vault that was stored there when the home was a bank. The broken-hearted young lady searched the house over and over for her lost love but in vain. Supposedly she died from a broken heart and continues to search for her love for all eternity.

Another version is that it is the spirit of Mrs. Sanford who lived many years in this house which was her and John's first married home.

When she and John married, her family built a lovely freestanding single room called the Oval Ballroom. It's octagonal on the outside and a splendid oval chamber within. Local legend associated the ballroom with one of the most-famous trials in North Carolina history. In 1850, Anne Simpson was accused of murdering her husband. The prosecutor contended she poisoned her husband by putting arsenic in his coffee in this very room.

The case began on the night of November 8, 1849, when Alexander Simpson, a wealthy carriage shop owner, died suddenly. Autopsy results revealed arsenic poisoning. Ann was the only suspect. A warrant was issued for Ann's arrest, and she was extradited from Cuba where she had fled after Alexander's death.

This was the first time a woman had ever been tried for murder in Cumberland County and possibly in the state of North Carolina. The testimony was titillating: letters hinting at infidelity. Ann's seamstress testified that Ann had showed her a letter from Alexander stating that she "loved another better than me. For the sake of your friends you may stay in my house ... Prepare a bed upstairs for me tomorrow. You can no longer be my wife."

Another piece of evidence was that Ann not only frequented a fortuneteller but also told fortunes herself. The fortuneteller, Polly Rising, foretold that Ann's husband would die within a week. Ann was reputed to have taken her husband's coffee cup, looked into the dregs, and murmured, "I see a sick bed, a coffin, and a dark and muddy road with clouds around."

Some damaging testimony came from a boarder who testified that Ann had served her husband coffee and syllabub, a combination of wine, milk, eggs, lemon and sugar, in the oval ballroom just before her husband got ill.

The most damning testimony came from the town druggist, Samuel J. Hinsdale, who confirmed that Ann Simpson had bought an ounce of arsenic just before her husband's death, which she told him was to kill rats.

Yet in spite of the overwhelming evidence, the jury took only three hours to acquit her. It is believed they were swayed by her attorney, former U.S. Senator D. K. McRae. His impassioned summation was,

You cannot give her peace -- you cannot restore her to joy. No more will the glad sun of prosperity shine upon her way, or the sweet flowers of pleasure spring up in her path. ... Her spring time and summer have faded out and all around, far as her eye can reach, is mantled with the white sheeting of misfortune's wintry snow. But, gentlemen, you can let her live. You can allow her for her allotted time to remain where mercy is sought and pardon be found.

Strange as it is, the story doesn't end here. Ann went to live in South Carolina. She remarried. When her second husband also died and traces of arsenic were found in his body, that jury convicted her and sentenced her to death. Because of the heinousness of her crime, they would not bury her in any Christian graveyard. Instead they sent her body, packed in a wine cask, back to her sister in Fayetteville. There, her sister buried her in a courtyard where the present courthouse now stands.

When workmen were preparing the site to build, they found an old keg, and inside was the skeleton of a young woman.

The Baker Haigh Nimocks House is the third of the group. It is an example of a low country house, believed to be built around 1804.

Art Center

Built in 1911 in an early program of federally financed post office construction, the Beaux Arts style of this stone-and-brick structure is typical of the governmental architecture of the time. Replaced in 1961 by the Federal Building on Green Street, it served as a public library. In 1987 it was extensively renovated and turned to yet another public use as the galleries and office of the Arts Council of Fayetteville/Cumberland County. It is now known simply as the Arts Center. Considered haunted by either an early postmaster or a female librarian, cool spots and noises abound. News channel 14 interviewed Deborah Mintz, executive director, in the catwalk of the center about renovations being done. Back at the studio, an editor who was editing the film asked the reporter, "Who is the woman in black?" the reporter said, "There is no other woman, just Deborah Mintz." The editor replied, "No, look." There just behind Deborah on the film was another woman dressed in black.

I spoke to Sharon Cagey who told me of an incident that happened to her. "I worked there for almost seven years without any incident. Then one night my husband was working on a report for his job and the computer went down, so he came in to the office to work on it. At about 8:30, someone called out 'You're the last ones here.' Not long after that, we started hearing a terrible clatter. He joked, 'It's the ggghooost.' We went upstairs and heard doors opening and closing, but there was no one else in the building. I couldn't get out of there quick enough and dreaded returning in the morning."

Kyle House

Another historic home that has its own permanent resident is the Kyle House. James Kyle was a Scotch immigrant who became a successful merchant in Fayetteville. He built this house after his first home was destroyed in the fire of 1831. He built it with walls 18 inches thick to provide insulation and fireproofing. The style is Greek revival and Italianate architecture.

His daughter, Annie, lived in the house. She had been a nurse during the Civil War. Later she rented it out. In 1960 it became one of the city offices. One night the assistant city manager was working late and saw an image descending from the attic. He felt very cold. After asking some family members, they revealed that the family had "seen things" there. They also confirmed the feeling of being watched that many people have in this house.

Cape Fear Botanical Garden

When you yearn for a touch of nature, it's time to head on over to the Cape Fear Botanical Gardens. This colorful 85-acre garden includes numerous species of native plants, wildflowers, and majestic oaks. It also boasts an authentic 1800s farmhouse and outbuildings. There are nature trails and a gazebo that seems to beckon you to come and rest in its shade.

Vander Light

If you are in the mood for just one more light legend, there is an interesting one just a few miles from Fayetteville in the little community of Vander.

On a dark and stormy night, railroad switchman Archer Matthews stepped out of the little train station to have a smoke. His lantern cast a small pool of light in the starless night. He had a few minutes before the next train was due. He heard a noise on the tracks and leaned over to investigate. The boards beneath his feet were wet, and Archer lost his balance and fell to the tracks below. He lay unconscious for a few moments. Just a few too many moments.

The approaching train was set to barrel past the empty station, as the engineer saw no one waiting to board. When the engineer spotted the tiny flicker of a lamp near the ground and finally saw the switchman's body, he slammed on the brakes. The train screeched against the metal track, but it was too late. Matthews was killed when tons of steel rammed his body.

If you go on a dark night to visit the place where the station once stood, you may see a glimmering light swinging back and forth over the tracks. If you get too close, it may disappear only to reappear just behind you. Skeptics say it is the swamp gas called will of the wisp, but old timers know the truth. It is Archer Matthews searching for the sound that scared him to death.

Fort Bragg

Fort Bragg was opened in 1918. At the end of WW1 the army saw the need for a field artillery training base. The army found the perfect spot near Fayetteville. The base was named for Confederate General Braxton Bragg, a native North Carolinian. Today it is one of the country's best-known bases and the home of America's Special Forces.

The Airborne & Special Operations Museum

The Airborne & Special Operations Museum is the only U. S. Army museum not located on an army base. It is conveniently located in downtown Fayetteville and offers a tribute to our fighting men and women around the world. The museum showcases the history of the Special Forces from 1940 to the present. It begins with the inception of the U.S. Army Parachute Test Platoon and ends with today's airborne and special operations units. WW II, Korea, Vietnam and the Gulf War were all interpreted very graphically. When I visited the museum, there were soldiers from each of those wars to tell us about what life was like as a Special Forces soldier in each of those wars. The Yarborough-Bank Vistascope Theater tried its best to make me dizzy with its specially filmed videos that put you into the action in the most-realistic way. If you think IMAXC is up close and personal, give this a shot. If you are afraid of heights, be prepared to hold onto your seat.

The Pitch, Roll, and Yaw Vista-Dome Motion Simulator really did succeed in making me dizzy. It was so realistic I was afraid "the plane" would crash and I would be killed. This is one you only want to pass up if you are pregnant or have a bad heart.

Leaving Fayetteville, I had to consider the price of freedom. This is a town where heroes past and present can be found both in the well-preserved museums and right out on the streets where a uniform is as common as a suit or jeans.

Chapel Hill, Durham, and Raleigh

The Carolina Inn

Telling the history of Chapel Hill and the University of North Carolina is like speaking of Siamese twins: You cannot tell one without the other. They share a joint birthday. On the day the first lot in the village was sold, October 12, 1793, the cornerstone for the first building at the university, Old East, was laid. This was the nation's first state university. So too the Carolina Inn's fate is interwoven with the city and the university. The city was originally named New Hope Chapel Hill in honor of the chapel on the hilltop that once stood where Carolina Inn stands today: right in the center of town.

The Carolina Inn came about because of one alumnus' sleepless night in a hotel from hell. John Sprunt Hill graduated from the university in 1889. He was staying at a hotel on Franklin Street, Chapel Hill's main thoroughfare. It was early fall and the heat was keeping him awake when as he later explained, he was invaded by "twelve or more big rats which suddenly fell upon a number of mice and chased them, squeaking with all their power, over and under my bed."

Being an intelligent and successful businessman, he did the sensible thing: He dressed, left his visitors to their pursuits and took a stroll on the moonlit campus. He sat on a rock under an oak tree and there "came the vision of the Carolina Inn."

Now, under those circumstances, you or I might have thought, "Yes, a new clean inn free of rodents would be nice," but Hill had the wherewithal and the clout to make his dream a reality. He had a vast personal fortune and many influential connections along with being a university trustee.

Hill contracted Arthur Nash, a Harvard and Ecole de Beau Arts-trained architect, to design the inn to fit in with the renovations going on at the same time to unify the appearance of the campus. Since Nash was already involved in this restoration, he was the perfect man for the job.

The inn was completed in 1924 and in 1935 Hill deeded it to the university. His plan was not for a grand hotel that would be a big income producer but rather a "home for returning sons and daughters of their alma mater."

During its first decade, the Carolina Inn transformed the reputation of accommodations in Chapel Hill. One of the university's most-famous alumni got his start right there in the Carolina Inn's ballroom. As a student, Andy Griffith worked in the dining hall as a busboy making $8 a week. When he first came to the university as a young freshman in 1944, he was homesick and not at all sure how he would do in this big new world so different from Mount Airy. He came to love Chapel Hill and the university, and in a later letter described the city as "one huge park" where the "sun is shining brilliantly and all the earth is blossoming."

He had reason to appreciate the university even more when he performed in the ballroom just two years after his graduation. The monologue he did for $25 that night, "What it was, was Football," was later recorded and set his feet on the path to stardom.

The war years saw an influx of servicemen and their families who came for training at the university. Much of the inn's accommodations were used to house those preparing to defend their country.

After the war, servicemen taking advantage of the G. I. Bill flocked to the University of North Carolina to pursue the dreams they had postponed to serve their country. It was in these years that the inn's favorite specter took up residence.

Dr. William Jacocks was a physician and UNC professor who had spent his younger years working as a physician in the international health division of the Rockefeller Foundation in India. He returned to Chapel Hill in 1948. His original plan was to stay at the hotel until he purchased a home, but he was so happy with the service at the inn, he decided to stay -- and stay he did. In life, he was a jolly man who was given to playing practical jokes on friends. He also was a meticulous researcher who did not want anyone to rearrange his papers. The activities in the hotel fit his personality. Guests today will smell flowers. He also moves items around. Keys will not work. Guests will be locked out of the suite, or the doors will stick and become unable to be opened. One time it was so bad, the staff had to remove the door to get into the suite.

Management believed that would end when electronic keys were introduced in the 1990s, but it continued. A great nephew of the ghostly doctor,

Frank Jacocks, had just a slight recollection of his ancestor. One thing he did recall of his great uncle: "He loved the University of North Carolina and Chapel Hill and the inn. He loved it so much there, it very well could be true."

They brought in a ghost hunter, Christopher Moon. He picked up many orbs and indicated that there was more than one presence in the inn. Most activity other than in Jacocks' suite occurs in the older section, particularly the ballroom.

Dr. Jacocks lived in suite 252, but contrary to popular legend, he did not die at the hotel. Apparently he still prefers that suite since that is where most of the paranormal activity takes place. No one ever feels threatened by the spirit. It's just that he wants to make his presence known. Bellmen and housekeepers have reported sightings, and many have heard noises and rustling of papers, but for the most part, it's just his fixation with keeping other people out of his suite that guests experience.

Today, the hotel offers accommodations to visitors with or without connection to the university. For former students of UNC there is an emotional bond. For others, it is a wonderful place to stay. Dining in the inn is not neglected either. Piedmont is the more casual dining area and Carolina Crossroads is the main dining room. It is casual rather than elegant and one of only two four-star restaurants in the state.

The Inn has been remodeled many times, but the essence of John Sprunt Hill's dream still remains. It is "home" when you are visiting Chapel Hill.

Gimghoul Castle

The Carolina Inn is not the only haunted spot in Chapel Hill. In the Historic Gimghoul District, you will find a stone castle. The building itself is the property of a secret fraternal society. The society was the brainchild of five university students. It began in fall of 1889. The group knew they wanted to father a society but were undecided as to its nature. That is until they attended a lecture by the then-university president, Dr. Battle. He told the story of a school mystery, the legend of Peter Dromgoole. The young founders instantly knew what direction their society would take. They formed the Order of Dromgoole, which they quickly changed to Gimgoole and then to Gimghoul.

The legend involves a young student named Peter Dromgoole. Peter was a rather headstrong and wild young man from Virginia, the son of wealthy and influential parents. He had a fondness for cards, drink, fast women and reckless living. That is until he met the love of his young life, Miss Fanny.

Peter forsook his wild ways and began to meet Fanny regularly at a spot called Piney Prospect near a small spring that today is called Miss Fanny's Spring. They pledged unending love there.

Unfortunately for Peter, Fanny had a former boyfriend who did not want to relinquish his claim on the lovely lady. He challenged Peter to a duel. The two young men and their seconds met one night at Piney Prospect. They stood back to back, and after their seconds failed to dissuade them, took 20 steps, then turned and fired. When the smoke cleared, Peter lay dead on the rocky ground. Suddenly the students realized the enormity of what they had done and hurriedly buried Peter under a large rock. They pledged never to tell what had occurred.

The next day, Fanny came to the spring to meet Peter. He never came, and the dejected young woman waited sitting upon the very rock where her lover lay in a shallow grave. She noticed a peculiar reddish stain on the rock but never associated it with Peter's non-appearance.

The legend goes that year after year Fanny still came to the rock waiting in vain for her love. An uncle of the dead boy came to the university to find out what had happened and claimed to have unearthed a different story. His version was that Peter, being the willful person he was, had a disagreement with a professor and refused to take any exams for that professor. The professor was going to fail him and to avoid the disgrace; Peter fled the school, joined the army under the name of his roommate, Williams, and later died in Europe. However, no evidence of any enlistment by either a "Williams" or a "Dromgoole" that match the date 1833 or the general age of Peter has ever been found.

Today, students who frequent the area after dark say strange things can be seen there. Perhaps it is the spirit of Fanny still searching, or maybe it is Peter's ghost who seeks to avenge his death. Whatever, many students believe the rock and the castle beyond are haunted.

Castle? No one mentioned a castle being there when Peter and Fanny met! Well, the castle is the next step in the story.

When the order's founders decided to use the legend as the basis for their secret society, they modeled it on the love story of Peter and Fanny and on Arthurian principals of chivalry. The order was limited to junior classmen or higher and faculty males. It remained popular and prospered well into the 20th century. Then in 1915 a Durham land speculator tried to purchase Battle Park from the university.

This was "sacred ground' to the order because it was there that Peter Dromgoole allegedly had been killed. They made a counter offer and purchased the land. In 1923 they sold their old lodge house and began construction of a grand castle befitting King Arthur himself. They divided Battle Park into thirds: one part was donated back to the university to be used as a park, one part was sold for individual residential development, and one part was the site of their stone castle that still stands in the Historic Gimghoul District neighborhood.

It's private property but you can easily see the castle from the road.

Horace Williams House

Chapel Hill is a city that is very interested in preserving its history. Thus it's fitting that the place that houses the Preservation Society of Chapel Hill is not only a historic structure but also a haunted one as well.

The Horace Williams House is one of Chapel Hill's oldest homes. The house at 610 East Rosemary Street began life in 1849 as a simple farmhouse. Benjamin S. Hedrick bought the property from the University of North Carolina for $300 in 1855.

Benjamin Hedrick was the only person ever dismissed by UNC for his political beliefs. He was an outspoken opponent of slavery and was burned in effigy by enraged students.

He got the last laugh when he returned during reconstruction to work with University President Andrew Johnson and North Carolina Governor Jonathan Worth to restore North Carolina to the Union. He is the one who added the octagonal room.

When he left in disgrace, he sold the house to H. Hosea Smith, another professor at the university, in 1857 for $1,500. Smith, while not as outspoken as Hedrick, was a New Englander and not a staunch supporter of the Confederacy either.

Several students set off a charge of gunpowder under his classroom chair in 1861 because he had not volunteered for the Confederate Army. He forgave his students and continued to teach his class, much less explosively, until the university closed temporarily during Reconstruction. He was a close friend of Governor Zebulon Vance, who visited the house frequently during Smith's tenure. Smith's son, Hoke, became governor of Georgia and later secretary of the interior under President Grover Cleveland.

The house next passed to George T. Winston, a professor of Latin and later president of UNC. He added the next addition comprised of the front parlor and the front porch, and he enclosed the entrance hall, which became the south parlor.

In 1897 it came into the possession of the last private owner, Horace Williams. It is Williams who gives the house its name and continues to reside in the house. He was a professor of philosophy at the university where he was considered somewhat of an eccentric. His students, who included novelist Thomas Wolfe, playwright Paul Green, United States Circuit Judge John J. Parker, United States Senator Josiah William Bailey, and historian and educator Albert Coates, loved him and spent many hours in his living room discussing the state of the world.

When he died in 1940, he bequeathed his beloved home and its furnishings to the university. Although the Preservation Society manages and maintains it, it is still the property of UNC because the provisions of Williams' will decreed it could never be sold or transferred.

Although the good professor has been dead more than half a century, he still enjoys his home. One university employee who rented the house claims Williams visited her. Residents have seen items move around, rocking chairs rocking by themselves and lights flashing, and hear footsteps in the dark and toilets flushing themselves.

The rumors of haunting were so consistent that the university brought in psychic investigators, Seven Paranormal Research, to determine who or what was in Dr. Williams' house. The investigation was done as a learning seminar and had 21 people present. Several people did sense a presence, but due to the large numbers, there was no conclusive evidence obtained.

Whether or not you experience anything paranormal in the house, its history and unique combination of architectural styles make it worth a visit.

North Carolina Botanical Garden

While in Chapel Hill, I had to take time to stop and smell the flowers- and the herbs ... and the trees ... and the ferns. The North Carolina Botanical Garden has all these and more. I started in the Totten Center.

The gardens have so much that you don't usually find in a garden, from carnivorous plants to an aquatic collection. There are raised beds where individuals with physical or emotional limitations, injuries, dementia and other issues can enjoy therapeutic gardening sessions with a trained horticultural therapist and volunteers. Admission is free.

Another unique feature of the garden is the Paul Green Cabin. This cabin was moved to the site in 1991. It belonged to Paul Green, a former teacher of philosophy and drama at UNC and the Pulitzer prize-winning author of many different types of play including the outdoor drama, The Lost Colony. He was inducted into the Theatre Hall of Fame in New York in 1993. His cabin has became a focal point in the field of ethno-botany, the relationship between plants and cultures, due to Green's interest in Southern culture in relation to the plants people used in the southeast. Green is believed to have re-constructed the cabin in 1925, and he used it as a writing studio for 26 years.

Orange County Historical Museum

For a museum with a broad scope, head over to Hillsborough, just next door to Chapel Hill. This museum covers the entire county with exhibits that look at the area peole form earliest to 20th century.l

Hillsborough is one of the oldest communities in the area. It was founded in 1754. Haunted Hillsborough Tours does historical ghost tours.

Alexander Dickson House

One of Hillsborough's oldest houses is the Alexander Dickson House. This house dates back to the late 18th century. It was moved from its original location a few miles southeast of Hillsborough where it had served as Confederate General Wade Hampton's headquarters and features an office that had been used by General Joseph Johnston prior to the surrender of his Confederate Army to General Sherman. Today this plain-style Quaker home is the Visitors Center of Hillsborough; you can tour it for free and collect information on all the Hillsborough attractions at the same time.

Burwell School

One of the most historically important sites in Hillsborough is the Burwell School Historic Site. The main house was built around 1821 by William Adams. It was purchased in 1835 by the Presbyterian Church for a parsonage for their new pastor, Robert Burwell, and his wife Anna. It became so much more over the years.

When the Burwells moved in, they had two children, John and Mary, and Anna was pregnant with the third of her eventual 12 children. Robert's salary was small, $400 a year, so Anna began a school for young ladies to supplement his income.

They constructed a two-room brick building just west of the home to use as a schoolroom. There were enough bricks left over to construct a brick "necessary."

The school evolved into their main focus. Robert resigned his pastorate to devote full time to the school. Eventually, they took in boarding students as well as local ones. The school only educated about 200 young women, but its importance lies in that many of these women also began schools of their own. The Burwells are considered one of the primary educational influences in women's education in North Carolina.

The Burwell School was also home to another famous person for several years. A North Carolina State Road Marker denotes it as the home of Elizabeth Hobbs Keckly.

Elizabeth, or Lizzie as she was called, was a young slave girl probably around 14 when she was loaned to Robert Burwell by his father in 1831 to accompany the Burwells to their new home in Hillsborough. She remained at the school from 1835 to 1840. Unlike most African Americans of the era, Lizzie was literate and kept a diary, which she later used to publish her memoirs, "Behind the Scenes," also referred to as "Thirty Years a Slave and Four Years in the White House."

Her years at the Burwell School reveal a different side of the Burwells and their prominent white neighbors. Lizzie began her life in Virginia. She was the child of Agnes Hobbs, a slave woman, and her owner, Col. Armisted Burwell. Her nominal father, George Hobbs, was owned by a neighbor and taken away from the family when Lizzie was around 7. Agnes was the plantation seamstress and taught young Lizzie her skills. They would serve her well in later years.

While at the Burwell School, she was beaten by a neighbor, William Bingham. Bingham was the village schoolmaster and a friend of the Burwells. Lizzie reflects that while Mr. Burwell was generally kind, Mrs. Burwell disliked her and used her influence to cause her husband to treat Lizzie more harshly. When she confronted Mr. Burwell as to why he had allowed her to be beaten, he struck her with a chair, knocking her down.

Things did not get better. She was raped and had a child by a neighbor of the Burwells, Alexander Kirkland. She named the child George after her "father" and shortly after that was sent away back to Virginia to serve Robert's younger sister, Ann Burwell Garland.

Mr. Garland was not prospering, to say the least. He moved the family to St. Louis to try and improve his fortunes but still had no luck. The family was very poor and the idea was brought up to put Agnes out to work as a seamstress. Lizzie was horrified and begged, "No, a thousand times no! I would rather work my fingers to the bone, bend over my sewing till the film of blindness gathered in my eyes; nay, even beg from street to street. I told Mr. Garland so, and he gave me permission to see what I could do. I was fortunate in obtaining work, and in a short time I had acquired something of a reputation as a seamstress and dressmaker. The best ladies in St. Louis were my patrons, and when my reputation was once established I never lacked for orders. With my needle I kept bread in the mouths of seventeen persons for two years and five months."

While in St. Louis, Lizzie married James Keckly, whom she believed to be a sober hardworking freed man. James was neither and within eight years died from his excesses.

Lizzie had often broached the idea of buying her freedom, and now she went about it in earnest. Some local women for whom she had sewn loaned her the necessary $1,200. At last, she and her son were free!

She went to Baltimore and then Washington and set up her own dressmaking business. Soon she was making the finest ballgowns for ladies in society's highest strata. Mrs. Robert E. Lee and Mrs. Jefferson Davis were among her clients. But what changed her life was when she fashioned a gown for Mary Todd Lincoln.

She became a close friend and confidante of Mrs. Lincoln and remained so until she published her book. She used the book to defend and explain the troubled first lady; however, Mrs. Lincoln felt her confidences had been misused and refused to speak to Lizzie again.

I could not find any references to any spirit in the school buildings, but the church and Old Town Cemetery next door are a different matter.

Presbyterian Church

The church Robert Burwell pastored continues to prosper. One man was a generous benefactor: Shepperd Strudwick, born in 1868, grew to love his church and his hobby, wood carving. Both loves have come together at the Hillsborough Presbyterian Church.

As a young man, he was restless and moved first to Richmond and then to Tennessee. However, he came back to his hometown of Hillsborough and became a staunch elder in his church. When he retired, he spent much of his time woodcarving. One of his pieces is a magnificent cross that hangs in the church.During the pastorate of the Reverend Charles Homer Reckard, in 1957, the church honored Sheppard Strudwick by the addition of Strudwick Hall.

After the hall was built, members and visitors to the church report seeing a man that resembles Strudwick entering the church and in the sanctuary.

The church brought in experts from Duke University's Rhine Research Center who found paranormal activity. In the course of the investigation, Duke investigators took several pictures.

The pictures had been sitting on a desk in the church; however, they soon disappeared.

Ayr Mount and Poet's Walk

Robert Burwell's friend Alexander Kirkland lived in one of the most-beautiful Federal-style homes in the Hillsborough area, Ayr Mount. The home was built in 1815 by his father, William, who emigrated from Ayr, Scotland, in the 1780s. William was not born to money. He earned his right to this magnificent home he built for and to enjoy with his wife Margaret and his 14 children.

When you visit Ayr Mount, it sits well back from Saint Mary's Road. But in 1815, its arrow-straight brick walk led straight to the old Halifax Road, which in turn had once been the Old Indian Trading Path. This was no accident; Kirkland's wealth was built on trade. He fit the stereotype of the thrifty Scot. He worked his way up the ladder of success from a lowly clerk to store owner and later as owner of a tannery and a cotton gin.

For the architect, the home is a treasure since it remained in the same family until it was purchased by preservationist Richard Jenrette in 1985. It has not been drastically altered since it was built. Jenrette donated the house, the furnishings and the grounds to Classical American Homes Preservation Trust, and today it's open to the public as a house museum. Ayr Mount is unique in several ways: It is built of brick where most homes of the period were frame, the woodwork is a mixture of Georgian and

Gothic, and it has its own resident spirit. The docent I spoke to said she had never seen or felt anything, but she did tell me they had brought in a psychic who did verify a presence in the home. It seemed to be localized in one place, which she did not reveal. She did tell me it is odd that many people when they reach that room do ask, "Do you have a ghost here?"

Leaving from Ayr Mount, take time to stroll the mile-long Poets Walk. The trail follows the Eno River, passes the ruins of an old tavern, and parallels the Old Indian Trading Path. The Indians who used the Old Trading Path are the Occaneechi Indians. You can also visit the nearby Occaneechi Indian Village, behind the Orange County Sheriff's Dept. It's a reconstructed 17th-century Occaneechi village on the banks of Eno River, close to where the tribe had its village site 300 years ago.

Regulators Marker

There is one more item nearby, a monument that marks the site where six Regulators were hanged on June 19, 1771, by the Royal Governor Tryon when they refused to pledge allegiance to the Crown following a battle at Alamance Creek. This is believed to be a precursor to the American Revolution. The Regulators were a group of North Carolina farmers who refused to accept the corruption of the king's officials and led a protest. They were captured and several were hanged. The graves of the six hanged here are reported to be on the nearby banks of the Eno River. The sign reads, "On this spot were hanged by the order of a Tory Court, June 19, 1771, MERRILL, MESSER, MATTER, PUGH, and two other Unknown Regulators."

As might be expected, the spirits of these early revolutionaries do not rest easy in their unknown graves. People wandering nearby at night have heard moans and sounds of men in distress.

Nash-Hooper House

How those brave Regulators must rejoice in the house just a few blocks away. The Nash-Hooper House is the only surviving residence of a signer of the Declaration of Independence in North Carolina. William Hooper was one of three North Carolina signers. It also has an interesting ghost story related to him.

The home was built in 1772 by Francis Nash, a brigadier general in the Continental Army who died during the Revolution.

William Hooper then bought the home and lived in it until his death in 1790. He was then buried in the adjourning Old Town Cemetery. His story doesn't end there, however. In 1894 Hooper's remains were moved to Guilford Courthouse National Military Park, N.C., but considering he had laid in rest for more than a hundred years, the body was so badly decomposed it was impossible to be certain all of Mr. Hooper was really moved. Legend is that he is seen walking the roads between the two burial spots searching for his missing parts.

Unfortunately, the home is not open to the public – the cemetery is, though -- but is well worth a drive past because of its historical significance.

As a university town, Chapel Hill has one of the nation's highest educated populations. They are one point of the famed Research Triangle that also includes Durham and Raleigh.

Duke Homestead

When you think of Durham, you probably think of tobacco, and there is one name associated irrevocably with tobacco and the city of Durham. Just outside Durham is a memorial to one man's resourcefulness. When a young farmer, Washington Duke, built his home in 1852 on his small farm, he never dreamed it would be a National Historic Landmark one day. But this two-story frame house was to become the birthplace of one of the largest industries in the United States.

He had begun experimenting with Bright Leaf Tobacco when the War Between the States broke out. He joined the Confederate Navy to help defend his home state even though he opposed slavery. He reached the rank of lieutenant and was captured by Union forces just days before the end of the war when they took Richmond. He was walking home with just a $5r Confederate bill in his pocket when he met some Union soldiers who traded him 50 cents American money for the bill. When he arrived at his plundered farm, that 50-cent piece was all he had to his name. That and four children.

He did find a little tobacco that the raiding Union Army had missed. With that tobacco he began his dream of a tobacco products factory again. He and the children began a small factory on the premises.

The factory was so successful that by 1872 he moved it into Durham and 10 years later began mass producing cigarettes. Today, that small farm where it all began is a living history museum.

Along with the farm and early factory buildings, there is another museum, the Tobacco Museum, which traces the history of tobacco.

Both of Washington Duke's wives died young. Mary Caroline Clinton, his first wife, died in 1847; she was just 22. His second wife, Artelia Romey, died in 1858 at the age of 29. However, one of these ladies may still be managing the Duke Homestead from beyond the grave. A former employee at the Duke Homestead claimed to have had an unnerving experience when he worked there. He said that when he sometimes spent the night at the homestead in the course of his job, many nights he saw a light coming from inside the empty farmhouse. He also reported seeing a woman, dressed in 19th-century clothing, through the window when there were no workers or visitors in there. Because of the clothing, it would most likely be one of Washington's wives.

Since I have never been a smoker, I was in for a new experience. I saw the growing tobacco and realized it was a beautiful plant. When we visited the drying barn, I was surprised at how pleasant the tobacco leaves smelled. Perhaps the thing that impressed me most was how modest the beginnings were of what was to become the largest tobacco manufacturing company in the United States, American Tobacco.

Duke University

There are those who begrudge a fortune made by the sale of tobacco. Well, the Duke family put a lot of that fortune to good use. One of the best things they did with their money was help fund Duke University.

Duke not only offers a first-rate education to thousands of young people, but it also provides several attractions a visitor should not miss. One of which is the Duke Chapel. The gothic spires of the chapel tower above the campus. This is no accident. In 1925, James B. Duke oversaw Duke University's West Campus' site; he placed the chapel on highest point. The chapel was the first building planned and the last one completed. It is also the only place on campus with a ghost story, which is really unique since colleges almost always have ghosts stories attached.

The chapel story goes like this: One night in the 1930s, several gravediggers were hired to quietly move the remains of three men from their family cemetery to the Memorial Chapel at Duke University. The remains to be removed were those of Washington Duke and his sons, James Buchanan Duke and Benjamin Newton Duke. The move was effected, but apparently James does not rest easily. A medium who investigated during the presidency of Terry Sandford claimed she "saw" James Duke dressed like Jesus in the crypt area of the chapel. She said he wanted her to arrange a meeting with Doris Duke to "find the truth," but the meeting never took place, so no one knows what "truth" he was seeking.

However, a phenomenon in the chapel occurs so frequently that it has been named the 'ghost chapel': A strange unexplainable shadow appears when the chapel is lighted and photographed from certain angles. So when you visit, do take your camera and shoot lots of night pictures.

Nasher Museum of Art

From the oldest building to one of the newest is just a short trip. Nasher Museum of Art is located on the Central Campus. It's named for Raymond D. Nasher who recently died. The museum opened in October 2005 with a large chunk of art donated from Nasher's private collection. The art there ranges from medieval to modern. The museum also features things not usually thought of as art such as a video of a modern version of *Rape of the Sabine Women*. I hate to admit it, but that didn't make a lot of sense to me. Maybe I lack something in art appreciation. Go see it for yourself and decide.

The museum also had a neat little café. As it was lunchtime, I checked it out. Since the museum is emphasizing contemporary art, the emphasis here is also on the latest trend, fresh and organic. It's food art on a plate.

Sarah P. Duke Gardens

After lunch it was time for a stroll in the park, the Sarah P. Duke Gardens. There are more than 5 miles of walkways to stroll surrounded by nature's most gorgeous floral creations.

Lemur Center

If you have planned ahead and called for a tour, you can enjoy more nature at Duke. The Lemur Center has the largest lemur refuge in the country, with 233 lemurs of several different species. These ancient prosimian relatives of monkeys, apes and humans developed on the island of Madagascar. Since they had few natural predators and lush habitats, they flourished until human overpopulation began crowding them out. The human population of Madagascar is doubling every 25 years, and one third of the lemur species have become extinct. This is a great place to observe these fascinating animals in natural-type surroundings. Remember you MUST have an appointment for a tour; you cannot just walk in and tour.

Greystone Manor

The Duke family had many relatives who also built mansions in Durham. Few of these have survived to offer a glimpse into the way of life of these tobacco millionaires. One such home is Greystone.Fortunately, it remained in the same family until it was purchased in 1998 by Randy and Leslie Brame who painstakingly restored it to its former glory. It was an inn or many years. It is no longer open to the public.

The Chauteasque-style beauty was built in 1910 for James Edward Stagg, a nephew of Dr. Bartlett Durham, the city's founder and a grand nephew of Washington Duke. His marriage to Mary Washington Lyon, Washington Duke's granddaughter, made the family as close to royalty as Durham has. In short, they were the cream de la cream of North Carolina society, and their mansion reflects their lofty station.

The two-and-a-half-story mansion was built of limestone blocks and brick with a granite foundation from Mr. Stagg's own quarry in Vance County, also named Greystone. The interior is decorated with Georgian-revival woodwork of mahogany, tiger oak and Italian walnut.

James was not destined to enjoy his home for long. He died in 1915 leaving behind his wife and their three children. When Mrs. Stagg died in 1945, she left the home to her youngest daughter, Mary, who, along with her husband, had already moved into the home to help her mother several years earlier.

In the '60s, the second floor of the home was divided into apartments while the family lived on the first. When the Brames bought it, they restored it with an eye to keeping the Stagg family heritage alive by keeping existing family pieces when possible or acquiring similar furnishings to replace missing pieces.

I stayed at the Greystone with some other journalists when it was an inn, and Leslie gave us a tour. She explained how important it was to her and her husband to preserve as much family history there as possible. "James' grandson told us that there had been a grandfather clock standing in the entryway. We found one from 1906 and put it in the same spot."

Some of her other finds include a 250-year-old Baccarat chandelier from France in the dining room and a 1910-matched pair of chandeliers from a New York penthouse that ended up in the morning room and the music room.

One of the things the Brames may have acquired along with the home was a quiet spirit. Leslie said she has not really seen anything, but people do sometimes mention strange happenings. While we were staying there, one of our number got a photo of an orb in the music room. Leslie could not account for who the spirit might be.

Both James and his wife died during their ownership of the house, and in researching, I found that the family had donated money to their church to purchase an organ and chimes, and Mary had donated funds to implement a music program at their church. Ironic that the presence manifested in the music room of a family so interested in music. Perhaps it is Mary or James enjoying the room that is so little changed since their lifetime.

Stagville Plantation

Another property connected to tobacco and indirectly to the Staggs is Stagville Plantation located about seven miles north of Durham. It grew from humble beginnings to a huge enterprise and one that still harbors a chilling reminder of the evils of slavery.

It all began when Richard Bennehan moved to North Carolina from Virginia in 1768. He found work operating a general store. He also found romance and married Mary Amis. The couple had two children, Rebecca and Thomas. In 1787 he bought 66 acres from widow Judith Stagg and opened his own general store located directly on the Old Indian Trading Path. The store prospered, and the same year he built the first section of his home. It's still standing today and open for tours.

In 1799 he added a two-story addition to his home. By this time he had 3,815 acres. When Rebecca, married Duncan Cameron, a wealthy Hillsborough lawyer, in 1803 the family land holdings increased again. In 1807 Duncan Cameron, Richard and his son Thomas merged their holdings to create the largest plantation in North Carolina: more than 30,000 acres. Naturally they needed laborers to plant and harvest the tobacco and other crops they grew, and the plantation became home to more than 900 enslaved people.

Rebecca and Duncan built Fairntosh Plantation for their home. By the time of the Civil War, the Stagville portion was under the control of grandson Paul Cameron. Paul had a knack for agriculture and had incorporated many new methods into the plantation, making it large and self-sufficient, almost a small town. By 1860, Stagville had reached its peak and by this point had added a two-story slave quarters and three-story barn structure.

The plantation eventually came into the possession of Liggett and Myers Tobacco Company. They worked it for 20 years, then in 1976 donated the land to the state. North Carolina then turned the property into a state historic site.

Today, Historic Stagville consists of 71 acres containing numerous historically significant structures; the home Richard Bennehan built in sections, four two-story, four-room slave houses, a pre-Revolutionary War farmer's house, a massive timber-framed barn, a modern visitor center and the Bennehan Family cemetery.

The ghost stories at Historic Stagville Plantation go way back. It seems like neighbors and passersby have reported strange lights in the windows of the former slave quarters and the sharecroppers for generations. Apparition of a young African-American girl has been reported frequently at the slave quarters. On one occasion, some groundskeepers fled in fright abandoning their equipment to the terrifying apparition. An African-American male has also been sighted in and near the large barn. Something in the barn has also triggered its fire and burglar alarms frequently with no apparent cause. On one of these occasions, the authorities witnessed the apparition of a male slave in the barn's loft.

The main house has also had unexplained events. Doors lock and unlock in front of the startled staff. Footsteps and murmuring voices are heard when no one else is there. One evening, the closing staff member was locking the main house for the night when she heard footsteps on the second floor. She went upstairs to check but found no one. She rapidly set the alarm and left. Although she waited in front for a good while, no one exited. The next morning, the motion detector in the main house had been triggered but had not set off the alarm. A skeleton key, which normally rests in the front door keyhole, had been moved to an antique couch several feet away. Perhaps the spirit was trying to escape its resting place or maybe just having some fun with the frightened docent.

Several paranormal investigators, Jim Hall, David Gurney and Waverly Hawthorne, researched Stagville and found some interesting phenomena. David observed what appeared to be a shadow moving in the barn and had a sudden unexplained pain in his head. He also saw what appeared to be a young African-American girl in the slave quarters. This was before the team had learned of the other sightings of this young girl. The team captured one orb that appeared to be genuine on the digital cameras. In the family cemetery, the entire group sensed a feeling of heaviness.

It would appear that several of the former slaves are still watching the goings-on at what was once their unwilling home.

Cabe Lands Cemetery

As cemeteries go, Durham has several old ones that are natural abodes of spirits. One you may want to explore while having a great outdoor hike through the picturesque woods of Eno River State Park. Just take the Cabe Lands Trail in the park to an abandoned cemetery. Its 1.2-mile trail will lead you past portions of an old mill works whose foundations are still visible. You'll also pass Cabe's Gorge, which is a particularly rocky area of the Enos River. The Enos Quarry is a popular swimming hole.

When you reach the cemetery, you may hear a man's voice, low but clear. He has been heard to say the words "noise, of about, miller, flags, and years," but no one knows what he may be speaking about.

Foster's Market

If all your explorations have made you hungry, fear not. Durham is a Mecca for unusual restaurants. For lunch I tried Foster's Market. Its deceptively simple appearance drew me in. I later found out the premises was once a lawn-mower repair shop.

I had a Grilled Chicken Fajita and enjoyed spreading out on the spacious back table since there were a few of us, but you could also sit outside on the Adirondack chairs in front or on either of the two porches as well.

The food was great, casual and homemade. You can have sandwiches, wraps, salads, soups and lots of other choices; everything from Chocolate Whoppers to fresh fruit pies in the desert department to enjoy with their own special coffee creations.

Foster's Market is the brainchild of Sara Foster. Sara was former director of catering for Martha Stewart and has remained friends with Martha ever since. She has brought her down-home-style dining to Durham and, judging by the great food and service, it is a hit.

Museum of Life and Science

The Museum of Life and Science might sound like a kids' discovery museum, but it is fun for all ages. When I visited it, Allison Savicz took me on a guided tour of the facility. It does have the typical discovery stuff inside where kids of all ages can learn about science by doing hands-on experiments. The aerospace exhibit is right up-to-date with an Apollo command module test vehicle. In fact, the Mercury Redstone Rocket in front of the museum has become a Durham landmark.

The Native North Carolina Wildlife exhibit is something adults as well as children can really enjoy.

Durham Bulls Athletic Park

Of course, there's something for sports fans. The Durham Bulls were made famous in the movie *Bull Durham* that was filmed in Durham; however, the movie was filmed at the old park. The spirit still lingers, but the new park which opened in 1995 was expanded to a 10,000-seat capacity.

American Tobacco Campus

We rambled through a complex of renovated historic brick buildings that were once the heart of the Duke's American Tobacco Company. The earliest structure in the complex was built in 1874 by the W.T. Blackwell Company, the original maker of Bull Durham Plug Tobacco. By the mid-20th century, these buildings had become eyesores instead of the landmarks they are today. That this revived heart of Durham has become a beautiful gathering spot instead of a scene of urban decay is due to a successful public-private partnership that included the Durham city and county government and Capitol Broadcasting Company, owners of WRAL-TV, and the Durham Bulls.

The refurbished buildings also showcase works by North Carolina artists. The most noticeable is a painted bronze Fire Boy, situated by the river's edge near the Symposium Cafe. The Fire Boy aims a hose, which sprouts real water that he brandishes at an imaginary fire. The newest addition is Fullsteam Brewery with a restaurant and taproom.

Page-Walker Arts & History Center

As you're leaving Durham for Raleigh, there is one place ghost-hunting, culture-loving travelers need to peruse; the Page-Walker Arts & History

Center in Cary. The center was built as a hotel in 1868 by Allison Francis Page, who is recognized as the founder of the town.

Cary began around the 1850s when a small settlement called Bradford's Ordinary found itself on a major railroad transportation route. Frank Page, as he was commonly called, was a Wake County farmer and lumberman. He and his wife, Catherine "Kate" Raboteau Page, bought 300 acres near the proposed railroad junction and named it "Cary" after Samuel Fenton Cary, a prominent Ohio prohibitionist he admired. Page developed the fledgling town and built a sawmill, a general store and a post office He was the first postmaster and later became the first mayor.

By 1985, the hotel was a deteriorating wreck headed for destruction until Friends of the Page-Walker Hotel joined with the Town of Cary to save it. Today it is listed on the National Register for Historic Places and provides a place for classes, events, performances, meetings and receptions; the gallery exhibits works of local and regional artists.

The old hotel retains a piece of history in the person of the town's founder, Allison Francis Page. Page is rumored to brush up against members of the audience as they view performances in the arts center.

Capitol Building

The third point of the research triangle is Raleigh, the capital city of North Carolina, with the emphasis on "Capitol," for it is none other than this historic building that is inhabited by so many entities from the other side that it has earned the title "The Most Haunted Capitol in America."

It's certainly not unusual to find a haunted public building, but the fact that public officials are not afraid to talk about the phenomena is astonishing. In most cases civil workers would rather die themselves than admit to any paranormal occurrences. Federal authorities could learn a lot from North Carolina's open mindedness. In fact, I have investigated in National Park buildings or battlefields where a ranger could fall over a ghost and still pretend nothing was there.

Instead of denying what everyone who worked in the capitol knew, the state in conjunction with Rhine Research Center in Durham, invited in Patty A. Wilson and Scott Crownover from the Pennsylvania-based Ghost Research Foundation to bring their crew and investigate the magnificent old building.

From the historical and architectural aspect, the building is a treasure. North Carolina's State Capitol is the least altered 19th-century state capitol in America. During the waning years of the 20th century, the capitol's interior was restored to resemble the building in its early years.

Raleigh became the state's permanent capital in 1792. Legend tells that Joel Lane, a local Revolutionary War colonel, convinced the planners to buy 1,000 acres of his Wake County property for 1,378 pounds sterling by relying on their weakness for a particularly intoxicating treat he offered at his tavern, Cherry Bounce. It is produced by mashing cherries, adding sugar and whiskey or brandy, and aging the mixture for several weeks.

Whatever the motive, a State House was constructed on the site near the center of the city and stood until it burned to the ground in 1831. The present State capitol was constructed from 1833 to 1840 and stands on the same site. The domed Greek revival building is 160 feet long by 140 feet wide and stands 97½ feet high. It was built entirely by hand with no power-driven tools or equipment.

Originally, the Capitol housed all state government offices. The executive branch occupied the first floor; the legislature the second floor; and the State Library and State Supreme Court the third floor. Later the state geologist was also crowded into the library space.

This was the site of the May 1861 Secession Convention, and the Ordinance of Secession was adopted and signed here. During the Civil War, war materials were also stockpiled in the building. Several Confederate officers who were killed in battle lay in state in the Capitol's rotunda.

In April 1865, the city of Raleigh was surrendered to General Sherman; however, Raleigh was much luckier than many other Southern capital cities. The State Capitol Building was not burned. During Reconstruction, one second floor room earned a dubious distinction; it was known as the "Third House" of the legislature because it was there that former Union General Milton Littlefield used the room to make his backroom deals and trade favors. The alcohol and cigars filled the room with smoke and fumes and offered Littlefield a perfect setting for his brand of politics. Littlefield had been a friend of Abraham Lincoln and came to North Carolina to promote fraudulent railroad schemes where he amassed a fortune in the climate of reconstruction politics. He was a charming dandy who was known for wearing a flower in his lapel and passing out money like it was water. He earned the nickname "Prince of Carpetbaggers."

Perhaps Littlefield is still hanging around the capitol. While Patty Wilson was interviewing Mr. Beck, the Capitol's historian, on the second floor where the House met, she observed a man who appeared behind Mr. Beck. She described him thus, "He appeared to be in his 30s and was dressed in clothing from the mid-to-late 1800s. He was dressed as a gentleman, had dark hair brushed to one side, and was quite pleasant-looking. The thing that struck me most about his appearance was his smile. He was laughing at us as we talked about the ghosts of the building and seemed immensely amused."

During the same investigation, another investigator took a digital photo of what appeared to be a bearded man dressed in 19th-century clothing smoking a cigar and looking at the camera. Both of these instances fit Milton Littlefield who was reported in life to be a very genial glad-handed type of politician who would have frequented the very areas where the phantoms have been seen.

Littlefield is not the only specter who seems to have been a public figure. There is a story of a governor back in the 1800s whose wife died while he was in office. Apparently he blamed the building for her death and after his death returned to roam the halls of the old Capitol.

The investigators got plenty of readings on their machines, but the most-interesting evidence comes from ordinary people who have had encounters with the supernatural in the Capitol.

James Barbot and Ernie Fuller were volunteers working on Christmas decorations in the second-floor rotunda. They set up the trees in small niches and, by the time the got to the last ones, found that the one in the northwest corner kept tilting for no reason. They straightened it again and made sure it was secure, but the next morning a staff member reported that the tree was badly listing again. James returned to securethe tree, and while he was working he was pushed over by an unseen hand.

Another person to experience unusual phenomena in the Capitol was Mr. Owen Jackson whenhe was a Capitol Police guard. He had worked the last shift, from 4:30 p.m. until 12:30 a.m. Right from the beginning strange things happened. His first week of working he heard someone singing

"Nearer My God to Thee." He searched the entire building for the source but found nothing, no person, radio or tape.

Throughout his stint as a guard, he heard doors slamming late at night when no one else was present, keys jingling, a man's footsteps, and a woman's piercing scream. One night he heard the sound of an armful of books dropping; not only was the room empty, but there were no books anywhere in it.

This "books falling" incident was doubly strange in that former Governor Hunt had a similar experience of books falling one night in the late 1970s from the same area. The governor had often had a sense of unexplainable presences at night when he worked alone in his first-floor office.

Mr. Jackson has several incidents that were much more than unexplained noises. One night when he was sitting down and about to rise, somebody laid a hand on his shoulder. He decided he really didn't want to go anywhere and remained sitting.

Another thing that was unnerving was the strange behavior of the elevator. It would come down and then return up without the door opening. No matter as far as Mr. Jackson was concerned. He wouldn't ride it when he was alone in the building: he didn't want to share that close of quarters with a ghost.

There were two instances when Mr. Jackson actually saw a presence. One time he saw the figure of a short, slender white lady wearing a blue choir robe with white trim. She came out from the men's room and walked through the closed double-glass entry doors before fading away on the other side.

Another instance occurred when he was leaving work. He looked up at the second floor windows as he was walking to his car and saw a man standing there in a Confederate uniform. The shade obscured the head and face and the window bottom cut off beyond the chest, but the brass buttons on the uniform were clearly visible.

Mr. John Johnson was a former custodian who worked the 4:30 to 7 a.m. shift for 18 years. He reported hearing a baby cry his first week on the job. He soon found that this was not unusual, as many of the other workers both then and now had heard the child's wailing, usually from the third floor in the early morning hours. He, too, had a strange experience with the elevator. Its doors closed, and it ascended to the second floor. He heard the doors open above him and tried to bring the elevator back by pressing the call button, but it would not return. He then walked up the stairs to the second floor but found no one there. Like Mr. Jackson, he too felt the stairs were safer than the elevator.

Some of the staff experienced unusual occurrences but refused to attribute them to anything paranormal. Samuel P. Townsend, Sr., who was the administrator of the state capitol from 1975 until 1998, was one such person. There was no place for "ghosts" in his lexicon. Still, some of his experiences needed a lot of rationalization to avoid acceptance of any spirit activity. He, too, heard the noises but explained them away as "the settling of an old building." One night he worked until the early morning hours and was heading home. Before he reached his car, he remembered one thing he had forgotten to do. He returned to the capitol and, as he passed into the senate chamber, saw another "person" approaching from the opposite direction. He sidestepped and then realized no one else was present. He decided the glare from outside lights caused the mantel and sign in front of it to appear to be a person approaching him.

Some other staff members are quite willing to accept the unacceptable when it appears to be the only explanation. Arlene "Dutchie" Sexsmith was at work in one of the senate rooms in August 2002. She was working late to clear her desk of some last-minute jobs before she left for vacation. When she heard the noises of doors opening and closing and voices talking, she assumed others were also working late, but when she left around 7 p.m. the noises were still drifting up to her from the first floor. As she locked her office and departed, all the noises ceased, and she realized the first floor was in darkness and all the other offices were already locked and empty; at least empty of any of her contemporary workers.

When Patty and her group were invited back to conduct a second investigation, they were able to obtain an audio recording of the woman crying or screaming on the third floor. The cries were also heard by two other investigators that evening.

Perhaps no one will ever know how many or who is haunting the old building, but one thing is certain: at least some of the haunts are of the Southern persuasion. The team tried an experiment by playing several Civil War songs on CD. When the CD reached "Battle Hymn of The Republic," it consistently skipped to the next track. They tested it outside and the song played fine. But one of the most conclusive pieces of evidence occurred when Steve, one of the team who is a native Southerner, sat in the senate chamber with his EVP. On tape he is heard to say clearly, "I know there's something up here. I sure hope it ain't no damn Yankee!"

An equally clear gruff male voice that was neither Steve's nor any other investigators, replied in a decided Southern drawl, "We're around here ...."

Governor's Mansion

Political ghosts are the norm in Raleigh as might be expected in a capital city as fraught with history as as Raleigh. They don't confine themselves to the capitol. Gov. Bob Scott in the early 1970s moved the bed of Gov. Daniel Fowle, who served in 1891, from what is known as "the Governor Fowle Bedroom." For many nights after the bed's removal, a knocking would be heard on the floor of the bedroom above where the bed had been put. The next governor returned the bed to its original room, but the Fowle bedroom remains unoccupied, many assume it is haunted by Fowle's ghost.

Holman House

One other historical home in Raleigh also boasts a ghost but this time a servant of a political figure instead of the pol himself. This ghost is called "the peg-legged ghost" and is said to haunt a concealed back staircase of the Holman House, built by William White, North Carolina's secretary of state from 1798 to 1810. Many people have heard him tramp up and down the steps. He is easily identified the distinctive tapping of his peg-leg. He is believed to be a former White family servant who, naturally in life, used only these back stairs.

Mordecai Historic Park

In another of Raleigh's haunted historical sites, it is the wife of one of the owners who patrols the home. The Mordecai House was built by Joel Lane, Raleigh's founder for his son, Henry. Henry's daughter, Margaret, married Moses Mordecai, a Raleigh lawyer and judge. They had two sons and a daughter. After Margaret died, Moses then married her sister, Ann, and had another child. Mordecai died in 1824. In his will he stipulated that the house be enlarged. This was done in 1826, giving the home its present Greek-revival look. By then the plantation had grown to one of the largest in Wake County. Its produced cotton, corn, wheat and other crops. Like most plantations it was worked almost entirely by slaves. The family remained in the home for five generations, so much of the original furniture and art remains.

Moses' son Henry had several children. One of them, his daughter, Mary Willis Mordecai, married William Turk and lived in the home until her death. There is reason to believe she remains there to this day.

Staff and visitors to the home have seen a woman dressed in Victorian clothing on the stairs and in the front room. The piano has been heard to play by itself, and her picture was thrown from a table.

The staff recently invited the Haunted North Carolina investigators to conduct a paranormal search of the home and grounds. They found evidence that the home and grounds do harbor a presence. Their batteries for electrical equipment drained inexplicably, and one member was sitting in a chair in Mary's bedroom on the second floor and felt it begin to shake.

Mordecai Historic Park also houses other historic buildings including Andrew Johnson's birthplace, a tiny home that was once behind a tavern where his mother cooked to help earn their meager living. Johnson's actual living quarters were upstairs over the kitchen. Even though much of the house is a reproduction, this building has also had a history of sightings. One child became very upset when he saw a man with a scar on his face appear and disappear. Thepark has several other historic structures.

Oakwood Cemetery

What better place to hunt for a good ghost story than a cemetery? Oakwood Cemetery began in 1867 during the Union occupation of Raleigh. The area where both Union and Confederate dead were interred was declared a federal cemetery. People were told they must move their Confederate soldiers or have them dug up by the Federals and tossed on the road. The citizens banned together and moved their dead to a new place, a small oak-filled parcel of land donated by George Mordecai. Oakwood now is the oldest private, nonprofit graveyard in Raleigh, home not just to 1,500 Confederate soldiers but also to businessmen, civic leaders and seven former governors.

A production by Raleigh-based Burning Coal Theatre Co. helped bring to life the stories of many of those interred in Oakwood. Although the actors portrayed the deceased, many of the inhabitants of the cemetery are rumored to roam the grounds.

One reenactment portrayed a Rebel soldier and his fiancé discussing how Confederate soldiers like him, who died in the Civil War, came to be interred there.

The name Red Upshaw may not mean anything to the average person, but an avid Gone with the Wind fan will recognize him as Margaret Mitchell's first husband. There is reason to believe he was the model for the Rhett Butler character in the novel.Berrian K. Upshaw was an ex-football player, gambler and sometimes bootlegger when he met the charming flapper, Margaret Mitchell. Their marriage was stormy and short-lived. Legend surrounds Berrien's death. One version is Berrian was ambushed and killed by the losers of an all-night card game in Galveston, Texas. Another version has him being caught cheating in that card game and the other players evened up the stakes permanently. In one more version he fell or was shoved out a window of the Alvin Hotel. Whatever the true cause, Red Upshaw, at age 47, died in Galveston, Texas, January 12, 1949. His death was ruled a suicide and the body returned to Raleigh for interment at Oakwood Cemetery.

Ironically, just seven months later, on August 12th, Margaret was killed while crossing a street in Atlanta by a drunken driver.As unpredictable as Red Upshaw was in life, it's anybody's guess whether you will find him still prowling around Oakwood looking for a drink and a good card game to wile away eternity.

Grave marker commemorating the Light Infantry dead

Poe House

Exhibit at The U.S. Army Airborne and Special Operations Museum

History Museum

Market Square

Capitol in Raleigh

Carolina Inn

Chapter 8 South Carolina

Charleston

Francis Marion Hotel

The Francis Marion Hotel, rising 12 stories, dominates the historic district. Built in 1924 by local investors at a cost of $1.5 million, it was the largest hotel in the Carolinas. They named it in honor of Francis Marion, the "Swamp Fox," a Revolutionary war hero and later senator for the state of South Carolina.

The 1920s was the Jazz Age especially in Charleston, home of the famous dance "the Charleston," and the city was in full bloom. The Francis Marion Hotel was the place to see and be seen. Flappers and their fedora-wearing escorts danced the night away in its Colonial Ballroom beneath the glittering brass chandeliers. Fires flickered in the marble fireplaces. It was America's Golden Age, and the Francis Marion was a part of it.

Into modern times, the hotel has still played host to celebrities. Elvis Presley stayed there when he was just beginning his career.

John F. Kennedy visited it many times when he was stationed in Charleston at the Department of Navel Intelligence. As a young ensign he was carrying on a rather serious affair with Inga Arvad. The FBI was watching Inga very closely as she was believed to be a Nazi spy. She professed a great admiration for Hitler and was rumored to have been his mistress at one time. Hitler had referred to her as a "perfect Nordic Beauty."

Kennedy and Arvad met at the Francis Marion Hotel so frequently, the FBI was able to plant a bug in "their" room. The affair ended when a columnist wrote about it in his column. "One of ex-ambassador Kennedy's eligible sons is the target of a Washington gal columnist's affections. So much so she has consulted her barrister about divorcing her exploring groom. Pa Kennedy no like."

"Pa" Kennedy immediately had John transferred to the South Pacific and his date with destiny.

As the years passed, the hotel, like the flappers who ushered in her opening, began to show her age. In 1996 the National Trust for Historic Preservation provided $12 million for a facelift. The hotel was renewed without losing any of her vintage charm; a lobby bar and business center were added, the front desk was remodeled and the elevators upgraded. All the guest bathrooms were fitted with marble floors and tub surrounds, new brass fixtures and pedestal sinks. The guestrooms were switched from keys to electronic door locks. Remote thermostats, artwork, k and coffeemakers, all the little touches that make a stay here so impressive, were added.

One thing was left as it was. The spirit who resides in the hotel did not depart. This is one time I can vouch of the spirit's authenticity, if not her identity, personally.

I was staying in a room on the 11th floor. Since I had a late breakfast meeting with Gayle Karolczyk, Then director of sales for the hotel, I awoke before my wake-up call. As I lay there deciding what I was going to wear, I suddenly sensed a person lying next to me. I was traveling alone, so I was stunned. For just a minute, I could see the bed as if I were floating above it. There was a small woman next to me. The woman was elderly, maybe in her 80s, and dressed all in beige: a beige linen or possibly heavy silk suit and a soft beige turban both of which might have been popular in the early 1950s. The lady was heavily made up with a lot of powder and discernible rouge. Then as fast as it began she was gone. I jumped up and considered the options; I knew I had not fallen back asleep; therefore, I must have seen something. It was too detailed for one of those "corner of my eye" sorts of sightings, which could be explained away by a shadow. No. Someone had really been here. I decided not to mention my experience to Gayle and see what her experiences or reports from others were.

Gayle and I met in the Swamp Fox Restaurant on the first floor. While we were dining on the fare from an especially generous buffet she told me of her encounter with "the ghost."

She was on the fourth floor with a tour and realized she had forgotten a key. She left the group there and turned to go downstairs. "When I turned, I saw a small person just boarding the elevator, but when I entered the car seconds later, no one was there. It unnerved me so that when I got to the office, I mentioned it to Joan, our sales assistant. She laughed. 'You saw Otis's wife?'" When Gayle asked Joan what she meant, Joan explained that there had long been a rumor that Mrs. Otis of the elevator family had died in the hotel and her spirit was the one haunting it. Another clue is that the most common experience guests report is about the elevator sometimes going unnaturally slowly and going up and down when no one had pushed a button to call it. The problem is none of us can find a link between any Otises and the Francis Marion or even Charleston. Elisha Graves Otis's wife died before the hotel was ever built. Perhaps it is a later Otis spouse who spurred the stories.

These are not the only clues. Another sighting was by a woman guest staying in an 11th-floor room. She saw a woman's face behind her in the bathroom mirror.

One more thing to take into consideration is that spirits from an original building that has been torn down often remain in new buildings. Prior to being a hotel, the Charleston Orphan Home occupied the site directly behind and may have extended into where the present hotel is now located. Certainly many of the children and probably some of the staff died there.

It's obvious that there is something here, but the mystery is who is this female phantom and why is she in the Francis Marion Hotel.

Fort Sumter National Monument

When you say "Charleston," most people will automatically think "Civil War" and "Fort Sumter." It was there that the conflagration turning brother against brother exploded into the most-bloody warfare American soil has ever known. At the crack of dawn on April 12, 1861, Confederate General Pierre Beauregard, in command of 50 cannons and by direct order from President Jefferson Davis, opened fire on his former West Point instructor and friend, Major Robert Anderson, commander of Union forces at Fort Sumter. On April 14th, the Stars and Bars was raised over the battered fort. The war for Southern independence had officially begun.

The Confederates held the fort for exactly four years. On April 14, 1865, now-Major General Anderson raised Old Glory over the battered fort. Grant put the 54th Massachusetts (Colored) Regiment, who had suffered many casualties in the attack on Fort Wagner (one of the batteries) in September of 1863, in charge of the fort. Many visitors have reported seeing apparitions of some of these African-American soldiers. Others have reported sounds of battle from the fort and the site where the former battery wharf once stood.

Another spirit reputed to roam the old fort is honor guardsman Daniel Hough, who was killed when his gun misfired as the U.S. flag was lowered at Fort Sumter after Col. Anderson surrendered the fort. Hough's burial at the fort was one of the last Union actions before their soldiers were evacuated. To balance this, visitors also report seeing the ghost of a Confederate soldier there also. Sumter is a powerful reminder of our national history and the ironies of war.

Harbor tour

As I looked out over Charleston Harbor, the captain explained the history of many of the structures I could see from the water.

One of the lesser-known facts of the War Between the States occurred on a little island called Shute's Folly Island in Charleston Harbor. Castle Pinckney was one of the forts designed to protect Charleston. It was built of brick and mortar shortly before the War of 1812. On December 27, 1860, just a week after South Carolina seceded from the Union, the Union forces there was forced to retreat to Fort Sumter. It is not known whether Castle Pinckney soldiers ever actually fired a shot, but it was the first Union fort to surrender to the Confederacy.

In the beginning of the war, Castle Pinckney was used as a Confederate prison. It was later returned to defensive service.

One East Battery is a magnificent home visible from the harbor. It was built between 1858 and 1861. It is divided into condominiums today, and the top floor unit sold just after Hurricane Hugo for $3.6 Million.

In February 1865 it had a front-row seat to the battle. While the Confederates were evacuating the city, a large gun at the nearby Battery blew up, severely damaging the home. During the evacuation, a guest at the house was Mary Boykin Chestnut, author of *A Diary from Dixie*, which gave a Southern woman's perspective of the events and people of the Civil War.

The history of the house involves one other famous person related to the Civil War. In 1926, the house was purchased by Mrs. Robert E. Lee, III, wife of the grandson of General Robert E. Lee.

Charleston was under siege for more than 500 days, the longest siege in North American history.

White Point Gardens (The Battery)

This beautiful park on the waterfront was once a scene that would rival a particularly grisly horror movie. Pirates were once the most-dreaded threat to the city of Charles Town. When Stede Bonnet and his crew were captured, the officials decided to make an example of them no one would ever forget.

They were all hanged on December 10, 1718, in White Point Park. The bodies were left swinging from the oak limbs for four days. Their corpses' eyes seemed to follow those who hurried past the gruesome sight. Today if you linger in the park alone after sundown, you may spot one or more of these tortured souls sulking around in the shadows in search of their executioners.

20 South Battery formerly Battery Carriage House Inn

The "Carriage House Gentleman" haunts the Inn. He likes to play pranks on the guests, particularly women, by lying down next to them in bed. When they awake and look at him, he disappears. The owners of the inn believe he was the son of an early 20th-century owner. He was a college student who became despondent and jumped off the roof, killing himself. He is usually seen in room 10.

Room 8 has a very different kind of phantom. This is the "Headless Torso." He is believed to be a Confederate soldier who was working on the battery during the day and perhaps retired to this area at night. He most likely was killed by an explosion, which blew off his head and limbs. In spite of his fearsome appearance, he is not believed to be malignant.

The house was originally built in 1843 by Samuel N. Stevens, a wealthy cotton factor. It was severely damaged during the Union siege and later bought by a Southern-born Union officer. He was not made welcome and finally sold the property.

It was sold several times, becoming an "hourly rental" in the 1940s for young navy sailors and the local "ladies of the evening."

The Citadel Museum

One other "act of war" occurred before Fort Sumter and was enacted by students at what was then called South Carolina Military Academy. The school had come into being in 1822 when the South Carolina Legislature passed an "An Act to Establish a Competent Force to act as a Municipal

Guard." It decreed in 1842 that these guard duties should be combined with an educational system.

On January 9, 1861, Citadel cadets fired on the U.S. steamer Star of the West, stopping the ship from supplying Fort Sumter with troops and supplies. This was the first overt act of the war.

The school continued to operate during the war, but classes were often disrupted when the cadets went to fight alongside their older counterparts. In 1910, the name of the school was officially changed to the Citadel, the Military College of South Carolina.

Today, the Citadel has a wonderful museum featuring photographs, uniforms, archival documents and more. The Citadel also has at least one documented ghost. "The Lost Cadet" is the spirit of a young student who was killed during the War Between the States. He is frequently seen around the Citadel buildings and seems to be looking for his lost pocketknife. If you spot him, he is easily identified since he is missing half of his head.

Old Exchange and Provost Dungeon

I took the Bulldog Ghost and Dungeon Tour, and this was one of the most-interesting places we went. Our guide, Stephen Beard, was very knowledgeable.

The Old Exchange and Provost Dungeon was completed around 1772. The Exchange served several functions: a meeting place, a customs house and a dungeon. The chosen site, the foot of Broad Street at the dead center of the waterfront at that time, was symbolic of Charles Town's rise to power in the colonies. The wealth of the city came from trade, indigo, rice and slaves. All flowed through this new building. The dungeon wall was the original Half Moon Battery and was the site of the former Court of the Guard where pirates like Stede Bonnet and his ilk were imprisoned before they were hanged. There is a display in the dungeon where chains block the pirate exhibit. Our guide told us that occasionally these chains swing for no apparent reason. Perhaps the imprisoned pirates are pushing them.

The dungeon has served other purposes as well. While patriots in Boston tossed taxed tea into Boston Harbor, Charleston patriots were a bit more practical. On December 22, 1773, a shipment of heavily taxed tea arrived in Charleston harbor. Patriots refused to allow the tea to be accepted. Robert Dalway Haliday, the royal customs collector, had the tea shipment seized, unloaded, and stored under the Exchange for non-payment of duties. The patriots were somewhat surprise by his action but did not protest as long as it remained safely stored.

The tea thus remained in storage until the British were forced out of power. The tea was then sold in 1776 to help fund the war against the British.

One other important item was stored in the dungeon. If you look through a small hole in the brick wall, you can see where kegs of gunpowder were hidden from the British. Throughout the entire British occupation of the city the gunpowder was never found.

Ghosts do disappear. No, not "disappear" as in fade away. They sometimes stop appearing. Perhaps they have found a way to cross over to the next step in their journey to eternity, or perhaps the reason they appeared in the first place ends. The spirit of Isaac Hayne at the Old Exchange and Provost Dungeon is an example of this. Colonel Isaac Hayne was a well-respected member of the Charleston community and an officer in the militia, perhaps the most famous person to be jailed in the dungeon.

During the British occupation of Charleston, he was captured and ordered to either take an oath of allegiance to the crown or be sent to a prison ship. At the time, his wife and children were ill with smallpox. He had only come to Charleston, in fact, to get them a doctor. Hayne then signed an agreement to act as a British subject as long as the British controlled the area.

By 1781, Francis Marion, Thomas Sumter and Andrew Pickens had regained control of most of South Carolina. Nathaniel Greene had arrived in the South, and Hayne felt the British had been repulsed and that his "allegiance due to a conqueror ceased with his expulsion from the subdued territory." He rejoined a South Carolina regiment of militia as a colonel.

Colonel Balfour, the British commandant of Charleston, captured Hayne and with a military tribunal instead of a trial, sentenced him to be hanged.

Hayne was held in the prison of the Provost Dungeon until his sentence was to be carried out. On August 2, 1781, the condemned man was led to the place of execution outside the city gates. On the route he passed the Perroneau house where his sister-in-law, Doris Perroneau, was caring for his children. When he passed by she called out to him, "Isaac, come back!" He replied gravely, "I will if I can."

For the next 80 years, mysterious footsteps have been heard on the stair of the Perroneau house, now the Hayne House Bed and Breakfast, and in the Provost Dungeon. Then on April 12, 1861, General Beauregard commenced firing upon Fort Sumter located in Charleston harbor. When the smoke cleared on April 14th, a new flag, the Stars and Bars, flew over the fort, and Isaac Hayne, who gave his life so the United States of America could be born, never again walked in Charleston.

The dungeon may have most of the ghosts, but the rest of the building is just as famous. George Washington enjoyed a week's worth of lavish entertainment in Charleston. Balls, dinners and concerts were held in the ballroom on the second floor of the Old Exchange. It was the stage for many of South Carolina's history-making events: the general Assembly was first convened there; the state constitution was ratified there; the delegates to the First Continental Congress were chosen in its Great Hall; and the Constitution of the United States of America was ratified there May 23, 1788.

Considering all the famous and infamous who have walked its halls, you can expect to find orbs, cold spots and sounds upstairs as well as in the dungeon.

Poogan's Porch

In 1976 when Bobby Ball and her family purchased the old home on Queen Street, they didn't know how much extra they were getting for the price. One item they discovered very quickly, a little white West Highland Terrier, was on their porch begging for a handout. These are restaurant people, so they naturally fed the hungry pooch. He, like all those who dine in the restaurant, liked the food and decided to make the porch his new home. The family adopted him and named their new restaurant by the name they had given the stray, Poogan's Porch. Over the years, the restaurant grew in popularity, and the guests loved having Poogan visit with them on the porch. Then in 1979, Poogan died. Visitors to the restaurant had grown to love him and always asked where he was. When the staff told them Poogan had passed away, they refused to believe them. "We just felt him by our feet." Or "He just brushed by under the table."

Poogan died of natural causes, but he has refused to pass on to his next life. This is where he plans on spending his eternity.

Poogan's not the only spirit cavorting around the restaurant. The other ghost is not as cute, and she certainly is not cuddly. She is believed to be Zoë St. Amand. Zoë and her sister, Elizabeth, lived in what is now Poogan's Porch until Elizabeth died. Between the 1940s and '50s, Zoë's mental health deteriorated to the point that she had to be put in a nursing home where she eventually died. However, she has returned to where her roots were, right there at 72 Queen Street. She often appears in black dress with white lace collar, wearing glasses and scowling at all these people in her home.

One incident occurred in the ladies restroom upstairs. The room is small, only meant to be occupied by one person. In 1995 a lady using the facilities looked in the mirror and saw a little old lady behind her. She turned, and no one was there. She turned and once again saw the ghostly reflection in the mirror next to her face. Needless to say, she fled the restroom and rapidly returned to her room across the street.

In another incident, a family member came in after hours to work on the plumbing. He poured a cup of coffee and headed to the back of the building. While there working, he heard a crash from the bar area and rushed there to see what had fallen. When he got to the bar, nothing was out of place so he returned to finish his work. When he reached for his coffee cup, he found it drained with a lipstick imprint on the rim. Zoë is French; naturally she likes coffee.

Former co-owner Bobbie was one of the family skeptics until she had her own run in with Zoë. One night as she tried to close the restaurant for the evening, she was having a problem with the alarm system and had to call one of the service technicians. Before she could even get off the phone with the technician, two of the heavy wooded bar stools crashed, almost impossible considering the sturdy construction. Next, the kitchen door slammed open, again nearly impossible, as it weighs some 40 pounds. When she checked in the kitchen, Bobbie realized she was alone and drew the only possible conclusion. Zoë made a believer of her that night.

All the food is good, but any true Southerner will fall in love with the biscuits and gravy. You know you are in good company when you dine at Poogan's Porch, too; Paul Newman, Joanne Woodward, Lauren Hutton, Jim Carrey, Jodie Foster, Joe Namath, Tennessee Williams, Barbara Streisand and James Brolin are just some of the celebrities who have sampled the hospitality there. In fact, it was the setting for the 1989 movie *Champagne Charlie*, starring Hugh Grant, much of which was filmed inside the restaurant. And, no, neither Poogan nor Zoë appear in the movie.

People from the Mills House Hotel just across the street have often called the police to tell them a little old lady is trapped in the restaurant. The police have gotten so used to Zoë's appearance, they don't come over to "rescue" the "little old lady."

Mills House Hotel

While the guests at Mills House Hotel are calling in reports about Zoë, they should be looking around their own rooms for phantoms. The Mills house has a long history of ghosts.

Otis Mills, one of the wealthiest men in Charleston, built the Mills House in 1853 on the site where the first Planters Hotel stood before moving to its more-famous spot at what is now the Dock Street Theater. He erected the Mills House as a hostelry for those who couldn't afford the more expensive hotels in Charleston. Mills was an ardent supporter of Southern independence, so at the start of the War Between the States, he sold all of his property, including his hotel, and purchased Confederate bonds. One of his more-famous guests was General Robert E. Lee, who stayed at Mills' hotel just before the war began. Rumors say his ghost is still seen by the light of the antique oil lamps that are still used in the halls.

Needless to say, after the War ended, Mills was left penniless. The house was reopened in 1870. It was still called the Mills House until 1897, when Mrs. W. W. Lawton purchased it and changed its name to the St. John Hotel. During the Charleston Exposition in 1900 it hosted many celebrities. President Theodore Roosevelt once stayed there before he was president. This was the first hotel in Charleston to offer electric lights.

In the 1960s, the hotel was completely renovated and is once again named for the man who built it.

CSS *H.L. Hunley*

One of the Civil War's greatest mysteries was partially solved in 1995 when Author Clive Cussler rediscovered a murky hulk in the waters off Charleston (The *Hunley* had been found earlier by Edward Spence, but the location was not recorded.). The enigma began in Feb. 17, 1864, when a top-secret Confederate submarine, *H.L. Hunley*, slipped through under the waters of Charleston Harbor headed for the Union ship, *USS Housatonic*.

The cigar-shaped vessel was hand-cranked by an eight-man crew. The *Hunley* succeeded in sinking the huge Union warship by means of a torpedo attached to a long pole. But after signaling its success, the *Hunley* never reached shore. Most people believed it was sunk along with its victim by the torpedo explosion. The sub had previously sunk twice, each time killing its passengers, but was recovered and put back into service. This time it remained on the bottom of the ocean until 2000 when it was raised. Its crew was buried with honors in the Magnolia Cemetery on Saturday, April 17th, 2004, after a week-long round of ceremonies honoring the ship and its crew. This was the last Confederate burial in history, obviously.

Many of the men who took part in the burial as honor guards report paranormal occurrences surrounding the Rebel sub. Re-enactors in Confederate uniform stood at attention guarding the remains of the crew.

They heard footsteps and a voice crying" "mother" and saw the shadow of a Confederate soldier. The strangest of the Hunley ghosts was nicknamed "the Adjuster" because they watched him adjust the positions of the straps on the soldiers' uniforms to more comfortable positions. They also noted the smell of fresh green apples. Steve Burt, the coordinator for the Honor Guard, believes the crewmembers may have taken apples with them as a snack. The guard members felt light touches and experienced a calm feeling of welcome from the spirits.

Randy Burbage, who was involved in digging for the crew members of the earlier sinkings believed buried near Johnson Hagood Stadium, felt he was guided to dig in spots where he had been told not to because he felt "a presence" guiding him to those bodies. Each time he followed that guidance he found another member of the *Hunley*. Five members had been buried at Hagood.

Bill Sharpe, who took a picture of the sub, later noted a crewman in it. He posted it on his website only to discover the next day the crewman was gone. He hurriedly took the page down.

Several months later I was at a re-enactment and met one of the Sons of Confederate Veterans who marched in the burial procession. He told me a fascinating story. After the burial, he and some friends went to a local restaurant for lunch. They were in period dress and laid their muskets down against a back wall of the restaurant. One of the group took a picture of them sitting at the table. The rifles against wall were in the background.

Someone else was there. A shadowy figure of a Confederate soldier stood near the guns. It was not a re-enactor. No one had been near the spot. No one mortal anyway. He showed me the picture and, unlike some hazy "ghost pictures," this one was clear. There was no mistaking the translucent figure as anything else but a Confederate soldier returned from the grave.

I have talked to many of the re-enactors who attended the Hunley ceremony, and almost all said they felt something unnatural.

Today, the famous Confederate sub is being studied and preserved in Charleston. You can visit, but it is a good idea to call ahead for tickets.

Joseph Manigault House

Joseph Manigaults was wealthy rice planter. He was also one of the French Huguenots who fled to Charleston to escape religious persecution in France. Joseph's brother, Gabriel, designed the home for the family's town house in 1803. Joseph had several plantations and only used the home when his family cam into town for a social event or business.

It is a beautifully simple Federal-style brick home with a period garden. The garden's centerpiece is a gate temple. Unbelievably, this house was due to be destroyed, but some of Charleston's ladies stepped in. They managed to save the home but had no funds to restore it. The home went through incarnations as a tenement, a USO (during WWII) and even had a gas station built in its yard and the gate temple turned into restrooms and tire storage. Fortunately, it came into the hands of the Charleston Museum and is open for tours.

Aiken-Rhett House

Another magnificent home, the Aiken-Rhett House is like stepping into a time warp. It is the most-unaltered antebellum home you can tour in Charleston. Many of the furnishings are still in the same room for which they were purchased. It belongs to the Historic Charleston Foundation, and instead of restoring it, the foundation has preserved it as it was a century ago, ghost and all.

It was built as a simple double house in 1817 (Charleston is known for "single" and "double" houses. The single was a house only one room wide and the double two rooms.) for John Robinson, a wealthy merchant and ship owner. When several of his ships were burned by the French, he lost the home to Governor William Aiken, Sr.

Akin used it for rental property and when he died left it to his wife and son. In 1833, the son, William Akin, Jr., who was in the railroad business and entertained lavishly and often remolded it, added 23 rooms and converted it to Greek revival style. William and his wife, Harriet, played host to the most-influential people in the country. General Beauregard used the home as his headquarters when he was in Charleston. President Jefferson Davis was also a guest here in November 1863. Harriet was a very cosmopolitan hostess who was close friends with John C. Calhoun's family. She was a world traveler, buying many of the home's furnishings in Europe when she accompanied her husband there. During the war, the home was looted by Union soldiers, and many of the pieces were lost forever.

When William died in 1887, Harriet lost her zest for life. She stopped giving and attending parties and turned the second-floor ballroom into her bedroom where she spent most of her time until her death in 1892.

When Harriet died, her daughter, Henrietta Rhett, inherited the home and closed off the ballroom. Harriet's last request was that her sanctuary be left untouched. And so it was until a descendant donated the house to the Charleston Museum in 1975. In 1995 its ownership was passed to the Historic Charleston Foundation.

The Aiken-Rhett House ballroom remained sealed for 82 years until the night two architects unlocked the room. They did not linger long in Harriet Aiken's chamber.

Two respected Charleston architects were working on drawings of the house for the museum. When they reached the second floor, they heard noises and felt a rush of cold air. They unlocked the ballroom door since the noises seemed to be coming for that room. They glimpsed an image in the mirror of a transparent old woman who seemed to have her mouth stretched in a silent scream. They are not the only ones to have seen "something" in the old mansion.

Others have glimpsed the figure of a man wearing a tri-cornered hat through a window of the parlor.

City Hall

In most cities, city hall is of no interest to visitors. Not so in Charleston. The building is a historical and architectural treasure. It was renovated and reopened in June 2007.

It was built at the dawn of the 19th century and designed by Gabriel Manigault in the Adamesque style. It was originally donated to the federal government to be a branch of the First Bank of the United States. In 1811 the bank's charter was revoked and the property deeded back to the City of Charleston. It became City Hall in 1818 and is still used for that purpose today. In fact, the corner where it stands, Broad and Meeting streets, was named by Robert Ripley "Four Corners of the Law" in his "Believe it or Not" column because it is the only occurrence of this particular conjunction in the country. The four buildings located there reflect four branches of law: the Charleston County Courthouse (state law), City Hall (municipal law), the Federal Building and U.S. Post Office (federal law), and Saint Michael's Episcopal Church (the law of God).

Inside you will find many famous portraits, including John Trumbull's portrait of George Washington and the hind end of a horse. Pierre G. T. Beauregard is honored with two portraits; in the earlier one, painted in 1861 when he was preparing the attack on Fort Sumter, he is still wearing the Federal uniform he wore as commander of West Point. Interestingly, the eyes of this portrait will follow you around the room. Another Beauregard portrait is a life-sized, full-length picture that hangs in the hall. Beauregard's sword, presented to him by the Ladies of New Orleans in honor of his capture of Ft. Sumter, is also on display. It hangs beneath the General's 1861 Portrait. Naturally along with all the memorabilia and paintings City Hall has a great ghost story.

While Beauregard was in Charleston preparing to attack Fort Sumter, a local politician was entrusted with a large sum of money collected for the Confederate cause. He held the money overnight at his home and the next morning, complained loudly that "someone" had stolen the money while he slept. Beauregard hurried to the man's home and located the money hidden behind a panel of the man's wall. Instead of accusing such a prominent citizen and perhaps casting the entire city in a bad light, he passed off the incident as being caused by mice dragging the hoard away to their nest. His tact won the respect of the entire city.

The story goes that he is frequently seen around City Hall keeping an eye on the politicians.

St Michael's Church

Charleston has been dubbed "the Holy City" because of the abundance of churches. Its oldest, St. Michael's, was built in 1761 on the site of the first Anglican Church built south of Virginia. The architecture is decidedly Gothic in the Sir Christopher Wren style.

A large, long double pew dominates the center of the church. This is called "The Governor's Pew." President George Washington in it on May 8, 1791. Seven decades later, General Robert E. Lee also occupied that pew. The church had a shell burst in it in 1865 during the Federal bombardment of the city, leaving a scar is at the base of the pulpit.

The church is home to an interesting ghostly legend. In the dawning years of the 19th century, when women were not supposed to bother their pretty little heads about finance, Dr. James Mackie died and bequeathed his entire fortune to his seven-year-old daughter, Harriet. The will stated that he left "my Estate both real and personal consisting of Negroes, horses, cattle, &c. to my daughter, Harriet Mackie, when she attains the age of 21 years or at the day of her marriage, which ever shall happen first."

When she was 17, Harriet fell in love and was to be married at St. Michael's. Days before her wedding, Harriet fell ill one night and died before morning. The fact that the girl was in perfect health the day before led to a lot of speculation. A motive was easily found in the remainder of her father's will: "If my daughter should die before the above-mentioned periods, then I give that part of my Estate which I have given to my daughter, to Captain Wm. Alston's two sons, John Alston and Wm. Alston."

The Alstons, his nephews, were questioned but released due to lack of evidence. Harriet was buried in her wedding dress. Jean Frangois Vallee painted a noted miniature of her in the dress. Unlike many funeral pictures, she has her eyes closed in the portrait.

Since that day, visitors to the church have occasionally seen a young woman in a wedding dress floating around the church. Our ghost tour guide, Stephen, told of taking a group into the church on a tour. One of the women in the group actually saw the woman for about three seconds. She had not been told the story as this was not a ghost tour but a history one.

St. Philip's Episcopal Church

St. Philip's might be called the "Bad Luck Church." It had more than its share. It was built on the current site of St. Michael's in 1680. Then it was destroyed by a hurricane in 1710. While the new church was under construction in 1713 at the present site, another hurricane blew it away. A fire burned the church to the ground 1835. Then in 1865, the Union army sighted on its tall steeple during bombardment of the city and scored a hit. Next, in 1927 a tornado knocked the steeple off. Its bishop, Father Guerry, was murdered by an angry clergyman in 1928. Hugo hit it in 1989, causing $4.5 million in damages.

It has managed to survive and thrive in spite of all the disasters. So they probably considered it another disaster when a photo of a spirit taken in their church cemetery surfaced.

It began around 10 p.m. on June 10, 1987. A couple had just gotten a new camera. So they decided to go out to see what they could find to photograph and try it out. Not much was available at that hour, so they decided to see how well it did in dim light. They went to St. Philip's cemetery. The woman knew there was a small gate that opened from the schoolyard. When they snuck into the schoolyard and found the gate closed, they took a few pictures through the fence and left.

When they got the pictures developed, they found a startling image that was not visible when they were looking in the cemetery. I saw the picture myself, and it does look like a woman kneeling at the tomb photographed from behind.

They were not believers in the supernatural, so they went back to the store where the pictures were developed and blamed the technician. Perhaps he was having a bad day, but he just told them he didn't alter the film and if they had a problem, take it up with Kodak. They actually shipped the camera and film back to Kodak. After examining both, Kodak informed the people it was not the fault of the camera or the film. They had captured what was there in front of them whether they liked it or not. The church obviously does not like it as they have a sign posted in the cemetery that reads: "There are no ghosts in this cemetery except the Holy Ghost."

The story began a lot earlier actually. A young 19th century woman named Sue Howard Hardy gave birth to a baby, but the infant died. Ironically, on June 10, 1888, exactly 90 years earlier than the modern photograph, that baby was buried in the same grave at which the photo was taken. A few days following the baby's death, the grieving Sue Howard Hardy passed away and was buried in the same grave with her child. She has been seen many times in this cemetery.

Another ghost in this cemetery is the Gray Man. There are several legends about how he came to be there. One version is that he is the spirit of a slave, Boney, who was freed for saving St. Philip's when it was on fire. He could not adjust to freedom and died. Boney was buried in his former master's slave cemetery but continues to hang around St. Philip's cemetery to watch over the church. The legend says anyone who sees him will die shortly.

Of course, there are a lot of famous people who seem to rest easily in the St. Philip's churchyard. Among them are John C. Calhoun, secretary of war and vice president of the United States; Edward Rutledge, signer of the Declaration of Independence; and Charles Pickney, signer of the Constitution.

Unitarian Cemetery

One other Charleston church is better known for its cemetery than the actual building. Do not miss seeing the church as well. It is the oldest Unitarian church in the South, begun in 1772. Some of the original building is still visible through all the renovations. The legend surrounding its cemetery is unique and may solve a literary mystery.

Annabelle Lee is one of Edgar Allan Poe's most-famous poems. Few people know it has a Charleston connection. On November 18, 1827, the brig Waltham sailed into Charleston. Aboard was a young man of just 18 years who had recently enlisted and was arriving at his army post at Ft. Moultrie on Sullivan's Island. Sullivan's Island guards the mouth of Charleston harbor.

The army was expecting Private Edgar A. Perry. They did not know that "Perry" was not his real name. His name was Poe, and he was probably using the alias to escape gambling debts. He had fallen out with his foster father, John Allan, and been "asked" to leave the University of Virginia because of his wild ways. Poe was young, wild, reckless and ethereal; the army was established, rigid, staid and down-to-earth. It was not a marriage made in heaven, but Poe had few choices. He had worn out his welcome in too many places.

Surprisingly in spite of his temperament, Poe/Perry was well-liked by his commanding officers and reached the rank of sergeant major, the highest rank an enlisted man can attain.

It was while stationed at Fort Moultrie that Poe wrote "The Gold Bug." The story's main character, Legrand, is modeled after a man Poe met on the island, Dr. Edmund Ravenel, a conchologist and professor at the Medical College. Ravenel was from a prominent Charleston family and maintained a house and a practice on Sullivan's Island. His family home and main office was on Meeting Street just across the street from the Nathaniel Russell House, now a house museum and the headquarters of the Historic Charleston Foundation. Ravenel and Poe shared an interest in shells and wandered the shore searching for interesting specimens.

Ravenel may have accepted Poe as a friend, but as a suitor for his daughter, Poe was decidedly not acceptable. The good doctor wanted his daughter to marry a Charleston blueblood with a fortune to match Ravenel's. So Poe and the young lady began to meet secretly in the Unitarian Cemetery. The Cemetery was and is wonderfully wooded and green, a very romantic place to meet. As was bound to happen, the doctor found out about his daughter's clandestine meetings and locked her in her room in order to put an end to the affair.

Meanwhile, Poe was transferred out in December 1828. He could not contact his love to say goodbye and left for Virginia heart stricken.

Summer arrived and brought its usual horde of biting mosquitoes to the coastal city. The young girl so recently released from her imprisonment must have welcomed a chance to be outdoors and may never have noticed the sting that carried the deadly yellow fever.

Her grieving father blamed Poe somehow for his daughter's death and vowed that even in death, he would not allow such an inappropriate suitor to bid the lovely young girl goodbye. He arranged for all the family plots to be dug up and disturbed so Poe would not know which was the true resting place of his love.

Sure enough, when Poe learned of her death, he returned to search for her grave but never found it. Today the grave is marked with a simple A.L.R. for her name, Annabelle Lee Ravenel. It is said that Annabelle Lee roams the Unitarian Cemetery searching for her lost love. Poe's immortal line about a "sepulcher by the sea" was all he knew of his first love's final resting place.

The Unitarian Cemetery is home to another unhappy spirit, Charleston's famous "Lady in White." The story is set in the late 1800s. It tells of Mary Bloomfield whose merchant husband had to go to Boston on business. He and Mary were very much in love and dreaded this separation. While in Boston, he became ill and was buried there. Meanwhile, in Charleston, Mary also became ill and longed for her husband's return. She died without ever knowing his fate and was buried in the Unitarian Cemetery. It seems she cannot rest until she finds her beloved spouse, and visitors to the graveyard frequently notice a dark-haired woman with upswept hair in a long white dress floating around among the gravestones always seeking someone she will never find.

Drayton Hall

First and foremost, Drayton Hall is a survivor. It's also one of the oldest and finest examples of Georgian-Palladian architecture in America. Seven generations of Draytons lived in the home, and some claim at least one of them is still there. It remained in nearly original condition through the years and is the only Ashley River plantation house to survive both the Revolution and the Civil War. It was built by Royal Judge John Drayton in 1742 as his country estate on the Ashley River.

John married Charlotta Bull, the daughter of the lieutenant royal governor, and had two children, William Henry and Charles. John outlived Charlotta and two other wives. When his third wife died, he married Rebecca Perry, the 17-year-old daughter of a neighboring plantation owner. When John died in 1779 while fleeing from the British army, he left Drayton Hall to Rebecca, not William Henry.

William Henry is the person most associated with Drayton Hall. Even though it was not his inheritance, it was his home for his entire life. He was educated in England as were most well-to-do planters' sons; however, he soon came to be a supporter of the rebelling colonies. He was one of the signers of the Articles of Confederation adopted by the fledgling nation.

William Henry is also one of the spirits who still roam the old home. When Elizabeth Baron, a well-respected trance medium, was invited to attempt to contact whoever haunted the mansion, she channeled William Henry Drayton. He spoke through her, stating, "I am here." She sensed a tormented soul who is greatly disturbed about past events. He spoke of a hanging that took place on the grounds, claiming he tried to stop the crime. He also said, "They were trying to protect me." Whether in regard to the people who were lynched or the perpetrators, it's hard to decide. He did say the people hanged were just fighting for their right to own property.

Baron also detected other presences, especially on the interior back stairway, which was a passage used by slaves to bring food up to the dining room from the kitchen.

Today, the 125-acre Drayton Hall National Historic Landmark offers visitors a rare glimpse of bygone days. The home is unfurnished and unrestored. It is as if the last living inhabitant just moved out and left the mansion to its ghostly inhabitants.

Dock Street Theater

Charleston from its beginning was a city of culture. It is home to the first building in the American Colonies designed as a theater. The Dock Street Theatre opened in Charleston on February 12, 1736.

In 1809 the building was converted into the Planters Hotel. It also housed a rather rowdy saloon, thus was a favorite spot for traveling actors until just before the Civil War when it fell into disrepair. Planters Punch originated in the Planters Hotel.

In the 1930s, the building was restored by the Works Progress Administration and once more serves its original function. The current theatre seats 464 patrons. The Charleston Stage Company performs there, and it is the home of the Spoleto Chamber Music Series.

One of the Planters Hotel's more-famous guests was Junius Brutus Booth, the father of President Lincoln's assassin. He stayed at the Planters Hotel when he acted in Othello in a nearby Charleston theater in 1838 and is still seen today in the restored theater. Many people have seen what they describe as a middle-aged man dressed in formal attire who disappears as you stare at him.

He is not alone at the theater. Visitors have seen a young woman dressed in a maroon dress on the second floor. She is believed to be a prostitute who died as a result of an illegal abortion during the building's stint as a hotel. The odd thing is she always seems to be walking on her knees. However, when you find out that the level of the second floor was raised by about a foot during the renovation, it suddenly makes sense: She is walking on the second floor of the building that existed in her lifetime.

City Market

City Market, built sometime between 1788 and 1807, is the heart of Old Charleston. Architecturally it is unique, built in the Roman-Revival style reminiscent of the Temple of Nike in Athens with skulls of sheep and bulls in a frieze around the top representing the Roman custom of sacrificing these animals to the gods. The first markets were meat markets, fish markets and product stands, but today you will find almost any product that can be sold. In the good old days, the market could be located by the presence of the buzzards that scavenged the offal tossed in the street by the vendors. These birds were more highly thought of then than they are today. They were known as "Charleston Eagles" and were protected by law.

On the second floor of the market you will find the Confederate Museum. If you are a fan of either military memorabilia or the War of Northern Aggression, you must visit this museum. Remember while in Charleston, "the War" is never referred to as the "Civil War." A native Charlestonian will quickly inform you "there was nothing civil about it" especially in South Carolina.

Old City Jail

In 1680, when Charleston was planned, a four-acre square on Magazine Street was set aside for public use. The site housed first a hospital, then a poor house, a workhouse for runaway slaves, Potters Field, a gunpowder arsenal and finally, in 1802, a jail. The Old Jail remained in use until 1939.

It is no wonder that this might be the most-haunted spot in all of haunted Charleston. Untold numbers of people were imprisoned in this thick-walled four-story building. Thousands of convicts were executed here. One of its most famous was America's first female serial killer, Lavenia Fisher. Lavina and John Fisher had an inn called Six Mile House just outside Charleston. Guests unfortunate enough to stop over at the Fishers' inn seldom left it the next morning -- at least not under their own power. Lavenia would charm the guests and feed them a fine meal – along with some oleander leaf-laced tea. John would then dispose of the bodies; he and Lavina lived well on the traveler's gold.

But all good things come to and end, and for the Fishers, that end came in the early 1820s when one of their proposed victims escaped alive and reported the goings on at the inn to the authorities. Throughout the trial, Lavina played on her exceptional good looks and charm, believing it would get her acquitted or at least pardoned, but on Feb. 18, 1820, she donned her old wedding dress and climbed on the gallows. Cocky to the end, she is reported to have said," If anyone has any words for the Devil, tell me now... I'll be seeing him in the morning."

Is it any wonder that the most commonly seen specter at the Old Jail is a woman wearing a white wedding gown?

One of the Old Jail's incarnation was as part of the School of the Building Arts. While renovating the building, many of the tradesmen came face to face with phantoms from the past. One blacksmith who was attempting to salvage the old ironwork was not a believer in the supernatural, but what he saw one night changed his mine forever.

He had been working on the building for about a year and had stayed behind when the other workers left to finish up a project. He was heading for the back exit through a long narrow hallway, his normal route, when he saw a tall grayish-complexioned man in a dark old-fashioned suit standing just to the right of the doorway. He shined his flashlight on the man and suddenly the man disappeared then reappeared to the left of the door. He was frightened when his light picked up the man's strange hollow eyes. He knew in spite of his former beliefs, the creature was not of this world.

When he finally got up the nerve to speak of his experience to his fellow workers, he was shocked to find many of the others had had similar experiences. Some had felt ghostly hands touch their shoulders or face only to find no one there when they turned to see who was behind them.

One carpenter who was working late one night heard footsteps over his head in the second floor. Only thing was the building was locked, and no one else was in the jail. When he went up to investigate, the footsteps stopped.

Another worker was walking up the spiral staircase to the third floor and heard footsteps following him. When he turned, he was alone on the stairs.

One of the rooms had lead-based material that needed to be removed. The workers were all wearing protective suits and masks. The room naturally was always kept locked due to the hazardous material and excessive dust, but one day when the workers entered there were some fat bare footprints in the dust. No one had access to the room except the hazardous material removal team and they took great care to keep all parts of their bodies covered. No one of them would have risked their health to play such a prank. It had to be the genuine article, a real ghost.

Considering the history of the building, it might be strange if there were no presences within.

Charleston Tea Garden

This is the only working tea garden in the country. It offers you a unique way to see how tea is produced. You also get a chance to sample some different flavors of tea.

Aquarium

Since its opening in May 2000, the South Carolina Aquarium has moved up to be the state's number-one attraction. It offers a lot. First off, it's located right at Charleston harbor and offers a breathtaking view.

Once inside, I was able to view so much of South Carolina's native marine and marsh life. From river otters to sharks, there are 60 exhibits that interpret the state's diversity: mountain streams, piedmont rivers, coastal swamps, salt marshes and ocean. You will find one ghost in there, the Ghost Crab.

Old Slave Mart Museum

The Old Slave Mart was opened in 1852. Here slaves, most from the West African region, were auctioned off. Most of these people were skilled rice planters and much sought after by the rice plantation owners in and around Charleston. In 1938 it was opened as the Slave Mart Museum, making it the oldest black museum of slave artifacts in America.

It is a good place to start learning about the Gullah culture, which is unique to the low country around Charleston, Savannah and the Sea Islands. One of the things they are most noted for is the beautiful Sweet Grass Basket. Check out the Old Marketplace to find some examples. African Americans were often not given credit for their inventions. All the praise went to the white owner or employer in later years. While you are in Charleston, you will have to try some She Crab Soup. When you do, give the praise for this delicacy to William Deas, a black butler of Robert Goodwyn Rhett, a former mayor of Charleston in the early 1900s. Deas created she-crab soup at 116 Broad Street, now the John Rutledge House Inn, as a treat when President Taft visited Charleston. The original builder of the house was John Rutledge, a signer of the declaration of Independence and chief justice of the U.S. Supreme Court.

The Gullahs brought their own folklore and ghost stories with them from Africa, and no trip to Charleston would be complete without visiting some of the places where their history and culture are displayed. Gallery Chuma just across from the visitor's center offers a look at the culture though art. It also offers an opportunity to learn more about the Gullah culture through Gullah books, crafts, storytelling, spirituals, tours and food.

One of the most popular ghost stores of the Gullah people is the Boo Hag story. "Hag" is Gullah for "ghost." Many of us have heard the expression "hag-ridden," and this story explains how it came about.

The Boo Hag is an ugly creature with a body the color and texture of raw meat. She roams the night looking for victims, but since her skinless appearance would be a dead giveaway, she steals the skin of some of her victims so she can walk around undetected.

Then while people are sleeping, she sheds her stolen skin and hides it nearby, then slips through a crack and "rides" her victims in their sleep. While being "ridden," the victim is rendered paralyzed and unable to resist. Should the victims resist, she might kill them instead and take the skin for her disguise.

The Gullah believe if you leave a broom by your bed, you are protected from the Hag as she becomes distracted and tries to count the straws, thus occupying herself until dawn when she is powerless.

Boone Hall Plantation

Boone Hall is also one of America's oldest working, living plantations. It has been growing crops for more than 320 years. However, the present-day mansion was actually reconstructed in 1936. The original plantation house and two later homes were destroyed by war, fire and nature. The reconstructed home is very accurate in appearance to what a plantation of the antebellum era would look like. The plantation offers a "slave street," one of very few in existence. It is so accurate that the 1980s TV miniseries *North and South* was filmed there.

Two impressive things have remained from earlier eras. The entrance lane of live oak trees was planted in 1743 by the son of Major John Boone, one of the early owners and its resident spirit. Visitors to the plantation have reported seeing a misty figure in a Confederate uniform trying to remove a bullet from a wounded ghostly comrade.

The Army of the Dead

No other city except New Orleans could hope to rival Charleston in the quantity and quality of its ghostly inhabitants, so I was not surprised when a native told me Charleston even has an entire army of ghosts.

The legend goes that around midnight the Confederate dead who died without knowing the war ended, rise up at night and march to the aid of General Robert E. Lee. They began in the last days of the war and still march on dark and moonless nights. They roll through the darkened streets with cannon and wagons. The sound of marching feet and rolling artillery can be heard at the midnight hour. But beware of trying to catch a glimpse of these undead soldiers. One laundress heard the sounds of this phantom army and slipped from her bed to see what was going on. She watched the ghostly parade, but when it had passed and she returned to her room, she found her right arm had been paralyzed; she never regained normal use of that arm.

Francis Marion Hotel

One East Battery

Poogan's Porch

Chapter 9 Tennessee

Chattanooga

Read House

New hotels come and go, but one Grande Dame of the old guard, The Read House refuses to be out-classed. It combines modern convenience and history in such a subtle blend you will fall in love with the place. It's not what you'd expect from a chain hotel, no matter how prestigious.

The Sheraton Read House began life as the Crutchfield House in 1847. Chattanooga was just emerging as a railway hot spot. Thomas Crutchfield and his family built their inn directly across from the rail terminal, insuring the inn's success. The trains turned Chattanooga into a boomtown, and the Crutchfields prospered.

As the dark era of the Civil War began, things changed in Chattanooga and for the hotel. One historic event that took place in the hotel lobby reflected the times to come. Jefferson Davis was a guest at the hotel on his way home to Mississippi after resigning from the U.S. Senate; Davis spoke briefly and temperately on the subject of secession. But it was still enough to enflame William Crutchfield, Thomas's brother. William called Davis a traitor and military despot. Davis demanded satisfaction. A duel was barely averted when Thomas Crutchfield, Jr., hurried his fiery brother out of sight. Some reports say Thomas was a Southern sympathizer. William's and Thomas's differences were a microcosm of Chattanooga and the entire state of Tennessee. It was deeply divided on this issue.

Some reports say William never enlisted but did act as an honorary captain in the Union Army at Chickamauga campaign and the siege of Chattanooga. However, Elizabeth Lyle Saxon, a relative of the Crutchfields, in her book published in 1905, stated: "Will Crutchfield ... was then a major on the Union General Wilder's staff and twenty-odd in number of his blood relations swept up in the gray-clad ranks of the Confederacy, to meet death. But he took no part in the hostilities after the first day, for the reason that he had a serious illness, which lasted a week. Years after he learned that his wife, whose sympathies were as strong for the South as were his for the

Union, had drugged him heavily, and so prevented his taking further part in the fratricidal strife."

Whether it was due to the "house divided" or commercial reasons, Thomas Crutchfield sold the hotel shortly before the war. The new owners never prospered. When the fighting swept into Chattanooga, the hotel was commandeered by the Union forces and converted into a hospital in 1863. The hotel survived the entire war only to burn to the ground in 1867.

That might have been the end of the line for the hotel had not a doctor named John T. Read stepped into the picture. By 1871 the city's economy had begun its slow recovery. Dr. Read and his son, Samuel, capitalized on this and built an even grander hotel on the old Crutchfield House site.

For the first time, the sign over the door was "Read House," the name by which it is still known. Samuel enhanced the hotel's reputation. The Read House became the place the elite chose to stay in Chattanooga.

In 1927 the original structure was replaced by the present 10-story Georgian-style brick-and-terra-cotta building. Those original materials would be far too costly to duplicate today: terrazzo floors inlaid with marble, paneling of quarter-sawed walnut, carved and gilded woodwork, mirrors recessed in massive arches, and a lobby beautifully defined by its soaring columns. Fortunately most of these exquisite features survived the re-dos over the years. A few such as a large mahogany bar were lost to architect's whims.

One priceless item was preserved by a small quirk of fate: During one of the later restorations, the contractor was redoing the Silver Ballroom on the second floor. It has a beautiful silver and crystal Waterford chandelier and some sconces that looked like wrought iron. The contractor ordered the sconces torn out as he thought they did not go with the "Silver" theme. A bellman, Howard Johnson, who had worked for the hotel for 27 years, said, "No don't take them out. Polish them."

The sconces turned out to be solid silver when polished. Naturally they still grace the ballroom today.

Of course, you wouldn't expect anything to be ordinary in a place like the Read House, and you would be right. It has played host to notables like Winston Churchill and Al Capone - fortunately not at the same time - Tallulah Bankhead, Gary Cooper and Tom Thumb. Dixie Carter and her husband, Hal Holbrook, were frequent guests. It even has its own resident ghost.

Annalisa Netherly was a living-breathing guest at the hotel in the late '20s when extended hotel stays were common. Not much is known of how she came to the Read House. Perhaps her husband brought her, or perhaps it was a "gentleman friend," but however she arrived, her spirit was destined to remain through the ages. Legend says her husband found her romantically entertaining another man and was so enraged he slit her throat, almost decapitating her in the bathtub of room 311. That's the room she is seen in most frequently.

She doesn't seem to like men, especially men who smoke. Ironically her room is on a smoking floor, so that creates some interesting situations. Al Capone also stayed in that room as a "guest" of the government when he was brought to trial in Chattanooga. Talk about your original "odd couple."

Many people have felt her presence; there are some who have seen her. Several years ago, a little boy stayed at the hotel with his parents. His mother asked the desk clerk, " I know this sounds strange, but does this hotel have a ghost?" Apparently the family had a ghost in their home, and the little boy, who was a sensitive, told his parents that it "felt like home" at the hotel.

Children seem to be much more naturally sensitive to spirits. One little girl was staying in the room with her parents. They noticed her talking to someone they could not see but dismissed it as just an imaginary friend. Children often do that. What got strange was when the girl asked for paper and crayons to draw the "pretty lady." Happy to keep the child entertained, the parents got the crayons and paper; however, when the girl drew a lady in 1920s clothing that she had never seen, they became alarmed and asked at the desk. The clerk told the story of Annalisa.

Some people who stayed in "Annalisa's room" would come to the desk in the night and asked to be changed as they "felt something" in the room.

One guest recalled that when she was napping on the sofa, the telephone started to ring. As she tried to wake up and answer the phone, she felt "someone pulling her up" as if to help her. This guest did not know she was staying in Annalisa's room at the time. She changed rooms when the full story came out.

When men are staying in the room, they bring out the trickster in Annalisa. Keys refuse to work, the TV or the lights flash off and on by themselves. I guess Annalisa doesn't like men. Considering how she died, is that not unusual?

Another tale of Annalisa is that she came to Chattanooga in the early 1920s to meet her fiancé, but it turned out he was already betrothed to another woman.

The tale has become blurred over time, and it is not clear whether Annalisa took her own life because of the rejection, or if her lover killed her to prevent his current sweetheart from learning of his duplicity.

Whichever tale is true, room 311 of the Read House is "Annalisa room."

While staying at the hotel, be sure to try its marvelous restaurant, Porter's Steakhouse.

The Crutchfields and Reads would all be proud that their names are commemorated in this hotel.

What more can you ask? Perhaps a city well worth visiting that has attractions to please the entire family? Well, Chattanooga has those in abundance.

Chattanooga's location on the Tennessee River made it a natural vacation playground. But for most of the 20th century one thing spoiled its image as a favored destination for tourists. It was America's dirtiest city. The Environmental Protection Agency officially named it that in 1969 just before Earth Day.

The Hotel Chalet at the Choo Choo

Read House is not the only haunted lodging in Chattanooga. Perhaps the city's most well-known landmark is the Chattanooga Choo-Choo. Most people know that what is now the lobby of the Hotel Chalet at the Choo Choo was once the railroad terminal. What many are not aware of is one of history's most ironic cases of déjà-vu. In 1871 it was the site of the magnificent Stanton House, one of the most-luxurious hotels of the era. The once-grand resort degenerated into an abandoned hulk. Then in 1905, Southern Railway acquired the property, leveled the hotel and built a showplace terminal. The 85-foot glass dome was the largest freestanding dome in the country at the time. Again the pendulum swung. The day of the passenger train passed, and once again a magnificent building had outlived its purpose. It, too, appeared destined to be razed.

Then in 1974, it again became a resort complex built around its unique history. The massive dome room is now the lobby for the 360-room hotel. The sleeper cars, once the ultimate luxury of the wealthy, now are offered as hotel rooms. You can have a real hotel room in the renovated hotel if you prefer. I stayed in one of the very upscale boxcars on a one visit and felt like a Victorian matron. There is a beautiful garden when you step out of the boxcar. I didn't see any of the spirits but felt like maybe Rockefeller or Carnegie was my neighbor in another boxcar. Others have seen the ghost of a conductor who is said to wander between the train cars. Ther is also a porter who helps passengers with their luggage and a Civil War soldier.

While there you must get a photo of Chattanooga's iconic Choo Choo parked just outside the hotel. The lobby has many artifacts from the days when it was a working train station.

Several of the dining cars have become restaurants. The complex offers a wide variety of eateries, ranging from the Silver Diner serving pizza to the elegant Diner in the Diner serving gourmet meals reminiscent of the golden era of the railroad. Their most-romantic restaurant is the Station House. All the wait staff are singers. You are royally entertained as you dine. The menu offers ample choices: steak, chicken, pasta and seafood. To end the evening, choose either Café Espresso, for a gourmet coffee and dessert, or the Victorian Lounge, where you can enjoy a cocktail surrounded by the ambience of a more-elegant era.

Chattanooga Aquarium

When the city decided to turn that soubrette around, it did so with a vengeance. When the Chattanooga Aquarium opened in 1992, the city was on the fast track to becoming one of America's favorite fun destinations. The Aquarium opened as the world's largest freshwater aquarium, but that was just the beginning. In May 2005 the city of Chattanooga unveiled its completed $120 million Waterfront Project.

The aquarium is housed in two stunning buildings with peaked glass spires that add a distinctive touch to Chattanooga's skyline.

You begin your River Journey on the fourth floor with the Seahorse Exhibit. If you always thought seahorses were all alike think again. Watch playful otters splash their way in a forest cove. Enter the steamy backwaters of the Mississippi Delta and observe the interaction of alligators, turtles, wading birds and other wildlife that make up the complex web of life in the steamy swamplands. Glimpse the variety of life that inhabits the rivers of the world. You can actually touch a prehistoric sturgeon or watch giant catfish skim along a river bottom. When you are saturated in freshwater wonders, move on, as do the rivers of the world, to the Ocean Journey.

It's hard to choose which you will like better. The original aquarium is larger, but the new addition is packed with color and adventure. From the tiny flying jewels in the butterfly garden that actually alight on your body, to the huge sharks you can actually touch, this is an adventure into another dimension. View the immense beauty of a coral reef teeming with thousands of colorful fish, from the large barracuda and shark to tiny minnows as only a diver could. Marvel at the Boneless Beauties Gallery where exotic sea life ranging from tiny luminous jellyfish to huge Pacific octopi awaits you.

An IMAX theater is also part of the aquarium complex.

River Walk

Leaving the Aquarium, you will be in the Passage. This park is more than a crossing from the city to the Riverwalk. It is an artistic recreation in stone, water and metal of the Cherokee Trail of Tears. Chattanooga is built on the site of Ross's Landing, the Cherokee trading post owned by Chief John Ross, and marks the beginning of the infamous Trail of Tears. The Passage was designed by five Cherokee artists from Oklahoma and depicts the culture and history of the People. Seven massive ceramic disks tell the history of the Cherokee Nation. At the river, seven fountains, representing the seven tribes of the Cherokee nation, spout forth the life-giving waters of the Tennessee River. However in 1867 the river took many lives with a devastating flood, that disaster left a spectral imprint on the riverwalk. The spirits of those killed by the flood are said to wander near Ross's Landing, They are joined by many spirits of Cherokee who died on the Trailof Tears and were unwilling to abandon their homes. Cold spots are felt and mysterious voices heard.

Directly in front of the aquarium, the city's River Pier ties the river and city even closer together.

Bluff View Art District

A stroll in either direction on the River Walk, leads to more exciting discoveries both old and new. The Hunter Museum of American Art now has a bridge connecting it and the entire Bluff View Art District to the waterfront. The Hunter has long been recognized as an outstanding museum, but now it has become more dynamic. It draws the visitor into the experience with an outdoor sculpture garden that offers jazz concerts atop the bluff, classes ranging from painting to cooking, and so much more. Keep the art experience alive and wander into the Bluff View Art District next.

Bluff View Art District is a spot that feeds the soul as well as the body. Perched on the cliffs overlooking the Tennessee River, it was once a neighborhood of magnificent homes and has been revived as a Mecca for artists. Culinary art is alive and well there, also. Dining at the Back Inn Café transports you to a little Italian bistro. The food is superb, music is mellow. And the view of the Tennessee River and the Sculpture Garden is breathtaking.

Of course the raison-de-etré for the district is the art, so be sure to visit the Hunter Museum of American Art, the Sculpture Garden, the River Gallery and, most of all, the glassblowers studio. Tommy Spake works miracles with molten glass. You can watch a work of art created before your eyes there. Of course, for overnight visitors, the Bluff View Inn offers unique accommodations furnished with original artwork and antiques.

Coolidge Park

All the newness isn't confined to the south side of the river. Coolidge Park offers a marriage of 21st-century technology with the old-fashioned town park. Like the old town park where neighbors gathered to picnic and celebrate holidays, it offers a large green space with a fountain and a carousel. But high tech interactive water jets power the fountain. Some spurt out of the mouths of its lions and bears, some from the ground. So if you wade, beware; the next jet of water could have your name on it.

The Carousel is the centerpiece of the park. It is the ultimate marriage of old and new. It began life in the workshop of Gustav Dentzel in 1895. It went to its first home in Rochester, NY, then moved on to Massachusetts and finally Atlanta. In the 1960s it was dismantled and its beautifully carved horses sold individually. The carousel sat rotting away in an old warehouse until a Chattanooga man, Charlie Walker, rescued it in the early 1980s. Still it was useless without horses. Charlie told Bud Ellis, a Tennessee carver, about this beautiful machine. Ellis founded "Friends of the Carousel" in Chattanooga and taught carousel's supporters how to carve.

While the carving was in progress, others restored the carousel to its original charm but with a high tech boost. It has new soft start and stop mechanisms, that are easier on its parts, and two band organs, a Wurlitzer and a new Stinson 57-2. The finished masterpiece was placed in a specially constructed building with rocking chair seats for those who choose to sit and watch the carousel whirl around. The old and new blend so skillfully, you can't spot where one ends and the other begins. But that isn't the important thing. What is important is the legacy of this work of art for Chattanooga children and visitors alike. The line at the bottom of the organ sums it up well: Dedicated to Children of All Ages.

The park can be accessed in both an old-and new-fashioned way also. You could drive over the Market Street or other bridges, or you could hoof it on the Walnut Street Bridge. The Walnut Street Bridge is an attraction in its own right. It was originally a "normal" bridge that you drove over. It became unsafe for automotive traffic and was destined to be demolished. But a lot of people didn't want to see the old landmark go. It was decided to preserve it and create the world's largest pedestrian bridge.

Southern Belle

The Tennessee River has shaped Chattanooga's destiny from the beginning, so it is only natural to want to get out on it while in Chattanooga. There are lots of ways to do this, but two of the most fun are the Southern Belle and the Chattanooga Ducks.

The Southern Belle takes you out for sightseeing/dining on a riverboat. Cruises vary from the morning sightseeing-only through lunch and dinner trips. Whichever one you choose, you will have fun. Food is plentiful. The narrator is well-informed about the sites you pass, and there is a touch of relaxing Southern steamboat music to top it off.

International Towing and Recovery Museum

One other museum that will interest the antique auto enthusiasts and history buffs alike is the International Towing & Recovery Hall of Fame and Museum. Chattanooga was chosen for the museum's location because the first tow truck was built there by Earnest Holmes in 1913. It consisted of three poles, a pulley and a chain hooked to the frame of a 1913 Cadillac. Holmes patented his invention and began the manufacture of tow trucks. The museum was dedicated in 1995; you can't help but get nostalgic when you look at the 1947 GMC Bubble Nose and other early tow trucks and paraphernalia.

Rock City, Ruby Falls and the Incline Railway

In all the excitement of the New Chattanooga, don't forget the old tried-and-true attractions. Ruby Falls, America's largest underground waterfalls, is a must. Also nearby is that perennial favorite, Rock City. To get up Lookout Mountain, Incline Railway is the most-direct route.

Raccoon Caverns is a must for those who want to explore more than 5.5 miles of underground wonders. It has been rated one of the top 10 caves in the United States.

Dining

Pluckett's Grocery or City Café Diner are my breakfast choices. Stir, in the Chattanooga Choo Complex, or Old Gilman's Grill are more upscale choices for dinner. Tony's Pasta Shop & Trattoria is delicious and filling when you are in the Bluff View Art District. Tony's has won the Times Free Press Best of the Best Award for Best Italian Restaurant in Chattanooga for three years in a row. You get to choose your pasta, sauce, and additions. The Wanderer is located in Hotel Indigo. For lunch after seeing the Lookout Mountain attractions, try The Purple Daisy in Historic St. Elmo.

Naughty Cat Café is a place where you can relax and sip a beverage when you visit with about 30 cats looking for a forever home. It's the only cat cafe in Chattanooga. Whitney Sickels and Heath Hanson wanted to help abandoned cats, so they began this project. It's a wonderful way to relax and you may even find a new housemate. They limited the age to over 11-year old children for the cats' safety. Since it gets busy, especially on weekends, I suggest making an appointment.

Tennessee Valley Railroad Museum

For a trip back in time, take a ride on the 1890-era steam locomotive and visit the Grand Junction Depot Turntable and shop. TVRM offers the only regularly scheduled passenger service in east Tennessee. You can choose between the Missionary Ridge Local or the trip to Chickamauga, GA, both round trips. If you are seeking a longer trip, TVRM offers several Dixie Land Excursions on select weekends throughout the year.

Most excursions include a lunch in the 1924 restored dining car.

Chickamauga

On September 19, 1863, the wooded hills of nearby Chickamauga rang with the clash of steel and the roar of gunfire as Confederate and Union troops locked in mortal combat in what was to become the bloodiest battle fought on Georgia soil. This battle calls attention to the "brother against brother" aspect of this war. When Lincoln was informed of the casualties at Chickamauga he was devastated. He also had a reason for personal grief. His brother- in law, Benjamin Helms, was one of the casualties. He was a Confederate officer who died at Chickamauga.

When the smoke cleared and the battle was done, the Confederates held the field with the Federals pushed back to Chattanooga. But at what price! They had lost more than 18,000 men out of their 66,000 soldiers. The Union Army left 16,000 bloody corpses at Chickamauga. Twenty-five years after the war, Chickamauga and Chattanooga National Military Park was officially dedicated on the anniversary of that bloody battle. Is it any wonder that countless visitors and staff alike have come face to face with the restless spirits whose life ended so abruptly on these rolling hills?

The federal government is the last to ever acknowledge the possibility of anything supernatural, yet it is ironic that the film it uses to interpret this park features two ghosts: a Union and a Confederate soldier, who meet on the centennial of the park's dedication. These two fellows discuss the battles from their respective points of view. The only thing both agree on is the fact they are both proud to be Americans. While waiting to see the film -- even if you never watch interpretive films at parks, do not miss this one -- you can view the Fuller Collection consisting of 355 weapons, many of them extremely rare. As you tour the battlefield watch for something the government does not admit exists there, ghosts.

The most commonly seen specter is "Old Green Eyes." Actually, he was seen at Chickamauga before the Civil War. According to John Fogerty, a Confederate re-enactor, who has visited the site many time, "Union soldiers atop Snodgrass hill claimed they saw this creature lurking among the many thousands of maimed and mangled bodies on the evening of September 20th, after the heaviest fighting there. The Indians who camped on the banks of the creek were the ones who named it "Chickamauga," "The River of Death" since they lost so many of the tribe to yellow fever there. That might account for the creature seen by the Union soldiers and described as having long black hair, long fangs, talon-like claws and a pumpkin-like head with blazing greenish-orange eyes.

Whether he is a Civil War phantom or an earlier demon, as the Native Americans believe, Old Green Eyes never fails to terrify anyone so unfortunate to cross his path.

Nicky Renolds, who worked as a ranger at the battlefield, tells a little about "Green Eyes." Visitors who come to the park look for the green eyes of a solider killed in battle, but that isn't the basis of the legend. The 125th Ohio Infantry, nicknamed "Opdycke's Tigers" or "The Tiger Regiment," fought heroically on Snodgrass Hill. Later a monument to the regiment was placed there, a statue of the regiment's leader, Emerson Opdycke, with a scene from the battle on a bas-relief slab. Atop the slab is a carved tiger. According to one legend, the green eyes belong to the tiger.

Other apparitions are more humanistic. There is the "Woman in White" reported frequently by visitors. She walks in the fields and disappears when approached. Specters appear frequently around the Hunt Cemetery and Lost Corners areas. Naturally many of the specters are soldiers. Nicky tells of a Yankee re-enactor in uniform who was walking at sunset on one of the maintenance roads. He spotted what he thought was a Confederate re-enactor and hailed him. The Rebel panicked and pointed the gun at him, then disappeared. To this day the re-enactor refuses to walk alone on that road.

John Fogerty knows one woman who actually visits the grave of "Johnny, the only Confederate with a known marked grave." This woman "talks" with Johnny and claims he hovers about and enjoys the attention. Many others have reported seeing him around the woods near Alexander Bridge Road.

John's girlfriend also had a strange experience near where the Poe Cabin had been. "She heard someone moving through the grass behind her, whirled around to see who it was and actually saw the grass being stepped on as if some unseen human was walking towards her. She said, 'Are you friend or foe?' and the thing turned away from her and paced into the woods."

Harper Harris, former historian at Kennesaw Civil War Museum and a Confederate re-enactor, tells of his first re-enactment at Chickamauga. "I shot on a cannon crew. I hadn't been with these guys long then. One day they said, 'We're shooting up at Chickamauga this weekend.' I thought that'd be great. They said 'Man, it's a real spooky place. We see some strange things every time we go up there.' I thought they were just pulling my leg. We camped out in front of Snodgrass Cabin. In the evening, we sat around the fireplace in the cabin. It got later and later, and everybody else had drifted off. I was sitting alone by the fireplace. I began hearing all kinds of noises and figured all the guys were playing tricks, so I just sat and ignored the noises. When I decided to turn in and headed out for my sleeping bag. I realized all the other guys were already asleep, so something else was making the noises. I stayed up all night long. I still don't like to be up there by myself."

Perhaps all the deaths that occurred there also attract death. For whatever reason, the battlefield is a favorite place for suicides.

The city of Chickamauga is also worth a visit. It was here that Union General Rosecrans had his headquarters just before the events leading to the Battle of Chickamauga. The town had what both sides needed desperately, water. Crawfish Springs, for which the town was originally named, bubbles up still adjoining the Gordon Lee Mansion. The mansion, completed in 1847, has recently been purchased by the city and will be renovated as it was in 1863. The mansion was used as a hospital by the Union soldiers although soldiers from both sides were treated there, with many Union doctors remaining behind to care for the wounded after the Southern victory. There are rumors of ghosts lurking behind the mansion's stately doors, but Richard Barclift, the present manager and former stepson of the owner, claims not. He admits that people have reported "things," but he says they could all be explained. Still, with that many deaths occurring in the building when it was used for a hospital, you can't help but wonder.

The town will make you feel you have stepped back in time. By the 150th anniversary of the Civil War, the city plans to have all of its electrical wiring underground and lighting put in place to look as the gaslights looked in that era.

Lee and Gordon's Mills, about 2 miles east of the center of town, is one of the oldest mills in the state of Georgia. The mill was built by James Gordon in 1836. It was used by Confederate General Braxton Bragg, commander of the Army of Tennessee, as his headquarters until September 10 when he moved his headquarters south to LaFayette, GA. Union troops then occupied the mill and surrounding area. Skirmishes between the two armies occurred until the major Battle of Chickamauga. The mill later served as a headquarters for Wheeler's cavalry until Union troops recaptured it in the winter of 1863. The City has recently entered into a lease agreement to operate the Mill also.

(Note: Chickamauga, Rock City and several of these sites are actually in Georgia not Tennessee, but since they are more easily accessed from Chattanooga and usually considered part of "Greater Chattanooga," I have included them here.)

If you haven't visited Chattanooga lately, you just haven't seen the "new" Chattanooga. This revitalized city rolls out the red carpet for visitors and even makes it easy to get around by providing free electric shuttle service.

It has succeeded in adding the new while not detracting from the glory of the old.

Nashville

Gaylord Opryland Hotel

Opryland Hotel is the "baby" of my historic hotels at only 30 years old, but it has packed a lot of history into those years. It opened in 1977 with 600 guestrooms and in just six years needed a major addition to accommodate the throngs of guests looking to visit its adjoining Opryland Theme Park and Grand Old Opry. In 1983 it added 467 additional rooms and its first signature atrium, the Garden Conservancy.

When it expanded again in 1996, it was the largest construction project in Nashville history at the time.

Today, the hotel has 2,881 rooms, and its Delta Atrium is reminiscent of the Louisiana bayou county with the convenience of New Orleans restraints thrown in for good measure. It is the largest non-casino hotel in the world. Guests can ride a "Delta Flatboat" through a guided tour of the atrium via the "Delta River" which had samples from more than 6,000 rivers throughout the world, including every registered river in the United States poured into it at the christening ceremony.

When I stayed there, my balcony overlooked the Delta, and it was all I could do to tear myself away from the window. I did leave my curtains open all the time so I could enjoy the view.

Walking about the grounds of the Opryland is like being in a small city. It even has a radio station. Historic WSM Nashville, the voice of the Grand Old Opry, is in the lobby. You can stand and look at the DJ's through the glass window as they play music: country, of course.

My favorite place to stroll in the hotel is the glass-enclosed atriums. You walk amid the 50,000 tropical plants and cascading waterfalls and envision a tropical rainforest, a rainforest with convenient restaurants and lounges.

Opryland Hotel is said to be haunted by the ghost of a "Mrs. McGavock." Several employees and guests claim they have seen her walking around the hotel. Opryland Hotel is one of the most luxurious hotels in the Volunteer State and is the last place one would think of as being haunted, so it's strange indeed to hear such tales.

Union Station Hotel

The Opryland is not the only hotel in town to boast a few specters from the past. The Union Station Hotel has a few interesting guests from days gone by. The soaring gothic-spired building began life as the train station for the Louisville & Nashville Railroad at the dawn of the 20th century. Guests on opening day, October 9, 1900, were welcomed into a lofty building fitting the era when the railroad was king. It sported a barrel-vaulted ceiling, Tiffany stained-glass, two live-alligator ponds and a bronze likeness of Mercury topping its multi-story clock tower. When the automobile replaced the train as the most-popular means of travel, the glorious station began to deteriorate and eventually closed in the 1970s. In the '80s, however, it was given a second chance to shine; it was opened as a boutique hotel. However, the renovations did not dispel the spirits who linger there.

One is the spirit of a man who used to work on the huge clock tower. He had to climb 11 flights of stairs to get to the clockworks. He was very devoted to his job, and after his death he has been seen in the tower.

The other specter dates to WWII. She is a young woman who was expecting her fiancé to return to the station but instead learned he had been killed overseas. She went to the station, climbed to the top of the staircase and threw herself to her death. People claim she still wanders the lobby waiting for her lover.

Hermitage Hotel

Still one other hotel with a ghostly history is the Hermitage. When Nashville's first million-dollar hotel opened its doors in 1910, it immediately became the favored meeting place of Nashville's upper crust as well as drawing its guests from the top levels of society, entertainment and politics. Over the years, the Hermitage has played host to six U.S. presidents and so many top-name stars it is almost impossible to count. It was one of the first hotels to admit women to its banquet honoring President Taft who was a guest in 1911.

Perhaps that explains the Lady in White who seems to float around in the building wearing a white nightgown. But the Southern belle who is seen only in the lobby is a different story. Her clothing is from an earlier era. Perhaps she is a remnant of what was on the site before the hotel was built, but that is just speculation. Another interesting phantom is the baby in room 910. People frequently report a baby crying incessantly from that room, but on checking the room is always empty when the crying occurs and it stops as soon as a bellman opens the door to check. One other unexplained phenomenon in the Hermitage is the lobby mirror. Occasionally, observers will notice a crack starting at the top then, with no repair, the crack will mysteriously disappear.

Fort Nashborough

Nashville started life as Fort Nashborough, a frontier fort strategically placed on the Tennessee River. A tiny trading post for the French fur traffic was established in 1710, and by 1779 it had become a permanent settlement. Relationships between the new settlers and the Cherokees were not good. The Battle of the Bluffs in 1781 almost wiped out the settlement. Perhaps that is the reason you may encounter Cherokee warriers and early settlers who died in that battle.

Nashborough changed its name to Nashville in 1784 and moved steadily forward until the Civil War. Nashville's location made it a strategic point due to the railroad and established riverboat connections to the Mississippi River. A recreation of that first settlement is preserved in its original location. Today that tiny settlement has grown into the city known around the world as "Music City." But it is so much more than the home of country music. For one thing, it is also known as "the Athens of the South" because of its dedication to the arts, and never forget that as the capital of Tennessee, it has a strong political heritage.

Hermitage

Part of that heritage is found in the home of our seventh president and his wife, Rachel. She left her mark on the Hermitage even more than Old Hickory himself. The Hermitage has been extensively restored to its 1830s splendor and reflects the taste of a president who was "a man of the people." But more than Jackson's presence is preserved in the Hermitage. His controversial wife, Rachel, chooses the spot and made it a home. Rachel Jackson was a pipe-smoking divorcee when "nice women didn't." During Jackson's presidential campaign, deemed the dirtiest in history, Rachel's reputation was tattered due to her marriage to Jackson before her divorce was finalized. Although they remarried afterward, this was a major issue in the campaign, one Jackson felt caused the death of his beloved Rachel shortly before his inauguration. When he left the White House, he never failed to spend time each evening in Rachel's garden where she was buried. At his death, he was buried beside her. You can still see traces of the flowers and herbs Rachel planted. Besides Rachel there are over 400 other bodies burried there including Jackson. It's only natural there are many report-sof the paranormal. People passing near Jackson's grave often smell cigar smoke although no one is smoking on the property. Others have seen Confederate soldiers there.

The Hermitage opened as a museum in 1889. The Jacksons were not aristocrats as earlier presidents were. He was a rough-and-tumble frontiersman who knew what it meant to work for a living. What began as a modest frontier farm grew, due to his hard work, to a prosperous and expansive cotton plantation seen at the present-day mansion. The exhibits there also show how his prosperous farm deteriorated after Jackson's death and its post-Civil War dilapidation.

The heritage of the enslaved people who did most of the work at the Hermitage also is preserved there. Jackson many have been bigoted when it came to Native Americans, but evidence indicates he treated his slaves fairly for a man of his time. In fact, many of them remained with the family after the Emancipation Proclamation as paid employees.

Perhaps that is why some of the phantoms found at the hermitage are African Americans. Caretakers have reported seeing a group of phantom slaves gathered on the balcony in front of Jackson's bedroom.

Reports of strange happenings at the Hermitage go way back. Jackson's daughter-in-law, Sarah Jackson, reports an incident when she was putting her children to bed. The sheet was mysteriously yanked off the children, who began squabbling as to who had done the deed. When she succeeded in getting them back to sleep, the sheet was pulled off once again. This time the children and Sarah knew it was not one of the kids playing a trick but some unearthly phenomenon. The children were never put in that room again. In fact, no one slept there after that.

After the home passed out of the Jackson family and was under the care of the Ladies Hermitage Association, paranormal events were still occurring. The house had become somewhat rundown by this time, and the ladies decided in order to prevent any further vandalism, two of them would spend the nights at the old home until a caretaker could be hired. The daylight hours passed pleasantly enough for the ladies, but at night while they slept on a mattress in the living room, they were awakened by the sounds of dishes crashing in the kitchen, chains rattling and the sound of a horseman riding frantically up and down the stairs. The ladies lit a kerosene lantern, and the noises stopped. They explored all over the house and found no reason for the noise. The next night they left the lantern burning, but again after they fell asleep the sound began and stopped when they began looking for the source of the disturbance.

Old Hickory seemed to quiet down once the restoration was completed, but there was one full body's image of a semi-transparent figure taken in one of the mansion's bedrooms that was shown on local television.

When you visit, look for Rachel's ghost in the garden. It was her favorite place in the Hermitage and the spot where the former president sat every evening after he retired to feel near his dear departed wife. Today you can visit the graves of both where they lie in the rose garden.

Capitol Building

By 1859 Nashville was no longer a small settlement. It had become a sophisticated state capital housing a fitting Capitol building. Located on a high hill in downtown Nashville, the massive limestone building is considered one of the most magnificent public buildings of its time, anywhere in the country.

Its tower is based on the monument of Lysicrates in Athens, Greece. The mastermind behind this achievement never lived to see his dream completed. William Strickland, the Philadelphia architect brought in to design the capitol, died in 1854 and is entombed above the cornerstone in the northeast corner. Strickland may not have walked the corridors of his creation in life, but many say his spirit as well as his body has never left the capitol. Lots of evidence points to not only the renowned architect's presence but his arch nemesis' phantom as well.

When Strickland was invited to build the edifice, the person in charge of keeping expenses in line was Samuel Morgan, president of the committee in charge of the building project. Right from the beginning, these two strong-willed men clashed. Morgan had his way in many respects by dint of outliving Strickland. However, Morgan is also entombed in the building at the southeast end.

Many security personnel have reported hearing the two loud voices arguing about details of the construction project late at night after all the visitors, politicians and workers have departed.

These two old rivals are not the only famous people buried on the capitol grounds. President and Mrs. James K. Polk also have their permanent earthly abode there.

An interesting fact I learned while touring the capitol shows that Tennessee women, although unable to vote, still made their influence felt in Tennessee when the 19th amendment came up for the vote. Tennessee was the state that cast the deciding vote. Harry Burn, a young legislator from east Tennessee, changed his vote when his mother sent him a telegram saying, "If it's close, just give us a chance." Harry did. And American women's right to vote became the law of the land.

A tour of the capitol building is a "must ." The history, the architecture and the ghosts would be enough to make it so, but it also has some interesting artwork. The huge floating ball in front fascinates me. You can turn it yourself and marvel at how something that heavy can float. Another great piece is the statue of Andrew Jackson in front. It is one of only three copies of the statue designed by artist Clark Mills in existence: this one, one in Jackson Square in New Orleans, and one in Washington, D.C. What makes the bronze so unique is only the two rear legs of the horse support the statue.

The seventh president may be riding in front of the Capitol, but it is rumored that the specter of his wife, Rachel, roams about in the tower of the building. People driving by at night have spotted her there often.

General Jackson Showboat

The landing for the General Jackson is near Opry Mills. The paddle wheeler is reminiscent of the old steamboats that plied the rivers of America a century ago. Its four massive decks offer a variety of dining and entertainment options as you gain a different prospective of Music City while cruising the Cumberland River.

Grand Old Opry

What the Vatican is to Catholics is what the Grand Old Opry is to country music fans. It's the mother church, the musical home of all the legends of country music. I have seen many stars perform in different venues, but there was none that thrilled me as much as watching George Jones sing "She Stopped Loving Him Today" as I perched on the edge of my seat in the balcony of the Grand Old Opry. Of course, having seen Porter Wagoner flash his sequined coat and Roy Acuff shuffle to the mike were all experiences I will treasure forever. Roy Acuff was so symbolic of American values during the WWII years that the Japanese were known to use the battle cry, "To hell with Roosevelt, to hell with Babe Ruth, and to hell with Roy Acuff!"

Roy Acuff may be still enjoying his time on the Opry stage. Stagehands who are closing the auditorium at night have experienced the lights coming back on and the curtains opening for no explainable reason. Many of them believe it is either Roy Acuff, who performed almost up to the day of his death and lived in a special house built on the Opry House grounds, or a stagehand who had a heart attack and died in a nearby hospital.

Ryman Auditorium

It is only natural that many of the stars who stood in the spotlight would want to remain on throughout eternity. However, the "new" home of the Opry is not old enough to have accumulated many phantoms. The world's longest-running radio show moved there in 1974 when it outgrew its original home, The Ryman Auditorium. The Ryman is old enough to have developed a large repertoire of phantoms.

The Ryman was not built originally as a home for the Opry. It's much older than that. It was constructed in 1892 by a rowdy steamboat captain named Tom Ryman. Captain Ryman "found" religion and built the auditorium as a home for the Union Gospel Tabernacle. He also used it as a town meeting hall, and in 1897 it was contracted to host a large Confederate veterans reunion. The only problem was there were so many attendees, a new balcony had to be added. The Confederate group donated the money for the balcony, and in return it was named the Confederate Gallery.

One of those veterans must have enjoyed the performance as he is reputed to still be hanging around. Many times at rehearsals, the stage manager will see a lone man dressed in gray sitting in the balcony and send up a security guard up to run him off only to find on one is there. When the guard gets back down and looks up the man has "returned."

The Gray Man is never seen at performances, just at rehearsals or when the building is closed.

When Tom Ryman passed away in 1904, the building was renamed in his honor. In 1943 the Ryman became the home of the Grand Ole Opry.

Over the years, other spirits have joined the Gray Man. The legendary captain himself is often heard. When there is a show that he feels is "improper," he will make so much noise, many patrons claim they cannot hear the performance.

Naturally, Hank Williams has been seen there. Performers and workers alike have encountered the legendary singer's spirit both onstage and in the back halls.

Another singer who met a tragic end is also seen in the Ryman; Patsy Cline has been glimpsed by many in the Ryman dressing rooms.

One other interesting legend is "the curse of the Grand Ole Opry." It refers to the abnormally large number of Grand Ole Opry entertainers who have met or narrowly averted untimely deaths. Since Hank Williams' premature death in 1953 at the age of only 29, some 37 people connected with the Opry have felt the wrath of "the curse." On March 5, 1963, Patsy Cline, Ramsey (Randy) Hughes, Hawkshaw Hawkins, and Cowboy (Lloyd) Copas were killed in the fiery crash of Hughes' Piper Comanche returning from a benefit show. Gentleman Jim Reeves was another plane crash victim on July 31, 1964, while touring. Stringbean (David Akeman) and his wife, Estelle, were killed by burglars in their own home after returning from a performance at the Ryman on November 10, 1973. On September 4, 1991, Dotty West, who had been fighting a string of bad luck, was killed in a car crash on her way to the Grand Ole Opry. Del Wood, a longtime Opry star, had a stroke on September 22, 1989, the day she was scheduled to appear on the Legendary Ladies of Country Music Show at the Opry House and died later the same day. The list goes on and on, right up to the present day. Gene Watson, most known for his hit "Farewell Party," was driving from Houston to perform on the Opry when his bus caught fire on the outskirts of Nashville. Fate was thwarted this time. Watson did get close enough to the flames to singe his hair but the bus was badly damaged. To make this even more thought-provoking, the accident occurred on Friday the 13th of July 2007. Of course all this could be just a coincidence but ….

Whether you believe in the curse or even the ghosts, no trip to Nashville is complete without a visit to this legendary music shrine. It was so "sacred" that when the Opry moved to its new home, a circle from the center of the Ryman stage floor was cut out and implanted in the new Grand Ole Opry House. Be sure to see the life-sized bronze sculpture of one woman who carved an unforgettable niche in what had been a male-dominated field without relying on her looks or build. Minnie Pearl shares the entryway with her long-time friend, Roy Acuff, in a life-sized bronze of the couple seated on a bench.

Tootsies Orchid Lounge

For every music hall, there is a nearby gathering spot where all the performers come to hang out before and after shows. In Nashville, it's Tootsies. It is located just across the alley from the Ryman, and many famous stars played there first. Hank Williams used it as his favorite watering hole when he performed at the Opry. It was close enough he could sneak over and belt down a few between shows. In those days, it was Mom's. It became Tootsie's when Tootsie Bess bought it in 1960. It became "Orchid" when Tootsie came there one day and found her inexpensive painter had painted it bright orchid. Tootsie helped many a singer and picker on their way to the top with jobs and handouts. Actually, Tootsie was the second Tootsie to own it. Tootsie Ross was an earlier owner.

It made the news in 2006 when Pamela Anderson and Kid Rock got married on its stage in a surprise wedding. Actually, it was the third wedding of the lovesick duo in the same month.

Several movies have been filmed in part in Tootsie's over the years including *W.W. & the Dixie Dance Kings* starring Bert Reynolds, *Coal Miner's Daughter* starring Sissy Spacek as Loretta Lynn, and *The Nashville Rebel* starring Tex Ritter, Porter Wagoner, Faron Young, Loretta Lynn, the Wilburn Brothers, and Waylon Jennings.

The lounge continues in Tootsie's tradition of hiring up-and-coming musicians to entertain there. Of course, Hank Williams' spirit is reported to not only frequent the lounge but has actually been photographed on the stage. The misty image has appeared in a national magazine.

Music Row

Music Row today is home to many of Music City's recording studios and other music-driven businesses. It once offered lots of honky tonk bars where you could find some great musicians who played their hearts out for tips. Music Row, which once spread for a 10-block radius around 16th Avenue, now named Music Square, is still worth a look for those interested in the music industry. However, if you are searching for the museums of the country stars and the future stars of tomorrow, the museums have moved out where there is more room to spread out and rent is cheaper. Today's musicians are making appointments to meet with potential agents in offices, not bars anymore. But the old stories and maybe the ghosts are still there. Many people have claimed to meet Hank Williams strolling down Music Row.

Studio B may or may not have any phantom inhabitants, but it has enough memories of stars and would-be stars that you really need to visit it. It was where almost all the early Nashville artists recorded; from Dolly and Porter to Elvis and countless others, all sang their hearts out in the tiny studio. Built in 1957 for RCA, it is Nashville's oldest surviving recording studio and the home of the "Nashville Sound." After RCA closed it down, it was reopened in 1977 by the Country Music Hall of Fame and Museum. It is now a separate tour. The studio has been restored to its original 1957 state, so inside you are bathed in the same lights Elvis had installed for his music recordings. I felt like there were so many presences in that studio when I took the tour.

The home located at 1111 16th Ave. S was once the happy dwelling of a prosperous German immigrant named Jacob Schnell, his wife, Jennie, and their children. Jacob had used his earnings as a grain merchant to build a mansion in a fashionable neighborhood and thus launch his three daughters and son into Nashville society. Unfortunately, the early 1900s were not a good time for people of German descent. War was brewing, and most people distrusted all things German.

Undaunted, Jacob decided to give a huge coming out ball for his daughters. The ballroom on the third floor was filled with catered food, an expensive orchestra and the expectant Schnell family. Unfortunately, few guests came to enjoy Jacob's extravaganza. In a fury that Nashvillians would snub his daughters so, he cursed the city and declared that the home should never be maintained. He moved back to his former dwelling above the grain shop and left his family in the maledicted mansion. Eventually, his wife died, his son left, and one daughter married. Two daughters, Lena and Bertha, remained and honored their father's wishes. Nothing in the home was ever repaired. When pipes burst, they went unmended, drapes rotted at the windows, paint peeled and wood rotted. Lena died first. Bertha remained with only her dog, Andy, for a companion and continued on her appointed course until her own death at age 84 on June 30, 1974.

By 1977, the house was demolished and a fine office building was built on the site. Jacob's curse was a part of another era.

Or was it? When Capital Records, the new tenant of the building, moved in, unexplained happenings plagued the company so much that a psychic was brought in to determine the unexplained cold spots and machinery malfunctions that had no natural explanation. The psychic found that the building was still inhabited by the spirits of the two shunned sisters who were very sad over the way they had been treated in life. The psychic claimed to have exorcised the two spirits. Still, Capital Records soon moved to a new location.

Country Music Hall of Fame

The Hall of Fame moved from its Music Row location on May 17, 2001. The $37-million facility is now located in downtown Nashville just a short distance from the Ryman. Its featured exhibits include "Sing Me Back Home: A Journey through Country Music," which offers a collection of original recordings, instruments, costumes, photographs, and memorabilia of country music's biggest and most-loved stars. The Hall of Fame Rotunda showcases bronze-cast faces of all the inductees to the Country Music Hall of Fame. The Ford Theatre, which also is used for small concerts, is also located within the building. No ghosts but lots of memories reside here.

Tennessee State Museum

To round off an "artfully" great day, drop in at the Tennessee State Museum. Like all good galleries, the State Museum offers rotating exhibits of the finest art available as well as the permanent exhibits that contribute to Tennessee history. For just plain fun art, it's hard to beat the wall mural behind the escalator there. Nude, but not lewd, whimsical folks of all descriptions hasten to a futuristic airport scene. Some are fat, some are skinny, some have fancifully colored hair and some have none. Thanks to strategically placed briefcases and handbags, all are presented in such a way as not to offend the most-sensitive viewer.

Parthenon

The greatest work of art in Nashville is Athena, Nashville's own resident goddess. This ivory and gold statue of the Goddess Athena is arrayed in all her armor and balancing Nike in her right hand. (No, Nike isn't the patron of tennis shoes. She is the Goddess of Victory.). Eight years in the making, Nashville sculptor Alan LeQuire's Athena is 42 feet tall, making her the largest indoor statue in the Western world.

Her home is among the sun-dappled trees of Centennial Park in her own Parthenon. It stands both a memoriam to times gone by and a beacon to the future ages. The Nashville Parthenon is a work of art in its own right. It was built for the 1896 Centennial Fair. After the fair, local citizens decided to make it a permanent fixture of the city. Both are exact replicas of the originals.

Riverfront Park

For a different type of art, head down to Riverfront Park. The Fox Trot Carousel is a combination of historical tribute, fine arts and just plain fun. The carousel, located downtown in Riverfront Park, includes many of Nashville's most-memorable citizens. Davy Crockett wrestles a bear. Sequoia is writing the Cherokee alphabet. Charlotte Robinson, wife of one of the city founders, is busy saving Fort Nashborough from an Indian raid. Anne Dallas Dudley, who led the fight for women's rights and became the first woman delegate at large to the Democratic Convention, is there. Modern Nashvillians are represented there as well. William Edmondson, an artist who was the first African American to have a solo show at New York's Museum of Modern Art, is hard at work carving a dove. Kitty Wells, first woman to be elected to the Grand Ole Opry, joins Lula Naff, who managed the Ryman Auditorium for 50 years and is credited with collecting the autographed photos, playbills and programs of those who performed there over the years. The rollicking work of moving art is the creation of artist Red Grooms, who might be described as a Carousel cowboy who has managed to round up Nashville's past and present in one horsing-around attraction.

Nashville Zoo

Nashville has a rather nice albeit small zoo. The habitats, Gibbon Islands, Unseen New World, Bamboo Trail, African Elephant Savannah, Hyacinth Macaw, Meerkat and Bongo exhibits, are nicely done. The zoo has the Patton Family Wild Animal Carousel. Take a ride on one of the 39 brightly colored, wooden animals. It's a treat for kids of all ages and features species currently found at the zoo as well as a giraffe and several other animals it is planning on acquiring. Where else can you ride a giant anteater or a clouded leopard cub?

The carousel is the work of Zsolt Hormay. He learned his expertise from the masters of imaging, Disney. He was responsible for the Tree of Life at Disney's Animal Kingdom.

While they do not have a lot of the larger animals, the well-maintained habitats and programs make the zoo worthy of a visit.

What sets the Nashville Zoo apart is the Old Croft Mansion. The home is the second-oldest in Nashville, dating to around 1810. It was built by Michael Dunn and his wife, Elizabeth Rains. She was the daughter of Captain John Rains, one of the original builders of Fort Nasborough.

The fifth and last generation of that family lived in the home until 1985. The two unmarried childless sisters, Margaret and Elise Croft, deeded the 300-plus-acre farm, with its slave quarters and other history intact and preserved almost as it was 100 years ago, to the Cumberland Museum to be used as a zoo in 1964 with a life estate for themselves. Margaret died in 1974 while Elise continued to run the farm up into her 70s. When Elise died and the farm passed into the hands of the Nashville Zoo, it realized it had a historical treasure and has taken care to preserve this unique site. It is open it for tours from August through October.

Most of the family, including Margaret and Elise, are buried in a nearby cemetery. Legend has it that at least one of the Croft sisters' spirit remains in the home. People had seen a woman looking out he windows late in the evening when the home is closed to the public. Others have heard phantom footsteps on the porches.

Belle Meade Plantation

Speaking of larger-than-life women, Nashville has a few of those. Belle Meade Plantation began in 1807 when John Harding purchased 250 acres six miles west of Nashville. He built a log house for his wife Suzanna. He had acquired more than 1,000 acres by 1816 and was gaining a reputation even then for breeding and boarding racehorses. In 1829 he moved his family into a new Federal-style house and named the place Belle Meade, meaning Beautiful Meadow.

After John's death, his son, General William Giles Harding, took over the reins of Belle Meade. The general was a widower until January 2, 1840, when he married Elizabeth Irwin McGavock. It was William who created the existing house in 1853. He had a new addition added that doubled the size of the building. The six limestone columns that were added to the front gave it the appearance of a Grecian temple.

In the years before the War Between the States, the farm grew to 3,500 acres with 136 enslaved people.

The general felt they needed the room as his family expanded. Elizabeth bore him nine children; however, only two girls survived to adulthood, Selene and Mary Elizabeth. There was a son, John Harding, Jr., from the general's first marriage.

The general was a strong supporter of the Confederacy and contributed large sums of money to it. He offered the plantation for the headquarters of Confederate Gen. James R. Chalmers of Nathan Bedford Forrest's cavalry. In December of 1864, the Union army attacked the mansion, and fierce fighting ensued in the front yard of the plantation. It was there that the 19-year-old Selena carved her place in history with a brave albeit foolish act. Despite the bullets flying around her, she remained on the porch waving her handkerchief to cheer on the Confederates. When you visit, be sure to look for the bullet holes. They can still be seen in the porch columns.

After Nashville's surrender, Harding was sent to Mackinaw Island in Michigan by the military governor, Andrew Johnson.

In time, brave Selena inherited the plantation. She and her husband, retired Confederate General William Hicks Jackson, played host to President Grover Cleveland and his new wife in 1884.

Belle Meade Plantation is known as the "Queen of Tennessee Plantations" and is renowned today for the famous racehorses such as Secretariat and Seabiscuit who trace their bloodlines to the plantation. It was transferred to the state and opened as a museum in 1953.

However, someone from the shadowy past still inhabits the mansion. A long-time costume designer at Belle Meade, Stina Fitch, used to come in early in the morning when no one else was present to arrange costumes for the docents. She frequently heard the sounds of another presence. Once she saw a figure in a dark suit in one of the hallway mirrors. It appeared to be walking just behind her, but when she turned around, no one was there.

Belmont Plantation

Belle Meade isn't the only plantation in Nashville with a strong female figure. Belmont Plantation was owned by Adelicia Acklen, a real life model for Scarlett O'Hara. When you visit Belmont, you will appreciate the scope of her talents.

Adelicia was born into a well-to-do Nashville family and related to President Hayes. When she was 22, she married Isaac Franklin of Sumner County, 28 years her senior and wealthy beyond belief. In the seven years of their marriage, Adelicia bore four children, none of whom survived childhood. When Franklin died, he left his widow an inheritance valued at approximately $1 million at that time. It included seven Louisiana cotton plantations, a 2,000-acre farm in Middle Tennessee, and 750 slaves, and made her one of the wealthiest women in America.

Three years later, she dipped into the matrimonial waters again. This time she wed Colonel Joseph A. S. Acklen but not before she had him sign an agreement leaving her in full control of her property. They built Belmont, a 20,000-square-foot Italian villa, for their use in the summer months. In winter they traveled to her Louisiana plantation. This time they had six children, only four of whom survived. The colonel was a worthy helpmate to her, and by 1860 he had helped her triple her fortune.

The mansion served as the headquarters for Union Gen. T. J. Wood during the Battle of Nashville. Union scouts used the 105-foot-tall brick water tower for a lookout and relay signal point. Perhaps for this reason the building was not damaged. During this time, Joseph had traveled to New Orleans to avoid the Union forces and died there. Adelicia had to rush to the Louisiana plantations to prevent the Confederate forces from burning her cotton. She must have been pretty good at convincing people to see things her way. As the battles raged in the South, she managed to smuggle her cotton out by convincing both sides she was going to turn over the profits to them. With one side guarding her by land and the other on the high seas, she transported it to Europe where she received almost a million dollars for the crop. Of course, she never got around to sharing the profits with either side. Three weeks after Lee's surrender, she and her children traveled to London to retrieve her money.

Three years seemed to be about how long the rich widow would grieve. She married Dr. William Archer Cheatham, a Nashville physician, in 1867. Of course, he also signed a prenuptial, giving her control of her vast fortune. This marriage lasted 20 years, until Adelicia sold Belmont and left both Nashville and the doctor. She moved to Washington and died about a year later on a shopping trip to New York. This remarkable woman managed to become one of the richest women in America at a time when women were supposed to be just pretty playthings.

Her home became first Ward-Belmont then Belmont University as it still is today. Some of the famous alumni of Belmont are Sarah Colley Cannon, AKA Minnie Pearl, Brad Paisley and Trisha Yerwood.

Perhaps some of these stars met Adelicia while attending classes, since she is reported to frequent the school. Since the mansion sits in the middle of the college, it is well protected by both alarms and security guards. These alarms, as well as lights and motion detectors in the mansion, frequently go off for no reason. Both guards and students have reported seeing Adelicia floating around. A psychic, who was not aware of the number of children who died prematurely there, investigated the school and reported that Adelicia was searching for her children and was afraid her home would be demolished due to campus renovation and expansion. Adelicia never causes any harm. But she has been at different places throughout the mansion and grounds. The school trustees now are very careful during expansions or renovations not to disturb the mansion. After all, it is Adelicia's home as well as a historical landmark. Belmont is open for tours seven days a week.

Carter Farm

At the time the War Between the States exploded into Tennessee, Confederate General John Bell Hood led his Army of Tennessee through a countryside torn in its loyalty. While Tennessee was nominally a Confederate state and 100,000 of its soldiers wore gray, there were 50,000 of its young men who chose to join the Union army. Hood planned to stop the Federals before they reached the capital. The result was the Battle of Franklin at Carter Farm, now Franklin is considered a suburb of Nashville,

Fountain Branch Carter, the family patriarch, built the house in 1830, and on November 29, 1864, the home stood right in the middle of the battlefield. Union General Cox had commandeered the house as a command post. The Carter family had been driven from their beds in the middle of the night as their home swarmed with enemy soldiers.

During the battle on following day, the Carters hid in the basement. Fountain Branch Carter was now elderly, and it was up to his oldest son, Lt. Colonel Moscow Branch Carter, to rally the family. He had been taken prisoner earlier and was home on parole. He took charge as the family, some neighbors, and their servants -- a total of 22 people -- took refuge in the home's basement.

The battle raged above their heads. When the two armies clashed, it was one of the bloodiest battle of the American Civil War. To exacerbate the situation, it was fought on one of the smallest battlefields of the war (only 2 miles long and 1-1/2 miles wide. Men beat and slashed one another to pieces in a mostly hand-to-hand situation. It has been called "the Gettysburg of the West."

Theodrick (Tod) Carter, one of Fountain Branch's sons who was fighting for the Confederacy, was an aide to General T. B. Smith. He had not visited since his enlistment early in the war. The young captain urged his mount forward and yelled to the men around him, "Follow me, boys, I'm almost home. Heaven and earth can't keep me out of this fight on my father's farm."

How prophetic those words proved. Tod was struck by several bullets. He died in his father's home two days later as a result of the bullet that lodged in his brain. True to his word, death had not stopped Tod from returning to his home. He still is found there. He has been seen there several times. One visitor to the home, now a historic museum commemorating the Battle of Franklin, saw the young man sitting on the side of the bed in the room where Tod died. The apparition looked at the visitor for a moment, then vanished.

Tod is not alone in the old house. Staff workers have heard the voice of a woman in the home, and many people have seen the apparition of a child, believed to be Annie Carter, Tod's younger sister.

Many of the poltergeist-style activities seem to fit Annie's personality. Objects will jump up and down or appear and disappear, and staff members have felt a child tugging on their shirtsleeves when they are alone in the home. Sally Carter, another family member, is reputed to haunt Franklin also. Sally acted as a Confederate spy passing valuable information between couriers and Confederate brass.

Clouston Hall

After the battle, the biggest necessity was for hospitals for the thousands of wounded Confederate soldiers and the far lesser number of Union casualties. One such home was Clouston Hall. The home had been constructed in 1828 by Edward Clouston, a wealthy landowner. The home has played host to all three of Tennessee's presidents: Andrew Jackson, James K. Polk and Andrew Johnson.

On the morning following the battle, it was pressed into service as a field hospital in the attempt to treat the never-ending procession of bleeding battered young soldiers.

The number of these men who did not survive is overwhelming. It's not surprising that several still remain here. Perhaps the events of the battle occurred so rapidly they could not believe they were really dead.

They have some feminine companionship in the mansion. Mr. Clouston's daughter, Annie, hanged herself from the entrance hall banister because her beau jilted her. Rather than face the shame that entailed for a girl of her era, she chose instead to cross over but somehow has not left her earthly dwelling place.

Strange events in the brick mansion are the norm. In 2000, a tenant died with a plastic bag over his head and a cord wrapped around his neck. Police determined it was self-inflicted.

The current owner once was moving a large antique secretary that had been blocking a door. When he returned home several hours later, the piece had been put back in the doorway. No one else had been in the house since he left. He had no explanation for the event but does not let it frighten him.

Carnton Plantation

Perhaps the most-famous home in Franklin is the Carnton Plantation, immortalized in Robert Hicks' best-selling novel, The Widow of the South. The book so closely follows the actual events and characters, sometimes renamed, that reading it will give you a feel for the actual Battle of Franklin and its aftermath.

The Carnton Plantation had been built in 1826 by former Nashville Mayor Randal McGavock. He was an important man in Tennessee and entertained two American presidents, James K. Polk and Andrew Jackson. Randal's son, John, inherited Carnton when his father died in 1843. The night of the battle, the second-story veranda was used by Gen. Nathan B. Forrest as a lookout point.

The carnage required a large hospital site. Carnton became that place. The Confederate wounded were brought there until the rooms were filled then placed on the porch. In the book, *Widow of the South*, Carrie Winder

McGavock was the one who nursed and watched hundreds of soldiers die and recorded their burial places so loved ones might have some closure is a real place. Actually, her husband, John, was present and oversaw the care and burial of the dead also. Their children Hattie (age nine) and Winder (age seven) helped attending the wounded.

The home's Historical Interpreter, Brad Kinnison, led me thought this beautiful Greek revival home furnished as it was in 1864. The entrance is a typical wide hall opening with rooms on both sides and stairs leading upstairs. The guest parlor, the most formal, is wallpapered and furnished elaborately. There is a gilt framed mirror over the fireplace, a piano, and several delicately curved brocaded chairs and sofa.

Another room downstairs that was used more informally has Carrie's portrait over the fireplace. A portrait of Hattie at age 18 on another wall. The clock and a music box are original to the family. One of the most interesting artifacts is the family bible. They kept newspaper clippings and photos stuck in it and recorded important dates. There are photographs of Carrie, John and the two children.

In the upstairs bedrooms the war becomes real for a visitor. In Winder's room, there is a makeshift operating table; a saw similar to today's hacksaw on it. Next to it is a table holding tools the surgeon would've used, file, pliers, probes, picks, hammers. Where the surgeon would have stood, the floor is stained dark with blood; blood over 150 years old. In one corner room there are excessive blood stains. Brad believes this is where amputated limbs were stacked.

The home was a private residence for many years after the war. Brad said, "A guy who lived here in the mid-20th century said he tried to get some of the blood stains out on the first floor but he couldn't carry the sander upstairs."

Under a glass protector, there is the actual record book of those buried in the cemetery. Brad requested I not photograph that relic.

Part of the tour is a walk to McGavock Confederate Cemetery, where nearly 1,500 Confederate soldiers lie. The McGavocks donated two acres adjourning the family plot and the slave graveyard for the cemetery. Soldiers had been buried on the plantation grounds and were reinterred here in 1866. Walking among the graves, which are divided into individual areas for each state that fought there, some headstones are marked by initials.

Many just say "Unknown." About 780 of the soldiers have been identified, the rest are unknown.

John and citizens of Franklin paid George Cuppett $5 per body to move the dead here. With the assistance of his brother, Marcellus, and two other men, Cuppett finished the job, recorded the known names in the record book, and placed a wooden marker on each grave. Marcellus died as a result of illness probably contracted handling the bodies. Since he was from Texas, his grave is near the Texas section. It would be strange if such a place did not have its specters. Many people, staff and visitors alike have seen some of them. One gift shop worker was in the home alone one fall evening while her mother, the special events director, led a ghost tour to the cemetery. She stepped out on the porch to watch as the lanterns from the tour bobbed in the distance; then she heard footsteps inside. Thinking someone was in there, she returned only to witness the apparition of a dark-haired woman in a 19th-century pink longsleeved dress. The woman appeared to be transparent, but the clothing looked solid. The phantom stepped out on the porch and waved in the direction of the graveyard. The worker ran screaming from the house.

Based on pictures, she was able to establish that it was Carrie McGavock whom she had seen. Carrie is not the only haunt hanging around the old mansion. A man in Confederate uniform believed to be General Patrick R. Cleburne is seen on the upstairs balcony. There also is a soldier who seems to guard the graveyard. He is said to watch you as you walk around the graves and follow you until you are safely out of the cemetery. One other spirit who is seen running and playing near the fence is believed to be one of the McGavock children who died before the battle. The girl is also seen inside the home playing the piano and has been photographed at a window. Franklin on Foot offers tours of both the town and Carnton Plantation and is a good way to learn about any new sightings.

Lotz House is another place I enjoyed visiting. Johann Albert Lotz was a master woodworker and piano maker from Saxony. He and his wife, Margaretha, built the house on land purchased from Fountain Branch Carter in 1858. Johann used the house as a showcase of his work, so you will see many interesting pieces of furniture, as well as the fireplaces' woodwork.

During the battle, the Lotzs took refuge in Mr. Carter's cellar. The Lutz's home sustained serious damage and, although Mr. Lotz repaired it, there are still remnants of the battle scars. Many of the rooms still have bloodstains on the floor. On the first floor, there is a burned trail where a fiery cannon ball landed and rolled.

They furnished the house as it was when the Lotzs lived there. There are many interesting artifacts, including pictures of the Lotzs.

Thomas Cartwright, Executive Director, gave me an informative tour of the home. There are also ghost tours.He has personally experienced some strange happenings. Items from the gift shop move around during the night and are found in the hall and other places. People have heard s woman crying for help and see an phantom child. The"lady in white" seems to be the most prevalent spirit there.

McLemore House

In the years that followed, the people of the South, both Black and white, had to learn a different way of life. The McLemore House tells some of that story. Ex-slave Harvey McLemore bought four lots from his former owner, W. S. McLemore, a former Confederate officer who subdivided 15 acres to form a middle-class African American community known as "Hard Bargain."Alma McLemore, President of the African-American Heritage Society in Franklin, told me, "in spite of W. S. being Harvey's former owner, they were friends."

Harvey built a small white clapboard home there in 1880. The McLemore Family remained in the home until 1997. It is the oldest remaining Black owned home in Franklin, Tennessee. Today, it is a museum that tells the side of the story from the former enslaved people's point of view.

Placards in the house tell of Harvey's family in later years with stories about people like his granddaughter, Maggie Mathews, who became a cosmetologist and operated a beauty parlor in the house as shown on the 1940 census. Maggie remained in the house until her death in 1989. There are artifacts and photos of African Americans from Franklin. One room contains records of these citizens who fought for our country from Buffalo Soldiers to a Tuskegee Airman. It's a small house with a big message. I didn't see or sense any spirits when I visited but it would not surprise me to learn there are some resident spirits here.

Hunter Museum of Art

Aquarium

The boxcar I stayed in

The lobby was once a train station

Belle Meade

Fort Nashboro

The holes shot in wall at Carter Farm during Battle of Franklin

The operating table at Carnton

Chapter 10 Texas

San Antonio

Menger Hotel

Almost certainly the fact that is it built on a battleground of the Alamo is what makes the Menger Hotel one of the most-haunted hotels in America. True the hotel is so colorful and unique it has no need of ghost stories to enhance its reputation. The spirits that inhabit the hotel range from the Alamo fighters to one of America's most-colorful presidents. They include the well known and the obscure among their resident phantom ranks.

The history of the Menger begins in 1859, just 23 years after the most-famous battle in Texas history. A German immigrant couple, William and Mary Menger, built a 50-room hotel on what was once a bloody battlefield adjoining the Alamo.

William A. Menger was a cooper by trade and was familiar with beer brewing. He came to San Antonio from Germany in 1847 when he was only 20. He met Mary Guenther, a widow nine years his senior, who ran a rooming house. They married in 1851 and in 1855 built a brewery/tavern, and since his beer was pretty strong they built a rooming house so the tavern patrons would not have to drive home. This worked so well, in 1859 he built an elegant hotel. By September it was already too small to accommodate his guests. He added 50 more rooms, making it the largest in the state. It drew some of the most-prestigious people in the state. Robert E. Lee and his sister stayed at the Menger, as did General Sherman -- not at the same time. Sam Houston signed in as "Sam Houston and horse." During the Civil War, the hotel shut down for a time. Many of the original Menger family furnishings are still displayed in the lobby.

After the Civil War, Confederate General Kirby Smith stayed at the hotel, in disguise. Fellow officer General Joseph Shelby recognized Kirby and ordered the band to play "Hail to the Chief," but that did not bring the general out of his room. Then Shelby ordered the band to play "Dixie." He stated, "That old man is Kirby Smith. If he were dead, that song would bring him out."

Sure enough General Smith came out of the room undisguised. The old general tried to speak three times but each time was overcome and broke down in tears. The following day, Shelby led the remnants of his Missouri Cavalry into Mexico. When they reached the Rio Grande, they slowly lowered the Stars and Bars into the river's muddy water where they buried it, along with the ostrich feather Shelby had worn in his hat throughout the war, rather than see it captured by Federal troops. Shelby never surrendered his flag or his regiment to the Union.

Major John Hermann Kampmann, a German emigrant who fought in the Civil War, was the next owner. The Kampmann family owned it from 1881 to 1943 when it passed into the hands of the Moody family. It was remodeled and the new wing added as it is today with the original hotel still preserved. In 1980 it received a State Historic Marker as the oldest continuously operating hotel west of the Mississippi. It has also been named as a Historic Hotel of America. U.S. Grant, Theodore Roosevelt, Benjamin Harrison, Woodrow Wilson, Howard Taft, William McKinley, Dwight Eisenhower, Ronald Reagan, Lyndon Johnson, Richard Nixon, Bill Clinton and George Bush have all visited the Menger.

Clinton commented, "Eating mango ice cream at the Menger is one of life's great pleasures."

The Menger is also designated as a "Literary Landmark." William Sidney Porter (O. Henry), Sidney Lanier, Oscar Wilde, Francis Parkinson Keyes, Earl Stanley Gardner, Robert Frost, Stephen Crane and Alex Haley are but a few of the great literary figures who have stayed at the Menger.

Ernesto Malacara, the Menger's former director of public relations, told me of some of the encounters at the Menger. He was coming into the lobby in the mezzanine in the old section one day and saw an elderly lady dressed in a blue dress with a beret perched on her hair. He noted she had on very unfeminine footwear, best described as "combat boots." She appeared to be knitting. Not recognizing her as a guest, he asked if he could help her. She replied very shortly, "No, I'm just fine." Mr. Malacara walked past and then looked right back and saw that the woman had disappeared.

Sally White is the best-known ghost. Sally was a chambermaid at the Menger in 1876. Her common-law husband shot her after an argument.

Sally ran toward the Menger but was carried back to her home where she died. The Menger paid $32 for Sally's funeral expenses. The receipt is in the lobby. Sally is frequently seen carrying a bundle of towels, but if you ask for towels she never takes them to your room.

Captain Richard King, founder of the King Ranch, kept a suite at the Menger. King died at 60 in 1885 in the big four-poster bed still in the King Suite. He has been seen in and around the suite named for him. One housekeeper watched him walk from the hall into his suite through the wall. He entered at the spot where the door used to be in his time.

Many guests have reported seeing a Confederate officer who looked like Robert E. Lee. However, Mr. Malacara said that when Lee stayed at the hotel shortly after its opening, he would have been wearing a United States uniform, not Confederate gray. He felt that the spectral soldier might be General Kirby Smith who did stay at the hotel at the war's end and would have been wearing his uniform. There is a resemblance between the two men that, combined with the general's uniform, could account for people mistaking one for the other.

There is a maitre de who is seen by custodians at night. The portly gentleman wearing formal attire will visit the dining room after the place is closed. He makes his way around the room, stopping at some of the tables as if asking if everything was satisfactory.

One of the Menger's most-distinguished phantoms is believed to be none other than Teddy Roosevelt. Roosevelt came to San Antonio in 1898 to gather recruits for a cavalry unit to go to Cuba and help him fight the Spanish-American War. His favorite method of recruitment was to gather a likely bunch of cowhands at the Menger bar and buy a few rounds while he eloquently preyed on their honor, patriotism and just plain fighting spirit. He was very successful although the local people referred to the new recruits as Teddy's Terrors instead of his chosen nickname, "The Rough Riders."

In life, the Menger Bar was one of Teddy Roosevelt's favorite hangouts. It appears death hasn't changed his preferences. One startled bartender was adding his receipts after closing one night. He had pulled the flap down that closed him in behind the bar to create more counter space to work on. He looked up to see a mustachioed man in an old-fashioned uniform at the end of the bar beckoning to him, but he knew the bar doors were closed and locked. When the man faded and disappeared, he didn't bother to raise the panel, just vaulted over it and out to the front desk. It took several minutes for the clerk to calm him enough to understand what he was trying to say: "I saw a ghost."

One night after closing, a janitor in the bar saw a man on the balcony wearing the same 1890s-era uniform. He went up to tell the man he had to leave, and when he got there no one was there.

Still another time, shortly before closing, there was only one couple in the bar. They had been drinking a bit and were not too steady on their feet. The man got up on one side of the stools and the woman on the opposite side of hers. At this point a man entered the bar and seemed to be heading on a collision course with the woman. Her companion stepped in between her and the oncoming stranger who just disappeared into thin air. Bet that sobered both of them up instantly!

Mr. Malacara recounted an instance when a distraught guest claimed he could not get any rest. He came out of the shower wearing only a towel to find a man dressed in buckskin in his room carrying on an argument with an invisible presence. The presence kept saying, "Are ya going to go or ya going to stay?" The guest demanded, "What are you doing in my room?" But the apparition paid him no mind. Finally the spirit disappeared, and the guest dressed and rushed down to the desk to tell them what had happened.

Perhaps two of the Alamo dead were rehashing the fateful moment when they decided their fate. After all, so much in San Antonio today relates back to what happened in that small mission over a century and a half ago.

The Alamo

There is no question. San Antonio is the heart of Texas. The heart of San Antonio lies in the middle of its 21st-century downtown. There, one piece of 18th-century architecture reigns supreme. It is not the tallest or the largest. Not even the grandest, but it is unquestionably San Antonio's crowning jewel. The Alamo! No other symbol in American history is more revered as a shrine to heroism in the cause of freedom. (Although in fact, we were taking Texas away from it former owner, Mexico.)

Originally one of a string of five missions built by Spanish friars with the help of local natives, it was named officially Mission San Antonio de Valero. Eventually it was secularized and the land returned to the natives who farmed it until the early 1800s when a Spanish military unit was stationed there. The soldiers nicknamed the post "Los Alamo" in memory of their hometown of Alamo de Parras in the province of Coahuila. The name stuck.

The Alamo continued to serve as a military barracks through the Mexican Revolution and was manned by Mexican General de Cós when the Texas Revolution broke out. The Texas rebels under Ben Milam took the Alamo and increased its fortifications.

A small band of Texans under Col. William B. Travis, with Jim Bowie in charge of the volunteers, held the small post on February 23, 1836, when a superior force of Mexicans under command of the Mexican president himself, General Antonio Lopez de Santa Ana, appeared at its gates and demanded surrender. Travis answered with a cannon shot over Santa Ana's head. Santa Ana declared, "No Quarter."

Men from 21 other states as well as England, Ireland, Scotland, Wales, Germany and Denmark rallied together to become one united force. Legend states that the young Travis drew a line in the sand with his sword and asked all who would stay and fight to the death to step across. All but one man did.

These men knew the consequences. One soldier, Daniel William Cloud from Kentucky, stated in a letter:

"If we succeed, the country is ours. It is immense in extent, and fertile in its soil and will amply reward our toil. If we fail, death in the cause of liberty and humanity is not cause for shuddering. Our rifles are by our side, and choice guns they are, we know what awaits us, and are prepared to meet it."

Travis, in his most-famous letter begging for reinforcements, states: "The enemy has demanded a surrender at discretion; otherwise, the garrison are to be put to the sword, if the fort is taken—I have answered the demand with a cannon shot, and our flag still waves proudly from the walls – I shall never surrender or retreat."

Travis and his men held against insurmountable odds for 13 days, but death was the final price for the approximately 189 defenders of the Alamo. (Historians differ in the actual number ranging from 150 to 250.)

Is it any wonder then that the ghost stories about the Alamo started immediately after the death of these heroic defenders? Those first tales begin with General Santa Ana's orders to raze the structure. He was furious and wished to extend his revenge to the actual structure as well as the men he had brutally executed. They had cost him more than 600 Mexican soldiers' lives. El Presidente was not a forgiving man. He ordered General Andrade to raze the Alamo, and there is no record he ever rescinded those orders. Yet when the Mexican army marched away to take on Sam Houston's rag tag army, the old mission still stood. Why? The stories abound from both Mexican sources as well as locals. They tell of the engineers and sappers General Andrade sent, commanded by Colonel Sanchez, going to the fort to carry out the orders. Much of the old fort was already in ruins from the siege, but they were stopped cold at the chapel.

According to the stories they told, they saw "something," actually several "somethings," standing guard over the walls. They reported "glowing men with flaming swords" who stopped them before they could touch a stone in the old chapel's wall. Some of the Mexican soldiers on that detail claimed that the figures they saw were six ghostly monks who materialized from the chapel walls and advanced on the wrecking crew waving flaming swords and screeching, "Do not touch the walls of the Alamo."

When General Andrade heard of Colonel Sanchez's failure to carry out the order, he returned to the Alamo himself with troops and a cannon. Andrade instructed his soldiers to fire the cannon at the front doors of the chapel, but before the men could comply, the ghostly apparitions reappeared with fiery swords in hand. The men fled in horror, but Andrade was a loyal officer and tried one last time. He stood his ground until he witnessed a wall of flame with the smoke taking the form of a large man who hurled fireballs at the stubborn general.

The monument in front of the Alamo, the Cenotaph, portrays this legend. It may be the only monument in the country that depicts a ghost. Built in 1940 by Italian-Texan sculptor Pompeo Coppini, it shows an ethereal figure with a torch rising toward the heavens. The battered bodies of the Alamo defenders lie near the base.

No one, only the ravages of time, has attempted to destroy the sacred chapel from that day on. However, time is a powerful element. The shrine was left to deteriorate and served a variety of trite uses. By the time Texas became part of the U.S., the facade of the chapel was a total wreck and the walls and long barracks in shambles. When the U. S. Army came to San

Antonio, it needed a warehouse to store grain and supplies. The Army Corp of Engineers rebuilt the walls of the chapel and re-roofed it. The present step-and-arch profile of the Alamo roof that's recognized the world over was not added until then.

When the army constructed Fort Sam Houston, it no longer had a use for the Alamo. In fact, title to the building and land was in dispute; both the city of San Antonio and the Catholic Archdiocese of Texas claimed it.

The Church won its claim and eventually sold the chapel and land it stood on to the state. The remainder of the Alamo was sold to a private interest. Much of it was torn down and the limestone blocks cannibalized to build other structures in San Antonio.

In 1894, the city used the mission as a police headquarters and jail. Prisoners were housed in the old barracks. Prisoners and police alike claimed to witness strange events within the old barracks and chapel.

The San Antonio Express News printed confirmed reports of paranormal activity at the Alamo. The articles recounted sightings of a ghostly sentry reportedly walking from east to west on the police station roof, strange shadows and moaning sounds. The guards and watchmen would not patrol the building after hours alone. Whether this was the cause or not, the city abandoned its plans for the Alamo in favor of a different jail site.

These reports from the late 1800s continue to this day. Many witnesses tell of a phantom sentry who patrols back and forth across the top of the Alamo. Some believe the ghostly guard is looking for a means of escape while others are convinced he guards the missing treasure of the Alamo.

The treasure stories began with rumors that during the final days of the siege, the defenders placed their valuables in a large bell and buried it within the fortress grounds. To this day it has never been found.

Certain figures have been observed repeatedly. One hot spring day, a park ranger encountered a man dressed in high boots, a plantation hat and a long overcoat. The suspicious figure was walking toward the library. As the ranger strode over to challenge this person, the figure faded and disappeared near the chapel. Others have observed this same figure numerous times in the courtyard of the Alamo. He has been seen both during the day and at night.

Generally the most-often repeated ghost story about the Alamo focuses on the spirit of a little boy who is rumored to haunt the park's gift shop.

Both visitors and park rangers alike claim to have seen a blond-haired little boy, somewhere between 10 and 12 years of age, staring out into the courtyard from one of the shop's high inaccessible windows. The small boy is only visible from the waist up and has never become a full-bodied apparition. Rangers who have searched the gift shop in hopes of finding a prankster have repeatedly come up empty-handed. They have reached the conclusion that there is no way a mortal person could perch him or herself in the window without something to climb up on or some way to support himself. The mystery only gets more convoluted when you consider the fact that the gift shop was not built until the 1930s.

Legend says that during the last days of the siege of the Alamo, a small boy was evacuated from the Mission. It is believed that this little boy's spirit returns to the same spot where he recalls last seeing a loved one alive. The ghostly child may appear to be looking down from the window at curious onlookers when in fact his eyes only search for a comforting glimpse of a father, brother, or other family member who made the ultimate sacrifice on the place where the shop now stands.

This is not the only child spirit present on the grounds of the shrine. Two young boys often attach themselves to groups touring the mission, then disappear. They are believed to be the sons, aged 9 and 12, of Alamo Artilleryman Anthony Wolfe. The boys were killed by the advancing Mexican soldiers who thought they were combatants.

Much of John Q Public's knowledge of events leading to the fall of the Alamo was learned not in a classroom but on the silver screen. John Wayne directed and played Davy Crockett in this $1.2-million epic. Wayne considered this a special film and strove to make everything as realistic as possible. He spent countless hours strolling the grounds of the real Alamo and immersing himself in the facts concerning the fateful battle. Since the real Alamo was now surrounded by 20th-century buildings, the Duke built a replica in Brackettville. The tragedy seemed to obsess him. As a result, he won an Oscar for best picture and educated millions of Americans about this part of Texas history.

After his death, his interest did not decrease, it seems. Countless visitors report seeing the Duke walking the grounds or conversing with spirits of the fort's original dead. A psychic called in confirmed that it was indeed the great John Wayne himself manifesting at the Alamo.

Still, even John Wayne is upstaged by the Alamo's most-famous specter, the real-life counterpart to Wayne's silver screen role. Rangers and visitors have observed a soldier dressed in buckskin clothing and sporting a flintlock rifle patrolling the grounds near the chapel. He has been observed at the same time by people standing at different positions on the grounds. Sometimes he wears a coonskin cap; other times he is bare-headed. All identify him as Davy Crockett.

The most frightening of Crockett's manifestations may be what is called a residual haunting. This type of haunting involves a reenacting of some traumatic scene that occurred in the hunted place. It is believed to be more of a psychic energy; think of it as a looping piece of extrasensory film. In this case, a ranger entered the long barracks one night and witnessed a nightmare. He saw a man dressed in the buckskin clothing typically worn by frontiersmen of that era. The man's semi-transparent body had been riddled with bullets and stood with his back up against the wall, fending off several ghostly Mexican soldiers who lunged with bayonets stabbing the valiant defender. Needless to say the ranger was very emotionally shaken.

Not all of the century phantoms associated with the Alamo perished there. Often on a March morning, just days after the anniversary, residents in the area hear horse's hooves striking modern pavement. Experts believe this is the spirit of James Allen, the last courier to leave the Alamo, before the massacre. Perhaps he is trying to return and report to Colonel Travis.

While Allen left in the call of duty, one other reported straggler is seen often walking the road from Nacatochis toward San Antonio. This apparition had actually spoken to passersby who stop to offer assistance to the strangely dressed pedestrian. He refuses all aid with the response that he "has to get back to the Alamo."

It is easy to place this phantom as Louis Moses Rose, known as the "Coward of the Alamo," since he is the only man to reputedly leave when Travis drew his famous line in the sand. Maybe he regrets his cowardly behavior and longs for another chance to prove his valor.

Not all of the specters are defenders, either. One is of an unknown Mexican boy in his mid-teens. Another is a tall, proud man wearing the uniform of a Mexican officer. He is believed to be General Manuel Fernandez de Castrillon, one of Santa Anna's regimental commanders, who had opposed the final assault. After the fall, six of the defenders surrendered to General Castrillon. He offered them clemency, but when he reported this to Santa Ana, the enraged commander refused to honor it. Instead he ordered the men hanged. Castrillon refused, stating such action was dishonorable. Instead, Santa Ana ordered his aides to kill the prisoners immediately. They hacked the helpless men to death with swords in front of the anguished general.

Another unexplained wraith appears frequently in the basement of the Alamo. Staff entering the storage area report seeing a tall Native American who either just disappears or walks through a solid wall that once housed a tunnel into the Menger Hotel across the street.

Mission Trails

The Alamo is just one of a series of five missions built in the area. The other missions on the Mission Trail are Mission Concepción, Mission San José, Mission San Juan Capistrano and Mission San Francisco de la Espada. I started at the visitor center located at 6701 San José Drive, adjacent to Mission San José. Interactive displays and a film about the history of the missions gave me some background for what I was going to be seeing. These missions still act as parish churches. If you only have time for two, make them San José and Concepción. These are the most complete and can be reached via the public bus system.

Mission San José y San Miguel de Aguayo is called the "Queen of the Texas Missions." It was most beautiful, most prosperous and the best fortified of all the San Antonio missions. San José is the most complete and includes the granary, 84 compartments that served as Indian quarters, an immense quadrangle enclosure and a restored gristmill that houses an original horizontal water wheel. The gristmill was rebuilt in 1930. It was an effort by the Franciscans to introduce wheat into the Indians' diet to supplement the ever-present maize. This mill also produced flour for the surrounding area. The oval "Rosa's Window," which opens into the sacristy, is covered with carvings. The angles and curves of this window, even weathered as they are by time, make it a true work of art.

There are stories of a phantom Franciscan priest who appears both inside the church and around the grounds. He is wearing a long dark blue robe and sometimes appears to be headless. Who he is is not known, but he is not alone. Parishioners have also seen an elderly lady dressed in about

1950s clothing who will appear and ask about the time of Masses. If you turn away for a few seconds, she will disappear.

Mission Nuestra Señora de la Purísma Concepción de Acuña, usually just referred to as Concepción, is one of the oldest unrestored stone churches in the United States. This mission was established in 1731; however, it took more than 20 years to complete the church. When you visit, you can still see traces of the brightly colored paintings that were used to adorn the interior walls of the mission.

Mission San Francisco de la Espada was founded in 1690 in a different location. Espada was relocated to San Antonio in 1731, but by 1778 the original adobe church structure was in ruin. The main stone church was never completed. The chapel, which was built originally as the sacristy for the church, dates from about 1884. It now serves as a small parish church. The Moorish-styled, arched doorway is the oldest portion of this mission, dating to about 1780.

A strange specter is seen there. A large black dog or wolf with a broken chain around his neck has been observed on the grounds. Once three priests, the elderly rector and two visiting younger clergymen saw the beast run across the yard. They immediately came out and searched the grounds but saw no trace of it. This story goes back generations. Some women who have lived in the area all their lives recall being warned as children not to go near the mission grounds at night because of a "great black beast." The phantom probably goes back to an earlier padre who kept such an animal as a pet and restrained him with the type of chain now seen on the phantom animal's neck.

Another spirit that is not so terrifying is of an Indian dressed in full ceremonial costume, who is seen at the chapel altar.

Mission San Juan Capistrano moved to San Antonio in 1731 from an earlier location in East Texas. Here also the church was never completed. The chapel houses rare figures of Christ and the Virgin made of cornstalk pith. Much of the original compound is preserved, providing an accurate picture of the early Spanish mission plan. Here too, an Indian man appears near the altar, then disappears.

Emily Morgan Hotel

The Menger is not the only hotel that has resident spirits. The Emily Morgan Hotel is named for Emily West, a free woman of color whom Col.

James Morgan contracted with to accompany him to Texas as housekeeper for one year. There are some historians who feel that Emily Morgan (Since most records refer to her as Col. Morgan's slave, she is known as "Emily Morgan") did more for the cause of Texas independence in her short encounter with Santa Aná than Sam Houston and all his troops that day.

The only documents mentioning her were her indentured-servant contract with Morgan and a letter by Isaac N. Moreland, an officer in Houston's army and later chief justice of Harris County. Moreland said he met her in April 1836, and she told him she had lost the papers attesting to her free status on the San Jacinto battlefield. He requested a Texas passport for her, which she apparently used to return to New York in 1837.

Emily was an attractive mulatto woman who was dedicated to the cause of Texas independence. She is credited with sexually entertaining Santa Aná just before the Battle of San Jacinto. She delayed him until the Texans attacked. William Bollaert recounts that fateful day in the following entry:

"The Battle of San Jacinto was probably lost to the Mexicans, owing to the influence of a Mulatta [sic] Girl (Emily) belonging to Colonel Morgan, who was closeted in the tent with General Santana, at the time the cry was made 'The enemy! They come! They come!' and detained Santa Aná so long, that order could not be restored readily again."

The Emily Morgan Hotel, located just across the street from the Alamo, was built as a hospital in 1928 and served that purpose until the late 1970s. The gargoyles carved over the first floor windows reflect various ailments, including the toothaches that would be treated here. One factor in the psychic activity here might be the nearly 950 bodies buried on the property, in part because this was a burial grounds for many of the defenders of the Alamo, but also it was used as a burial grounds for the mission prior to that. The basement of the Emily Morgan was used for a morgue; thus it is one of the most-active areas. Sightings have been reported on the 8th and 14th floors also. Guests have seen phantoms and complained of the electrical service turning off and on for no reason. The lobby has also been the scene of cold spots and strange noises.

Gunter Hotel

In 1837, just one year after the fall of the Alamo, a new inn opened its doors downtown, the Frontier Inn. It changed hands twice before becoming the Gunter Hotel. At one time, it functioned as housing for U.S. Army personnel. One of its most-famous guests was Robert E. Lee, who was stationed there in the 1840s.

Then at the turn of the century, Jot Gunter and a group of investors decided San Antonio needed a palatial new hotel. So they purchased the property and added six new stories, making it at eight stories the largest building at that time in San Antonio. It opened, amid much fanfare, on November 20, 1909.

It was in 1965 that something happened to change the hotel forever. February 6, a blond man in his late 30s, calling himself "Albert Knox," checked into room 636 at the Gunter. For the next three days, he was often seen coming and going in the company of by a tall, slender, blond woman.

Then on February 8, the afternoon maid, Maria Luisa Guerra, entered the room in spite of the "Do Not Disturb" sign. What she saw made her blood run cold. A bloodstained man holding a bloody bundle in his arms rushed past her out the door. The room was covered in blood, and the sheets were soaked with it.

After police calmed the hysterical maid enough to speak, they searched the room and found evidence that the man and woman had been there and indications that he had shot the woman and perhaps butchered the body in the tub.

The police tracked down the suspect, Walter Emerick, who, using the different alias "Robert Ashley," had checked into room 536 at the St. Anthony Hotel just a few blocks away. He had wanted room 636, but it was not available. When the police reached the door of the suspect's room, a shot rang out from inside. Walter Emerick took his own life with the same gun used at the Gunter. He left an officially unsolved murder and lots of questions. Who was the dead woman? No one matching her description was reported missing. What had he done with the body? It was never found, but he had purchased a very large meat grinder the previous week at a downtown department store. Could he have actually ground her up and flushed her down the toilet? Another possibility was that there was so much construction going on in San Antonio at the time, the killer could easily have entombed the "package" containing the remains of the victim in a place due to have concrete poured on top of it. It would have become a grisly part of some new building.

One thing is sure: Both staff and hotel guests have reported strange happenings from time to time. Many people have seen the ghostly figure of woman wearing a bloodstained white dress or gown. Guests have reported sounds of hammering and grinding coming from room 636, but when checked, it was unoccupied. Once the image of a strange woman appeared in Christmas pictures taken at the hotel.

There are also reports of women dressed like 1930s flappers seen here.

In spite of or perhaps because of the mystery, the Gunter is a great place to stay. In 2007 it was officially added to the National Register of Historic Places.

Crowne Plaza St. Anthony

The St. Anthony where Walter Emerick fled to take his own life has many spirits of its own, but strangely enough, Emerick does not seem to be one of them.

The hotel has a long and interesting-enough history to account for a whole collection of phantoms. It was built in 1909. It played hosts to presidents and celebrities. It continually expanded and was in the process of its third building in December of 1941. Naturally, construction stopped, but the hotel flourished.

The war effort became the foremost thing on people's minds. Entertainers like Lucille Ball, Fred Astaire, and Judy Garland came there promoting war bonds. Secret meetings of President Eisenhower, the Rockefellers, General Douglas MacArthur, Eleanor Roosevelt and Princess Grace of Monaco were held there. There were several bases located in and around the San Antonio area. Afterward, the hotel continued in its tradition of gracious service.

Employees and guests have long known there is something else there as well. Many staff members have experienced something paranormal in the basement area near the male employee locker room. Guests have feelings of being followed on the 10th floor, and the doors to the roof garden, long shut down, open by themselves. Other guests have reported mysterious footsteps and even seen a pair of spirits sitting in a "vacant" room having cocktails. One of the strangest phantoms has been a mysterious pair of black-stocking-clad legs that appear and disappear in a stall of the mezzanine level ladies' powder room. This mystery was solved when Dorcia Schultz Williams along with the then-management staff of the hotel brought in two psychics to investigate. They were able to communicate with the owner of the legs.

She had been in the stall when she experienced a sharp pain in her chest and feared a heart attack. She did recover her strength enough to get out and meet her son, who took her to a hospital where she recovered. She told them her name was "Claire" or "Clara."

In the closed down area of the rooftop garden, they discovered a sad young lady from the World War II era wearing a white evening gown. She had spent a happy evening with her fiancé, who subsequently went oversees and never returned.

There is also the spirit of a former Hispanic maid named Anita who enjoyed her job there and continues to come to the hotel after her death.

Many guests have heard thumps or whacks on their doors only to find no one there. Perhaps if you visit, you, too, will encounter one of the many spirits of the Saint Anthony.

Crockett Hotel

This hotel is located where Davy Crockett defended the southeast palisade of the Alamo. A staff member saw a ghostly figure in the executive office. Legend has it that the phantom there is none other than Davy Crockett himself.

In 1909 a fraternal organization built the current six-story building to serve as a hotel and fraternal lodge. In 1927, a second seven-story west wing was added. The building was again renovated in 1982, earning it a place on the National Register of Historic Structures. In 2007, Crockett Hotel was completely renovated while still preserving its historic character. Perhaps all this renovation has stirred up its spirits.

La Villita

I discovered La Villita accidentally as I walked around the downtown area of San Antonio. It was hot, and I was walking along the sidewalk next to the traffic flowing all around. Then I saw the little village right in the middle of town. It was as if I had stepped into the past, the early 19th century. No more pavement, skyscrapers and traffic. Instead I was surrounded by old-style colonial buildings of adobe or limestone and narrow streets of brick. The little shops of artists and craftsmen -- glass blower, spinners, weavers, potters, painters, jewelery makers, stained glass makers – were sprinkled with a few small restaurants. Many of the shop owners were dressed in colonial Spanish costume. I had discovered a treasure.

Locals had also been slow to discover the potential in La Villita as well. One of the earliest settlements, this little village on the east bank of the San Antonio River has stood for some 200 years. It was considered a squalid area of squatters until a flood in 1819 destroyed much of the west bank of the San Antonio River. La Villita survived the flood with little damage due to its higher elevation on the east bank. Instantly the area became more desirable.

It had originally been settled due to the proximity to the Alamo. For the same reason, in the 1830s it became a meeting area for the revolutionaries. The treaty recognizing the defeat of Mexican troops at Bexar was signed in the "Cos House" in La Villita.

In the early 1900s, La Villita declined. It became a slum filled with cheap rooming houses and worse.

But in 1939, the city recognized the potential there. The Villita Ordinance established the area as an arts and crafts center dedicated to Pan-American harmony. It was named a National Historic District.

Chamade Jewelry Store reports items moving around on their own. Voices have been heard when no one is in the shop at night. People have seen a young woman in a white dress and apron. Perhaps a baker from lng ago as once the store was a bakery.

Another shop, Starving Artist's Gallery, is visited by a ghost dressed in nineteenth century clothing. La Villita House, once home to an Alsatian immigrant named Cirilus Gissi, is very active. Ruores are the imigaant burried gold on the property and is searching for it. People havealso seen a little girl spirit here.possibly Gissi's granddaughter. La Villita is haunted by a beheaded Comanche Ithat seem to be looking for his head. Not far from La Villa amurders wer hund from trees along the San Antonio River. Legend says you can hear screams and moaning coming from the trees

Riverwalk

From the rear of La Villita you can step down to the Paseo del Rio, commonly known as the Riverwalk. When you enter the Riverwalk here, you are at the Arneson River Theatre, a unique outdoor theatre where spectators sit on grassy steps on one side of the river facing the stage on the other bank. Events ranging from a Mariachi Festival, a Saint Patrick's Day show,

Fiesta Noche del Rio and Coffins on Parade at Halloween are all offered at the theater. The Riverwalk is San Antonio's pride and joy. The city has good reason to be proud of this attraction.

However, this was not always so. Unbelievable as it may seem to anyone who has visited the Riverwalk, the river was almost cemented over and used as a sewer.

A damaging flood in 1921 killed 50 people and caused millions of dollars in property damage. People clamored to do away with the "dangerous" San Antonio River. Fortunately, San Antonio Conservation Society stepped in, and the idea of a Riverwalk was born. When HemisFair, the World's Fair in 1968, was set in San Antonio, the Riverwalk, which had been mostly a park-like area, was developed into the marvelous attraction it is today. Cobblestone walkways line both banks of the river, and footbridges are arranged at intervals to get from one side to the other. Small boats offer sightseeing, and you can dine aboard open-air, candlelit cruisers. River taxies make it a snap to travel between Rivercenter, a dining and entertainment complex, and the Henry B. Gonzalez Convention Center.

Rivercenter is located at the head of the river, which is reputed to be one of the places some of the Alamo defenders' bodies were burned. Visitors and employees of the mall have seen strange shadows, particularly in the area where the photo center is now located.

Both banks offer sidewalk cafes, specialty boutiques, nightclubs and entrances into the high-rise hotels. The dining offers a choice of any kind of food imaginable. I tried Casa Rio, one of the first restaurants on the Riverwalk. I waited to sit under the colorful umbrellas near the riverbank and had the beef fajitas. Both food and atmosphere were perfect. There are tons of restaurants along the Riverwalk, and judging from the happy customers sauntering away after a meal, all live up to their appearance.

Schilo's Delicatessen

The back upstairs wall of Casa Rio is shared with a deli on Commerce Street. I had lunch there one day mainly to try the root beer, which is world-famous. Everything else about the place is equally good. I feasted on the Ruben and a cup of split pea soup and really enjoyed it. It's much cheaper than the places on the Riverwalk. . had heard rumors of an Indian ghost that bounced between there and Casa Rio as well as a spirit that pinches employees and turns lights off and on, but I could not confirm anything at either place.

Market Square

While I'm on the subject of food, be sure to visit Market Square. This colorful bit of old Mexico in the heart of the city has a long tradition. Beginning in the early years of the 19th century there was a market in San Antonio. The present site became the official marketplace around 1892. The original market stood until 1938 when it was replaced by the building that now know as El Mercado, The Market. Here you can find almost anything. It is a cross between a department store, an indoor flea market and a Mexican market.

Aside from the actual market, Market Square offers much more. Boutiques, craft shops, art galleries and restaurants will let you happily spend the day shopping and dining. Mi Tierra is the granddaddy of Tex-Mex food. There you can have a substantial lunch for under $7 in a swirl of Mexicano art and Christmas lights. This place turns out some of the best sweet treats in its bakery, and best of all it never closes.

Spanish Governor's Mansion

The Spanish Governor's Palace was constructed in the first half of the 18th century. In spite of its name, it never was the governor's home. Instead it served as the residence and headquarters for the local presidio captain, a type of military administrator. The simple one-story masonry structure, built in the Spanish Colonial style, could not be considered a palace, either. But it is an interesting building to visit when trying to get the feel of the history and culture of San Antonio.

The front doors are mysterious. They are inscribed with symbols that relate the story of the history of Spanish America. Reading from the top right side of the door down: The seashells represent la Nina, la Pinta, and la Santa Maria. The dragons represent the dangers the first settlers faced, and the baby face represents the new land, America. There are arms for protection and flowers representing the bounty of America. Continuing on the left-hand door reading from the bottom up: The medallion of the head of the Spanish Conquistador represents the Spanish conquistador who came into this land of flowers and riches. The shields show the conquest of the dangers and the native people.

The interior is furnished as it would have been in the pre-independence period. There is even a private chapel for the administrator to use. In the rear is a large patio with a well and a shrine to the Virgin Mary. It is there that the event leading to the most-horrific ghost legend is centered.

After the end of Spanish sovereignty, the building was privatized and owned by many people for many uses. Eventually it was bought by E. Hermann Altgelt, a German ex-Confederate who made his fortune in real estate and the practice of law. He was the founder of the town of Comfort in Texas hill country. He moved to San Antonio in 1866, continued his practice of law, and increased his real estate holdings.

In 1929, the city acquired the property and began restoration to preserve the unique house museum. It was at this time that the stories began to be whispered. Whether based on old paperwork or just hand-me-down tales, it was said she had been raped by the Spanish soldiers and the body thrown into the well.

When this building was renovated, the skeleton of a woman was found in the well. Apparently, the woman had been raped and killed by a mob of Spanish soldiers. Since the discovery of the skeleton the woman's spirit has been said to haunt the premises. Quite possibly the haunting occurred before that but was never reported or it began because of the restoration, which commonly triggers more phenomena. Who she was or how she happened to fall into such a fate no one knows, but what is known is she is still there in spirit. Moans and cries are heard coming from the well, and shadowy figures are seen.

Since she is not the only departed soul in the palace, no one can be sure exactly who they are seeing. A small child's body has also been found in the wall, but no one knows how it died. One apparition that has been identified is that of Jim Bowie's wife, Ursala Veramendi Bowie, who appears near the doorway that leads from the kitchen to the dining hall.

Ursala was the daughter of Juan Martín Veramendi, the vice governor. She grew up in the palace and spent time there while waiting for her husband to return from his travels. Tragically, the marriage her and Bowie was cut short by Ursala's death and those of their child and newborn infant. They, along with her father and much of their family, died when an epidemic of Asiatic cholera struck in 1833. Bowie was devastated by the death as this had been a real love affair, not just a marriage of alliance.

Whoever is causing the hauntings, many objects move mysteriously and strange things have happened.

San Fernando Cathedral

This first non-mission house of worship dates back to the same period. It was built by a group of Canary Islanders who settled here in 1731. Not much remains of that original structure, but the current edifice boasts Gothic Revival towers that look as if they harbor ghostly secrets. The church's history parallels the city's. James Bowie was married to Ursula de Veramendi there in 1831, and Gen. Santa Ana raised the flag of "no quarter, no mercy" from the tower of the church in 1836. Even Pope John Paul II visited this old cathedral.

Just inside the nave is a casket claiming to bear some of the bones of three of the Alamo defenders, Travis, Crockett and Bowie. Supposedly, the remnants were gathered by Texas hero Juan Seguin after the battle and brought to the church. The archdiocese has refused to allow any testing to be done, and it is generally believed that the bones are not those of the Alamo heroes.

The plaza in front of the church is believed to be haunted by very malevolent spirits. I spoke with a few vendors who claim to not want to be there after dark. As to whether they are able to breach the portals of the holy cathedral, that is open to speculation.

The Saga, a fantastic light show is shone on the front wall of the cathedral several nights a week. It is free and trlls the history of San Antonio.

Yturri-Edmunds Home

Manuel Yturri Castillo received a land grant in 1824 from the Mexican government of a small tract of land formerly belonging to the Mission Conception. A few years later, around 1840 to 1860, he built a small adobe blockhouse. Over the years, his descendants added a mill powered by the Conception Aqueduct.

Manuel's youngest granddaughter, Ernestine, was the last of the family to live in the house. Ernestine became a teacher like her mother, Manuel's daughter, Vincenta. Ernestine and her older sister, Josephine, spent their lives in the home. Both Josephine and her mother claimed to see a vision of the Blessed Mother in the back yard. In honor of that, Ernestine built a small grotto there. When Ernestine died, she left the home to the San Antonio Conservation Society Foundation so young people would continue to be taught by her donation. Today, that house is one of few remaining in San Antonio. Several other structures have been moved to this location to preserve them as well. It is operated as a house museum as is the other property owned by the foundation, Steves Homestead.

There is evidence that Miss Ernestine has not left her beloved home. Why would she? This was where she chose to spend her life teaching; why not eternity as well? Staff members have experienced cold spots and even caught fleeting glimpses of Miss Ernestine. There is a clock that stopped when she died and is said to be cursed. Several years ago, vandals broke into the home and stole the clock. One can only hope the clock's curse will take its vengeance on those thieves.

San Antonio Botanical Garden

This extensive garden was once a limestone quarry. Today it is a great place to go to observe the plants of Texas as well as flora from around the world. The Native Texas Trail consists of plant communities characteristic of the Hill Country (Edwards Plateau), East Texas Piney Woods, and South Texas. Although fairly close in distance, they are vastly different in soil, plant life, topography, and weather, thus producing totally divergent plant systems. Sprinkled through are several early-Texas houses to give you a better feel for each region.

The Lucile Halsell Conservatory is a huge collection of glass buildings that allow plants from all over the world to flourish there. You can find older flower varieties in the Old Fashioned Garden and for a quick snack there is the Carriage House Kitchen.

There are stories of a nightrider in the garden. He is supposed to be the botanical garden's answer to the Headless Horseman, but no one seems to have any idea why he haunts or who he is.

Brackenridge Park

Brackenridge Park sits at the headwaters of the San Antonio River, a 433-acre refuge in the heart of the city. It houses the San Antonio Zoo as well as Japanese Tea gardens, a golf course and plenty of natural parkland that abounds in wild life. Laszlo Ujhazi, an avid Hungarian hunter lived there. When he died in 1870, he was burried ther but later hi remins we shipped back to Hungary to be burried inhis homeland. Apparently he like

San Antonio better as his sopirit along wiht his hunting dogs had returned to roam the park.

Another spirit is around also. His daughter, Helen Madarasz, was brutally raped and burned to death here in 1899. Her killer had never been found. No surprise, she is often seen and heard n the park.

San Antonio's first zoo consists of a collection of animals assembled in San Pedro Park in the 1800s, not an impressive place. In 1914, Colonel George W. Brackenridge, founder of the San Antonio Express-News, gave the city a collection of buffalo, elk, deer, monkeys, a pair of lions, and four bears and the land where he placed them. That became known as Brackenridge Park, and his collection became the nucleus of the San Antonio Zoo.

Today the zoo is the third-largest, and ranked as one of the best, in the country.

Jose Antonio Navarro State Historical Park

The residence of José Antonio Navarro is one of the most-historically important sites in San Antonio. Navarro was a signer of the Texas Declaration of Independence and one of the drafters of the Constitution of the Republic of Texas. Navarro favored annexation of Texas to the United States and was the only Tejano delegate to the Convention of 1845, which was scheduled to decide on the annexation question. He helped write the first state constitution and worked to protect Tejano citizenship rights. A true Texan, Navarro supported secession from the United States in 1861. He saw four sons leave to fight in the Confederate army. He died in 1871. The site, located in downtown San Antonio, is now a state historic site.

A state employee who spent the night in the home during the restoration reported a face staring out of the attic dormer window. He had slept in the same room Navarro died in, and he awoke in the middle of the night with the feeling he was not alone. When he went outside, he saw the face peering down, but when he went to the attic, no one was there.

Two different sensitives visiting the home at different times both saw a young man "hiding" in the home. He appeared to be out of breath and bleeding profusely from a leg wound. Navarro's brother Eugenio had been shot by an assailant. He bled to death in the home in 1834 at the age of 34.

Other apparitions include a Confederate soldier, perhaps one of Navarro's sons or one of their comrades; a child, believed to have died in a fire; and a prostitute and a bartender, most likely from the days when the house had been converted into a bar.

Considering Navarro's life, you should spot the "Spirit of Texas Independence" there for sure.

Witte Museum

This museum of South Texas history, culture, and natural science came into being mostly through the efforts of one woman, Ellen Schultz Quillin. Quillin was a botany teacher at the Old Main High School. She and her students managed to buy a collection of rocks, artifacts and minerals that was the real start of the museum. She badgered the powers that be for a natural science museum and finally succeeded in bringing the Witte into being. It became her life. She could be found in the museum almost until the day of her death, so it is no surprise that workers still see her there. She is most active in the attic where she kept a library and worked on her book, The Story of the Witte Museum. Today her museum is filled with dinosaur skeletons, cave drawings, wildlife dioramas, some live animals, an American Indian display and so much more.

Many staff members have heard sounds of chairs scraping the floor, felt cold spots, had papers move around their desks. Several have even seen Ms. Quillin. One man felt a hand on his shoulder in the attic. He won't go up there alone anymore. A security guard reports that he has seen Ms. Quinlin's ghost many times.

Tower of the Americas

To get a birds-eye view of San Antonio, visit the observation level of the Tower of the Americas. Built for the HemisFair in 1968, this 750-foot-high tower is one of the tallest freestanding structures in the Western Hemisphere. The deck sits at the equivalent of 59 stories and offers spectacular night viewing. Also found in the tower are: Skies over Texas, a 4D theatre ride that takes visitors on a trip shy high trip across Texas; Eyes over Texas, a rotating restaurant which offers a 360 degree view; and the Observation Deck.

The tower is located in HemisFair Park.

Institute of Texan Cultures

Poles. Germans. Irish. Chinese. People from all parts of the globe came to Texas. All over the state, these settlers left pieces of their culture stitched into the patchwork quilt that is the state of Texas. Want to take a closer look at all the pieces of that great quilt? Visit the Institute of Texas Culture. It's one of the three campuses of the University of Texas at San Antonio that is also a museum dedicated to the better understanding the cultural diversity that has made Texas great. It originally opened in 1968 as the Texas Pavilion at HemisFair, the world's fair held in San Antonio. It met such a vital need; it never closed, just grew larger and better over the years.

When I visited the first time, I met two of the staff members who proved invaluable: Willie Mendez, an archeologist, and J. Rhett Rushing, in the research department. These two guys not only gave me lots of insight into the workings of the museum but had a wealth of information about that other species that isn't officially recognized at the museum but definitely is there, the ghosts of the Institute of Texas Culture.

Believe me there are enough of them to warrant their own book.

Willy was working one Sunday morning, walking the exhibits to be sure all was in order. A few days before, a woman had said there seemed to be some bugs on the clay in one exhibit. He had ordered the production crew to remove the exhibit until it could be corrected. He walked by the exhibit and found it still up. He had just seen the exhibit manager and another worker in the front of the museum when he saw two men pass by him going to the back of the museum. He called out to them "Look at this. They did not take it down to clean."

When they did not answer, he looked back and saw that the two men had not moved and were still standing way up in the front area of the museum. They could not have passed him and returned there that quickly. Needless to say, he rushed back up front. He was not too surprised as he had heard so many strange stories about the things people saw and heard in the museum.

There is one exhibit dedicated to Native-American spirituality. Within the exhibit is a Shaman's Cave where you may enter and listen to a tape telling of the Native American's beliefs. One night nearing closing time, a security guard making his rounds looked in the cave and saw lady in mid- or late 20s. She had packages and appeared to be resting. He started to leave her to her meditations but realized it was almost closing time, so he turned to tell her. She was gone. He called Willy, and they both searched the area, but no lady fitting the description was found.

Although Willie did not see that lady, he did see a small black boy near the Tree of Life in same area at a different time. Again the child disappeared without a trace.

Several years ago, Willy had an office in a different area. He never was comfortable as he always felt a "heaviness" there. One Sunday, he was doing research on a "Bigfoot exhibit" and headed for his office to work on that. He and the security guards were the only ones supposed to be in the building then. He heard what sounded like doors opening and closing, so he called security. They said no one was upstairs, but he continued hearing the sounds. As he stood in the hall, the left had a light on but the right section was dark. He decided to play a trick on the guard he was sure was up there. He waited until the sound was right behind the door, then he yanked open the door and started to yell, "Hey, got you!" Instead of startling the guard he was sure was right there, he got the shock of his life. No one was there.

Later they moved the offices, and new people were placed in that section. Several weeks later, security interviewed him about the office area. They said the new people using the office were hearing strange noises.

One day he got a partial answer to some of his questions. He was escorting a Native-American dancer, Liz, to show her where she was going to be performing. As they approached the cave area, she said, "You have people here."

He thought duh, yes, it's a museum but politely replied "Yes, we have an event going on and expect about 600 people."

"No," she interrupted. "You have people."

By now he realized what she meant. He had heard a lot of stories about the woman in the cave. She continued. "I feel somebody inside the cave. She is a woman, and she is lying in there with her head pointed east (away from where the speakers were located), and there is another young woman on the outside of the cave. They mean no harm. They are just here to see that the pottery is okay."

Willie remembered the security guard describing the woman as having short hair, so he asked about that. "She can't be Native American can she?"

"Oh yes, she is. Her hair is pulled up in a bun."

He also questioned her about the other person he had seen, not mentioning the sex or age.

She responded, "I see him, too. He is a boy, and he is naked. I have no idea how he got here. He is not one of the Native Americans, and they did not bring him in."

Liz had no explanation for the boy ghost and neither did Willie, but I have been told by psychics that spirits attract other spirits. So perhaps the boy was a lost soul from either a later or earlier era who just attached to the group for that reason.

Rhett Rushing also recalled several incidents. There is a hearse in the museum that was built in the 1850s by French Alcacians in Casperville, Texas. Aside from its primary use, it has a false bottom, which indicates it was used at a later date to haul brandy during prohibition. The security guards at night will find a door open, close it and check back on the next round, and it will be open again. Psychics checked it and found orbs and heard moans moving from the hearse to the rear entrance. The chief of police investigated and found no explanation. It also happened when it was in the warehouse in Casperville.

One of the best-documented incidents he told me was about the groundskeeper named Gerald. Gerald was mildly mentally handicapped. He could always be found working outside and did not often interact with people inside, but he did always go in to the vending machines to buy snacks for breakfast and lunch. He usually said hello to whoever passed him at these times.

Vivace Lemmons was one who always said "hello" to the young man. One Monday, she came into work and saw Gerald at the machines. She was very surprised to see him wearing a brown suit and red tie instead of his usual coveralls. Later that day, she was shocked to hear some co-workers discussing Gerald's funeral. When she asked, they told her Gerald died the week before and had been buried over the weekend. She reported her sighting to Rhett, and he told her she was not the only person to see the deceased groundskeeper. Another male worker had seen Gerald that morning also. The groundskeeper was coming out of the snack bar area counting some change. In separate interviews both described Gerald as wearing "a tan suit with a blue tie." Those who attended the funeral noted that he was buried wearing "a tan suit and a blue tie."

Another phenomenon occurs in the building and has been experienced by many, including Rhett and his two sons, 8 and 12. On the second floor on the opposite corner of the building from the library was the residence of Henderson Shuffler, the institute's first director. Henderson was in the habit of smoking his pipe and strolling from his apartment to the library to pick out a few books to read in solitude.

He was bringing a few books from home to place in the library. His younger son stopped at the library door and exclaimed, "I smell something burning!"

The 12 year old moved closer and commented, "It's burning fruit."

When Rhett reached the spot, he recognized the smell as fruit-flavored pipe tobacco. The two boys had never been around anyone smoking a pipe, so they were confused about what the smell was. He commented, "No one has smoked in this building for the past 25 years."

This is a fairly common occurrence when the museum is closed. In September 2006, Rhett brought in a ghost hunting team. He had them stay overnight in the building. When they reached the library area, all 12 team members not only smelled the pipe, but their electric magnetic meters all went wild at that point. They also got a voice on the EVP near the hearse, but no one could make out what it was saying.

Willie also had an incident with the former director. Again he was working on a Sunday and took the elevator up to the offices on the second floor. He stressed that this floor was blocked to the general public on the elevator and no one can get into the floor since it is all offices. He went into the restroom and found both faucets turned on. No one else had been up there that day. Strangely enough when he mentioned it to a woman co-worker, she said the same thing had happened to her, only this time in the ladies room. Could the former director be trying to make his presence felt this way, too?

Even if you aren't lucky enough to see a ghost at the Institute of Texas Cultures, you will see one spirit, the spirit of the people from every corner of the globe who made Texas what it is today.

Austin

Driskill Hotel

It was in the 1830s the first permanent white settlers established a village they named Waterloo at the site of present day Austin. By 1839, it was chosen to be the capital of the Republic of Texas. The city was renamed after Stephen F. Austin, "the father of Texas." With the arrival of the politicians, the town's population burgeoned to 856 people. When the Republic became one of the United States, it clearly stated in two elections that it wanted Austin to remain the capital of the new state.

When a young high roller from Tennessee named Jessie Driskill came to Austin in 1869, the city was on its way to being a metropolis. Driskill had already made and lost one fortune during the Civil War. The young Irishman, who held the rank of Colonel, had furnished cattle to the Confederate Army and the Texas Rangers. Unfortunately, he had been paid in Confederate money so by the end of the war, he had no money and no cattle.

By 1884, he had rebuilt another fortune and decided to invest some of it in a luxurious hotel to complement the new capital building being erected on the city's highest spot.

Driskill purchased an entire city block for his hotel for the outrageous sum of $7,500. When the Driskill opened in December of 1886, the Daily Statesman called it "One of the Finest Hotels in the Whole Country." Two weeks later the Driskill began a tradition by hosting the inaugural ball for Texas Governor Sul Ross. Later governors have followed this tradition including William P. Hobby, Miriam (Ma) Ferguson, Dan Moody, John Connelly, and Ann Richards who all hosted their balls in the Driskill's magnificent ballroom.

But for Driskill, fortunes were "Easy come. Easy go." When an early freeze in 1888, killed off much of his herd, Driskill was forced to sell the hotel. It passed through several hands until it came into possession of Major George W. Littlefield in 1895, who proclaimed that "it would never close again."

Social, political and entertainment bigwigs all stayed at the Driskill. In October 1898, Austin's first long-distance telephone call was placed from the lobby. Over the years the Driskill has played host to almost every sitting president since it opened. Lyndon Johnson's first date with Lady Bird was breakfast at the Driskill.

One of the interesting things about the hotel is that every room is different. The art alone is worth visiting the hotel to view it.

Littlefield was almost proven wrong in 1969 when the hotel was destined to be razed and a new modern hotel to be constructed on the site. Fortunately, local citizens banned together and saved this Texas treasure for posterity – and the ghosts that roam the building.

Yes, there are more than one here at the Driskill. It is only fitting that Colonel Driskill should still inhabit his masterpiece. Many people have seen him standing with a hand on a chair; a common position he assumed when he was alive. Ed Van de Vort, a local historian who since passed away. told me of a woman who was arranging a meeting of a New Age group at the hotel. One of hotel staff, Janice, was showing the woman around. When they reached the stair landing where Col. Driskill's portrait hangs, the woman stopped and stared at it for a moment. She then asked "How did he die?"

Janice answered, "A stroke." The visitor replied, "He was in great pain."

Ed also gave me a tour of the hotel. When we reached the Maximillan Room, he pointed out the mirrors. They had been destined for Emperor Maximillan and consort Carlotta's Palace in Mexico but instead found their way into a Texas pawnshop. In the 1930's the hotel bought them and had them installed in the grand Maximillan Ball room. The same lady who had commented on Driskill's pain was shown the ballroom as a possible venue for the meeting. She saw an apparition of a woman with a young boy sitting in the corner. She claimed the boy was "very sad." The woman was wearing a long flowing white dress of the style popular in France in the mid 1800s.

Carlotta? Perhaps. Yet the mirrors never had any contact with her except possibly when they were chosen. The boy presents a confirmation that the woman was indeed Carlotta. During their short but turbulent reign as rulers of Mexico bolstered only by Napoleon III's troops, the couple were childless. In an effort to legitimatize their rule, they adopted the grandson of a former emperor of Mexico, Agustín de Iturbide y Arámburu. The child also named Agustín was taken from his home to live with the royal couple and given the title "His Highness, the Prince of Iturbide." That is enough to make any child sad.

Carlotta, who ended her days completely insane, would not be very good company with which to spend eternity. Luckily there are lots of other phantoms in the Driskill. Besides the stories I gleaned from Ed, I spoke with "Maverick" who leads tours for Austin Ghost Tours. (This tour is great way to learn more about haunted Austin.)

Maverick also had an interesting story about "Carlotta" in the Maximillan Room. He was having lunch with a friend who is a makeup consultant. The friend commented to him "You do know the Driskill is haunted?"

He replied that he did and asked why she mentioned it. She replied with this story: "I was there for a fashion show and they had me set up in a large room with a lot of mirrors. (Maximillan Room) I was seated in a spot where when I looked up at the mirror, I had a view of the door. I was looking in the mirror and saw the door open and a woman with long blond hair and a long flowing white gown enter. I looked over to the door to greet her thinking it was one of the models and no one was there. When I looked back in the mirror, there she was." (History is unclear about the color of Carlotta's hair but as she was a Hapsburg, it is likely she was blond.)

One of the most common specters seen at the Driskill is "The Bride." Actually, there are two "brides" one is believed to have committed suicide after being jilted in the 1920. She is seen mostly in the ladies restroom.

The more commonly seen one dates to the 1980's era. She is often seen on the stairs or in the hall of the fourth floor carrying lots of bags. In life, she came to Austin from Huston Her fiancé had just informed her that never planned to marry her. She came to Austin to think things over. The last people who saw her in life were the bartender who remembered her ordering a diet Coke and the bell man who remembered her walking across the lobby to the elevator loaded down with shopping bags To get revenge, she had hit him where it hurts most; in his pocketbook. She maxed out his credit cards with a grand shopping spree of more than $40,000 then went to her room, picked up a pillow to muffle the sound and killed herself with a bullet to her stomach. She wasn't found until three days later when a housekeeper wondered aobut the constant "Do not disturb" sign.

One group attempted a séance using a Ouija Board and got an answer from a female spirit with the initials DB or Deeb. Another instance of a female specter trying to communicate was a bit more direct. It happened when two women were working late one night in an office with a curtained window to the lobby. One worker heard someone knocking on the window and opened it to see what the problem was. They were confronted with an angry gesticulating young woman who disappeared in front of their eyes.

Back in 1999, two young women came to stay at the hotel. They wanted to stay on the old side but were told it was under repair. Late that night, they snuck into the old side of the hotel. The floors were all covered with black plastic and all the wall trim had been removed. They noticed a woman get off the elevator and go to room 27. The hall was dark but they saw that the woman was carrying a lot of bags as if she had just returned from shopping but it was 2A.M.

The two young guests called down to her, "Don't you mind staying in a room with all this construction going on?"

The woman did not turn to face them but replied as if from a great distance, "No I don't mind at all."

Somewhat frightened by her tone, they quickly left for the better lit area in the new section. As they turned the corner, they noticed the woman was no longer by the door and must have entered the room.

When they checked out next morning they complained to the concierge, "Why did you let that woman stay in the old section but not us?"

He replied that no one was stating in that section but the women were so insistent that they had seen a guest enter room 27 that he took the master key and brought them over to show them the room. He opened the door of room 27; there was no furniture in it; plastic draped the floor. There were not even any fixtures in the bathroom. It was then that the women realized they had seen "The Bride."

Still another episode where The Bride made her presence felt when singer, Annie Lennox, was staying at the Driskill in the 1980s. She was getting ready for her show and unpacked two dresses, to try and decide which to wear. She left them on the bed and went in to take a shower. When she came out only one of the dresses was still on the bed. The other was neatly hanging in the closet. Annie knew no one could have come into the room as the safety lock was on the door. Needless to say, she accepted the phantom decision and wore the dress on the bed.

Perhaps the saddest of the Hotel's wraiths is a young girl about four or five. The child accompanied her father, a U.S. senator from another area of Texas, to the hotel for a big political meeting. They were going down the stairs from the mezzanine and the little girl was bouncing a wooden ball. The ball slipped out of her reach and, as she tried to grasp it, she tumbled down the stairs breaking her neck. Ever since, the child is heard bouncing her ball and giggling loudly on the stairs. The desk clerks have become so used to it that they just loudly say "Shhhh." The phantom quiets down.

Recently, Maverick was coming up the stairs with a woman friend. He had not told her the story of the senator's daughter when she trued to him and asked, "Is there a child's ghost here?"

Maverick replied, "Yes. Why?" to see what she would say.

The woman continued, "It just felt as if my two year old was tugging at my skirt and I looked down before realizing she isn't with me."

Obviously, the child is still around and searching for her parents.

Some of the spooks are still just having fun, Texas style. In the 1920 when the elevators were first installed people would summon an elevator. When the doors opened they would be confronted by the sounds of a wild party going on but no one would be in the car.

Another group of shades hanging around are still doing their jobs. A long dead housekeeper, Mrs. Rogers is sometimes seen arranging flowers where desk used to be.

And a night watchman is still making his rounds on the top floor. He always smoked a cigar. People today often smell the smoke. Both of these people died around the turn of the century.

One episodes happened to a brand new security guard. He was on his second week on the job and on the stairwell between the fifth and sixth floor. This is the highest point that the original hotel reached. He stopped and bent over to tie his shoe when someone tapped him on the back and said in a gruff male voice, "Do you have a match?"

Having heard the stories he knew Col. Driskill smoked cigars. Not daring to turn around he rushed down to the lobby for human companionship. The desk clerk remarked "Are you alright, you look kind of white."

The terrified watchman replied, "I don't know! I heard all the stories but I never believed them but I think I just met Col. Driskill."

A manager in the café had to go down to the basement to get some tins. /while he was there, all the generators and lights went out then a single one went back on and he felt someone brush past him and felt a cold spot. Then the lights came back on. Needless to say, her hurried back upstairs and was not anxious to return to the basement.

For spirits of a different kind a visit to the Driskill Bar. The bar is a true Texas experience. Their furnishing are plush but masculine. Overstuffed leather couches, light fixtures made of guns, spurs and little lampshades, a copper-plated ceiling, longhorn cattle mounted on the wall and bar chairs with cow-print backs make this a really comfortable meeting spot. It's not crowded and has plenty of Texas style seating arrangements spaced around that give the feeling of having a drink at Southfork while waiting for J.R. to come swaggering through the door.

You can even order from the bar menu but I suggest you visit the Grill Room to really take advantage of the superb food prepared under the watchful eye of Executive Chef Josh Watkins. He is so good he actually took on Bobby Flay in an Iron Chef episode on The Food Chanel. Have one of their famous beef dishes. This is Texas after all.

For a lunch or breakfast try the 1886 Café and Bakery located in the front of the hotel. I had Mama's Meatloaf served with Garlic Mashed Potatoes, Green Beans and Mushroom Gravy. Yumieee!

The Littlefield House

The hotel's savior, Major George Littlefield, was also a benefactor to the University of Texas. His somewhat spooky 1893 Victorian home is still in use on the college campus. After George died, his wife Alice lived in the house until her death in 1935. The house then passed on to the university.

Even solid university personnel sometimes feel that Alice did not ever leave her home. Strange occurrences have been difficult to explain without bring in the paranormal. The sound of footsteps and a piano playing in the empty home are not what could be considered normal. The first floor is not occupied on a regular basis. It is used for special functions. Resource Development Special Programs staff use the second floor for office space.

Some pretty spooky thing have happened to them. One event planner, noted that after the staff returned after winter break, they found two candelabrums, which had been firmly ensconced on the mantle in the middle parlor, lying on the floor several feet from their original position There was no logical way they could have gotten there as no one had been in the house over the break. The same worker noted that when she brought her young granddaughter into the house for the first time, the child noted, "Someone dead is here."Alice was reputed to be a somewhat disturbed woman and some of her paintings add credibility to that rumor. The one on display in the home is somber to say the least.

The home is not open to the public but you cansee it froemthe grounds.

State Capitol Building

Austin is clearly the head of Texas and the top spot in Austin literally and figuratively is the State Capitol Building. It was the third capitol building and its grandeur made up for the lack of any style in the earlier buildings. Completed in 1888, the Sunset Red granite Renaissance Revival building is reminiscent of an ancient Italian church. It was the winning design from a national competition. Austin, Texas is one of only two Southern state capitols not occupied by Union troops during the War Between the States. (Tallahassee, Florida is the other.)

The grounds themselves have been haunted long before the capitol was built. Before the settlers arrived it is believed that an Indian scout stole a Comanche maiden. The girl's father killed the scout and the girl stabbed herself and died next to her lover. The Texas scout and his lover and are still seen occasionally.

One of the best documented murders that took place in the capitol is that of Col. Robert Marshal Love, Comptroller of Public Accounts for Texas in 1901. Love had a strong law enforcement background having been a sheriff and United States Marshal. His murder relates back to that part of his career when he had helped oust the last reconstruction Governor who refused to give up his office to the newly elected Governor Richard Coke. There is a rumor that Love literally kicked Davis out of the capitol.

Love was shot in his office near the east wing of the capitol on June 30, 1903 by W. G. Hill, a member of the former administration. The Arlington Journal described the event; "Comptroller of Public Accounts, Hon. R. M. Love, was shot to death in his office at Austin Tuesday morning by W.

G. Hill; a former employee of the department, Mr. Love was shot twice and died shortly after. His last words were a prayer for mercy on the man who killed him.

S. J. Stevens, chief bookkeeper in the department, ran to Mr. Love's assistance and grappled with Hill. In the scuffle Hill's pistol was again discharged, whether with suicidal intent or aimed for Stevens is not known, but the ball entered Hill's chest and he died a few hours afterward."

Love was laid in the rotunda where he died. His final words were "I have no idea why he shot me. May the Lord bless him and forgive him. I cannot say more."

Today, many people report seeing a "nice man" dressed in a suit dating to the early 1900s. He has even spoken to some. When security approaches him, he just walks through a wall.

The capitol is the largest state capitol in the United States. With 8.5 acres of floor space and nearly 500 rooms including the newer underground area, there is room for lots of haunting.

The spirits in the capitol are harmless but beware of the place called "The Shark Tank." It's an atrium which is the only part of the underground area visible from above ground. Many lawyers frequently gather here as this is the only part of the underground capitol where you can get cell phone service.

Governor's Mansion

Across from the capitol is the Governor's Mansion. The Greek revival style buff brick building was built in 1856. It's the oldest remaining public building in downtown Austin and the fourth oldest governor's mansion continuously occupied in the United States. It's open for tours.

While touring, keep a lookout for some of its previous inhabitants who just won't leave. Naturally, Sam Houston is still there. He is seen in his bedroom. Both Governor Mark White who was governor in the 1980s, and his wife, had stated they saw "Old Sam."

The building has a colorful history since opening in 1856, (Check out the links below.) Paranormal activity includes occupants reporting seeing the former Texas hero, Republic of Texas President, and Governor, Sam Houston in his bedroom in the Mansion. Sam Houston served as governor from 1859 to 1861. Both the wife and daughter of Governor Mark White had encounters with the spirit of "Old Sam" back in the 80's.

Another specter in the mansion is not a political figure. He is the 19-year-old nephew of Governor Pendleton Murrah (1863-1865) who shot himself in an upstairs bedroom when the niece of his uncle's wife refused his proposal. To this day, moans, footsteps and cold spots are reported in that bedroom. People have seen doorknobs turn of their own volition.

Texas State Cemetery

From Stephen Austin to Barbara Jordan, everybody who was somebody in Texas, lies beneath its rolling green hills. It's hard to pick the most interesting personages but some of my favorites are: Joanna Troutman, called the Betsy Ross of Texas. She designed and made the Lone Stat Flag for the Republic of Texas. She lived in Georgia and had never visited Texas until her remains were moved here in 1913.

Edmund Jackson Davis, possibly the most hated man in Texas; he was the last Reconstruction Governor who refused to leave office until he was kicked out by Marshal Love. After his death his brother erected the tallest monument in the cemetery; an obelisk meant to insult and irritate the relatives of the Confederate veterans buried nearby.

The Fergusons, James and Miriam Amanda Ferguson, The only Texas husband-wife team of governors. James swept the Texas Gubernatorial election in 1914 on an anti-prohibition platform. He returned to office in 1916 but was impeached for mishandling of funds among other charges. He attempted to prevent the probation that impeached officers could not hold other state offices by resigning the day before the impeachment went into effect.

When he was not allowed to run for the governorship in 1924, his wife tossed her bonnet into the ring. "Ma" Ferguson, as she was called because of her initials and her devotion to her husband and children, ran against a candidate endorsed by the Ku Klux Klan. She promised the people of Texas if she was elected they would get "two for the price of one" because she would rely totally on "Pa's" experience. As any student of Southern politics could have predicted, she won by a landslide. She was the first woman governor of Texas and only the second in the United states. (Nelly Ross had been inaugurated fifteen days earlier in Wyoming.)

Her term was marked by strife and she allegedly pardoned an average of 100 convicts a month. Both she and "Pa" were accused of accepting large bribes of land and cash for favors and were accused of awarding lucrative state contracts to family and friends. However, a threat to impeach "Ma" failed. She was defeated for re-nomination in 1926 but ran again in 1930 and was again defeated. She persisted and in 1932 again declared for the governorship. Running on an anti-waste, anti-graft, anti-political favoritism platform, (That is not a joke. She really promised those things with a straight face and the voters ate it up.) she won in November to secure her second term as Governor of Texas. She continued her course of liberal pardoning and parole policies. This term, no one objected too much as every convict paroled or pardoned eased the fiscal burden on the state during the depression.

Never a quitter, "Ma" Ferguson, now 65, did make a run once more for governor in 1940. She claimed she could not resist a "popular draft." Even though she was defeated, there were still over 100,000 voters who were willing to send her back to the governor's Mansion once more. When "Pa" in 1944, Miriam Ferguson retired to private life in Austin and died of heart failure on June 25, 1961.

Apparently Texans have a good sense of humor about less than honest governors. The story was told that at her second inaugural ball at the Driskill Hotel, of course, someone bumped into her while dancing. The gentleman turned and said "Pardon me, Ma." She replied, "See Pa in his office tomorrow about that."

General Albert Sidney Johnston's tomb is the most elaborate. It is graced with a life sized recumbent stature of the general carved by the Elizabeth Ney known as the "Madwoman of Austin". Johnston was killed at Shiloh and remained on his horse giving orders as he bled to death. Johnston had served as Texas Secretary of War under Governor Lamar.

There's a entire section devoted to Confederate veterans and widows with over 2,000 Confederate dead. The last widow was interred in 1963.

Ann Richards who was buried in the State Cemetery September 2006 making her the fourteenth governor buried there. You will also find nine Confederate Generals, five famous authors, two Revolutionary War heroes, one Union soldier, hundreds of interesting stories and a few ghosts.

The Bob Bullock Texas State History Museum

The Bob Bullock Museum is the best place to learn the history of Texas. with three floors crammed full of what Texas is all about. 35-foot-tall bronze Lone Star sculpture greets visitors in front of the Museum, and a colorful terrazzo floor in the Museum's rotunda features a campfire scene featuring events from Texas' colorful past. In Texas, everything is larger than life .

The museum is filled with characters that arise straight from our history books as well as lesser known figures that are every bit as colorful. Texas was the only state to be an independent republic.

There have been six flags to fly over Texas: The Spanish, French, Mexican, Confederacy, United States, and Republic of Texas, before it became a state and because of that, was the only state to enter the United States by treaty instead of territorial annexation. In that treaty, it staked its claim to one of the most unique states. For instance, the Texas flag is the only state flag that can legally be flown at the same height as the United States flag.

It's history contributed the Texas brand of hero. In most states, the biggest heroes were usually native born sons or daughters. Not so with Texas. William B. Travis, Jim Bowie, Davy Crockett, the best known defenders of the Alamo, were all born elsewhere. Sam Houston, considered by many as the Father of Texas, was actually born in Virginia and served as governor of Tennessee before moving to Texas.

Mexico, when it was still a Spanish province, had originally opened its borders to land hungry gringos to fill the wide open spaces of their state of Tejas-Coahuila. By the time they realized their mistake, the state was filled with many former American citizens who continued to trade with the U.S. and maintain ties with it. Mexico had recently won its independence from Spain. Santa Anna, the president, took steps to curb the frightening U. S. influence in his young country but it was too late.

Stephen F. Austin and Santa Anna belonged to the same free masonry lodge in Mexico City. Texas' fight for independence from Mexico, General Sam Houston, a Mason, spared Mexican General Santa Ana's life after recognizing him as a brother Mason. In fact, Travis, Bowie and Crockett were also Masons, but that did not influence Santa Anna at the Alamo. Suzanna Dickerson was one of the few people spared at the Alamo. She is the only woman to appear on the museum's façade. Had Santa Ana not been so ruthless in slaying all the defenders of that small mission stronghold, history might have been very different.

As it was, "Remember the Alamo" became the Texan's rallying cry. The final battle for Texan independence occurred at the small hamlet of San Jacinto on April 21, 1836 and lasted only 13 fateful minutes. When it ended, Texas declared itself a free and independent republic.

The San Jacinto Monument commemorating that event rises 570 feet, taller than either the Washington Monument or the Statue of Liberty.

Yes, Texas is unique and proud of it! This museum tells its glorious story.

Moonlight Towers

Moonlight Towers, once employed in many U. S. cities, are now unique to Austin. They are an official state landmarks thus designated in April 1970, and were placed on the National Register of Historic Places July 12, 1976. The tower I visited was near the state cemetery but they are all around the older section of the city. The original 31towers have dwindled down to 17. Historical markers tell the story of the towers. The tower in Zilker Park is lit each December with over 3,000 colored lights making it the "world's largest Christmas tree."

The real story of the lights started almost a decade before their installation. On New Year's Eve, 1884, one of America's earliest serial killers struck in Austin. The Servant Girl Annihilator, as the reporters called him began his killing spree with African American women, usually domestics. He axed, bludgeoned, cut, mutilated and raped victims he usually dragged from their own beds or snatched near their homes. On Christmas Eve of 1885, he changed his style and switched to white victims. The case was never solved and the killings ended after the two Christmas Eve murders. People had begun to speculate that the attacks which left seven women and one man dead had a supernatural origin and ghost stories still are attached to the scenes. Ironically none of the crime scene houses are still standing.

The crime spree left people feeling unsafe and a motion was started to install the now famous lights. Strangely enough, the murders in Austin may have been committed by the same person who came to be called Jack the Ripper in White Castle. A Malay ships cook named Maurice was living in Austin at a seedy hotel called The Pearl. The Pearl was located very near the area where the killing took place. Maurice left Austin in January of

1886, just weeks after the last murder. Later, when he came under Scotland Yard's scrutiny for the Jack the Ripper murders, The London Times quoted him as having threatened to kill White Chapel prostitutes. Both cases has similarities in the way the victims were militated. Neither series of crimes were ever proved to be committed by Maurice but then neither case has been closed.

History doesn't record whether Maurice ever returned to Austin but if he did and was the Servant Girl Annihilator perhaps the Moonlight Towers cast too much light on the streets of 19th century Austin for him to strike again.

Bat Bridge

Another famous resident of Austin dislikes light also. If someone remarks that Austin is "batty," they are not trying to insult the local politicians. The largest urban colony of bats in North America, some 1.5 million or so Mexican free-tail bats, live beneath The Congress Avenue Bridge that spans Town Lake in downtown Austin. Their nightly food foreys especially from mid-March to November, occur at dusk. The small flying mammals blanket the sky as they head for the batty equivelant of the golden arches. This event has become one of the most unusual tourist attractions in Texas. There are several points from which to view the phenomenon. and an information kiosk is located on the north bank of the river, just east of the bridge. No, they are not vampire bats and are not dangerous unless you happen to be a mosquito or small flying insect, their favorite snack.

Paramount Theater

Old theaters always have their specters. The Paramount is no exception. One of the most common phantoms around the Paramount is a man smoking a cigar. Visitors, actors and staff have all had occasions when they smell cigar smoke even though no one is smoking in the theater.

One of the most alarming events happened to the daughter of a director. It was a closed rehearsal. The daughter had sat back in the balcony to see how the show would look from there. She smelled smoke and looked to her left. There was a man in a gray suit sitting there smoking a cigar. She bolted downstairs and looked to see if he was following her. To her amazement, he had disappeared but there was still a cloud of smoke over the seat he had occupied.

The phantom is believed to be a cigar smoking projectionist who worked at the theater in the 1950s. And talk about lightning not striking twice, there is another projectionist from a different era who is only seen in the projection room.

The Paramount originally opened on October 11, 1915, as the Majestic Theatre. They were a top vaudeville venue, booking acts like Harry Houdini. With the advent of silent film, the theater needed a major overhaul. In 1930, the theater was renamed the "Paramount" given wall-to-wall carpeting, upholstered chairs, and adding a state-of-the-art sound system. The Paramount continued to offer live theatre. Stars such as the Marx Brothers, Helen Hayes, Orson Welles, Sarah Bernhardt, Lillian Russell, John Philip Sousa, the Barrymores, Lillian Gish, and George M. Cohan trod its boards.

But by the dawn of the 70s the Paramount Theatre was in disrepair again. A trio of entrepreneurs with more vision than money took on the task of keeping this grand old thespian alive and well. It was a challenge but on February 2, 1975, the Paramount had its first live show in years, a concert with the Dave Brubeck quartet. The theater also began screening the old classics such as *Top Hat, Citizen Kane* and *An American in Paris.*

Shortly after this, the Paramount was awarded its state historical marker by its place in the national register of historic places, which qualified it for federal restoration funds.

It hosted world premiere of the film version of *The Best Little Whorehouse in Texas* back in 1982. It is back in the limelight showing classics and hosting live performances of big name entertainment and Broadway shows.

Rhambo Building

The area between Sixth Street and Chesar Chavez (First Street) ranging for about five blocks either side of Congress St. is considered "hip." It's Austin's live music venues. There you will find art, restaurants and boutiques as well as the music spots. It's also where you find some unique ghost stories.

One of the most intriguing and best documented ones is found at what is now David Grimes Photography Studio. David calls his place "The Hideout" and it is exactly that for a whole range of shades from Austin's less darker past. David had come to terms with a ghost lady named Pearl, a little girl spirit known as "The Shy One" and a boogie scooting remote control car with a mind of its own. But the most intriguing specter is a laughing African American man who had been detected by psychics and heard by many. The psychic said the man is laughing because he never though he would be his own client. There is quite a story behind this soul with the strange sense of humor.

In 1901, William M. Tears, Austin's most prominent black undertaker, hired a young apprentice, Nathan Rhambo. Rhambo was handsome, polite, and well respected. He moved on to his own establishment between 1915 and 1920. By 1929 Rhambo's funeral home was advertising "Superior Ambulance Service" and "Courteous Attendants." Rhambe had joined the local Baptist Church and married. He had become wealthy in the process and he flaunted that wealth. He was even rumored to have a white mistress. Whether it was the money he flashed or the interracial affair, he had aroused some resentment. On June 21, 1932, Rhambo was approached by a well dressed young man who asked the undertaker to accompany him just out of town to fetch a recently deceased relative. They left in Rhambo's black Buick. The next day, Rhambo was found about 130 miles from Austin. He had been shot in the head and beaten. Within 24 hours, the police arrested Carl Stewart. Rhambo's employees identified him as the man with whom Rhambo had left on the night of his death. Police also arrested two of Rhambo's employees citing a conspiracy to rob and kill Rhambo for his money. However, a local paper had reported that Rhambo was still wearing a diamond ring when the body was found.

Stewart came into court with three prominent white Austin lawyers. The attorneys did the unthinkable; they questioned the methods and veracity of the arresting officers, all white. None of this did Stewart any good; the jury found him guilty and sentencing him to the electric chair after only thirty five minutes of deliberation.

The question was never publicly asked "How did a young black robber afford the best legal minds in Austin?" "Were these lawyers paid by a jealous white husband or a group of wealthy white supremacists?"

Perhaps they is why Nathan Rhambo still is waiting around his old funeral parlor and hoping for justice to finally be served? One thing is sure he has a great sense of humor to be able to laugh about his own murder after all these years.

Port Aransas

Tarpon Inn

It's a small magic island. Mustang Island is what it's called now, but before the first English settler, the Karankawa Indians and the pirates who frequented its sandy beaches called it "Wild Horse Island." They were referring to the herds of wild mustangs that roamed the 18-mile stretch of beach land separated from Padre Island by a narrow channel.

Legends tell that somewhere on Mustang Island is hidden a Spanish dagger with a silver spike driven through the hilt. The dagger belonged to Jean Lafitte, who had settled on Galveston after leaving New Orleans. If you find the dagger, you have found the place Lafitte buried a chest of gold and jewels.

An island that boasted golden sand beaches, soft gulf breezes, plentiful game and rich soil would not long remain the free domain of native people or wild pirates. Sober settlers were foreordained, and they arrived in the person of an Englishman from Lancaster, Robert Ainsworth Mercer, in 1853. Mercer established El Mar Rancho and brought his wife and children to the island. Other settlers, including the Stephenson family, followed, and the town began to thrive. A lighthouse was built to aid in shipping.

The Civil War affected the island more than most mainland communities. It was a big supplier of beef, hides and other supplies to the Confederate forces. The Union sent the U.S.S. Afton; its men leveled the small community on Mustang Island in February of 1862, burning most of the houses, structures, warehouses, piers, docks and wharf.

By the time the Union had captured the island, the lens had been removed from the lighthouse lantern and hidden in the marsh somewhere behind the tower. The light was vital because it controlled the nighttime pass. Without that light, Union ships could only safely travel the treacherous pass in daytime. This vastly limited Union's blockade of the coastline.

The island passed back and forth between North and South during the war, driving the settlers from what was left of their homes.

In 1866, the settlers returned with newcomers. By now there were about 50 settlers on Mustang Island.

As the island thrived, the need for a jetty was seen. One of the original settlers, Frank Stephenson, used some of the old Civil War barracks to build a two-story structure to house workers building the south jetty called the Mansfield Jetty. After the workers left in 1886, Stephenson converted the structure into a hotel called the Tarpon Inn. He correctly planned on capturing a piece of the tarpon fishing trade currently in full swing. At that time, the town called "Ropesville" was renamed "Tarpon."

In 1897, he sold the hotel to Mary Hatfield and her son, Ed Cotter. A fire ravaged the hotel, destroying it totally in 1900. In 1904, two new structures were built. The hurricane of 1919 destroyed the main structure but left the smaller one repairable. The inn was rebuilt and again sold in 1923 to James M. Ellis, who rebuilt the inn to resemble the original barracks.

Over the years, the inn's famous guests included President Franklin D. Roosevelt, who visited the inn but did not stay overnight. He fished there in 1937 and left behind a signed fish scale as a memento of his visit, and Duncan Hines, who was married and spent his honeymoon there. Other famous names include Hedy Lamarr, Victor McLaughlin, Billy Mitchell, Amee Semple McPherson and Clyde Beatty along with his lion. That gave the maid reason to be cautious.

When you cross on the ferry from Aransas Pass, you enter a different zone -- the relaxation zone. The inn today offers a rustic escape from the stresses of civilization. Each of the 24 rooms open onto the longest porch in Texas. No television and no phone really let you "get away from it all." They do have WiFi if you must connect with civilization.

In 1986, in commemoration of the inn's centennial, mortar tiles were made on the property, and guests, former owners and island residents made their handprints in the wet cement along with comments. The tiles now form the sidewalk in front of the inn.

As might be expected in a building this old, numerous strange events have been reported. Guests have heard voices in showers and footsteps above the second floor and felt cold spots. There is no third floor, just an attic for the footsteps to originate in. One guest even reported the bathroom glowed pink.

The management discounts these tales but does admit there is "something in what used to be the restaurant area." The desk clerk suggested I speak to Julie Caraker, the restaurant's former manager.

I set up a meeting with Julie the next morning for breakfast on the mainland. She was a wealth of information. First to understand what happened in Beulah's, the restaurant-cum-event facility, you need to get oriented.

Beulah's has had different names. It was originally called the "Silver King." The main inn building faces the street. Behind it is a garden enclosed by a small bungalow to the left side and a long narrow building to the rear. The swimming pool is also back there. These two buildings were used as Beulah's Restaurant and now serve as venues for weddings and special events. The long narrow building to the rear is the remaining building that was repaired and used for the inn after the hurricane of 1919. The smaller building was the main restaurant. The long building had an office and a walk-in cooler. Restaurant staff would go to the walk-in and get supplies and then bring them to the main restaurant. Julie said, "At first the old building was where we would encounter the ghosts. But later they began coming into the new building."

Julie came to the island first as a teenager. Even then she heard people talk of the ghosts. Beulah May Williams, who was head housekeeper at the inn for many years and in whose honor the Silver King was renamed, claimed she had heard a ghost in the kitchen even then. She was off duty one day and passing by the kitchen when she heard a din and clatter comparable to the busiest day, yet she knew the restaurant was closed that day. She went in anyway to check and found everything still in its place as if nothing had happened.

Julie had heard these stories as a teen, so she was not too surprised at the things that happened. She explained that the fire in the main building caused a lot of damage. A cook who worked there then lost her pearl necklace in the fire and now comes back looking for it.

Not only has Julie seen her, but two other former employees, Kent Marsh, an evening chef, and Mike Burvosa, another staff member, saw a middle-aged woman with her hair pulled back into a tight bun who appeared to be searching for something.

Julie's "favorite" phantom is a former cook called "Sammy." She recalled one day when they had been shorthanded and she had to help with the cooking. She claims not to be the world's greatest cook, so this morning while she was cooking, "I just seemed to get everything mixed in right.

I was surprised at how well it was going when I realized it had not been me making these decisions. I had help. Sammy was directing me as I cooked."

He played tricks sometimes, too. Julie told of one day while she was mopping the hardwood floor. "Now I tend to twirl, so when I looked down and saw a spin mark I thought I had done it, but then I looked back over the floor and all the way back there where it had been clear before were these little marks. Sammy had been following me."

The University of Texas Marine Science Institute

For those of you who are interested in marine life, visit the Marine Science Center. The visitor's center is a virtual natural history lab. There are seven aquaria displays that feature typical Texas coastal habitats and the organisms that live in them, including Spartina, black mangrove marsh, oyster reef, open bay bottom, rock jetty and offshore artificial reefs. Educational movies are shown Monday through Thursday at 3 p.m. There are other displays, which feature current and past research projects and are a great way to understand the marine biology that surrounds the island.

The university also offers several Elderhostel programs. Elderhostel is an educational/travel adventure for adults over 55 usually with an educational focus. They sponsor two Elderhostel Adventures Afloat programs annually on hotel barge, R/B River Explorer. One begins in New Orleans and barges the Intracoastal Waterway through the swamps and bayous and ends in Galveston, TX. The other begins in Galveston and barges the Intracoastal Waterway through the salt marshes of Texas, including Aransas National Wildlife Refuge, a habitat for the endangered whooping cranes. A trip to the King Ranch, recognizable as the inspiration for the movie Giant, ends in Port Isabel, Texas.

Another project, the Wetlands Education Center, 3.5 acres between the UTMSI Visitors Center and the South Jetty, consisting of marsh/seagrass ponds landscaped and planted with various seagrasses and natural coastal vegetation. The public can stroll the boardwalk and observe migratory waterfowl and resident marsh birds.

The Regional Transportation Authority (RTA) in cooperation with the City provides a trolley, which loops around town and the beach for a great overview of the area. You can board anywhere along the route. The trip lasts about one hour depending on traffic and conditions. There may be places you want to explore, so you can get off and re-board at any of the stops.

When you pass the big dunes near UTMSI, there is an old gun bunker from World War II. Cannons were placed there to protect the shipping pass. The residents also used them to hide in during hurricanes in 1919 and 1930.

Birding Centers

One of the most-popular activities, the Whooping Crane Festival, draws birders from across the nation. It's held the last weekend in February.

Currently two of the five official birding centers that make up the Texas Birding Trail stretching along the coast from East Texas to the Rio Grande Valley are located in Port Aransas; the Leonabell Turnbull Birding Center on Ross Avenue and the Joan and Scott Holt Paradise Pond Birding Center off Cut-off Road However, almost any place on the island is a potential birding spot. The Flats, marshy places that get inundated daily, are good spots to look for wading birds. Island Mooring Marina is a favorite haunt of the Brown Pelican.

Dolphin Watch Tour

One of my favorite things to do when the opportunity arises is to go dolphin watching. Here the opportunity was docked at Woody's Sports Center, the place to go for any type of charter boat. This is also the place to rent anything water- or nature-related.

The *Island Queen II* offers private charter fishing trips, for up to 99 passengers with 65 fishing at a time. The *Queen* fishes the bay waters. My vessel of choice was the *Mustang*, a boat especially designed to bring people closer to the sea. She is a large stable vessel great for watching wildlife. It offers birding trips to observe egrets, herons, spoonbills, gulls, pelicans, curlews and many more, then gives you a taste of sea life by means of a pulled shrimp trawl net which the crew dumps into a sample bin to observe the crabs, shrimp and fish that inhabit this region.

But dolphins were what I wanted to see, and that is what I got. We cruised out past the Lydia Ann Lighthouse. (I just bet it has a juicy ghost story, but I could not find it.) We spotted a pod of dolphins that seemed to enjoy following the boat and doing fantastic gymnastic tricks for our entertainment. We then returned to the wharf just at sunset.

Mustang Island State Park

Next morning I just had to make a quick swing through Mustang Island State Park. Imagine five miles of beach on the Gulf of Mexico at sunrise. It offers picnicking, fishing, swimming, hiking and mountain biking on 5 miles of open beach, sunbathing, hiking, surfing, and excellent birding, especially during spring and fall migrations. Interpretive ecological tours are available by request. Naturally they have camping, both primitive and developed. Did I mention all that sun sand and blue water? If I were a pirate, this is where I would have stashed my treasure.

One thing to remember about buried pirate treasure, however, is there is always a swashbuckling phantom left behind to guard this ill-gotten gold for all eternity. Perhaps if you search diligently among the shifting sand dunes of Mustang Island, you may not only uncover Jean Lafitte's treasure but come face to face with the Corsair from New Orleans himself. It's that kind of timeless place.

McAllen

Casa De Palmas

When I headed from Port Aransas to McAllen, I could see the countryside becoming more tropical. This entire Rio Grande Valley is a modern-day Garden of Eden. Gaze up into any tree, and you will most likely spot a colorful bird. Look in the tall grasses or bushes, and there will be a fluttering butterfly.

When you reach McAllen, you are almost as far south in Texas as you can go. The city nestles up against it neighbor, Mexico, with just the easygoing Rio Grande between.

It's a peaceful city and rather new as cities go. McAllen traces its beginnings to an immigrant from Londonderry, Ireland: John McAllen. McAllen first settled in Matamoros, Mexico, then he met John Young, who employed him as a clerk in his store in Brownsville.

When Young died, McAllen married his widow, Salomé Ballí Young, the heir to half of the vast Santa Anita Ranch, part of an old Spanish land grant. McAllen and Young's son, John J. Young, joined forces and ran the ranch together. By 1904, it had attracted a few settlers and became known as West McAllen. The railroad arrived a year later. By 1907, another group had started a town called West McAllen. By 1911, the two settlements had joined together as the town of McAllen.

At its founding, the town had a population of 150, but by 1920 it had jumped to 5,300 residents. The rapid rise in population was also triggered by the influx of Texas National Guardsmen who were stationed in McAllen to combat the bandits who would rustle cattle and then herd them over the Mexican border to sell.

The need for a hotel was apparent. The city had a parcel of land it used as a city park. The builder purchased that land and built a 57-room red-tiled Spanish-style structure with 24-inch-thick walls and an outer patio enclosing the twin-towered building.

The hotel was landscaped with a row of stately palms across the front. Today McAllen is known as the City of Palms, and the hotel has grown to three floors, 141 rooms, 24 suites with eight meeting rooms and 6,500 sq. ft. of total meeting space. Its Spanish Room offers a fine-dining experience for breakfast, lunch and dinner, and the Cantina Lomax, a bar located in the lobby, is the perfect spot to unwind after a long trip. It still retains the original charm that made it a focal point in the early days of the city.

The Casa has played host to some big names over the years. Anthony Quinn and Marlon Brando stayed there during the filming of Viva Zapata. Other stars like Bing Crosby, Jose Greco, Pedro Infante, Vickie Carr and Bob Hope enjoyed the hospitality. Political figures as diverse as Lyndon Johnson and Fidel Castro visited it – not at the same time. Castro snuck over from Mexico one summer evening to stay at the famous hotel and meet with former Cuban President Carlos Prío Socarrás, who had been ousted by Batista.

There is another "guest" who has stayed on at the Casa De Palmas long after her time. She was a former employee of the hotel who also lived on the third floor. In her lifetime, she was extremely conscientious and treated her job as desk clerk there as her whole life. When she died, people began reporting sightings, especially on the third floor. Others have seen her bustling around the lobby late at night when no one else is around. Perhaps she just wants to be sure your stay is just right.

LaBorde House

Just a few miles west of McAllen is another haunted hotel. It's called LaBorde House, and it's right in the middle of tiny Rio Grande City, one of the oldest settlements in South Texas,

Henry Clay Davis, a Kentuckian, moved to the area and married María Hilaria de la Garza, the granddaughter of Francisco de la Garza Martínez who owned all the land. When Davis' wife acquired the land, he designed a port city with broad straight streets, modeled on the capital city, Austin. He planned to take advantage of the river access for steamboats to become a leading port town. (Unfortunately, in the 1950s, the river changed course and now flows about a mile from its former bed.) The establishment of Fort Ringgold in 1848, right next to town, assured its growth and permanence.

In 1899, a French immigrant named Francois LaBorde moved into his Paris-designed home. It was a blend of European, Creole and Texas-border styles with shady verandahs, courtyard and a patio. Over the years, it has served as a boarding house, a smuggler's haven, as well as the elegant home of the LaBordes. The LaBordes fell on hard times, and one of the daughters even resorted to prostitution to keep the building in the family.

Legend says she was in love with a Confederate soldier who rejected her. In desperation, she committed suicide in the room that is called "The Red Room" today.

The LaBordes operated the house as a hotel until 1930. The house has been restored to its turn-of-the-century grandeur and once again functions as a small hotel. A restaurant, El Patio, is also part of the hotel. It features many historic photos of Rio Grande City.

The hotel seems to be inhabited by many specters from its colorful past. Along with the LaBorde daughter, there are another suicide and two children who drowned but don't seem to realize they are dead. Some people have even sighted a floating body. Visitors have had someone tap their heads in an empty room. Other guests have found their closets reorganized and small objects like lipsticks vanish. The lights flicker, and a strange chill descends on the hallway. The scent of perfume unlike any worn by a present guest sometimes wafts down the stairs.

A psychic investigating group with the unlikely name "PIMPS" recently checked the hotel out and found numerous orbs, cold spots and EVR sounds. The investigators even photographed a partial apparition.

Old Fort Ringgold

There are other interesting sites in Rio Grande City, such as Lopez-Tijerina Complex, a replica of the Lourdes Grotto and Old Fort Ringgold. Fort Ringgold was established during the Mexican War. It was named after Major Samuel Ringgold, the first United States Army officer to die from wounds received in the battle of Palo Alto. Henry Clay Davis' heirs sold 350 acres to the government for $20,000 in 1878 for the post known initially as the Post at Davis Landing.

In the 19th century Fort Ringgold hosted a number of prominent military figures, including Robert E. Lee, John J. Pershing, and possibly Jefferson Davis.

The Rio Grande Consolidated Independent School District purchased the property in 1949 but continues to maintain the standing buildings, the most famous being the Lee House, where Lee resided in 1860 while he was investigating Juan Cortina's revolt against Texas.

Museum of South Texas History

The Spanish Mission Revival-style jail built in 1909 now serves as home to this museum located in nearby Edinburg, which showcases the rich history and culture of the Rio Grande Valley. The jail itself has a great history. It has an inside gallows that was only used once. The unlucky "usee" was Abram Ortiz, who had been convicted of rape and murder and executed in 1913. Ortiz and another man, Domingo Gonzalas, were accused of waylaying a Mexican couple, Mr. and Mrs. Martinez. Ortiz killed the husband and raped the wife, who later escaped and led lawmen to Ortiz. Gonzalas had fled to Mexico.

Ortiz and his family insisted he was innocent to no avail. Many people since have heard Ortiz' ghost which haunts the jail. He is known to clank his shackles, create cold spots and moan. The most eerie report is that the noose, which is displayed hanging in the tower room used for the gallows, sometimes sways and a shadow of a hanging man is seen on the walls.

In the 1930s the building was turned into the fire station and city hall. The firemen's sleeping quarters were on the second floor, with a pole to slide down to the trucks. Many of the firemen reported their sleep being disturbed by the ghostly noises coming from the tower room. Today, the gallows and trap door can be seen; however, the trap door is welded shut.

After the fire department moved, the building slowly deteriorated until the mid-1960s when it was chosen as the home for the newly-organized Hidalgo County Historical Museum, which later grew into the large museum it is today. While the old jail is still one of the most-popular attractions, the museum offers so much more.

Everyday life such as a telegraph office and ranch wagons are portrayed. Also many little-known facts, such as the possibility that Poncho Villa had visited the valley, are supported by a rifle and ornate silver saddle belonging to the famed Mexican outlaw. This museum will give you a glimpse of what life in the South Rio Grande Valley was like in days gone by.

International Museum of Art and Science

Opened in 1969, the International Museum of Arts and Science, a Smithsonian-affiliated institution, has provided residents and visitors alike with programs and exhibits related to both art and science.

There are five galleries and a children's area, Discovery Pavilion, with lots of hands-on exhibits, and an outside area, RioScape, similar to a playground but themed to the journey of the Rio Grande River from the mountains to McAllen.

Many traveling exhibits also grace its art collection including Folk Art, Fine Art and Decorative Arts.

Quinta Mazatlan

One of the few remaining hacienda adobe homes in Texas, Quinta Mazatlan, combines history, culture and nature. Today, it is part of the World Birding Center network. Built in 1835 by Jason Chilton Matthews and his wife, Marcia Jamieson Matthews, the home has had only two owners before coming into the hands of the city of McAllen. Top this off with a layer of ghost stories, and you have a very interesting site.

Jason Matthews led a pretty colorful life. He traveled the globe collecting artifacts and stories during World War I. He visited at least 11 countries and fought alongside Lawrence of Arabia.

When he picked a spot to settle for the rest of his life, you know it would not be ordinary. Oh no! Mathews and his wife decided to live at the "Crossroads of the Western Hemisphere." They settled in McAllen in 1935 and built Quinta Mazatlan. Literally, Matthews personally built much of his new home. He perched it on the highest knoll in McAllen and began working with adobe blocks. His first experiment was an adobe-block bathing pool. Using no drainage, he simply drained and refilled whenever the water became dirty by means of a freshwater well with a six-inch-diameter pipe attached to an airplane engine. He was able to fill the pool less than 30 minutes.

Next he built the cottage and hootch. The hootch was his personal hideaway. He could climb in by means of a rope ladder, then pull the ladder up behind him when he desired solitude for his writing. Then after mastering the technique he built the main house. He coated each block, inside and out, in the house with aluminum sulfate paint in the belief that it would prevent radar waves from penetrating the building. For the front doors, he hired famous Swiss woodcarver Peter Mansbendel to recreate the front doors of the Spanish Governor's Palace in San Antonio, Texas. The doors feature two gargoyles and two cherubs, carved in the likeness of his own children. Along the back of the hacienda is a stately hall known as the Cedar Hall. The exposed ceiling beams of this impressive room are made of rough-cut Lebanese cedar trees presented to Matthews by the King of Lebanon in appreciation for his fight alongside Lawrence of Arabia in Lebanon's War of Independence from the Turks.

Another interesting item is the rosewood piano, which belonged to Jefferson Davis.

In his spare time, Matthews published a very conservative right wing magazine, American Mercury Magazine.

Many people, employees and visitors, have sensed a presence in the building and feel that the mansion is haunted. Most agree it is Jason Matthews who is naturally reluctant to leave his home even though he died in 1964. Marcia had died the previous year.

The mansion sat vacant for four years until Frank and Marilyn Schultz bought the estate. They restored and expanded the home, adding beautiful stone patios and planting exotic flowers, shrubs and trees. They also encouraged the regrowth of the native thornscrub. After living there for 30 years and raising their family in the historic mansion, The Shultzes put Quinta Mazatlan up for auction in 1998. Fortunately the city won out over developers who lusted after this prime commercial site. Quinta Mazatlan and its wildlife were saved.

In 1985, the Texas Historical Commission recognized Quinta Mazatlan as a Historical Landmark; now the mansion combines that history with a nature sanctuary to become part of the World Birding Center.

Bentsen-Rio Grande Valley State Park

The crown jewel of the Birding Center is the Bentsen-Rio Grande Valley State Park. Here in the Birding Center headquarters, you may catch a glimpse of a plain chachalaca, green jay, great kiskadee or least grebe. These rare birds are called "valley specialties" because they are found nowhere else in the United States except deepest south Texas. Here, spotting a "Mexican vagrant" is not reason to call INS. These are birds from across the Rio Grande that often fly over to the American side.

Bentsen-RGV State Park adjoins over 1,700 acres of federal refuge land, so there is ample room to spread out in your search for rare birds. If you wish to camp out, the park offers several sites by reservation only.

The park offers bird walks, night hikes, owl prowls, stargazing, tram tours, hawk watches, butterfly walks, dragonfly walks, nature hikes and lunch with a naturalist in the park's café where he will answer your questions.

The park also has a tram and four nature trails ranging from 1/4 mile to 2 miles. It has a two-story Hawk Observation Tower with a 210-foot-long handicapped access ramp, two observation decks and two handicapped-accessible bird blinds.

Nearby Lower Rio Grande Valley Wildlife Refuge is another spot where you will find great birding, too.

La Lomita

This was originally a Spanish mission built in 1865 by the Oblate order of priests. It's located just a few miles south of Mission, Texas, and the chapel is still opened to the public. It's on the National Register of Historic Places, and the chapel has its resident ghost.

One legend is the priests were having sexual relations with the nuns. Unwanted pregnancies were aborted, and any children were slaughtered and buried nearby. Some Mexican peasants found out what was happening and killed two of the priests. One escaped, but the mission was closed down. The large mission building became Tropical Texas Center for Mental Health and Mental Retardation, until that, too, closed down.

Los Ebanos Ferry

To grasp the feeling of how close and accessible our Mexican neighbors are, you need to visit Los Ebanos Ferry. For me the drive to Los Ebanos was a trip in time. As we left McAllen, the road became more winding, and with each twist, it was as if a few decades had skipped lonely highway. It is in the southwestern corner of Hidalgo County, just about three miles off Expressway 83 in 2007, but by the time we had driven through a little village with few houses that seemed lived-in and the remains of several buildings that were once groceries, shops and even some walls of what was once an elementary school, I had the feeling that I wandered into a ghost town from long ago. When we reached a railroad crossing, the road degenerated to almost nothing but a winding trail. Then we reached the river, the tiny border station and a relic of history, the last hand-pulled ferry to cross from the United States to Mexico.

The village has its ghost stories, and driving the lonely road into it will make a believer out of the most-hardened skeptic. The two most-likely candidates for the phantom seen in Los Ebanos are one of two people: General Juan Flores Salinas or Dr. A. A. J. Austin.

In the 1870s, the ferry operating there was often used by cattle rustlers. In one instance in 1874, Captain L. H. McNelly led his band of Texas Rangers to recover cattle being taken to General Juan Flores Salinas' Las Cuevas Ranch. In the skirmish, the general was killed. Local citizens erected a monument to him in Díaz-Ordaz, the nearest town on the Mexican side. I have no idea why a rustler deserved a statue, but he could very likely be the phantom.

Another possibility is Dr. Austin, a colorful pharmacist and physician who owned a ranch, brickyard, gravel pit and drugstore at Los Ebanos. He was known as Doctor Paloma (Dr. Dove) due to his habit of always wearing white suits and riding a white horse. Although he had moved to Mission before his death, it is possible he returns to the place he enjoyed as a young man.

I arrived too late to ride the ferry over -- it closes at 3 p.m. – but if you do make the trip, be aware the nearest town is about three miles away.

La Llorona

While you are along that placid river, you might look about for La Llorona. According to a legend common to many places along the Rio Grande, La Llorona is a female spirit doomed by her own actions to haunt the earth forever. The story is she was a beautiful peasant who had several children by an aristocrat, who eventually left her. In a fit of despair she drowned her children in the Rio Grande. When she realized what she had done, she knew she could never get to heaven and drowned herself in the river.

She is doomed to haunt the river, weeping for her lost children. She appears to men as a beautiful woman, but when they follow her, she turns into either a woman with the head of a donkey or a fleshless skull that attacks and scratches them with sharp, pointed nails.

Dining in McAllen

I sampled two of the local restaurants, Espana for dinner and Republic of Rio Grande for lunch. Espana is one of those fine restaurants that would be at home in any cosmopolitan city in the world. It offers Mediterranean food in an elegant setting. I chose the Chicken Marengo, grilled chicken breast, topped with a sauce of white wine, diced tomatoes, onions, mushrooms and garlic, served with bleu cheese crumbles and pecans. It was mouthwatering and more than I could eat. Espana also has a large selection of steak, seafood and veal.

Two of my favorite restaurants are owned by one award-winning chef, Larry Delgado, and his wife, Jessica. Salt -New American Table in the Art District has a Chef's Table facing the kitchen so we could watch our food being prepared. The ravioli is fantastic. If they have truffles for dessert, get them no matter how full you are.

Chef Larry's House Wine & Bistro opened in 2008. It rivals Salt but has a whole unique personality. There are wine racks surrounding the tables and a full bar. I loved his Bee Sting Flatbread.

Another restaurant I love in McAllen is Republic of the Rio Grande. Besides the fantastic food, it has great atmosphere. The courtyard with its fountain makes you feel you're in an old Mexican mission. I had the House Salad and Stuffed Chili Fritos, hand-breaded Anaheim peppers stuffed with goat cheese, cream cheese, chorizo, and fried to a golden brown.

The Alamo

Statue of Travis drawing line in sand in Menger lobby

Teddy Roosevelt display at bar in Menger Hotel

Mission San Jose

San Fernando Cathedral

Austin Capitol Building

Lobby of Driskill Hotel

Tarpon Inn

Chapter 11 Virginia

Virginia Beach

Cavalier Hotel

The year was 1926, the heyday of the big band sound, the Charleston, the flappers and the Cavalier Hotel in Virginia Beach. Calvin Coolidge was president, and prohibition was the law of the land. When this brand new hotel was completed, it had used more bricks than had ever before been used in a single building in the state of Virginia. The Cavalier Golf Course was the best in the area, with some holes modeled after the famous North Berwick and St. Andrews in Scotland, and Chicago's golf club at Fox Chapel. The hotel sported a beautiful sunken garden whose flowers were used to decorate guestrooms and public areas of the hotel. It still offers the largest hotel ballroom in Virginia. It originally contained 195 guestrooms and 350 acres (290 acres of golf course and 60 acres of hotel property). It opened on April 4-9, 1927, with a grand celebration and guests from the highest walks of life. While prohibition lasted, hotel limos were available to transport guests to nearby speakeasies.

The Cavalier hired the biggest and best bands in the world: Tommy Dorsey, Frank Sinatra, Benny Goodman, Xavier Cugat, Cab Calloway, Glen Miller, Lawrence Welk and Bing Crosby.

The hotel even provided a stock-brokerage office, which had a ticker tape directly from the New York Stock Exchange. There was a special dining room for the chauffeurs of the rich and famous who poured into this plush retreat. The radio station, WSEA, came live from the Cavalier. On June 10, 1927, Mayor Tyler of Norfolk, using WSEA facilities, was the first American to welcome home Charles Lindberg as he was passing the Old Cape Henry Lighthouse on his way to Washington, D.C., for the completion of his record-breaking flight.

Over the years, the Cavalier has hosted seven U.S. presidents: Calvin Coolidge, Herbert Hoover, Harry Truman, Dwight Eisenhower, John Kennedy, Lyndon Johnson and Richard Nixon. Gerald Ford, Jimmy Carter, and George Bush have spoken at the hotel for various functions.

Movie stars loved the Cavalier. F. Scott Fitzgerald, Judy Garland, Will Rogers, Bette Davis, Jean Harlow, Mary Pickford, Betty Grable and Fatty Arbuckle were guests at various times.

One famous guest came in April of 1929. According to many visitors and former employees of the hotel, he never left. Adolph Coors, the founder of Coors Brewery, was traveling around the country protesting the unfairness of prohibition. After dumping 17,000 gallons of beer into Clear Creek, he turned his brewery into a malted milk producer under contract to Hershey's and was also producing pottery, but beer was his first love and he wanted to be able to legally brew it again.

He was staying in a room on the sixth floor. One morning during his stay, on the evening of June 5, an employee was leaving the hotel. She saw what she thought was a pile of clothes lying on the lawn and went over to pick them up. She was shocked to discover that the clothes were on a body, the body of Adolph Coors. When the coroner, Dr. John Woodhouse, arrived on the scene, he did not wait for an autopsy to tell the crowds that Mr. Coors had died as a result of a fall from his sixth-floor window.

The following day, The Virginia-Pilot, a local newspaper, printed this obituary: "Adolph Herman Joseph Coors, aged 82, retired pottery manufacturer of Golden Colorado, was killed instantly yesterday by a fall from a window of a Virginia Beach hotel, where he was stopping …."

The New York Times published a different version: it stated he died of a coronary while dressing in his room. He left a note that some people interpreted as a suicide note, directing that the estate pay his hotel expenses.

Within the next two months after his death, the sightings of Adolph Coors were so widespread that many local people insisted the suicide was just a hoax designed to draw attention to his campaign to repeal prohibition. They insisted that he was not dead, as they had seen him on the sixth floor or in the lobby or on the grounds or stepping off an elevator. He has even been seen in the kitchen and dining room. Since then, he has been seen numerous times by many different people.

There were so many people having encounters, the hotel decided to try and find out what was happening. Hotel officials did not want to acknowledge the possibility of a ghost at first, so what they did was print up a questionnaire about their guests' stay. In it, along with the normal questions such as "How did you enjoy your stay?" they added "Did anything unusual happen during your stay?"

Many of the guests reported that their towels kept changing colors. They would use one and hang it on the rack and when they returned to the bathroom, it would be a different color. No one was ever able to figure out how that was happening.

Perhaps he regretted his decision to end his life. Perhaps the fake obituary in the Times angered him and he wants to let people know what really happened.

Mr. Coors is not the only spirit in the Cavalier. He has a lot of ghostly company. There's a bride who died on her honeymoon, the victims of a double murder, a manager who committed suicide, a little girl who drowned in the pool, a sailor who roams the halls, and even a phantom cat.

Early in WWII, the U.S. Navy requisitioned the Cavalier Hotel as a Radar Training School. Space was at such a premium that even the stables were pressed into service as living quarters for some of the sailors. The swimming pool was drained and used as a classroom with blackout curtains placed over the glass ceiling and windows. Even though living space was cramped, the sailors ate well. The Cavalier retained its chefs, who fixed some of the best Navy meals ever served.

The training school remained at the hotel from October 3, 1942, until June 1, 1945. Then, for the next year, the Navy retained 130 rooms to house single officers.

It was during the Radar Training School time, 1944, that a young sailor met a WAVE who was also stationed at the hotel. They fell in love, married and raised their family. They planned a second honeymoon at the Cavalier for their 47th anniversary. However, just three months before their anniversary, the no-longer-young sailor died. His widow gifted the Cavalier Hotel with the flag that had been draped over his coffin. For both of them, the Cavalier on the Hill was a special place, the place where they found eternal love. The flag flies over Cavalier on the Hill still.

I would not be surprised if the spirit of the sailor is not this very man, strolling down the halls where he found so much happiness because it was right after the flag was first raised that people began reporting seeing the apparition of the sailor.

After the war, trends changed. The automobile replaced train service. The Cavalier Oceanfront opened in 1973, and for a time, the original Cavalier on the Hill closed.

Cavalier on the Hill had too much history and grace to remain closed for too long. It reopened in 1976. Today, it is still as gracious and timeless as it was in 1927. If you stay at the Cavalier, my suggestion is request the "old" hotel, Cavalier on the Hill. In fact, the Travel Channel did a half-hour program on the ghosts at the Cavalier.

Association for Research and Enlightenment

Anyone who has done any research at all on psychic phenomena is well aware of the name Edgar Cayce, who is widely known as the "Father of Holistic Medicine," and his Association for Research and Enlightenment (ARE). For any who are not familiar, Edgar Cayce was unquestionably the greatest psychic of the 20th century. Cayce was born in 1877 to a poor farming family near Hopkinsville, Kentucky. He was brought up with a strict fundamentalist church background. Forced to drop out of school after completing eighth grade due to family finances, he moved from job to job. During a stint of selling insurance, he suffered laryngitis and could not speak. He then turned to photography to earn a living. A hypnotist suggested Cayce try and discover the reason for his laryngitis under hypnosis. Cayce agreed and while in a trance estate diagnosed and cured his condition. The hypnotist, Al Layne, was amazed at Cayce's ability under hypnosis and suggested he begin giving readings for others. Cayce agreed but would not charge for his service. The readings became so successful; Cayce began doing it full time for donations.

At one point a businessman tried to use Cayce to control the stock market. This was not what he wanted to use his gift for, so Cayce began having a secretary or his wife present for all readings. Since he was in a trance, he was not aware of what he said in the readings. Often he displayed knowledge of anatomy that was comparable to a learned physician's rather than a grade-school dropout's.

While he was in a trance one day, he casually mentioned reincarnation and the patient's former life as the reason for a certain illness. At this point, he became alarmed because of his staunch religious beliefs. Gradually, he came to accept the truth of his readings and began giving "life readings" which dealt with the karma involved in a former life coming back to affect the person in this life.

Gradually, he was successful in opening a hospital that worked with his usually homeopathic cures and an institute to study his readings related to reincarnation and prophecy. By this time he was being called "the Sleeping Prophet" and "the Greatest Seer of the Twentieth Century."

He felt called to move to Virginia Beach to open his hospital and continue his readings. Al Chewning, Virginia Beach's top ghost hunter, spoke of this: "Edgar Cayce felt that Virginia Beach was a very strong area metaphysically. Does that have any correlation to the presence of, or absence of, ghosts? I don't know."

Since Virginia Beach has an abundance of ghosts, there could be a relationship between Cayce's feelings regarding its strong metaphysical field and spirit manifestation.

Whatever, a visit to Cayce's ARE when in Virginia Beach is almost mandatory. I was invited to have a massage and tour the facility. The spa is located in the original Edgar Cayce Hospital building and offers many spa services. My massage was the best I ever had.

I walked over afterward for my meeting with Una Marcotte who gave me a tour of the ARE facility and Research Library. I even took the simple card test to determine if I was psychic. I failed miserably, but I did come away with a lot more knowledge, and that wonderful relaxed feeling stayed with me for the rest of the day.

Ferry Plantation House

"I be not a witch." So said Grace Sherwood. It took 300 years, but finally, the powers that be believed her. On July 10, 2006, Mayor of Virginia Beach Meyera Oerdorf read the letter from Virginia Governor Timothy M. Kaine officially exonerating Grace Sherwood of the charge of witchcraft imposed on her in early 1706. To find out more about "the Witch of Pungo," as Grace was called, I visited Ferry Plantation House.

The present-day farmhouse dates to the early 19th century. Before that it was the location of a tavern owned by Anthony Walke in the 1770s, and prior to that in 1735 it was the location of the Princess Anne County Courthouse where Grace was tried and ordered "witch-dunked" in the adjacent Lynnhaven River. It is also believed that she was imprisoned for seven years in a cellar where the present house now stands.

I met with Belinda Nash, probably the greatest fan of Grace Sherwood and the museum director at Ferry Plantation House and co-author of *Ghosts, Witches and Weird Tales of Virginia Beach.*

The house was built in 1830 by George and Elizabeth Walke MacIntosh from the old bricks of the original home to replace that earlier home of her ancestor, Anthony Walke, which burned in 1828. It is restored to its 1830-era condition.

As soon as Belinda ushered me in, I could feel that there were presences in this place. Remember I am not really a psychic, so they had to be screaming out their presence for me to feel them.

Belinda told me of the 11 spirits - that have been counted so far - residing in the house. "We know about them and we know the names."

Before the home came into the hands of the Friends of the Ferry Plantation House, there were people reporting strange phenomena. Two men, Dr. Mayo and Mr. Weathersby, used to house-sit on weekends when former owner Mrs. Howren, the last private owner, went into assisted living in 1980. There was a bench where Dr. Mayo would sit every night when he was there, and he witnessed an African-American male figure who appeared to be a servant. This wraith walked across the room and then vanished through the wall. He has been identified by the ARE group of parapsychologists as a former slave called Henry. They also say he doesn't want to leave as this is the only home he knows.

During the years when the site housed the Walke Tavern, it was also a convenient place for ship captains trying to avoid duty by slipping in and unloading their illegal cargo, including human freight. Archeologists have found indications that there were once tunnels or perhaps shallow conduits where the cargo was hurried into the house and the unfortunate African captives were then chained in a dark basement room until they could be sold. Henry may have been one of these sad souls.

One of the more-fortunate early residents of the house was seen regularly by Belinda's granddaughter, Kathlene, from a very early age. General Thomas Hoones Williamson was born at the plantation in 1813. He grew up as a member of the influential Walke family. He served in the Confederate army under Stonewall Jackson and was a professor of engineering at Virginia Military Institute and, by avocation, was an artist. He painted the watercolor of the original Walke home from his childhood memories. He died in 1888, but he is not gone.

Belinda told me of a time when she was working in the Ferry Plantation Home and her little granddaughter was only two. It was a crisp fall day, and a draft was seeping up through the floorboards on the first floor, so Belinda decided to work on the second floor that day. As they were heading up the stairs, Kathlene pointed to the top of the stairs and said, "Nanny, someone is there."

Belinda reassured the child that it was probably just a shadow. She herself had not seen anything in the house yet, but she had heard unnatural footsteps often. When they prepared to leave, the child assured her grandmother, "The man with the dirty shirt is here again."

Several months later when Kathlene had turned three and her speech skill had progressed, they were again working on the house. This time they were painting the green room on the second floor. When a storm came up, Belinda decided as soon as the rain stopped, they would go home. While she was cleaning and putting up the tools, Kathlene mentioned the mysterious man again. "Nanny, what is he painting?" The girl was looking up as if at a very tall person, so Belinda thought the child was remembering a tall plasterer who had worked on the house. The child insisted that was not who she meant. This man was old and had a beard.

A few weeks later the mystery was solved. Again they were on the second floor. Belinda was working, and Kathlene was drawing at a little table with some crayons. The child asked for some paints instead. Belinda told her there were none at the house. The little girl pointed out to the hallway and stated, "The man with the dirty shirt is painting a picture. Can I have some of his paint?"

The description and the fact that "the man with the dirty shirt" was painting a picture, not a wall as Belinda had first assumed, made it clear whom the child was seeing. Perhaps Thomas Williamson was remembering the happy times he had spent in his old home.

There are two children's spirits often seen in the home as well: a little girl in a long dress who appears to be looking for someone or something and a mischievous boy of about 8 or 10, who likes to play tricks. Psychics have said the little boy is named Eric.

There are several other spirits who reside in Ferry Plantation, but the saddest is that of Grace Sherwood. It is only natural that Grace would return to the scene of her trial and dunking. Many people have seen her. Others have seen a light winking over the river where she was dunked.

One former resident of the house was fixing dinner in the kitchen one evening when she saw Grace came out of the dining room in front of her and walk through the pantry door. The viewer described her: "She was young, slender with long dark hair and wearing a long gown. She never looked at me."

Some neighbors in the subdivision around Ferry Plantation whose back deck faces the farmhouse reported that the chairs on their deck will be moved off the deck at night and lined up on the lawn looking at the farm.

They also have witnessed an apparition matching the description of Grace moving through their home. They have frequently awakened in the night to hear the sounds of a party coming from their own living room.

After all, who has a better right to haunt the scene of her trial and imprisonment than the former "Witch of Pungo?"

Francis Land House

The Francis Land House was built between 1805 and 1810. It remained in the Land family for several generations, then passed into private hands. It has been a dairy farm, and in the 1950s, '60s and early '70s it was the home of the Rose Hall Dress Shop for the Ladies and their Daughters.

The home is a great example of 19th-century architecture. It offers tours with costumed docents. At the time I updated this it was trmporarly closed for renovation.

Adam Thoroughgood House

In the mid-1600s, Virginia Beach was a place filled with bears, deer and other wildlife and mostly uninhabited by humans. However, it was here that a former indentured servant rose to the highest echelons of Virginia society. His wealth was based on tobacco. By the time of his death at age 35 in 1640, Adam Thoroughgood owned more than 7,000 acres of land.

It was in 1636 that he acquired the tract where the home bearing his name stands. The Adam Thoroughgood House Foundation has discovered that this house was not completed in 1640 but may have been built by his son or grandson. Regardless of its builder, it is one of Virginia's architectural treasures, a brick home built in 1640 of traditional English design and workmanship. The bricks used were sun dried -- one even bears the mark of a bear scratch - and the style was of the type of English manor house young Adam could only have gaped at from afar. It is surrounded by the same type of garden the young Adam might have aspired to work in had he not ventured over the ocean.

The house today is owned and maintained as a house museum by the Adam Thoroughgood House Foundation. Over the years they have found that all of the former residents may not have departed at their deaths. Several docents have found that no matter how carefully they make the bed, it sometimes shows the imprint of a body as if someone has lain on top of the covers to take a short nap.

Another interesting thing happens sometimes when furniture is rearranged. The staff will return the next morning to find it put back in the original positions. This sounds like a male ghost to me. Men always hate to have furniture rearranged.

Belinda Nash, a co-author of *Ghost Witches and Weird Tales of Virginia Beach* and my host at Ferry Plantation, had an interesting experience when she arrived at the Adam Throughgood House for a meeting of the Bayside History Trail Association one spring afternoon. She had parked in the lot next to another car with an out-of-state license and was heading to the door when she remembered she had forgotten her notebook. As she headed back, the family from the other car approached her and asked if the house was open for tours. She informed them it was but today it was closed and she was just coming there for a meeting. The family insisted that there were people in the house because they had seen "a line of workers dressed in colonial costume walking around in the back yard. When we walked around back to try and follow them, they were nowhere to be seen." The baffled tourists assumed "the workers" had entered the house through the back door. However when Belinda asked the person on duty at the museum if anyone had been working in the yard just before she arrived, he answered, "No one has been working out there at all today."

Old Coast Guard Station

One of America's first lifesaving stations began with a series of 20-by-40-foot boathouses. The idea was to have one station every seven miles. In 1874 there was a small community already in Cape Henry, but in 1878 there was nothing where station is today.

The current building was built in 1903. Surfmen worked in the station six months out of the year. A man would walk from each station along the beach. About halfway between the stations, he would meet with the man from the next station and exchange badges and then return to the station and repeat the drill again before the shift ended. If they found a shipwreck, they signaled the boat with a flare they carried and ran back to the station to sound the alert; the rest of the crew brought out the lifeboat to help. They would bring the survivors and the bodies back to the station.

The roads were such that you could only get into Norfolk, where the nearest doctor, coroner and cemetery were located, in good weather. Bodies from shipwrecks often could not be transported until the weather cleared and roads were passable. In cases of hurricanes, that could be a week or more, so the bodies were stored in the attic.

In 1915, the U. S. Coast Guard was formed and took over. In 1969 the old building was decommissioned.

To prepare it for use as a museum, workers moved the building, and in doing so they turned it 90 degrees. Unexplained things were reported even then. Workmen often had to spend an hour looking for their tools; they would be scattered. Jackets would be moved. Lunches would be missing.

When the museum staff moved in, there were lots of electrical problems. They were burning out light bulbs a case a week. Even more startling manifestations began to occur. In the upper gallery people heard sounds like someone moving things around. Al Chewning says he has heard sounds like someone dragging something across the attic floor.

Many people have strange feelings about the building, feelings like someone is behind them. Women have just started crying for no reason. Cold spots are very common.

A full-figured apparition was seen by one female employee. It happened on a Sunday afternoon. She was almost done working in the closed building, and she walked into the lower gallery and saw a man dressed in an old-fashioned three-piece suit with big lapels. She told him, "Sir, the museum is closed. You will have to leave."

He left. Right in front of her eyes! She also left – very rapidly.

Many people have seen the upper torso of a man in a sailor suit in one of the upstairs tower windows where the surfmen slept. This happens so frequently that it has caused problems. People would call 911. Police would come out, find the building locked and call the manager. He would come out and unlock the building. They would search and find nothing. This happened so frequently that one of the employees found an old picture of one of the surfmen who worked the station. She had it blown up life-sized, cut out and pasted on a piece of plywood. They then placed that in one of the upstairs tower windows so that now when the police get a call they can just dismiss the caller with "Oh yes, we know who that is."

Besides its resident spirits, the station is filled with artifacts pertaining to shipwrecks and man's relationship with the sea.

Norwegian Lady

One of the most-famous shipwrecks in the area involved a Norwegian ship, On Good Friday, March 27, 1891, the Norwegian barque *Dictator*, based out of Moss, Norway, was having troubles. To compound her problems, the ship ran into a storm off Virginia Beach.

Captain Jorgensen was watching for Cape Henry, believing the lighthouse would guide him into port, but when the crew spotted what they believed was Cape Henry, no light was shining. Believing that the light, fueled by oil, might have been extinguished due to the weather, they decided to put ashore anyway.

It was not Cape Henry but a spot called False Cape Henry, and the ship ran aground. It lost both of its lifeboats. The Dictator had a crew of 15 and the captain's wife and son aboard.

The men from the station worked from dawn to dark in the high winds and seas at rescue efforts. Eight of the 17 persons aboard were saved, but among those missing were Johanne Jørgensen, the captain's pregnant young wife, and their four-year-old son, Carl Zealand Jørgensen. The captain and one other sailor washed ashore alive. They found all the other bodies, including Johanne's, but the child's body was not located.

The crew and surfmen searched until Easter Sunday. By then the despondent captain and the remains of his crew left for Baltimore and a ship back to Norway.

Several days later, a young fisherman walking on the beach near a village a few miles away found the body of a young boy. He took it to the local preacher, but since the preacher was not awake yet, he left it on the doorstep. The preacher, knowing it was not a child from his village, quietly buried it in the local cemetery. Not wanting to upset his parishioners, he didn't mention it. The following morning, everyone in the village was talking about the crying baby. Since no one in the village had a young child, they were perplexed. This occurred again for morning after morning. The villagers searched to no avail. Finally, a young man from the village rode into Virginia Beach and heard people talking about the shipwreck and the lost child.

The man rushed back to his village and organized a search party. They went to the preacher to ask for his prayers. The preacher told them about the body he had buried, but the men insisted that the child they sought was alive still as they had heard it crying in the night.

Naturally, no living child was ever found. Does that ghostly little boy still cry sometimes in the night? The area today is False Cape State Park, and many campers and rangers have reported hearing a baby cry.

Someone did find the remains of the ship's wooden figurehead and set it up in a vertical position facing the ocean near the boardwalk as a memorial to the people who had lost their lives in the shipwreck. It became known as the "Norwegian Lady," and was a landmark for some 60 years.

However, wind, salt air and hurricanes took their toll, and the figurehead became weathered and eroded. Finally Hurricane Barbara in 1953 damaged it so badly the city removed it and placed it in storage until it could be renovated. When they looked for it a few years later, it had disappeared.

The people of Virginia Beach were upset. They began a drive to raise money to replace their statue. The drive was successful in part due to a substantial contribution from the Norwegian Shipping Association. They raised enough funds to purchase not just a replacement for Virginia Beach but a second one to be placed in Moss, Norway. They commissioned Ornulf Bast, a Norwegian sculptor, to create two 9-foot bronze replicas of the original figurehead. Both statues were unveiled on September 22, 1962. The statues face each other across the ocean. The inscriptions read: "I am the Norwegian Lady. I stand here, as my sister before me, to wish all men of the sea safe return home."

Cape Henry Lighthouse

This lighthouse, constructed at the dangerous junction where the Chesapeake Bay meets the Atlantic Ocean, deserves its place in history. It was the first public building constructed with money from the brand new

United States of America. In 1792, President George Washington climbed the 90-foot tower to ignite the flame that would guide ships away from treacherous shoals.

In 1881, it was closed and replaced with a 163-foot tower in the mistaken belief that the old structure was in danger of falling into the sea. The newer tower is still active and sits 350-feet away from the original. Both are located at Fort Story Army Base. They are among the 12 "historic light stations" in Virginia recognized by the NPS.

Several people have reported hearing ghostly footsteps follow them in the area around the old lighthouse. I wouldn't be a bit surprised to discover a ghostly former keeper hanging around.

Be aware that you must have valid identification and will be subjected to a thorough search before you are allowed on the base. For non-citizens, a passport is required. There are also height requirements to enter the lighthouse, so if you have a small child, check ahead.

Virginia Aquarium & Marine Science Center

For fish and sea life in a different context, make sure to visit the Virginia Aquarium & Marine Science Center. It's the state's largest aquarium and one of the most popular in the nation. From sea turtles to sharks, this is a way to get up close and personal with the denizens of the deep.

It offers more than 700,000 gallons of aquariums, 300 hands-on exhibits, an IMAX 3D Theater, a great nature trail that connects the two pavilions that make up the aquarium and an outdoor aviary where you can view hundreds of the marsh birds native to Virginia Beach's shore.

The aquarium continues to expand to meet the need for knowledge in today's world. Restless Planet, their newest addition, is scheduled to open in late 2008 and will feature the spectacular forces that have shaped Virginia's environment from 400 million years ago to today.

The aquarium is not just a showplace; it is actively involved in rescue missions involving sea life.

Whale Watching Tour

A Whale Watching Tour with Rudee Tours is a two-hour excursion that guarantee sightings December thru February. The humpback whales put on a show for us. They were breaching, so the entire body was visible. Some were just breaking the waterline and flipping their enormous tails. A narrator explained about whale behaviors.

The upper deck is the best spot for watching, but the boat has bathrooms, a snack bar, a full bar, and a heated indoor cabin as well. Rudee Tours has several different tours if you are there at other times. If you get seasick, go sit in the lower rear and stare at the ocean. This will help banish that queasy stomach.

First Landing State Park

For nature lovers, this is a must. Located on Chesapeake Bay, it's Virginia's most-visited state park. It was built by the Civilian Conservation Corps in the 1930s to commemorate where Captain John Smith landed in 1607 on his way to establishing the first permanent English settlement at Jamestown.

Here is your opportunity for boating, swimming, nature and history programs, hiking, biking and picnicking. It boasts a boat launch, cabins and 19 miles of trails on 2,888 acres. It also offers campsites, some with bay access, with water and electric hook-ups. Be sure and see the Replica Indian Village along Cape Henry Trail.

The beach with its dunes might be the place to hunt for Blackbeard's treasure, which is rumored to be buried somewhere nearby.

Histories and Haunts Ghost Tour

This tour is a great way to learn the history of many of Virginia Beach's famous haunts. It is owned by local author, actor and historian Al Chewning, a retired Virginia Beach firefighter with a degree in history and a love for teaching. His tour combines the two in a way I found fascinating. It was a great help to me in my search for interesting haunted spots in Virginia Beach.

Three famous statures

Virginia Beach has three famous statues. Cape Henry Memorial Cross marks the site of the landing of the settlers who established the first permanent English Colony in North America at Jamestown.

Neptune, the god of the sea created by sculptor, Paul DiPasquale, stands on the beachfront at the entrance to Neptune Park. He is a reminder to respect and protect our ocean.

A bronze statue of Grace Sherwood, The Witch of Pungo, stands in front of Sentara Independence Hospital. Sherwood was the last person tried for witchcraft in Virginia in 1706. She was tried by "Ducking" a process where she was tied hand and foot and tossed into Witchduck Point in the

Lynnhaven River. If she sank and drowned, she was innocent; if she floated to the surface and survived, she was guilty. It was a bit of a no-win situation. She did untie her hands and swim to the surface and was then sentenced to seven years in jail. On July 10, 2006, 300 years after her trial, Virginia Governor Tim Kaine reversed that verdict and restored her reputation as an honest midwife and healer.

Aside from the many sculptures, Virginia Beach has many murals.

Mount Trashmore Park

If you are seeking a peaceful place to walk or just relax, try Mount Trashmore Park. This unique park, a few miles from the beach, went from landfill to park with gardens, lakes, and mountains. The "mountain" has the Virginia State Emblem on top of it. You can take stairs to the top where you can walk the trail. The park has a children's playground, baseball, tennis courts, skate park, and other sports offerings.

Dining

Blue Pete's

For dinner, I visited Blue Pete's, located in Pungo, about 20 minutes from the resort area of Virginia Beach. I was not disappointed, either, in the food or in its ghost stories. Blue Pete's is named for the little duck-like bird, the American coot, locally known as the "blue pete." The then owner, K. C. Knauer, told me that the place is very haunted. She later sold it to Nicholas and Aristotle Cleanthes, twin brothers. She and many of her staff have had some strange experiences over the years. While I dug into my Seafood Sampler filled with crab cakes, shrimp, scallops and flounder and a side of sweet potato bread smeared generously with orange marmalade, I could look out over the water and watch all kinds of birds searching for their dinner as well.

Blue Pete's began life as a rough bar located on a rustic wooden building built on stilts over the water. K.C. came over and told me about the history. "The original place was a rough-and-tumble bar back in the 1970s. It was just a shack with four tables and a bar. Boaters and fishermen would pull in by boar and come in for a drink and then clean their fish on the back dock. They were a really wild bunch. All of them had guns and would sit on the back dock and shoot at things."

I noted that the brick looked really old, and she told me that earlier there had been a tiny post office here. She said she felt the ghosts were patrons who had hung out here in the early bar years and had such a good time they didn't want to leave.

When she first got the restaurant, neither she nor any of her employers knew anything about it being haunted but started hearing things. Around 11:30 they would start hearing voices when no one was there. One of the strangest phenomena happened shortly after K.C. bought the restaurant. She said, "There were two separate tables. There was a woman in one group who had a baby sitting in a booster seat. She got up and went to the restroom. When the mother was returning, the chair she had been sitting in right next to her baby just spun out into the middle of the floor. It moved about three feet. It was like someone had been sitting there admiring the baby and saw the mother returning so they jumped up. Everybody in the place turned to look. Funny thing, the two groups became friends and came back together about a year later."

She also said she had actually once seen the figure of a woman run across the room. "I thought it was strange. She never set off the motion detector. She was dressed in a '70s kind of outfit, a lime green jumpsuit, and she had short blond hair."

Tiffany, a former waitress at Blue Pete's, told me about what happened to her one night. "It was just me and the kitchen manager, Rocco. We were getting ready to set the alarm and leave. Then we heard a loud thump thump in the back dining room. He about jumped out of his skin. He's about 6-foot-2, but he jumped. I'm trying to find the light. I'm not going to walk into the room with no light on. He stayed in the front and wouldn't even help me look. When I looked in the room, no one was there. We went outside and looked, but no one was anywhere around. It was spooky."

Rocco had just been there early one morning by himself with his little boy, Anthony. Anthony was about 2 and had just learned to say "carry you," which of course meant "pick me up." Rocco left the room for a minute, and when he came back in, Anthony was in the middle of the floor with his hands out to an unseen entity saying, "Carry you." Rocco grabbed his son and took him back home.

On another occasion, Jessie, who also worked there, and Rocco heard somebody in front room. Two tray holders went down behind them, bam bam! "They screamed like girls and ran out of the room," KC said. Brittany, KC's daughter, was working one day and heard a sneeze from the restroom. When she went in to check, no one was in there.

There are are two other dining spots I recommend. Cactus Jack's Southwest Grill for casual Southwest style dining. When we visited on a Saturday night, Joe Heilman was playing guitar and singing. There is also entertainment on Friday and Wednesday. Waterman's Surfside Grille if you want upscale offers delicious seafood. Both have full-service bars.

Grace Sherwood, statue after pardoned as Witch of Pungo

Lobby of Cavalier Hotel

Edgar Casey Institute

Fort Henry old lighthouse

Cavalier Hotel

Thorowgood House

www.ingramcontent.com/pod-product-compliance
Lightning Source LLC
Chambersburg PA
CBHW070934180426
43192CB00039B/2183